LONG SHOT

A SOLDIER, A SENATOR, *A SERIOUS SIN*
AN EPIC LOUISIANA ELECTION

By TYLER BRIDGES and JEREMY ALFORD

The
LISBURN
PRESS

The Lisburn Press
www.TheLisburnPress.com

THE LISBURN PRESS
3115 OLD FORGE DRIVE
BATON ROUGE, LOUISIANA 70808

LONG SHOT

PUBLISHED IN THE UNITED STATES OF AMERICA

Visit our website at TheLisburnPress.com.

First edition published in November 2016

Cover layout by Compose Digital Design
Cover photos courtesy of Louisiana Public Broadcasting
Text design by Ashley Powell
Editing by Clancy DuBos
Copy Editor Patricia Stallman

Library of Congress Cataloging-in-Publication Data is available.

IBSN: 978-0-692-79533-0

For information regarding special discounts for bulk purchases, please
contact Jeremy Alford at JJA@LaPolitics.com

Printed in Canada.

This book is printed on acid-free paper.

To my daughter Luciana—if I have passed on to you the love of reading that I gained from my parents, I will be a happy daddy.

And in memory of C.B. Forgotston, who taught me so much about Louisiana politics (1945-2016).
—*T.B.*

For my wife Karron, who is smarter than I am,
infinitely more lovely, and the best friend
and mother imaginable.
You are the center of my universe.

And in memory of my friend and mentor,
John Maginnis (1948-2014),
who would have truly enjoyed just how weird
the 2015 race for governor was at times.
I always enjoyed watching history with him.
—*J.A.*

CONTENTS

FOREWORDS

By James Carville and Mary Matalin

He Said: "An Election that Defied the Odds"

Every state in America has its uniqueness, but no state stands out quite like Louisiana. From our legal traditions rooted in Roman law and the Napoleonic Code to our annual *laissez les bons temps rouler* Mardi Gras celebrations, from our world-renowned musicians and literary giants to our Cajun and Creole cuisine, Louisiana strikes most Americans as a foreign country that happens to lie within the Lower 48—one that speaks English only in a manner of speaking but happily accepts U.S. currency. We like it that way.

So it's no surprise that Louisiana's brand of American democracy likewise stands out as sometimes hard to fathom but always full of surprises. In his classic book, *The Earl of Louisiana,* the great A.J. Liebling compared Louisiana's politics in 1959 to the politics of Lebanon. Not much has changed since then. Every state has its share of political shenanigans, crooks, and liars, but ours have elevated hijinks to an art form. We seem to like that about ourselves, too.

But the truth is, for all our uniqueness, Louisianans are as passionate about America as we are about our gumbo. It's always been that way. Exhibit A: The largest individual financier of the American Revolution lived in New Orleans in the 1770s. Oliver Pollock, an Irish immigrant who made his fortune in the Crescent City, underwrote George Rogers Clark's Campaign of the West and gave America's fledgling rebellion the modern equivalent of $1 billion. That kind of passion continues right through today. Exhibit B: Louisiana sent more men and women, per capita, to fight in the First Gulf War (Desert Storm) than any other state in the nation. Here's something else about Louisiana that's uniquely American: We love an underdog. Just ask any New Orleans Saints fan.

I make these points lest you think that the story you're about to read could happen only in Louisiana. Well, maybe this *particular* story could have happened only in the Bayou State, but the notion of a small-town legislator taking on—and beating—a national political juggernaut is a profoundly American tale. It's *Mr. Smith Goes to Washington* come to life, with a much more colorful cast of characters. Ultimately, it's the story of one man who saw an opportunity that no one else saw and kept working to make it happen even when everyone else—including his own natural constituency—told him he couldn't succeed. Turns out he was right and the world was wrong. Political parties matter, but candidates matter more.

Artfully told by two of Louisiana's most respected political writers—Tyler Bridges and Jeremy Alford—*Long Shot* unfolds like a James Lee Burke novel. We all know how this saga ends, but the backstory leading up to that ending is so compelling that you won't want to put this book down. In the end, I think readers will conclude that while Louisiana will always retain its quirky, lovable uniqueness, this David-versus-Goliath tale of an election that defied the odds holds lessons for every candidate—and every voter—in America.

—*James Carville*

She Said: "Both Unique and Foretold"

"We do things different here."

If you are considering a career in national political consulting, two pieces of advice: (1) read this book; and (2) collect a nickel every time a state operative adamantly asserts the above. You will make a ton of coin.

Such a notion is inescapably inherent in my husband's take on the Louisiana governor's race of 2015, which he calls "An Election That Defied the Odds." The claim is at the same time both true and false. From decades of experience spanning every state in this great union, as well as dozens of foreign countries, James and I can agree on this rudimentary Politics 101 point: Every state *is* unique.

But they are all unique in the same way.

That is to say, all politics is driven by human nature, which is infinitely unique yet stubbornly predictable. Myriad external influences can radically impact political outcomes, but they cannot alter essential human nature. So yes, Louisiana is unique, in too many extraordinary and beautiful ways to count, but relative to John Bel Edwards' ostensibly unpredictable victory, my own view is that his triumph was easily foreseen.

Yes, as this book details, Louisiana employs numerous electoral oddities, which, while discombobulating to outsiders, are well internalized by natives and therefore to be discounted as dispositive factors (such as the jungle primary, ancient and ever shifting alliances, etc.) in the ultimate outcome of elections. What was both unique and foretold about the Louisiana election of 2015 was its occurrence in the midst of an era of an unfolding political transition.

Like other politicians before him in recent years, Edwards' victory was the product of an emergent and hardening political zeitgeist that rewards outsiders and eschews "establishment" insiders, no matter how competent or popular, or for that matter, incompetent or loathed. True, Democrat Mary Landrieu was defeated by an insider Republican, Bill Cassidy, but despite her demonstrable record of bringing home fat stacks of blubbery bacon, her association with an ever expanding, encroaching establishment dwarfed his mini-establishment bona fides. And while Republican David Vitter was a darling of anti-establishment conservatives, his membership in a GOP majority unable or unwilling to thwart the uncontrollable bureaucratic burgeoning was his Achilles heel, despite conventional wisdom attributing his downfall to "the recent unpleasantness" of marital indiscretions, which Louisiana voters (who are remarkably merciful) had forgiven.

Edwards ably rode to victory on this wave of frustration, anxiety, and burning anger with a dismissive establishment. In this context, to all but those who attributed the righteous voter anger to bigotry or provincialism, the John Bel Edwards upset of Vitter was predictable. Though the entire 2015 field pursued a common sense strategic imperative to mesh with the vote-determinate demands of human nature, Edwards was unique in the way voters were demanding.

In a period of global political turmoil and uncertainty, human nature recoils and reverts to First Principles, which (in a largely free, or perceived to be free, electoral system) seek the "virtuous citizen" model for leadership (one Socrates failed to find and died trying to discover). Edwards' public and personal history hit the contemporary mark of the virtuous citizen for Louisianans: pro-life, pro-Second Amendment, West Point grad, Army Ranger, Catholic, good family. His soft spoken and humble demeanor contrasted colorfully with the neon bombast of what passes for today's statesmen.

In modern history, Louisiana has a solid record of political prescience. In a program instituted by RNC Chairman Lee Atwater (for whom I served as chief of staff), the first Southern "switcher" from Yellow Dog Democrat to new Republican was then-Governor Buddy Roemer in 1991. In a political blink of the eye, the solid blue South is now gloriously ruby red. And while the politically correct groupthink master class attributes this astounding realignment to race, its true origin lies in the Democratic Party's rejection of the commonly held values and centuries-old traditions of the South, which were inherited from Enlightenment Europe. First and foremost, personal and state sovereignty, individual liberty, and the non-arbitrary rule of law.

Not dissimilarly, Landrieu's and Vitter's defeats resulted from the same voter perception of rejection—of the voters themselves and their long revered values—by a force that increasingly appears to be the one-party centralized power of a protected class. One based not on merit or effort. One that unfairly and arbitrarily redistributes the wealth and equity, and hence the freedom, of the citizens it

iv

professes to protect.

Contemporary American democratic upheavals are the modern political equivalent of monarchical beheadings. This timeless and ageless story of human beings reasserting their inherent longing for self-determination is beautifully rendered by its knowledgeable and thoughtful chroniclers. It is at once a look back into our collective history and souls, and a telling portent of the way forward.

—*Mary Matalin*

Part One

"The past is never dead. It's not even past."
—*William Faulkner*

1

A Hall of Fame Election

Of course Louisiana has a hall of fame for its political class. What else would one expect in a state where politics is as much a spectator sport as football? The Louisiana Political Museum and Hall of Fame fills a renovated, wood-paneled train depot in the north Louisiana hamlet of Winnfield, birthplace of Huey and Earl Long, neither of whom needed a hall of fame to affirm his place in the Bayou State's annals of political immortality. New classes of inductees arrive each year, leaving behind written records of their accomplishments, faded photographs of their proudest moments, and other mementoes of public lives. Generation after generation they come, all claiming their own sliver of immortality, the ultimate political prize in Louisiana—next to winning the governor's race.

The layers of chatter rose to a level just shy of deafening on the afternoon of Saturday, February 7, 2015, as staffers and volunteers readied seven new display cases for the annual induction ceremony. The reception in the main exhibit room, followed by a banquet at the Winnfield Civic Center, unofficially launched what would become an unforgettable election season. Local candidates and statewide contenders worked the crowded room. A photojournalist from the *Winn Parish Enterprise* asked the families of new inductees to pose for a glowing spread that appeared in the following Wednesday's edition.

An unmistakable big-fish, small-pond vibe filled the museum; this crowd would have it no other way. No strangers here. Louisiana politics is personal, its history intimate. No combination of anecdotes, memorabilia, or recorded speeches could match that sense of *affaire*, that recognition that we're all in on the joke. Football, crawfish, music, fishing, hunting, fairs, festivals, religion, gambling, meat pies, and Mardi Gras—at some point these and all other touchstones of Louisiana's unique culture intersect with its politics. Which is why, in the state named for the vast territory that Thomas Jefferson bought from Napoleon Bonaparte for less than 3 cents an acre, politics is *life*.

Since its inception, Louisiana has stood apart from the rest of America in almost every respect. French was its dominant language even after statehood, prompting Congress to require Louisiana's first constitution to safeguard the rights of English speakers. Its legal tradition is still uniquely grounded in the Napoleonic Code rather than English common law. But Louisiana is in no way a strictly Francophonic culture. Whereas other states are majority White Anglo-Saxon Protestant, with varying populations of African Americans and Hispanics, Louisiana's electorate is roughly one-third African American, with the rest fairly evenly split among rural WASPs, Catholic Cajuns (descendants of French-speaking Canadians exiled in 1765), and urban and suburban whites whose political and religious affiliations run the gamut. Also part of the mix: contingents of Asians, Hispanics, Italians, Irish, Lebanese, Yugoslavs, Germans, and Native Americans—thus the familiar description of Louisiana as a cultural gumbo.

The diverse attendees at the Hall of Fame induction ceremony spoke dissonant strains of the Queen's English, but their passion for Louisiana's blood sport gave them a common language. Inside the train depot, they created a verbal sonata that had serenaded political events for generations, from the piney woods of north Louisiana to the sleepy bayous of Acadiana to the double-parlored mansions on St. Charles Avenue in New Orleans. Loud laughter, whispered rumors, and "How's your momma" sounded the notes of a familiar overture. The din hung heavy in the air, like wet moss, below strings of white Christmas lights in the old depot's main hall. The mood was equal parts excitement and intimacy—fueled by alcohol, budding intrigue, and exaggerated storytelling. For the *cognoscenti* under those lights, a trip to the Louisiana Political Museum and Hall of Fame in Winnfield— especially in a statewide election year—was akin to older Catholics' holy days of obligation. It was a pilgrimage they dared not skip.

A strange admixture of self-absorption and theater was the order of the day, so when a young woman dropped a plastic cup of white wine, few noticed at first. It puddled just long enough on the rustic wood floor to reflect the white lights above. That's when Billy Nungesser, the former Plaquemines Parish president who was running for lieutenant governor for a second time after a failed 2011 bid, dropped to the floor on all fours before anyone else could make a move. He dabbed the wine from the woman's shoes with a napkin in his left hand and then, with his right, pushed a pinch of paper napkins into the crevices of the floor to sop up the rest of the spill. It was fussy work for a bulky guy who had made a fortune in the family business of feeding roughnecks and roustabouts on offshore oil rigs, but success in politics demands a certain adaptability.

Though the election season was barely underway, already

Nungesser had earned a reputation for attending practically every event open—and quite a few closed—to the public. Earlier that afternoon a staffer for one of his opponents remarked, "Billy would attend the opening of an envelope." Now he was on the floor rescuing a damsel in distress, at least in cocktail party ethos. With a hand on one knee for leverage, Nungesser pushed himself up off the floor. He asked the young woman if she was okay and then introduced himself to the small group that gathered 'round. After a few pleasantries, a man placed his hand in the small of Nungesser's back and said softly over a few chuckles: "You know, a Louisiana politician never stands taller than when he's on all fours kissing somebody's ass." Nungesser chortled back, nodding his head in affirmation. Yes, everyone truly was in on the joke. In Louisiana, retail politics and exaggerated chivalry are kissin' cousins.

As the roar of conversations overtook the room again, some found distraction in the museum's many exhibits. *Oh, look, there's a campaign t-shirt for Cecil Picard. See that, they have Hunt Downer's gavel when he was House speaker. Is that Rodney Alexander on that poster? Did you see the John Georges campaign sign in the men's bathroom?*

The buzz of the crowd underscored the significance of the 2015 race for governor—the first open contest for Louisiana's premier political post in eight years. The outgoing incumbent, Republican Bobby Jindal, would finish his constitutionally imposed limit of two terms in just eleven months. He was facing, for the 2015–16 fiscal year, a $1.4 billion budget hole that was certain to bleed into the next governor's term. The go-to factoid of the afternoon, however, was that only one declared candidate for governor was already a member of the Political Hall of Fame: state Representative John Bel Edwards, a Democrat from the small town of Amite, a 70-mile drive northwest from New Orleans. Ironically, Edwards also was the least known of the major candidates.

Edwards had officially launched his dark-horse bid for governor two years earlier. He had served nearly two terms as minority leader, fighting Jindal's ideological conservatism at every turn with mixed results in the GOP-controlled House. Those efforts hardly earned him a spot in the Hall of Fame, though. Edwards was the scion of a legendary family of sheriffs in his native Tangipahoa Parish, and the previous year the entire Edwards clan received the "Political Family of Officeholders Award." The Edwards family was inducted as a group.

Despite Edwards' brush with immortality, many inside the Political Hall of Fame that afternoon didn't know much about him, if they knew him at all. They definitely had no idea what the West

Point graduate and former Army Ranger had in store for the state over the course of the next nine months. Had they known, they might have looked differently at the rest of the established field, which was confined to Republicans: United States Senator David Vitter of Metairie, coldly calculating but strategically brilliant, a scorched-earth campaigner and the *de facto* leader of Louisiana's GOP; Public Service Commissioner Scott Angelle of Breaux Bridge, a personable Cajun and former Democrat who had held senior posts for two governors; and Lieutenant Governor Jay Dardenne of Baton Rouge, a veteran office-holder and the quintessential good government candidate.

Edwards, ultimately, was the one to watch. He and his then-handful of allies were about to mount a campaign that would defy the odds, resurrect Vitter's 2007 prostitution scandal in an unforgettable showdown, and give Louisiana one of its best long-shot political narratives in decades. Edwards may have coasted into the Political Hall of Fame on the coattails of his family, but the 2015 election would prove that history, luck, and a "breeze of hope"—a phrase he would use in many future speeches—were indeed at his back.

Ironically, Edwards did not attend the Hall of Fame ceremony on that Saturday afternoon in 2015, when so many saw him as the Democratic sacrificial lamb in a race destined to end in Vitter's election. Recent contests, after all, had proved what "the fundamentals" and the so-called experts were telling everyone: Louisiana wasn't just trending Republican; it was barreling headlong down a ruby-red highway. White Democrats like Edwards were a dying breed in the South. Between 2004 and 2015, white voters in the Bayou State fled the party of Jefferson and Jackson at an alarming rate, with more than 225,000 changing their registrations, mostly to Republican. It had been a long slide. In 1978, 90 percent of Louisiana voters were Democrats. Heading into this election season, that share was closer to 46 percent, compared to the GOP's 28 percent. Louisiana also had a massive hidden electorate—Democrats who voted Republican without officially switching parties. Meanwhile, African-American registration had increased over the previous eight years to slightly more than 31 percent. Women, who accounted for 55 percent of the state's registered voters, would find themselves heavily targeted in the governor's race. These statistics, vital to the strategies of candidates seeking any office in any state, would factor into the 2015 Louisiana governor's race in a big way, as would polling data.

Every early poll showed Vitter comfortably if not commandingly in front—and a solid majority of voters was promising to vote for any Republican over any Democrat. The most frequently asked question across the state, and likely in the old Winnfield train depot that February afternoon, was, "Can *anybody* beat Vitter?" Edwards certainly believed he could, but few others did—despite floor-to-ceiling evidence to the contrary right there, in the Hall of Fame. Though the cumulative number of inductees neared 200 that day, only two dozen Republicans ranked among them. The rest were Democrats. Like Edwards.

Experts roundly predicted Vitter would face Edwards in a classic right-versus-left runoff, drown him in money, and trounce him on Election Day. That, in fact, was the heart of Vitter's strategy from Day One. In the end, the two men spent roughly $11 million each, and Edwards won handily. Besides Edwards' storybook upset, the big news of the campaign was the unprecedented level of activity by political action committees, particularly super PACs, which accounted for 41 percent of all spending—some $20 million. That was certainly no fluke, as super PACs had begun playing in state elections across America. In that sense, the 2015 Louisiana gubernatorial election was a political slice of Americana, served with a dash of Cajun spice.

The election also marked a major shift in political messaging. The last time Louisiana had an open election for governor, in 2007, Apple had just introduced the iPhone, iPads did not yet exist, and Internet advertising for campaigns was still a novelty. In 2007, the 24-hour news cycle, just creeping into Louisiana, wouldn't peak until eight years later, when social media established its own foothold among voters. Fundraising was relatively straightforward, and newspapers were still almost exclusively paper. In ways that strategists are still counting, the 2015 election cycle changed Louisiana's political landscape far more than Edwards and his "breeze of hope" could have imagined.

The changes that overtook Louisiana in the past few decades were much like those that changed America's political landscape. Former Governor Edwin Edwards—no relation to John Bel Edwards—was Louisiana's answer to Bill Clinton. In fact, he presaged Clinton by at least a decade. His era in Louisiana politics spanned the 1970s through the mid-1990s, a time marked by fast and loose governance, as well as skirt chasing and scandals of every sort. Edwards' relevance had long since ended by the time the 2015 election cycle kicked off at the Political Hall of Fame inductions.

The Bobby Jindal Era, which was defined by legislative term limits, governmental austerity, ideological agendas, culture wars, and, above all, national ambitions, had already supplanted the earlier Edwards reign. Now, as the crowd watched Billy Nungesser mop the floor with napkins in Winnfield, the Jindal era, too, was coming to a close, though Jindal was still in office and in the early thrall of his presidential aspirations.

The ensuing months would usher in a new era of mostly cautious politicians who dared not campaign too close to the edge or in ways that revealed too much about themselves, other than their Christian bona fides. Cell phone cameras, private investigators, and trackers—photographers whom special interests or campaigns had hired to trail opposing candidates and record *everything*—were transforming Louisiana's, and America's, old style of personalized politics.

Somehow, John Bel Edwards and his campaign team found a way to cut through all the noise, establish the little-known Democrat as relevant, and snatch from Vitter what seemed like certain victory to most who attended the Political Hall of Fame gala that wintry Saturday in February. In retrospect, the 2015 gubernatorial election deserves a display case of its own in Winnfield's old train depot.

What follows is the story of how Edwards grabbed the campaign narrative, how Vitter lost his political grip, and how a cast of characters as colorful as any of Louisiana's political immortals made it all happen.

Many who read this tale no doubt will say, "That could happen only in Louisiana." They would be wrong, for John Bel Edwards' rise is no more or less remarkable than Barack Obama's or Donald Trump's on the national scene, or Mitt Romney's in Massachusetts, or Ann Richards' in Texas. None of them was supposed to succeed, yet they all upended favored opponents by connecting with voters in a way their foes could neither foresee nor forestall.

Every election is a unique event, but people are pretty much the same everywhere. That's why the story of Edwards' improbable victory against overwhelming odds is one that, while unfolding against the colorful backdrop of Louisiana's backroads and bayous, barrooms and ballrooms, could literally happen anywhere in America.

2

"That Crap in the Mail"

The Democratic Party volunteers working the phone bank had gone home. The last robocalls had reminded targeted voters, one last time, to cast their ballots that day. It was after 8 p.m. on October 22, 2011, which meant that the polls had closed in Louisiana's statewide primary.

The big news that evening: Bobby Jindal, the *wunderkind* of Louisiana politics, had crushed his virtually unknown and egregiously underfunded Democratic opponent—a 39-year-old public school teacher who had never before run for office. He had won his second term as the state's Republican governor.

Despite Jindal's easy re-election, however—and despite the Democratic Party's failure to field a major candidate for any of the seven statewide offices up for grabs that day—the men and women who sat around the conference table at party headquarters in downtown Baton Rouge had expected a good night. What they cared most about that evening, and where they had focused their energies for the past several months, was the fate of a handful of white incumbent Democrats seeking re-election to the state House and Senate in rural districts that Republicans viewed as ripe for the picking.

As the returns trickled in, the Democratic operatives who huddled inside their party's war room felt confident they would retain most, if not all, of those battleground legislative seats. Even if the media and everyone else saw the primary results as a GOP sweep—and a Democratic apocalypse—they hoped that day to sow the seeds of their party's comeback.

Perhaps no one was more confident that evening than the man who had run the campaign for the House candidates. His name was John Bel Edwards. He was on the ballot, too, and easily beat his opponent that night to win re-election to House District 72 in Tangipahoa Parish, a bucolic enclave of small towns and piney woods about 50 miles northwest of New Orleans. As the leader of the House Democratic

Caucus, the 45-year-old Edwards had spent months traveling the state to assist other candidates the GOP had targeted. Though few realized Edwards' goals at the time, the little-known state representative from Tangipahoa had as much riding on that night as anybody running for statewide office. Maybe more.

In early 2011, Edwards and other House Democratic leaders—Karen St. Germain from the Cajun town of Pierre Part, Sam Jones from the coastal city of Franklin, and Patricia Smith from the capital city of Baton Rouge—had viewed the fall elections with trepidation. They had seen how Republicans whacked Democrats across the country the previous November by tying them to President Barack Obama and his unpopular Affordable Care Act, which the Republicans had derisively dubbed *Obamacare*. Senator David Vitter, the Louisiana GOP's whacker-in-chief, had cruised to victory in the November 2010 elections by painting his opponent, Congressman Charlie Melancon, as Obama's best friend in the Bayou State.

Edwards, St. Germain, Jones, and Smith had no doubt that Republicans would turn to the same playbook in Louisiana's 2011 elections. What's more, Democrats had been on a losing streak in Louisiana, as in other southern states. For generations the dominant force in state politics, the Democrats, in 2007, captured only two of Louisiana's seven statewide constitutional offices. Then, in February 2011, one of those winners, Attorney General Buddy Caldwell, turned Republican only months before the statewide elections. The other statewide Democrat, Lieutenant Governor Mitch Landrieu, who had won the New Orleans mayor's race in 2010, saw a Republican succeed him in a special election later that year.

Going into the 2011 elections, United States Senator Mary Landrieu was the only Democrat holding statewide office, having won a hard-fought re-election battle in 2008—ironically, on Obama's coattails. Republicans, meanwhile, steadily picked off Democrats in the state Legislature. Vitter and Republican House Speaker Jim Tucker began warning rural white Democrats that they had a choice: They could switch parties or face political extinction in the 2011 elections. It was classic Hardball 101, Louisiana style.

Their goal was simple: gain a majority of the 105-member House before the next election cycle began.

The GOP's job of turning Democratic lawmakers into newbie Republicans was made easier by the popularity of Governor Jindal, who rode to victory in 2007 on a wave of voter dissatisfaction with the state's response, two years earlier, to Hurricane Katrina. When the 36-year-old governor took office in January 2008, expectations ran sky-high. A Brown University graduate and a Rhodes Scholar who, at age 24, had led the state Department of Health and Hospitals, Jindal was hailed in a glowing *60 Minutes* profile in March 2009 as "a young man in a hurry."

He had campaigned on the promise of transforming Louisiana government: no more spending one-time money on recurring state needs; a top-to-bottom overhaul of Louisiana's lax ethics laws; smaller government; support for education vouchers and homeschooling programs; and an end to the so-called "Good Ole Boy" way of doing business. To all that, Jindal added a large dose of Christian values—which meant championing the nation's toughest anti-abortion laws—and staunch support of gun ownership rights. While those promises made up Jindal's core political values, one additional vow trumped all the others: No matter how small the tax or how great the need, he would oppose anything that even remotely smacked of a tax increase.

This pledge was more than a promise; it was an ideology, and Jindal would soon show his credentials as an ideologue of the highest order. He was an enthusiastic early signer of the "no tax" pledge proffered by anti-tax fanatic Grover Norquist. Jindal would resist *any* pressure to back away from that vow. Not one inch.

In his first term, Jindal won virtually all of his legislative battles—especially those involving the state budget. In 2008, Louisiana had a nearly $1 billion surplus, thanks to the economic boom spurred by post-Katrina recovery spending. That surplus, which Jindal and lawmakers spent in their first year, gave them a false sense of flush economic times. Jindal at first opposed, then supported a 2008 bill to roll back the personal income tax brackets and rates that voters had approved in 2002. Although the previous income tax structure—known as the Stelly Plan—was sound fiscal policy, voters in 2008, in the face of the $1 billion surplus, answered the demagogic cries for its repeal. Jindal saw the oncoming freight train and gingerly hopped on board. In no time, he took credit for "the largest tax cut in Louisiana history."

When the recovery money dried up, the repeal of Stelly led to an outsized impact on the state's coffers, an impact that increased with each passing year. The annual "hit" started out as $300 million and ultimately grew to more than $800 million. Jindal was not about to raise taxes, so he and his lawmakers began to cut. The cuts fell hardest on public hospitals and universities.

In the early years, Jindal and the lawmakers glossed over the annual deficits by plugging the holes with one-time money—something the governor had promised, as a candidate, he wouldn't do. While good governmental watchdogs warned against that practice, voters and lawmakers turned a blind eye, because taxes went down.

Jindal, however, didn't just oppose new taxes; he started giving business and industry big tax breaks at the same time, all in the name of "economic development." What was great PR for Jindal in the short run put tremendous pressure on state finances, forcing more raids on diminishing pools of cash reserves. Moody's Investors Service came to call the use of one-time funds "Louisiana's structural deficit."

The bubble had to burst at some point—but not during Jindal's first term. All voters saw were glowing statements from Jindal about lower taxes, affirmation of Christian values, tough laws against sex predators, and claims that the new ethics laws constituted a "gold standard." To all appearances, his 2007 campaign had never ended.

One by one, in the face of Jindal's popularity and mounting pressure from Vitter and Tucker, legislative Democrats began caving, and Republicans picked up additional seats during special elections. On December 17, 2010, Vitter and Tucker accomplished their goal when state Representative Noble Ellington—a champion, in earlier days, of populist Democratic Governor Edwin Edwards—left the Democratic Party to become a Republican, giving the GOP 53 votes in the 105-member House. "This is a day to celebrate the next step in what will be more conservative change in the State of Louisiana," crowed Tucker.

Now attention turned to the state Senate, where Democrats clung to a 20–19 majority. A mere five days after Ellington's party switch, Jindal helped push the Senate into the GOP column when, on December 22, he appointed state Senator Nick Gautreaux to head the Louisiana Office of Motor Vehicles. It wasn't a coincidence that Gautreaux was a Democrat. On February 19, state Representative Jonathan Perry, a Republican, won the special election to replace Gautreaux. Going into the 2011 statewide elections, Republicans held both legislative chambers in Louisiana for the first time since Reconstruction.

The GOP was on a roll, and party leaders had every expectation of increasing their ranks in the House in the 2011 elections. Democrats had other plans.

Led by Edwards, the Democrats resolved not to go down without a fight; they even held out a glimmer of hope. At their request, Raymond "Coach" Blanco—the gregarious, politically savvy husband of former Governor Kathleen Blanco—commissioned a poll in May 2010 in the Crowley-based district of state Representative Jack Montoucet, a first-term Democrat. Crowley, the "Rice Capital of the World," is a quintessentially Cajun town nestled in Louisiana's agri-petro belt west of Lafayette. Though Cajuns are conservative, they stick with those they know and trust, regardless of party. The poll showed that voters in Montoucet's district didn't like Jindal's cuts to health care and to public colleges and universities. They disliked his frequent campaign trips outside Louisiana even more. The poll also showed that voters favored some Democratic issues, such as equal pay for women. While cause for hope, those results covered only a single House district. The Democrats needed more data.

Edwards and his colleagues decided to coordinate strategy and messaging for all their candidates in 2011, with professional advice from consultants who had experience taking on the GOP in other states. On April 20 of that year, they put the first piece in place when they hired pollster Jim Kitchens. The 62-year-old Kitchens had earned a Ph.D. in political communications from the University of Florida, had taught in Texas and Alabama, and lived in Orlando.

Kitchens was a political veteran who had made his name as the pollster for Jim Wright of Texas, when Wright was the Democrats' majority leader in Congress in the 1970s. That role took him all over the country. In 1991, he conducted his first poll in Louisiana for the Louisiana Association of Trial Lawyers (a natural ally of the Democrats) and later conducted many surveys in the state. Kitchens liked working in Louisiana; state legislators were close to their constituents, and Louisianans really loved their state. "It's my favorite Third World country," he joked to friends.

When Kitchens interviewed with Edwards and his team in March 2011 for the project coordinating House campaigns, he told them, "I never look at a poll and say *This is how things are*. I look at a poll and think how we can change things for the better."

Around that time, the Democratic House leaders hired another Florida-based firm, Mad Dog Mail, to handle direct mail, a key piece of every campaign's strategy. In the final weeks of a campaign, "hit pieces" arriving via mail inundate targeted voters. Postal workers, art directors, and media consultants all work extra hard to get the massive batches of missives delivered on time. Voters may spend a few seconds looking at them, or no time at all—depending on conception and execution of each clever piece.

Mad Dog's lead in Louisiana would be Jennifer J. Smith. A native of Alabama, the 40-year-old Smith had worked as a reporter in Georgia before deciding to take an active role electing Democrats. When she came to Baton Rouge to interview, Smith told Edwards and the others that she had just served as the general consultant for the Alabama Democratic Party during the 2010 legislative elections. The work had not gone well. The anti-Obama mail that tagged her candidates as liberals, she said, had prompted more than one-third of reliable white Democratic voters to stay home.

"The Republican wave was bigger than we expected," Smith told

Edwards, "and now it's coming your way."

How might Edwards & Co. stand up to that wave? They commissioned Kitchens' first poll in May. The results did not inspire optimism.

Obama had a 38 percent favorable rating in Louisiana, while Jindal's was 66 percent. About 70 percent of voters saw the election as a chance to send Obama a message—not a kind one. Only 32 percent of voters said Democrats best represented their families' interests, while 48 percent said Republicans did. As Kitchens mulled over the data at home in central Florida, he devised a strategy for overcoming those numbers.

"We have to change the dynamic so it won't be a referendum on Jindal or Obama," Kitchens advised his new clients. "We can't win that fight. We have to radically localize the races, to make the election about the needs in each community. You need to show what your candidates have done for their communities, how they represent the values of their communities."

Edwards liked that message. It tracked what he and his team were thinking and seeing, and it resonated in his gut. Edwards was the brother, son, grandson, and great-grandson of sheriffs, Louisiana's quintessential retail politicians. His team would tailor each race to each Democratic candidate. Jennifer Smith and Mad Dog Media came up with the tagline for the overall campaign: "Put Louisiana First." They all liked it.

The best message in the world wouldn't matter, however, if the caucus lacked money to put behind it. Smith brought aboard a 34-year-old political consultant from Florida, Eric Foglesong, to oversee fundraising. At 6 feet 4 inches, Foglesong towered over most people. He leapt at the chance to serve as the House Democrats' political consultant, though that meant moving to Baton Rouge for the duration of the election season, leaving his wife to raise their three-month-old daughter and two young boys near Orlando. On Foglesong's first day, Edwards handed him a binder with bios of the 10 most vulnerable white Democrats in the Legislature. That number soon dropped to nine when state Representative Taylor Barras of New Iberia switched to the GOP, another sign that Democrats faced an uphill battle.

With Foglesong's help, Edwards raised money where he could—from lobbyists, trial attorneys, unions, and others sympathetic to the cause—but as of June the caucus had only $300,000. Meantime, the Republican Party and the Louisiana Committee for a Republican Majority, an outside Super PAC that Vitter had organized, had raised at least $2 million—and the Republicans had the *O-bomb*. Obama.

Returning to the strategy extracted from Kitchens' poll, Jennifer

Smith and Foglesong told each of their candidates to emphasize local issues, to tout every road and infrastructure project they had brought back to their districts, and, above all, to avoid any discussion of Obama and national Democratic issues. "We need to inoculate our candidates before the Obama mail hits," Foglesong said.

Of course, the Democrats planned to send out their own mail pieces. Foglesong and Smith thought that striking photographs of the candidates would make a positive impression during the 10 to 30 seconds that voters looked at a mailer before tossing it into the trash. The two consultants therefore began traveling the state with a photographer in tow to capture their candidates in favorable settings. On July 14, Foglesong, Smith, and the photographer, Amy Mikler, followed John Bel as he made several stops in his district. Mikler shot him talking to a group of seniors and meeting with several blue-collar workers. She also posed him wearing hunting garb while walking in the woods with his nine-year-old son, John Miller, shotguns over their shoulders. Another picture showed Edwards standing next to a large John Deere tractor with its owner, Jack Liuzza, a strawberry farmer and long-time friend of the family, who was known to everyone as "Mr. Jack." Foglesong liked the photos, but he wanted something with Edwards and a dog. The Edwards family dog was a Dachshund named Fred. *Too frou-frou,* Foglesong thought. Then he noticed Mr. Jack's dog, a white Labrador named Mo. *Perfect.*

They went out onto a wooden dock behind Mr. Jack's house so Mikler could take an evocative father-and-son shot of John Bel and John Miller dipping fishing lines into a pond. Then Foglesong noticed an orange rubber "bumper" (a fetch toy used by dog owners and trainers) lying on the dock. "Mr. Jack," Eric asked, "if I throw the baton into the water, will Mo jump in to retrieve it?"

"Absolutely," Mr. Jack replied.

Foglesong turned to Mikler. "If I do that, can you get a good photo of the dog jumping into the pond? Can we make the shot work?"

"It's going to look really cool," Mikler replied.

The photograph captured Mo in mid-flight, with Edwards pointing toward the leaping dog and John Miller standing next to him. Edwards would use it on much of his campaign literature, to great effect.

One of the incumbents high on the Republicans' hit list was Jack Montoucet, the Cajun lawmaker whose district Coach Blanco had polled a year earlier. Nearly all the seats that white Democrats held in Acadiana had gone Republican. Logic said that Montoucet's would be next. Jindal was popular in the district; Obama wasn't. Indeed, Kitchens' May 2011 poll showed that voters in Montoucet's district generally preferred, by a 44 to 28 margin, a Republican holding the seat. But elections are realities, not abstractions, and that's where Democrats felt they had a fighting chance.

Montoucet, 63, had grown up in the district, on a farm outside of Scott, just west of Lafayette. True to his Cajun roots, as a toddler, he spoke French with his parents and grandparents and didn't learn English until he started school. At age 17, he and a buddy enlisted in the Marines, and for two years he worked as a heavy equipment operator on the island of Okinawa. Later, back home, he worked at his dad's mechanic shop and then joined the Lafayette Fire Department, rising to the rank of chief. After his retirement, he began farming alligators and soon opened a company that distributed gator meat across Louisiana and overseas.

Because of his interest in politics and public service, Montoucet had an itch to run for office. His wife Sandra said she would support scratching that itch—once. In 2007, Montoucet ran in House District 42, an open seat. He won. Over the next four years, he faithfully voted against abortion and in favor of gun rights, and he brought home key infrastructure projects. Kitchens' poll showed that Montoucet enjoyed a 50 percent approval rating in the district, with only 10 percent of voters viewing him unfavorably. The poll also showed three issues that worked in Montoucet's favor: Voters liked his work in bringing an alternative energy plant to Crowley, his opposition to a pay raise for legislators, and his efforts to identify French-speaking state employees who could assist French tourists visiting Acadiana. On those issues, at least, Montoucet seemed well positioned to withstand the Republican onslaught.

Then the first anti-Obama mailer blanketed Montoucet's district in late September. He was standing in his family room when a friend called with the news: The mailer called him a liberal and described him as a confidant of Obama. As he listened, Montoucet grew angrier by the second. "This whole thing is a lie," he blurted out. "I've never met Obama or spoken to him. This is bullshit."

Sandra cut him short. "Settle down," she said. "You're always drinking coffee with people in the district. Everybody has your cell phone number. You're out there every day. Get a feel for what people say." Sandra had a point. As Montoucet made the rounds in the ensuing days—even as more mailers tied him to Obama—he found that many people weren't buying the Republican message. "I saw that crap in the mail," folks told him. "It was horrible. We know better." Montoucet felt reassured.

Along with the others, Democratic operative Jennifer Smith had been waiting for the anti-Obama mailers to hit. When they did, she flashed back to a refrain often associated with hurricanes: "I hope our defenses hold," she told herself. (In south Louisiana parlance, "Please, God, let the levees hold against the rising tide.") As she and Foglesong checked with their candidates over the next few days, they learned that the defenses indeed seemed strong. And for the offense, Jared Arsement, a University of New Orleans film school graduate who lived in Lafayette and was close to Kathleen and Raymond Blanco, produced tailor-made TV ads that the vulnerable Democrats used to return fire.

The attack mailers kept coming. On October 13—nine days before the primary—a particularly nasty anti-Obama mailer hit. Edwards convened a conference call. "We have prepared ourselves to deal with this," Edwards, an ex-Army Ranger and former commander in the 82nd Airborne Division, assured the troops. "We have insulated our candidates by consistently pushing our 'Louisiana First' message. The Republican ads will not work in this election cycle. It's important to reinforce that message with our candidates."

Foglesong sent an advisory memo to all Democratic candidates titled, "Response to Obama Ads." His first suggestion was critical: Do not alert local newspaper or TV stations about the mailers. "This will not help you stay on message," he wrote, "and will only serve to broaden the impact of the piece."

The memo went on to detail how to address the issue, depending on the audience. Before a white or racially mixed crowd, the message should be: "You can be sure of one thing when you vote for me— I'll put Louisiana First. I'll fight to protect Louisiana families and Louisiana jobs from the Wall Street interests that want to hijack the state." Before African-American crowds, the message was blunt: "The David Duke forces are back in Louisiana—this time spearheaded by David Vitter and his Washington, D .C.-style racist attacks on African-American voters." The memo ended by urging candidates to make sure that African-American ministers in their districts had seen the mailer and could denounce it from the pulpit.

Jim Kitchens began tracking polls in key legislative districts. Several days before the primary, he checked the latest results and said to himself, "It looks like our plan is working." Still, no one could be sure.

On October 22, the day of the primary election, staffers who had worked on the Democratic House campaign showed up one by one at party headquarters on Government Street in downtown Baton Rouge. Someone pushed two tables end-to-end in the main room to create a long conference table. They fielded calls and checked with their candidates after the polls closed. By 8:30 p.m., they were constantly refreshing the secretary of state's website to check the results. *James*

Armes has 54 percent of the vote with one third of the precincts in, someone shouted. *Dorothy Sue Hill has 60 percent of the vote with half of the precincts counted*, someone else yelled a few minutes later. Nervousness around the table gave way to growing excitement and then fist bumps when staffers called out a winner. By 10 p.m., the results were in: The nine white Democratic representatives the Republicans had targeted had won outright in the primary.

In the state Senate, several vulnerable white Democrats likewise won re-election in conservative rural districts. Among them were Ben Nevers in the mill town of Bogalusa, Eric LaFleur in Cajun-inflected Ville Platte, and Gary Smith in Norco, about 20 miles up the Mississippi River from New Orleans. All three ran coordinated campaigns that stressed their local roots and the "Louisiana First" message. Edwards and his team believed they had pulled off an improbable victory by finding a weakness in the Republican strategy and exploiting it—although some Republicans had foreseen the losses and, near the end, had pulled out of races they deemed unwinnable.

The Democrats' streak continued four weeks later when first-time candidates Gene Reynolds from Minden, in northwest Louisiana, and Stephen Ortego from Carencro, just outside Lafayette, won runoffs that, only a few months earlier, some strategists had expected them to lose. In all, after Labor Day, the Democrats' ranks in the House had dropped by only a single seat. They would be in the minority in both the House and Senate, and the party had been shut out of the seven statewide elected offices, but the results could have been much worse. Though the old saw says that *people learn more from their failures than their successes*, that didn't happen. Not this time. Edwards sensed he was on to something.

As Eric Foglesong was packing up on election night, Edwards asked him to join his family the following evening for supper at his home in Roseland, just outside Amite in Tangipahoa Parish. On the hour-long drive the next day, Foglesong reflected on what they had accomplished and wondered what might lie ahead. He arrived after the family had already finished eating. Donna Edwards got him a plate of turkey with all the fixings, and her husband sat with Foglesong while he ate. After dinner, Edwards invited Foglesong to join him on the pool deck behind the family home. The night was chilly. Edwards threw wood into the outdoor fireplace, lit a fire, and brought out a bottle of Maker's Mark, Foglesong's favorite bourbon.

Across Louisiana and in rural enclaves across America that

same November night, hunters likewise gathered 'round fires and recounted their exploits taking deer, ducks, squirrels, and other prey earlier that day. The closest that Edwards, a lifelong country boy, had come to hunting that season was the photoshoot, months earlier, of him and John Miller walking through the woods with unloaded shotguns slung over their shoulders. On this night, however, Edwards and Foglesong were *hunters*, celebrating the taking of a different kind of prey—one that was hunting them as well. The two men settled into wooden Adirondack chairs and replayed the highlights of the election. They laughed at memorable anecdotes and spoke with pride at how the campaign had exceeded expectations. By now, Foglesong sensed that Edwards had something else on his mind.

Indeed, he did. Edwards leaned toward Foglesong and said, "I'm thinking very seriously about running for governor. What do you think?" The question didn't surprise Foglesong. As they had crisscrossed the state helping other candidates, Foglesong had told Edwards more than once that he had met Democrats who said to him, "One day, John Bel is going to be a great governor."

"You're a state representative," Foglesong told Edwards. "But what you've just accomplished—raising more than $1 million and recruiting and assisting candidates in every corner of the state—is equivalent to running a statewide race. You could repeat that effort in 2015 and be successful."

Edwards nodded. "I'm not independently wealthy," he said. "I'd have to spend a lot of time campaigning and take time away from my law practice, right?"

"Yes," Foglesong replied. "You'd have to campaign nearly full time."

The conversation turned to Mitch Landrieu, who won election twice as lieutenant governor before winning the New Orleans mayoral race in 2010. Landrieu obviously had bigger ambitions. Would he run? If he did, he would easily eclipse Edwards' effort. They noted that Mary Landrieu, Mitch's sister and Louisiana's senior senator, faced a run for re-election in 2014. That was certain to be another tough race—with Obama at the center of the Republican barrage.

Would conservative Louisiana elect two "liberal Landrieus" to statewide office in the space of one year? Mary's fate in 2014 would certainly influence her brother's decision, but either way, both men concluded, Mitch Landrieu would recognize that he couldn't be elected governor—at least, not in 2015.

"John Bel," Foglesong said, "you're a different Democrat.

You've got a great personal story, and you're conservative on abortion and guns. You know how Republicans like to beat up Democrats on those issues."

They drained their glasses and called it a night. Edwards walked Foglesong out to his car. As they said their goodbyes, Foglesong made one final point. "If you do run, count me in," he said. Edwards smiled and waved as Foglesong drove off.

3

"What If Things Go Bad?"

The water tower behind Spartan Field grew larger as John Diez drove his Ford F-150 down Burnside Avenue. "G O N Z A L E S" painted across its tank in large block letters easily gave up its locale. A black cast iron pot appeared to the left of the "G," a nod to the late Governor John McKeithen's proclaiming Gonzales the "Jambalaya Capital of the World" in 1968.

While making jambalaya is serious business everywhere in south Louisiana, the people of Gonzales are especially intent: Do you cook it with wood or propane? Pork or chicken? Caramelized onions with a dark stock or, heaven forbid, Kitchen Bouquet? Kids growing up in this corner of south Louisiana know how to make their rice properly *pop* in a jambalaya before they learn how to drive.

Painted to the right of the "S" was a Spartan, the mascot of East Ascension High School, where the football field sat in the shadow of the water tower and across Burnside Avenue from Diez's Magellan Strategies office, the site of an all-Republican election results watch party later that night. The list of invitees was small but the people high -powered.

The evening before, in the parking lot of the football field, local candidates had enjoyed prime politicking time. Better still, the team had delivered a hometown win, as East Ascension beat Baton Rouge Catholic 36–29. Nothing went better with Friday night football in Gonzales than fall elections the next morning.

As Diez pulled into his parking lot that Saturday morning on October 22, 2011, he knew that those same tailgaters from the night before were beginning to show up at their voting precincts, as were voters across Louisiana. The ballot that day was long, crowded with candidates vying for scores of public offices—from governor to the Legislature, from parish police jury seats to assessors, from sheriffs to ward constables. The 41-year-old Diez was focused on the legislative contests.

That day marked the end of Diez's second election cycle as the executive director of the Louisiana Committee for a Republican Majority, whose stated purpose was to wrest control of the Louisiana House and Senate from the Democrats and put it squarely into GOP hands. Launched in 2006, LCRM had at its disposal an army of GOP influencers happy to write checks and twist arms. The committee's strategy relied heavily on term limits opening up seats in rural districts that Democrats had held for generations.

A year after its ambitious beginnings, during the 2007 election season, LCRM and Diez launched assaults on Democrats in rural communities across the state. They gained enough seats in the House and Senate to scare many surviving white Democrats into dropping their "D's" and embracing "R's." The Republicans took the House in late 2010 for the first time since Reconstruction, and by the time Mardi Gras ended in early 2011, the GOP had captured the Louisiana Senate as well. Republican control of the Legislature marked a seismic shift in Louisiana's political landscape. Diez's job in the summer and autumn of 2011 was to build on that shift and to position the conservative movement for even bigger statewide gains.

As he parked his truck, Diez couldn't help thinking, *What if things go bad?* Questions raced through his head. *If things go bad, how do I explain to the donors why 2011 didn't live up to 2007? Did we set expectations too high? And did I fail to manage them? How will this election impact our goals going forward?* With a touch of gallows humor, Diez allowed himself a small laugh. *Will I wake up tomorrow with a horse head in my bed? Why does Louisiana politics remind me of* The Godfather*?*

Once he entered his office, he realized that months of hectic phone calls and noisy meetings had ended abruptly. He was alone. As the names of clients raced through his mind, one name resurfaced again and again: David Vitter, the junior senator from Metairie. Vitter had been responsible for giving life to LCRM, and the party credited him for the group's success. For a budding Republican consultant like Diez, nabbing Vitter as a client was the grand prize. Not only had Diez worked with the senator's campaign team, he had also scored the LCRM gig to oversee polling, predictive data modeling, and voter analysis for the legislative races in 2011. Vitter would be Diez's special guest that evening, along with Kyle Ruckert, his chief of staff and campaign manager.

Diez paced around his office, reviewing countless scenarios to answer his question: *What if things go bad?*

Campaign strategies, paths to victory, and messaging often coexist more inside the heads of consultants and pollsters than anyplace else.

Diez's head was full. He finally settled into his personal office and from behind his L-shaped desk started stacking empty blue cans of Skoal. He had first engaged in this ritual, amusing to some and disgusting to others, while at the Republican National Committee seven years earlier. During the course of an election cycle, Diez would keep all his empty cans of dipping tobacco and stack them into miniature pyramids, small castles, or any other shape he found cathartic.

That Saturday morning, he had a lot on his mind. In addition to helping Republicans maintain a majority in the state House and Senate, and possibly build upon it, he had been watching a pair of competitive statewide races that would play out that evening. He knew that the contests for lieutenant governor and secretary of state had long ago entered the orbit of David Vitter, Diez's cornerstone client. Those races looked to be very close.

Lieutenant Governor Jay Dardenne was defending himself against a challenge by Plaquemines Parish President Billy Nungesser, who had developed a close relationship with Vitter and was benefitting from the alliance. Dardenne had won the lieutenant governor slot the previous year, in 2010, via a special election to replace Mitch Landrieu, who had won election as mayor of New Orleans. After 14 years in the state Senate, then four as secretary of state, Dardenne, the new lieutenant governor, posed a threat to Vitter, who gave no quarter to anyone who even thought about crossing him—or running against him. For his part, Nungesser used his personal wealth to bolster his campaign kitty.

The race for lieutenant governor pitted Dardenne's moderate and academic brand against Nungesser's husky conservatism—backed, of course, by Vitter's hardball politics of precision. The race got nasty at times, with Dardenne and Nungesser exchanging broadsides at a furious pace.

Though Vitter was not on the ballot, he had plenty of skin in the game. That's why Diez was not smiling as he stacked one blue Skoal can atop another. A long-term plan that was positioning Vitter as a primary influencer—in races up and down the ballot—had come together. Back in the 2007 cycle, Vitter had successfully backed then-state Representative Mike Strain for agriculture commissioner over incumbent Bob Odom, a Democrat. Now Vitter was getting involved in more statewide races—and quite a few legislative contests as well.

In addition to the lieutenant governor's race, Vitter had staked out a position in the election for secretary of state. When Dardenne vacated the seat to ascend to the position of lieutenant governor, his chief deputy, Tom Schedler, automatically took over as interim secretary of state. Now Schedler—who had served in the state Senate with Dardenne while Vitter was still in the Louisiana House—was seeking a full four-year term. Opposing Schedler was House Speaker Jim Tucker, a Vitter ally who was instrumental in turning the new Republican majority into conservative policy inside the rails of the lower chamber.

With Vitter backing Nungesser against Dardenne, and Tucker against Dardenne's hand-picked successor, the only two competitive statewide races on the October 2011 ballot appeared to pit Vitter against Dardenne.

For Diez, the Dardenne-versus-Vitter aspect of the election cycle presented a conundrum. He was working not only for Vitter and LCRM in a handful of hard-fought legislative contests, but also for Dardenne in the race for lieutenant governor. While the old adage, "It's easier to get forgiveness than permission," might work with the mild-mannered Dardenne, Vitter was not the sort to give *either* permission *or* forgiveness. In fact, in the preceding months, Vitter and Ruckert had made pointed comments about Diez working for Dardenne.

Fortunately for Diez, Vitter's camp had on its radar a target more important than Dardenne: the senator's real political enemy, Governor Bobby Jindal, who was expected to win re-election handily that evening. Nominally the top Republican in Louisiana, Jindal was Vitter's only rival for the hearts and minds—and money and loyalty—of Bayou State Republicans. The bad blood between them ran deep, their feud due in part to their similarities, but mostly to their conflicting ambitions. Both were Rhodes Scholars, Vitter at Harvard and Jindal at Brown, and both looked to conquer Louisiana politics as conservative Republicans. The similarities ended there.

After losing the governor's race to Democrat Kathleen Blanco four years earlier, now, on July 16, 2007, Jindal reintroduced himself to Louisiana voters, spending the day announcing for governor in each of the state's major media markets, the largest of which is New Orleans. That afternoon, at exactly the same time Jindal appeared in Kenner at the Airport Hilton, Vitter upstaged him with his own nationally televised confession of a "very serious sin" in connection with the "D.C. Madam" prostitution ring.

After Vitter's name surfaced in the scandal, Jindal was the only major Republican in the state who failed to give the senator an unqualified statement of support as he began his long, methodical march to political redemption. After that, the two men never passed up a chance to snipe at one another. In 2010, for example, Jindal chose not to endorse Vitter for re-election to the Senate. Although Jindal's refusal to support the senator did not affect the election's outcome—a rout of Vitter's Democratic opponent and a large dose of salvation for the senator—Vitter never forgot the slight.

A year later, in the statewide primary that brought Diez to his office that Saturday morning, Vitter gave Jindal a left-handed endorsement for re-election by urging voters to help make the governor "bolder"—a reference to the increasingly frequent criticism that Jindal shied away from the toughest issues. Despite their mutual enmity and thinly veiled shots at each other, both men had won big victories since their feud went public.

By late afternoon, Diez was browning meat in the big cast iron pot as Ascension Parish Sheriff Jeff Wiley pulled up. The bespectacled sheriff, jovial and beyond balding, exited his SUV and walked toward Diez.

"So the senator is really coming?" Wiley asked.

"Yeah," Diez replied, stirring his jambalaya. "They're on their way."

Wiley looked around at the empty parking lot, then at Diez. The sheriff eyed the cast iron pot and the stack of paper plates and plastic forks on Diez's tailgate. No tables. No chairs. Wiley could hear the traffic blowing by. He looked again at Diez.

"This is the setup?" the sheriff asked.

"Yes, Martha Stewart. This is the setup," Diez replied with a laugh.

Diez knew Vitter didn't want to get dressed up that night or meet with a big crowd. Parking lot jambalaya served with cold Miller Lite and election returns—with only a few close political allies—sounded about right. For all of Vitter's in-your-face politics, he was often unassuming. At that very moment, Vitter was getting into the passenger side of his Honda Civic at his home in Metairie, with Ruckert behind the wheel. The two men traded quick updates on races in which LCRM had played a major role, but mostly they listened to the radio, flipping between pre-sets to listen to sports talk and the news on WWL–AM, the state's only 50,000-watt radio station. They would reach Gonzales within the hour.

Ruckert and Vitter had turned heads in 2007 with the first showing for the Louisiana Committee for a Republican Majority. This election, however, offered fewer open seats. With an electorate already trending red, some districts no longer revolved around the question of which candidates were Republican, but rather to what degree the candidates kept the party faith, a development that strategists considered the byproduct of earlier successes.

As the sun began to set that Saturday afternoon, Ruckert and Vitter exited Interstate 10 and put the wheels of the senator's Honda Civic onto Gonzales terra. Vitter had planned a low-key evening with just one stop before joining Diez for parking lot jambalaya. Former Gonzales Mayor Johnny Berthelot, who was running in House District 88, had grown up just two blocks from Gonzales City Hall, and he was the great-nephew of "Tee Joe" Gonzales, the city's first mayor. As one of the nine House candidates LCRM had recruited, Berthelot benefitted from the group's handling of his direct mail, radio ads, and robocalls. Berthelot was expected to run away with the House seat that night, and he thanked Vitter when the senator and Ruckert made a quick stop to greet him at the Clarion Inn and Conference Center.

Around 7 p.m.—an hour before polls closed—Vitter and Ruckert finally reached Diez's Magellan Strategies office on Burnside Avenue. The senator was just fine with the parking lot setup; he knew everyone in attendance and slipped in effortlessly. Diez made sure everyone had a Miller Lite. They all stood around the jambalaya pot sipping from their cans. Wiley spoke first. He brought up the topic the others had been thinking about a lot recently.

"You know you want to run for governor," Wiley said, motioning to Vitter with a beer in his hand. "You'd be a good governor."

Vitter just shrugged. He had heard such talk before, and he had a variety of stock answers, most of which Ruckert had already heard. "I'm not committed to anything right now," Vitter told the sheriff.

As Vitter's closest confidant, Ruckert knew different. Roughly a month earlier, Ruckert had asked the same question while he and Vitter reviewed legislative races from the offices of the National Republican Senatorial Committee in Washington, D.C.

"What are you going to do?" Ruckert had asked, sensing his boss was more likely than not to run for governor in 2015.

"It's 50–50," replied Vitter. That, at least, was an acknowledgement that the senator was giving the race serious consideration.

Diez's parking lot was neither the time nor the place for Vitter to declare his intentions. He had other scores to settle first, beginning with the elections that night for lieutenant governor, secretary of state, and the Legislature. Joel DiGrado, Vitter's communications director, joined the senator and Ruckert as they moved from the parking lot to a secluded cubicle in Diez's office. They had finished eating their jambalaya, but the beer kept coming. With polls now closed, Ruckert turned on a computer and went to the secretary of state's website. The numbers were trickling in, giving hints of what the night had in store. Johnny Berthelot, as predicted, was going to crush his competition in the Gonzales-based House district.

Diez began cleaning up the tailgate of his pickup. He had a good idea of the results Vitter and Ruckert would see that night, as did they. LCRM would have a respectable showing, but it wouldn't repeat the crushing victories of 2007. Somehow the Louisiana Democratic Party had woken up, and Diez had spent weeks trying to figure out what had happened. Yes, the Democrats saw what LCRM had done in 2007 and knew what was coming. But something else had changed.

In Diez's mind, that something was state Representative John Bel Edwards, who chaired the House Democratic Caucus as a freshman lawmaker and was seeking re-election that night. Diez, having identified Edwards as the Democrats' new legislative ringleader, felt a surge of energy pushing back against LCRM's efforts—primarily for seats held by white, rural Democrats. He thought Edwards was a "Democratic Jim Tucker."

The Vitter–Ruckert–Diez game plan in 2011 called for playing smarter, not harder—and focusing on the statewide races of concern to the senator. Democrats under Edwards' stewardship had employed the same "smarter, not harder" strategy, but had focused on the legislative races. Those who hovered around Vitter and Ruckert that evening, on October 22, 2011, noted that the two men seemed primarily more attuned to the statewide races for lieutenant governor and secretary of state.

Ruckert would hit *refresh* on the computer's browser, new election figures would appear on the screen, and with his boss he would try to make sense of the numbers. Very little conversation was necessary. After years of working together, Ruckert and Vitter had their own communicative body language. A certain look or a nod conveyed more than a spoken sentence between the two of them.

Judging by their unspoken reactions to the numbers on the screen, the night was not going well for their chosen candidates, Billy Nungesser and Jim Tucker. *Refresh.* Jay Dardenne would remain lieutenant governor, setting him up perfectly for a run for governor in 2015. *Refresh.* Dardenne's chosen successor for secretary of state, Schedler, held a razor-thin lead. *Refresh.* Dardenne knocked out Nungesser with 53 percent of the vote. *Refresh.* Tucker lost to Schedler by just 8,400 votes out of 890,000.

At 10:45 p.m., Vitter and Ruckert slowly made their way outside. The pair began the return drive to Metairie in the darkness of Interstate 10, catching up on legislative races and assessing the blowback from the Nungesser and Tucker defeats. By the time Vitter's Honda Civic made it through LaPlace and over the Bonnet Carre Spillway into Vitter's home parish of Jefferson, fatigue kicked in. They had flown in from D.C. the day before at 6 a.m. and had spent most of the time that followed in another plane zipping around Louisiana with Nungesser and Sammy Kershaw, the country music legend who had mounted unsuccessful bids for lieutenant governor in 2007 and 2010. This time

Kershaw was backing Nungesser. The two had fought a long primary battle.

The 2011 election cycle gave Republicans 58 of the 105 House seats and 24 of the 39 Senate seats—a total gain of 10 seats in the Legislature from the previous February. Though the wins didn't repeat 2007's huge gains, the needle still moved in the party's direction. Term limits had not been as helpful this year, and, in addition, LCRM targeted districts that had historically voted just 52 percent for Republicans in major elections—whereas in 2007 the baseline measure of GOP support was 67 percent. LCRM stakeholders had to raise the bar on themselves, because they had already picked the low-hanging fruit four years earlier.

The night's big disappointments for Team Vitter were the losses Nungesser and Tucker suffered, but both of those races were intramural in nature—Republican versus Republican. The Democrats were so wounded after 2007 that they barely competed in the 2011 statewide races, and no one knew when they would truly compete again. The October 2011 primary may not have given Vitter the political boost he wanted, but he was still the GOP's most visible leader riding the crest of a Republican tsunami, which is why many conservatives expected him to run for governor in 2015.

The question of who else might appear on the 2015 ballot would serve as grist for cocktail party chatter and opinion columns over the next several months. For the next three-plus years, no one could say for sure which potential candidates would actually run. The race to succeed Bobby Jindal—and the emergence of a surprise Democratic candidate, someone beyond the usual list of names—seemed far away as Ruckert and Vitter arrived at the senator's home in Metairie. But that race, and that candidate, were already headed their way .

4

"He'll Be Here Next Year, and I'll Be Gone"

On the morning of July 2, 1984, John Bel Edwards awoke from a fitful sleep at the Cornwall Inn in the village of Cornwall-on-Hudson in New York state. The seventeen-year-old had a lot on his mind. The day before, he had gone to Mass with his family and girlfriend Donna Hutto one last time at St. Helena Catholic Church in his hometown of Amite. During the service, Edwards' mother, Dora Jean, and Donna both cried at the thought of his leaving. After lunch at the home of Dora Jean's mother, Grandma Miller, they all drove to New Orleans International Airport to see him off.

The seventh of eight children in a small country town, John Bel had rarely spent time away from Amite or his family. He had flown only once before—in the fourth grade—when he traveled with a friend's family to Disney World. Now, as the Edwards clan stood in the terminal at the New Orleans airport, everyone knew they wouldn't see him for months. And his destination this time was the polar opposite of the Magic Kingdom.

After long hugs and more tears and a last look back at Donna and his family, John Bel boarded the plane and flew to Newark International Airport. By the time his bus arrived at the Cornwall Inn, the night clerk had given away his room. The teenager had nowhere else to go, so the clerk rolled a cot into the inn's restaurant, where Edwards spent his final night before entering the United States Military Academy at West Point.

When he awoke the next morning, he knew he would soon enter a very different world, and he knew the first few weeks would be brutal, beginning in just a few hours with Reception Day. He grabbed his bag of civilian clothes and rode the bus to West Point.

R-Day begins Basic Cadet Training, also known as Beast Barracks. Inside Eisenhower Hall, families learned they had 90 seconds to say goodbye to their loved ones. Edwards watched the others; he was already on his own. After 90 seconds, the academy began the process of dehumanizing high school class presidents, football stars, and valedictorians so that they could transform into West Point cadets, willing to obey their superiors without question and, ultimately, die for their country.

Edwards and the other new cadets changed into black low-quarter shoes, black socks, black shorts, and white t-shirts with their names stamped on them. Scared stiff, they rushed from station to station, where they collected uniforms, New Cadet handbooks, duffel bags, and canteens and received vaccinations and company assignments. Their heads freshly shaved, they learned how to salute, how to stand at attention, how to walk double time at 120 steps per minute—with one foot always on the ground—and how to answer an upperclassman in one of only four responses: "Yes, sir," "No, sir," "No excuse, sir," and "Sir, I do not understand."

When in formation, they learned, they could speak only after an upperclassman, an officer, or a noncommissioned officer had addressed them. Outside of formation, they could address an upperclassman only after asking, "Sir, may I ask a question?" They had to walk along the wall inside buildings and to square each corner, whether or not anyone else was there. At each stage of R-Day, seniors yelled at them when they didn't perform perfectly, especially when they began to learn how to form up and march.

Although exactly 1,460 young men and women began R-Day on July 2, 1984, the hazing and stress prompted dozens to quit the same day. Edwards, too, had thoughts of leaving, but he kept telling himself that life at the academy had to get better at some point. And even if it didn't, he couldn't let his family down.

John Bel Edwards hailed from a line of achievers in Tangipahoa Parish. Immigrants of English descent from the Tidewater region of Virginia and the Carolinas had settled Tangipahoa—an Indian word for "ear of corn" or "gatherer of corn"—after the Revolutionary War. Many had been Tories fleeing persecution from the newly triumphant Americans. Among the piney woods, they found safety and large tracts of cheap land. Eventually, Tangipahoa Parish was carved out of four neighboring parishes and chartered in 1869. Its northernmost town, Kentwood, later the birthplace of Britney Spears, lies on the Louisiana side of the Mississippi border.

Then, in the late 19th Century, Sicilians migrated to Tangipahoa, many establishing truck farms along the Illinois Central rail line that bisected the parish north to south.

In the state's history, the parish is best known for its regional nickname, "Bloody Tangipahoa," because feuds and grudges between rival clans in the 1890s and early 1900s led to ambushes by one group of white settlers against another on rural roads. The blood feuds only begat more killings. John Bel's great-grandfather, Millard F. Edwards, who was instrumental as a deputy sheriff in stopping one spate of violence in the 1890s, went on to serve on the parish school board, as the local postmaster, and ultimately, in 1898, as the appointed sheriff of Tangipahoa Parish, a position he held for two years.

One of Millard's sons, Frank M. Edwards, lettered for three LSU football teams as a lineman during the sport's early days, captaining the 1905 squad in his final year. Frank M. Edwards was elected to the state House of Representatives from Tangipahoa Parish in 1916, left to serve as a captain in the Louisiana 161st Infantry in World War I, and won a second four-year state House term in 1924. He was elected sheriff of Tangipahoa in 1928 and won re-election every four years until 1948, when a man named Tom Sanders defeated him. Frank M. Edwards won one more election, a four-year term in the state Senate in 1956, before losing his 1960 re-election bid. He died a year later.

Throughout his career, Frank M. Edwards stood firmly in the camp of Huey Long and his brother Earl, the patron saints of Louisiana's unique brand of Democratic populism.

Frank had only one child, Frank Edwards Jr., and the family lived on a farm outside of Amite. At Amite High School, Frank Jr. met his future wife, Dora Jean Miller. "He was gorgeous, absolutely gorgeous," Dora Jean recalled years later. "And he was very smart. He had the best way with people—giving advice to whoever asked him." They married in 1956, after she had finished nursing school and while he was a student at LSU Law School.

Beginning in 1958, back in Amite, they had eight children over the next 10 years. "We were Catholics," Mrs. Edwards explained later with a laugh. The first child, Alice, was followed by seven boys: Frank III, Andrew, Clay, Chris, Morgan, John Bel, and Daniel. John Bel was born on September 16, 1966. The second part of his first name came from the last name of his paternal grandmother, Lilian Bel.

Although Amite was the parish seat, it claimed only about 4,000 residents; several other towns in Tangipahoa Parish dwarfed it. The biggest was Hammond, which was home to the state's third largest four-year public university, Southeastern Louisiana University. As in other rural parishes, government institutions—the sheriff's office, the Charity Hospital, the school board, and a military installation at Hammond Municipal Airport—were the largest employers. The population in 1960 had reached 60,000—double the number of residents in 1920—and Tangipahoa's population continued to grow.

As in other rural parishes in south Louisiana, the politics were generally conservative, with a populist tinge. All elected officials were Democrats. By the mid-1960s, whites constituted about two-thirds of the parish population and African Americans one-third.

In keeping with its nickname—"Bloody Tangipahoa"—the parish saw its share of racial strife over the years. Between the late 1800s and 1950, at least two dozen lynchings were reported in Tangipahoa. By the 1960s, public oppression gave way to quieter but tense race relations, as was common across the rural South.

In 1968, Frank Edwards Jr. won election as the family's third-generation sheriff when he forged a coalition of poor whites, Italian immigrants, and African Americans to defeat, narrowly, Tom Sanders, avenging his father's loss to Sanders 20 years earlier. Soon thereafter, as schools and government jobs desegregated, Frank Jr. became the first Tangipahoa sheriff to hire African-American deputies empowered to arrest white offenders and to investigate crimes in white households. With the help of his kids, who campaigned with him door to door and licked stamps to send out mailers, Sheriff Edwards won re-election in 1972. That same year, he was elected as a delegate to the special assembly that rewrote Louisiana's Constitution. Again, in 1975, he won re-election as sheriff.

Children in the large Edwards household had to follow certain rules. They had to "Yes, sir" and "No, sir" their father and "Yes, ma'am" and "No, ma'am" their mother. They had to attend Mass every Sunday at St. Helena Catholic Church, where the family filled an entire pew. Further, the children enjoyed few luxuries. Because their parents had to raise and clothe so many children, the boys wore mostly hand-me-downs. The occasional family night out meant hamburgers at Sullivan's Drive-In in Amite.

In the late 1960s, the Edwards family moved into a rambling, four-bedroom house at 411 East Mulberry Street, only 100 yards from the parish courthouse. The sheriff and his wife took one bedroom, Alice had another, and the boys were divided between the other two. John Bel shared the downstairs bedroom with the brothers on either side of him in age, Morgan and Daniel.

Frank Edwards Jr. had grown up on a 600-acre farm about 10 miles east of Amite. "My husband was a country boy at heart," Dora Jean said later, explaining why, while he was sheriff, he decided to operate a dairy. He first leased, from a friend, farmland between Amite and Independence to the south where he kept 75 cows. The dairy performed well enough that the sheriff moved it to the larger 600-acre site where he had grown up and where his mother still lived.

The family moved out there as well and for about 18 months lived in a one-room structure with a concrete floor and a tin roof.

Everyone slept in that one room, the eight children in double bunk beds. A makeshift bathroom stood tucked away in a corner. In the summertime, as the room had no air conditioning, the family installed fans. During the winter, the parents put up plywood shutters and brought in a wood- burning stove. The conditions were rough, but the family treated the stay as if it were an extended camping trip.

The boys had to milk cows, bale hay, build fences, and plant corn. They ended workdays during the hot, humid summer by jumping from a bluff into Big Creek. On weekends, when hired hands worked at the dairy, they visited the family's fishing camp, reachable only by boat, in Manchac, a tiny isthmus separating Lake Pontchartrain from Lake Maurepas.

The day after Christmas every year, Sheriff Edwards took the seven boys on camping trips that evolved over the years as a central part of family lore. They would float down the Tangipahoa River until New Year's Eve, sometimes as far as Lake Pontchartrain. Braving cold and rain, they added the beans, onions, and potatoes they had brought to large cast iron pots and cooked them with whatever they caught fishing or hunting. Dessert consisted of leftover Christmas pumpkin pie, John Bel's particular favorite.

Dora Jean had grown up poor—her father was electrocuted in a workplace accident in New Orleans when she was two years old. Afterward, Dora Jean's mother, who had only a seventh grade education, moved with her five children to Amite. There, Mrs. Miller scraped by on hard work and help from her sister and brother-in-law, who lived across the street.

Though Dora Jean had studied nursing, she devoted herself full time to motherhood after her children began arriving, nearly one every year. Later, in 1971, she decided to put her education back to use, as the family could use the money. Within a year, she was caring for patients in Independence at Lallie Kemp Charity Hospital, which was part of Louisiana's sprawling state-operated Charity Hospital System, established by Huey Long in the 1930s to give poor people access to free (or affordable) health care. Nursing allowed Dora Jean to offer her warmth and kindness to Lallie Kemp's patients.

"At the charity hospital," *The Times-Picayune*'s Kevin Litten reported in 2015, "Dora Jean remembers asking a patient why he wasn't taking the medicines he was prescribed for a chronic medical condition. He told her if he spent the money to buy the prescriptions, 'I can't eat.' She said the answer horrified her, but she would hear that story again and again." She was also dismayed to discover the difficulty patients had to overcome even to "make it to the hospital for care. Many would arrive after days of looking for transportation," and afterward, they often waited hours for rides home. "'When you see how hard it is to get to a charity hospital, you wonder what it's like if the hospital wasn't there,' she said. 'Everybody ought to spend time working in a charity hospital just to see what goes on and how badly they're needed .'"

When Sheriff Edwards ran for a fourth term in 1979, he had a real fight on his hands. He was under investigation by federal authorities for drug smuggling, and he faced allegations that he had used prison inmates to work on the family's fishing camp in Manchac. He was also accused of having the sheriff's department rent an airstrip on his dairy.

His family stoutly defended him, claiming that the federal investigation was politically motivated and that any mistakes the sheriff made were the result of his over-generous nature. "If you were a friend, he'd do something he could to help you," remembered Frank Edwards III, his eldest son, who became the police chief of Independence. "He had friends who were accused of burning their properties down. He had friends who made whiskey. He had friends from all walks of life."

When seven men challenged the sheriff in 1979, he purchased a full-page ad in the *Hammond Daily Star*, appearing in a photo with his large family under a headline that read, "Why Change?...When we already have the best." With Frank Edwards as sheriff, the ad read, Tangipahoa Parish had "LESS DOPE, LESS CRIME AND THE BEST IN LAW ENFORCEMENT." Then, when a popular town marshal named Gordon Anderson from Hammond appeared to offer the sheriff his strongest challenge, Sheriff Edwards savaged the man. He ran another full-page ad headlined "CORRUPTION?" that contained copies of canceled checks and receipts from Anderson's office as evidence of wrongdoing.

Sheriff Edwards led the October primary but fell short of the majority he needed for outright victory. Nevertheless, he had bloodied Anderson so badly that his main challenger finished third, out of the money. A little-known realtor and state wildlife agent named Eddie Layrisson finished second with 27 percent of the vote, behind Sheriff Edwards' 36 percent. Layrisson had outworked both men by visiting every residence in Tangipahoa Parish.

The incumbent sheriff now turned his fire on Layrisson, claiming that his challenger was a dope-smoking draft dodger because he had taken graduate classes in 1969 at the University of California at Berkeley. Layrisson dismissed these and other allegations hurled at him by the desperate sheriff. On Election Day, Anderson's voters swung behind Layrisson, giving him 54 percent of the vote, an outcome that few could have foreseen only a few months earlier. A second outcome was the Edwards family's lesson in political reality.

Over the previous dozen years, holiday gifts had flowed to their home—pot roasts, cookies, fruitcakes, loaves of bread, and bottles of Early Times, Sheriff Edwards' favorite bourbon. After he lost the November runoff, however, the sheriff received not a single Christmas gift from constituents and vendors.

And Sheriff Edwards would face more tough times with the budget before he left office.

The following July, when Layrisson took over, the newcomer found that his predecessor had sold almost all the sheriff's office vehicles to balance a yawning budget deficit, forcing Layrisson to borrow patrol vehicles from 17 other sheriffs over the next two years. In addition, because Sheriff Edwards had also sold the sheriff's office furniture, Layrisson had to scrounge surplus furniture from federal and state offices. The resulting negative publicity further damaged the former sheriff's reputation.

After his loss, the ex-sheriff returned to practicing law while continuing to operate the dairy. The defeat ate at him. He split up with his wife for a time and was often depressed. The couple went through marital counseling that also involved the children. "It was a very difficult time for the family and for me as well to go through that," John Bel Edwards recalled years later, fumbling for words. "You don't think your parents are ever going to separate. I do remember how painful it was for me and for my siblings."

John Bel Edwards resolved then that he would do everything he could to make sure that he never put his own children through that experience. "I would do everything possible to make sure that my children didn't live in a house where my wife and I were separated," he said years later. He added, however, that he had never believed his father did anything wrong and that his father was his hero. "I will tell you that I think about my dad every day still," he said of his father, who died in 2014.

Did his father's legal and political troubles prompt John Bel to commit to a more righteous path? He put it this way: "I tried to make sure that nobody questions my honesty or my integrity. That's very important."

In time, Frank and Dora Jean Edwards reunited, and the former sheriff decided to try to avenge his 1979 defeat by challenging Layrisson in 1983. He went on the attack again, but Layrisson won outright in the primary, with 58 percent to 36 percent for the former sheriff, and with two other challengers splitting the other 6 percent. After Frank Edwards' 1983 defeat, Edwin W. Edwards, newly elected to a third term as governor—and not related to the Tangipahoa

Edwards family—bailed out the former sheriff by naming him an assistant commissioner in the Division of Administration. While Frank Edwards held that job, the family dairy failed, a victim of low milk prices and high fertilizer costs. The family lost the dairy and the 600-acre parcel of land.

By the early 1980s, the former sheriff's seventh child, John Bel, had earned a reputation among teachers and other students at Amite High School as a smart, can-do kid. At Westside Middle School, he gave his sixth grade English teacher Anagene Mobley a ceramic apple to hold pencils as a Christmas present. Somehow, one day, it broke. As the school year was ending, Mobley discovered a replacement on her desk. When she asked the class who had brought it, no one would take credit, but John Bel's smile gave him away.

John Bel indulged in his share of boyhood mischief, too. In December 1980, while a freshman at Amite High, he went out one Saturday night with two of his older brothers. They ended up at the Hi-Ho BBQ, the local hangout just south of Amite on Highway 51. A bottle of pink champagne appeared, and John Bel proceeded to get drunk for the first time in his life. The following morning, as his head ached, he tried to get his younger brother Daniel to do his yard work. Daniel declined, and his parents found out about the previous night's antics. They made John Bel spend the entire day mowing the lawn, raking leaves, and pulling weeds. His only solace was the New Orleans Saints game on the radio. In the midst of their worst season ever, the Saints were 0-14 at that point. But as John Bel worked his way through the hangover, the Saints pulled out a 21–20 victory over the New York Jets for their only victory that year.

Growing up in Amite, John Bel's life centered on family, church, and sports. In 1981, he added a new element to the mix: Donna Hutto, a petite, brunette cheerleader who had moved to Amite three years earlier when her father took a job there with International Paper Company. Donna was a year younger than John Bel, but they had noticed each other at school and at church dances on Friday nights after the high school football games.

Donna wasn't allowed to date. On December 14, 1981, John Bel went to her house so they could watch television together. On the porch, as they said goodbye, he fidgeted for several moments before asking her if she would be his girlfriend. She said yes, and they kissed. From then on, they watched TV together on Friday nights. On Saturday nights, after *Love Boat* and *Fantasy Island*, but just as *Saturday Night Live* was beginning at 10:30 p.m., John Bel would have to leave.

In the fall of 1982, his junior year, John Bel won the job of Amite High School's starting quarterback. The year before, the Warriors hadn't won a game. The new coach, Gary Hendry, was old school. To toughen up the team, he introduced something the boys called *the Purple Cracker*. It consisted of two pieces of plywood—painted purple—that created an open-ended chute barely wide enough for one player. On a coach's whistle, one player took a handoff and had to bull through the narrow chute behind an offensive lineman whose task was to push a defender back—or get pushed back into the ball carrier. For 15 to 20 minutes at practice, pairs of linemen would take turns colliding as the rest of the team hooted and hollered.

John Bel wasn't fast, but at 5'11" and 175 pounds, he was sturdy enough that tackling him sometimes took more than one defender. He had a decent throwing arm, but Coach Hendry rarely called passes. Though the Warriors won only two games that year, John Bel made all-district as quarterback.

The team fared better in John Bel's senior year, posting a 6–4 record. Against Salmen High School, located in the larger city of Slidell, he and his center, Mark Vining, noticed that Salmen had no defender playing nose tackle. On the sideline, John Bel and Vining agreed that if they saw the same defense the next time they walked to the line of scrimmage, Vining would hike the ball as soon as John Bel positioned his hands to take the snap. The first time they did that, John Bel gained five yards. Every few downs, they ran the same play until Salmen changed its defense. By the end of the game, John Bel had gained almost 100 yards and had led his team to victory. When the Warriors lost on the road, John Bel, as team captain, made sure no one talked on the bus ride back to Amite. He wanted his teammates to focus on the downside of defeat.

Though John Bel once again made all-district as quarterback, he was an even better baseball pitcher. With a fastball, a curve, and a changeup, he won more games than he lost and made the all-district team each of his four years at Amite High. His junior and senior years on the ball field were especially sweet for his parents, because his catcher was his younger brother Daniel.

John Bel's oldest brother, Frank III, who had joined the ROTC while at Southeastern Louisiana University in Hammond, was now an Army officer. John Bel planned to follow a similar career path. One day early in his senior year, his baseball coach received a recruiting letter from West Point asking if he knew of any top student athletes who might qualify for the prestigious military academy. The coach gave the letter to John Bel, who was president of the community service-oriented Key Club in his junior and senior years and was on his way to serving as the 1984 class valedictorian. John Bel immediately set his sights on West Point.

His father, though no longer sheriff, secured the necessary

recommendations from Louisiana Senators Russell Long and J. Bennett Johnston. John Bel, however, was applying late, perhaps too late. But one day a colonel called the family home from West Point and told Dora Jean that her son had been accepted to the United States Military Academy. She would later say that day was one of the proudest days of her life .

John Bel made it through R-Day in July 1984, exhausted but unscathed. Two days later, he and the other new cadets stood at attention for what seemed like hours under a boiling sun to mark Independence Day. Some cadets fainted.

School didn't get easier once classes began. The upperclassmen harassed the new cadets during meals, demanding that they recite obscure facts—such as the definition of leather—while trying to eat. This often meant they didn't have enough time to finish their food when someone barked out the order—"Regiment, rise!"—and they all had to leave the mess hall. The new cadets learned to welcome a drill in which squads of 12, carrying M-16s, had to reach a simulated enemy bunker without getting shot with blanks that registered on detectors worn by each would-be soldier. To reach the bunker required crawling through mud and over rocks and past bushes that nicked them up. The cadets welcomed that drill, however, because it took them away from the hazing upperclassmen, and they had time to eat all their rations.

It was during these exercises that another new cadet named Murray Starkel noticed John Bel for the first time—Edwards had an uncanny ability to make it to the enemy bunker on a regular basis, and he was one of the few who did. After the drill ended and Starkel walked with the other "casualties" to the bunker, he would see Edwards with a big grin on his face wolfing down MREs.

By the time Dora Jean saw her son during Plebe–Parent Weekend in March, she too noticed something about him: The constant stress and lack of ready access to food, she would later recall, had left him "skinny, skinny, skinny." He had dropped to about 165 pounds.

One of the notable features at West Point is the cadet Honor Code, which is carved into a marble monument on post: "A cadet will not lie, cheat, steal, or tolerate those who do." All cadets lived in fear of violating the code, knowingly or unknowingly, because a violation could lead to expulsion.

Each company had a liaison to the committee that investigated Honor Code violations. During Edwards' freshman, sophomore, and junior years at West Point, his fellow cadets chose him to serve as his company's liaison—a measure of the respect he had gained among his peers. Then, in his senior year, the cadets chose him to oversee the investigations committee for the entire corps. When an infraction was alleged, he had to decide whether the case warranted a full investigation and hearing. On such occasions, Edwards had to put together a cross-section of cadets for a hearing to determine whether an Honor Code infraction had in fact occurred.

West Point lore holds that only 2 percent of the cadet candidates who enter the academy with a steady girlfriend have that same girlfriend when they graduate. Edwards and Donna were determined to belong to the so-called "2 Percent Club." They spoke on the phone most Sunday nights and wrote letters to each other weekly. She traveled to West Point whenever possible—once or twice a year, always accompanied by sorority sisters from the University of Southern Mississippi, where she majored in education. Donna's friends often served as dates for Edwards' friends at West Point dances. Finally, in May 1988, she attended John Bel's graduation ceremony, for which Vice President George H.W. Bush delivered the commencement address.

Of the 1,460 cadets who had arrived for R-Day nearly four years earlier, 986 graduated. Their class motto was: "No task is too great." Edwards earned his Bachelor of Science degree—he majored in American history with a heavy load of engineering courses—and his officer's commission as a 2nd Lieutenant.

During the fall semester of his senior year, when each of the cadets had to choose a branch of the Army, Edwards selected the infantry. Because he was one of the top students in his class, he got his first choice for a post—Hawaii. First, however, he had to get through Ranger School—a 65-day course designed to stress students physically to a point just short of breaking them—starting at Fort Benning, Georgia. Only half of those who entered Ranger School made it through. Soldiers had to pass a physical fitness test—49 pushups in two minutes, 59 sit-ups in two minutes, and a five-mile run in less than 40 minutes—then calmly walk across a log suspended 35 feet above a pond, jump into the pond, and ditch their rifles and 65 to 75 pounds of gear while submerged. They also had to reach a specific location at night without a flashlight.

They had to perform all of these tasks with less than four hours sleep per night over the 65 days of Ranger School. To stay awake, like other Army Ranger candidates, Edwards took coffee grounds from packets of instant coffee in his MREs and placed them between his cheek and gum and occasionally dabbed them with his tongue for a jolt. Any soldier caught napping faced expulsion.

Failure to complete a task also led to expulsion. Edwards thought he was going to fail when he twisted a knee during a 2 a.m. drill that involved hand-to-hand combat. The pain was excruciating, and his group had to complete a run several hours later. Edwards decided to begin the run but figured he wouldn't be able to keep up. After about a half-hour, however, when the group reached the turnaround point at the four-mile mark, he realized he could make it the whole way. It was a lesson in perseverance that he would remember years later.

From Fort Benning, Edwards moved to the remote Camp Merrill, also in Georgia, where he had to scale mountains, again without enough food or sleep. After that, he had to parachute into Eglin Air Force Base in Florida, where he led small units through swamps and across rivers—the only part of Ranger School that might have seemed easy to a south Louisiana country boy—to capture enemy targets.

The soldiers then moved on to Dugway Proving Ground in Utah, where they scaled even bigger mountains in sub-freezing temperatures. By the time Ranger School ended, Edwards was exhausted, but he had passed the course and earned the Ranger Tab above his unit patch. Weeks later, on March 4, 1989, he and Donna said their vows at St. Helena Catholic Church in Amite, drove to New Orleans for their honeymoon, and moved to Oahu. In Hawaii, he was chosen as a general's aide, a post many ambitious young officers see as a pathway to the Army's top echelons. Edwards' military career was on a fast track.

He was away training when Donna learned in 1991 that she was pregnant. The good news came with a flashing red sign: Their child would be born with spina bifida, a congenital defect that leaves an opening in the spinal cord that can prevent nerves along the spine from passing along simple messages such as "Move your feet" or "It's time to go to the bathroom." Though she had already miscarried once, Donna's doctor counseled that she have an abortion and try to get pregnant again. Their child, the doctor said, would likely be unable to walk and would have severe learning disabilities. Donna was devastated.

Her husband hurried back from his training mission. In a parking lot at the Honolulu airport, she broke the news along with the doctor's recommendation. "No, we're going to do this together, and we'll make it through," Edwards told his wife. She was relieved, because she, too, didn't want to abort their child. "We'll love this child no matter what," he said. Their daughter Samantha was born on March 17, 1992.

She was actually healthier than expected, but required surgery immediately after her birth, and another surgery 17 days later, when doctors placed a shunt in her head to release spinal fluid build-up. Samantha had yet another operation within the year. When Edwards and Donna celebrated their daughter's first birthday in 1993 at Fort Bragg, they still didn't know if she would ever walk.

Edwards continued to serve frequently away from his young

family's new post. By then he commanded a 120-troop Army Ranger rifle company in the 82nd Airborne Division, training often with jumps at 2 a.m., the best time to take an enemy airfield—the most likely target scenario. When his unit was on call, it had to be ready for wheels up within 18 hours to travel anywhere in the world.

In 1994, he and his company boarded an aircraft at Pope Air Force Base in North Carolina, ready to drop into Haiti to force the military government there to establish democratic rule. Their destination, as part of Operation Uphold Democracy, was an urban area. Any resistance would lead to widespread bloodshed among the outgunned Haitian population, a prospect that Edwards did not relish. The mission was canceled at the last minute, however, before Edwards' plane took off. "I ended up being a peacetime soldier," he said later. "And look, I was not one of those people who felt like their life would not be complete if they did not engage in combat. I am not going to tell you I was disappointed, because that was not going to happen without a tremendous loss of life—not on our side, on their side."

While he was gone during his training missions, Donna worked constantly with Samantha to strengthen her legs. She was determined to help her daughter beat the odds. And she did. By age three, Samantha was walking, albeit imperfectly because her legs were weak. Her health continued to be an issue; when her shunt failed in October 1995, she required two emergency procedures. Donna was nine months pregnant at the time with their second child, whom they named Sarah Ellen. The new baby had issues, too, during childbirth. She ruptured Donna's uterus when Donna delivered in November 1995, briefly endangering both of their lives.

By then, Edwards had admitted to his wife that he missed his large family. He also expressed concern about living so far away from both of their families, given Samantha's health challenges. Meantime, Edwards' Army career was taking off: He had been accepted to a program that called for the family to move to Oslo, Norway. But after eight years in the Army, he decided to retire as a captain, without seeing combat. He would return home to attend law school. While still in the Army, he took the Law School Admission Test and won admission to LSU Law School, which his father had attended.

In August 1996, on the first day of classes, some 120 freshmen gathered in LSU's Paul M. Hebert Law Center auditorium for orientation. Howard L'Enfant, the acting chancellor, reminded students that the law school experienced a high attrition rate among first-year students. "Look to your right," L'Enfant said. "Look to your left. One of you will not be here next fall." Ryan Gatti, 22, was among the students listening to L'Enfant. He had been class valedictorian at

Airline High School in Bossier City in northwest Louisiana before breezing through LSU in two-and-a-half years. Feeling a bit cocky, he turned to the balding guy to his right to size up the competition. "Hey, old man," he asked, "what have you been doing since you got out of college?" John Bel Edwards, who was 29, smiled and said, "Well, after I got out of West Point, I was a company commander for the 82nd Airborne Division." Gatti's confidence tanked.

"I was at the Kappa Sig house a year ago, and this guy was defending the country," Gatti said to himself. "He'll be here next year, and I won't." Gatti, however, went on to graduate and was elected to the state Senate from Bossier Parish in 2015.

After classes began, Gatti saw Edwards every time he went to the law library. He also noticed that Edwards was prepared whenever a professor grilled him in class using the Socratic Method. In fact, Edwards rarely socialized with the younger students and did not join any of the law school's extracurricular organizations. He and Donna lived in the married student dorms at LSU that first year, but, needing more help than her husband could provide as a full-time law student, Donna and their two daughters often stayed with her parents in Natchez, Mississippi. Edwards finished his freshman year first in his class, earning a spot on the prestigious law review, reserved for those among the top 10 percent of law students. By his third year, he and Donna lived with Samantha and Sarah Ellen in a friend's house in Amite. He didn't have the money to buy a place of their own.

Edwards left for LSU at the crack of dawn every school day, attended class, studied in the library afterward, and then left school at 5 p.m. so he could spend the night at home with his family without having to study there. He graduated third in his class in 1999, earning the additional academic honor of Order of the Coif.

After graduation, he spent a year clerking for Associate Justice James Dennis at the Louisiana Supreme Court, then returned home to Amite to practice at his father's law firm, which included his younger brother, Daniel. He would later describe himself as having a typical small-town lawyer's practice, handling wills, incorporation papers, contracts, and minor disputes. The law firm also represented individuals and businesses alleging they had been wrongfully injured in accidents. The firm was part of a $9 million settlement involving a freight train derailment in 2002 that spilled hydrochloric acid in Amite and forced several hundred residents to evacuate for three days.

In the meantime, the election defeats of Frank Edwards Jr. were an open wound for the family. Finally, in 2003, after years of planning, Daniel Edwards ran for sheriff. Incumbent Eddie Layrisson, who had twice beaten Frank Edwards Jr., decided not to seek re-election due to health issues. With John Bel as his campaign manager, Daniel won the race and became the fourth generation of his family to serve as sheriff. Four years later, it was John Bel's turn.

He had wanted to serve in the Legislature, and with the law firm on sound financial footing, he got his chance when term limits forced the popular state representative, Robby Carter, to give up his seat representing District 72 in the Louisiana House of Representatives. "In a small area like that, you don't ruffle as many feathers running for an open seat as if you run against an incumbent," Edwards said later.

The district, one of the poorest in the state, included not only the area of Tangipahoa Parish that encompassed Amite but also St. Helena, East Feliciana, and West Feliciana Parishes to the west. Many of the residents worked for various branches of government, including the massive state maximum security prison at Angola.

Those parishes, like rural parishes throughout the state, were trending Republican by then, beginning with elections at the top of the ticket for president. Nonetheless, Edwards ran as a Democrat, in part because roughly 55 percent of District 72's residents were African American. Edwards also explained to anyone who asked that he had always been a Democrat and saw no need to change. He won the seat easily and, just as he had done at West Point and at LSU law school, quickly gained the respect of his House colleagues.

In 2010, though just a freshman, he was elected chair of the House Democratic Caucus. In 2011, as United States Senator David Vitter and state House Speaker Jim Tucker targeted rural white Democrats for extinction, Edwards waltzed to re-election in his own rural district—and spearheaded the House Democrats' successful defense against the GOP siege.

5

"Another Governor Edwards?"

Springtime does not last long in Louisiana, though it is a welcome respite when it arrives. The weather typically goes from cold and humid to scorching and humid in the space of a few weeks. During those splendid weeks, Louisianans celebrate everything from jazz to crawfish to Cajun culture to strawberries and more. In the springtime, life in the Bayou State is pure joy—except for members of the Louisiana Legislature. For them, springtime after 2008 meant long days arguing over how to balance the demand for government programs and services with the limited money available in an anti-tax atmosphere. For those in the minority party, it was a particularly miserable time.

Despite their surprise victories in the 2011 legislative elections, Louisiana Democrats watched their plans go south after Bobby Jindal took his second oath of office in January 2012. The governor's priority was "reforming" public education in Louisiana from top to bottom. Conservatives had sought such changes for years, but until now they had achieved only incremental success. One of Jindal's measures—summarily approved by lawmakers—weakened the rules for teacher tenure and made acquiring the treasured form of job protection more difficult for future teachers. Another bill expanded Jindal's voucher program from a pilot project in New Orleans to a statewide program that would allow nearly 8,000 students in poorly performing public schools to attend designated private schools—some of them newly formed by Jindal supporters—on public dollars. A third measure aimed to remake the state's pre-kindergarten system but did not provide the needed funding. In pushing the three measures, Jindal and his legislative allies overrode teacher union objections that lawmakers were approving, too hastily, changes that were unconstitutional and would harm public schools.

Late one afternoon during the legislative session, seatmates John Bel Edwards and Sam Jones sat at their side-by-side desks in the rear of the House Chamber lamenting their fate. Jones lived in the coastal town of Franklin, in St. Mary Parish, which sits—much like Jones' seat in the House Chamber—on the southernmost reaches of the Cajun Triangle. Edwards and Jones sided with the teachers, but they lost battle after battle. They were tired and frustrated, and it showed.

The defeats also crystallized certain political realities for Edwards. He realized that his colleagues had approved fundamental, far-reaching changes to the state's public education system because that's what the governor wanted. He now had a clear idea of the awesome power that emanated from "the Fourth Floor"—insider-speak for the governor's office, which is located on the fourth floor of the state Capitol. Edwards rallied House Democrats against Jindal's policies, but Democrats were a minority in both the House and Senate, and Jindal had too many weapons at his disposal. "I'm one of 105 in the House, and there are 39 more [in the Senate] across the hall," he thought.

As Edwards and Jones exchanged frustrations about Jindal and their shared belief that he was leading the state in the wrong direction, Edwards suddenly turned and looked intently at his friend. "Sam, I've had enough of fighting with this guy," he said. "I'm not running for re-election. It's time to go big or go home, because I can't do much in the Legislature."

Edwards paused before adding, "I'm running for governor."

Jones took a deep breath and asked, "Are you serious?"

"Yes, I'm serious."

"Let's do it," Jones said. "You can win. You have what it takes."

Before he got too carried away, Edwards admitted that he needed to clear this decision with a higher authority: his wife Donna. "She has veto power," he said. Jones understood.

The aspiring candidate and his wife discussed it at home in Rosedale, just north of Amite, while preparing dinner and cleaning up afterward. "Donna, this state is really messed up," he said. "I think I have a lot to offer. I think it will be hard, given current trends, but I really believe we can win if we work really hard." Donna had concerns. She told her husband that running for governor would mean lots of time away from the family, and juggling those demands with the needs of Samantha, Sarah Ellen, and John Miller wouldn't be easy. For that matter, given her own work as a music teacher at Southeastern University Lab School, a K–8 public school in Hammond, she hadn't found the role of a legislator's wife an easy one.

Edwards said he understood her concerns but put it all on the line: "I can't do this without you being there for me." Donna had supported her husband's career choices from Day One. She didn't have to give this one much thought. "Whatever you feel like you want to do, I'll support you," she said.

The next time Edwards and Jones talked, Edwards said that Donna was in. He had at least two people in his corner. It was a start.

One hot Friday mid-day after the session ended, Edwards was working at his law office in downtown Amite. "Come on, let's go to lunch," he told his law partner, Brad Stevens. Joining them were Edwards' brother Daniel, now in his third term as sheriff of Tangipahoa Parish, and his father Frank Jr., who had himself served three terms as sheriff.

The four men got into Daniel's Suburban. Normally, they would have lunched at Ardillo's or Mike's Catfish Inn, but when they turned north onto Highway 51, Stevens knew they were going to have an important conversation. They drove more than 20 minutes and pulled into a dirt parking lot outside an unadorned rectangular roadhouse just north of the town of Kentwood, about a mile shy of the Mississippi line. It was Skinney's, a restaurant well known to locals for its BBQ, fried chicken, and seafood. Though the three Edwardses were political celebrities in Tangipahoa Parish, they could eat in relative anonymity at Skinney's, where the bill of fare took center stage. They ordered fried chicken livers as an appetizer and chased them with BBQ ribs.

As the food began arriving, John Bel broke the news to his father, brother, and law partner. "I am going to run for governor, and this is how I'm going to win," he told them. "The more Republicans who get into the race, the better it is for me. If I can keep the Democratic side clean, I can make the runoff. If I face David Vitter, I can win."

The three men peppered him with questions, and Edwards had ready answers. Unlike national Democrats, he was pro-life and pro-gun, and he had a voting record to back that up. That part of his record, his Catholicism (a key selling point in south Louisiana), his West Point credentials, and his military service would appeal to conservative Democrats, independents, and even some Republicans— particularly against the scandalized Vitter, who had detractors in every voter demographic, including among Republicans. At the same time, because Edwards had championed public education, equal pay for women, and social programs favored by African Americans, he could speak to the Democratic Party's base. In many ways, he had the same profile as the state's last Democratic governor, Kathleen Blanco.

After Edwards outlined his strategy, everyone at the table pledged to support him. Now he could count on five votes. Not exactly a juggernaut, but he had the support of those he needed most.

On July 20, Edwards took another step when he drove to the home of Raymond and Kathleen Blanco in Lafayette. Kathleen had risen through the political ranks to win election as the state's first woman governor in 2003 and was riding high until Hurricane Katrina hit in 2005. Afterward, the criticism of how she had handled the natural disaster was so fierce that she chose not to seek re-election in 2007.

From Lafayette, the Blancos had watched Edwards closely. He had consistently stood up to Jindal—and he seemed to relish doing so—when other Democrats voted with the governor or offered only token opposition. Kathleen emphasized that while Edwards had a good personal story and could appeal to conservative Democrats, he absolutely had to spend lots of time raising money to make sure he had the funds to get his message across. She reminded him that she had announced for governor in 1991 but had bowed out long before qualifying opened because she ran out of money. Edwards said he understood, noting that he had helped raise $1 million for House Democrats in 2011.

Kathleen felt comfortable enough with Edwards to ask if he had any skeletons in his closet that might provide fodder for Vitter or any other Republican candidate. Edwards said he couldn't think of anything and then added, "The only woman I've ever slept with was my wife"—a pointed reference to Vitter's notorious connection to a prostitution ring operated by the D.C. Madam, Deborah Jeane Palfrey.

Edwards planned to use the prostitution scandal to snipe at Vitter, but others cautioned him not to lay his own morality on too thick. At one meeting, when he told a group of men that he had always been faithful to his wife, Coach Blanco pulled him aside afterward and warned, "Let me tell you something: Don't be confessing anything. Half of those guys have mistresses. You're going to cost yourself votes." Edwards looked at Coach as if the former first husband was crazy.

In the coming months, Edwards quietly told more folks of his plans to run. He broke the news to his distant cousin Andrew Edwards in December 2012 while they drove to a fishing trip. "I can't think of a better candidate," responded Andrew, who soon became Edwards' campaign treasurer. Andrew paused and added, "David Vitter said all sorts of nasty things about Charlie Melancon. Are you ready for that?"

"I spent four years at West Point and eight years in the Army Airborne Rangers," John Bel replied. "David Vitter puts no fear in my heart."

Others were generally supportive...but a second-term state House Democrat winning the governor's office in a state that hadn't elected a Democrat statewide since 2008? To most, especially those who did not know Edwards, the notion seemed quixotic if not impossible. He took that response in stride and continued putting the pieces of his campaign into place.

In January 2013, he made his first campaign hire—Chris Binder, a 25-year-old New Orleans native who had served as deputy director of the House Democrats' 2011 legislative campaigns. As Edwards' personal assistant, Binder could learn statewide politics from the ground up. Besides, he liked Edwards' down-to-earth manner. Edwards also brought aboard a key volunteer, Mary-Patricia Wray, a 27-year-old Ohio native who had come to Louisiana five years earlier to pursue a law degree at Loyola University.

Wray had gotten her start in state politics as a lobbyist for the Louisiana Federation of Teachers, the statewide teachers union, and in that capacity she had come to admire Edwards as they worked on legislation. She noted that he typically came better prepared to debate bills than did the lobbyists and legislators who had sponsored the legislation. In a state where politicians traditionally moved up by playing the deal-cutting inside game, Wray possessed a remarkable grasp of how to deliver a winning message to voters and key constituency groups. She had no qualms about telling men—including older men—how they could work more effectively. Though her direct manner sometimes got her into trouble, Wray worked hard to fit in and quickly gained respect within the small circle of Edwards advisers.

Edwards hired Jim Kitchens to serve as his campaign pollster. The two had gotten to know each other when Kitchens conducted surveys in 2011 for the key House Democratic campaigns that Edwards directed. Edwards and Kitchens' political sequel started much like the 2011 legislative campaigns began: Edwards had hired the right pollster, but he couldn't afford to commission a poll.

In January 2013, Edwards attended the Washington Mardi Gras Ball, a blowout party in the nation's capital for Louisiana's political insiders. There he met with Jared Arsement, the young media whiz who had crafted the TV ads for the House Democrats' 2011 legislative campaigns. They reminisced a bit about those successes before Edwards got to the point: He was running for governor and he wanted Arsement on his team. It was an easy sell. Though Arsement privately gave Edwards little chance of winning, he figured the work would, if nothing else, add to his experience.

While in Washington, Edwards also slipped off to meet with officials at the Democratic Governors Association. He told them that he planned to run in 2015 and that the group shouldn't automatically support the state's leading Democrat, New Orleans Mayor Mitch Landrieu, should the mayor decide to run. The DGA officials gave him no commitment, but that was nothing new.

Back in Louisiana, Edwards drove to Lafayette for another

political skull session at the Blancos' home. At that meeting, after listening to everyone, Edwards decided he would wait until after the 60-day 2013 legislative session ended in June before officially announcing his plans to get in the race. He was all set, or so he thought.

Then Jim Engster, the king of political talk radio, who broadcast on WRKF–89.3 FM in Baton Rouge, invited Edwards to appear on his show on February 20, 2013—not long after Edwards' strategy session with Coach and Kathleen Blanco. Edwards took a seat in the studio directly across from Engster, pulled a microphone close to his face, and they began. During the first segment, Engster asked Edwards to comment on Jindal's radical plan to scrap the state income tax and replace it with the nation's highest combined state and local sales tax in the upcoming legislative session. Edwards said he opposed that idea because higher sales taxes would disproportionately hurt Louisiana's poorest citizens. The plan, he said, also would harm businesses by ending business tax breaks. "I think it's a real problem," he told Engster. The soon-to-be-candidate for governor was clearly warming to the idea of running against Republican orthodoxy.

A caller named Bruce asked about the prospects for expanding Medicaid for the working poor, given Jindal's opposition. That led Edwards to say that the expansion would benefit not just the working poor but the entire state. A caller named Jim asked about the cuts in state aid to LSU and a news report that the university was in decline. "No state that we want to emulate undertakes these drastic cuts to higher education," Edwards said. "You just cannot cut your way to prosperity." Another home run. *This was fun.*

They broke for a commercial. Back on the air, Engster threw Edwards a curve ball: "Before we go back to the phone lines, are you running for governor"?

A more experienced politician would have anticipated the question and had a canned response ready. Not Edwards. He wasn't ready to hit the curveball. He took an audible breath before answering. "Jim, that's ah, that's ah, an interesting question," he replied, trying to decide whether to play it safe and say he was considering the idea or didn't know. He opted instead to give the honest answer, but he stumbled over his words. "I do intend, ah, to run in 2015," Edwards said, clearly not yet comfortable in the role of *officially a candidate.* "Um, I just know from my six years now in the Legislature that, that I believe we're heading in the wrong direction, and we're getting there in a hurry. We've got to change course quickly. Quite frankly, my ability to influence things in the Legislature is certainly limited."

Engster gave no quarter to the floundering would-be candidate. "Is the state ready for another Governor Edwards?" he asked. John

Bel Edwards is no relation to the "other" Governor (Edwin) Edwards, but their shared last name could certainly cut both ways among voters in light of the former governor's populist Democratic appeal and his federal conviction on corruption charges.

Edwards laughed nervously. "You know, I hadn't been asked that question before," he said. "I certainly, I certainly will run on my own ideas."

Mary-Patricia Wray was sitting in her 1999 Acura Integra outside the state Capitol listening to the show. She silently cheered Edwards' answers on the topics of Jindal's tax plan, health care, and higher education. But when she heard Edwards announce his intention to run for governor—and trip over his words—a wave of panic swept over her. *This definitely was not the way to announce.* Indeed, the state's major newspapers would bury the news. Wray was not alone in her disappointment. Donna Edwards also was not pleased, but for different reasons. She and John Bel hadn't yet prepared their three children for their dad's candidacy.

Oops.

For Edwards, deprived of the boost that typically follows a traditional campaign announcement, a difficult race had just become even more difficult. Edwards figured he couldn't do anything but forge ahead. He drove to Lafayette a few days after the Engster show for a meeting at the home of Jared Arsement.

Kathleen and Raymond Blanco drove over from their home nearby, while Sam Jones came from Franklin. Wray drove from Baton Rouge, as did Eric Foglesong, who had managed the successful 2011 House legislative campaigns. "Okay, the cat is out the bag," someone said after they sat down. "What do we do now?"

Over pizza, Edwards told them he was already moving forward with plans for his first fundraisers. He would need money to pay for his travels around the state and to cover Chris Binder's salary. The group also agreed that Arsement would craft a video biography to introduce the voters to Edwards.

On March 21, he attended a breakfast at the unionized Loews Hotel in New Orleans, one of the few union shop hotels in the state. The meeting was organized by Tiger Hammond, president of the AFL–CIO in metro New Orleans. Others in attendance included Louis Reine, president of the Louisiana AFL–CIO, and officials from about 20 local unions. When Hammond sent out the invitation and asked each union rep to bring a check, some of them asked: "Who is John Bel Edwards?"

"That's exactly why we need to hold this event," Hammond replied. "You need to get to know who he is and educate your membership. It may take a whole year to do that. He's married to his high school sweetheart. She's a public school teacher. He has been fighting for working families in the Legislature."

Edwards and the union leaders sat at a rectangular table, and after the breakfast plates had been cleared away, he stood up and described how he had repeatedly opposed Jindal and voted with teachers and workers. Of course, he mentioned that Donna was a union member. As a legislator, he noted, he had a pro-union voting record. He sketched his bio—graduating from West Point, serving as an Army Ranger company commander, belonging to the Florida Parishes Skeet and Gun Club, serving as a Eucharistic minister at the St. Helena Catholic Church in Amite. "They're not going to out-God me, out-gun me or out-patriotic me," he said. The local union officials liked what they had heard.

As Edwards was leaving, Hammond handed checks totaling $8,000 to Chris Binder, the candidate's aide. The amount did not represent a large haul financially, but early commitments from that many union leaders counted for much more than money. Support from the union members behind those checks, crucial to any Democrat running statewide, represented a major breakthrough for his nascent campaign.

In the weeks after Edwards inadvertently announced his campaign on Engster's show, the candidate and his wife noted that their three children—Samantha, Sarah Ellen, and John Miller—were uneasy with this new chapter in their young lives. What would it mean to *them* to have their dad running for governor? If he won, what would life be like in the Governor's Mansion? Edwards and Donna took their children to Lafayette on March 24 to meet with the Blancos and several of their daughters. It was Palm Sunday.

The Edwardses attended Mass with the Blancos at their home church, the Cathedral of St. John the Evangelist in Lafayette. From there, they all went to the Blancos' home in central Lafayette, a yellow cottage where they had returned after four years in the Governor's Mansion. It was an unpretentious four-bedroom house where the most striking feature was the George Rodrigue painting that the artist gave Kathleen just after her election as governor in 2003. Rodrigue, who had gained world renown as "the Blue Dog artist," loved telling the story of how Coach, his high school history teacher in New Iberia, had kicked him out of class and into the rain one day for doodling and not completing his assignments. The painting, which hung in a bedroom, featured Blanco amidst a Louisiana oak, the state Capitol, a Blue Dog, and the statue that stands in front of the Evangeline Oak. The Edwardses admired it, and afterward they sat down at the long dining room table for seafood gumbo that the former governor had prepared.

After lunch, the group repaired to the sunken family room. There, the Blancos' daughters explained that campaigns could get rough. They advised the Edwards children to avoid following the governor's race on social media. Kathleen leaned in to offer additional advice: Be careful what you say to strangers—especially reporters. "Things can go wrong in an instant if the family says something wrong," she said. Kathleen's comment brought back a memory for her oldest child, 47-year-old Karmen. In 1987, Kathleen was running for re-election to the Louisiana House of Representatives against a man named Luke LeBlanc, who had chosen not to seek re-election four years earlier but had decided that he wanted his seat back. During that 1987 campaign, recalled Karmen, LeBlanc "said the worst things about my mother. He said she wanted to let rapists of children out of prison. He ran ads in the newspaper saying this. I got pretty upset about that. I came home one day and found my mother taping up the ads on the dining room wall. I was aghast and asked her what she was doing. She said we needed to understand that he was running the ads because she had gotten to him. 'I'm beating his butt,' she said." Everybody laughed.

"Vicious things might be said about your father during the campaign," Karmen told the Edwards kids. "If so, it's because he is beating their butt."

The conversation turned lighter when the Blancos shared memories of living in the Governor's Mansion. They noted an unusual feature of life there: While the State Police guarded the premises, the family's servants were inmates who had been convicted of serious crimes—including murder—but who had shown they could be trusted to serve the state's first family. Kathleen said the Edwardses would soon get over their nervousness about the crimes the Mansion staffers had committed and, in time, appreciate their help. She noted that she had raised six children and had welcomed no longer having to cook or clean house.

That prompted Karmen to tell the story of what she called "the magic table." It was the dining table in the back of the Mansion on the first floor, where the family gathered for meals. "Food will magically appear that you don't have to cook," Karmen said with a smile, "and plates will magically disappear that you don't have to wash." Karmen also marveled that you could leave your clothes in a pile in the morning and find them washed and folded that night. On the drive back to Amite, the Edwards children said they felt better about his running for governor.

Two weeks later, on April 4, the campaign organized its first formal event: a $2,500-per-couple fundraiser at the Jacmel Inn, a rambling

100-year-old home on a tree-shaded street in downtown Hammond, not far from Amite. The old home was now the finest restaurant in Tangipahoa Parish and a fitting place for Edwards to start raising the kind of money he would need to run for governor. Dozens of couples gathered around tables on the brick patio. Most of them were from Tangipahoa and knew Edwards as well as his extended family. With their popular sheriff, John Bel's brother Daniel, doing much of the asking, they were happy to donate. Everyone quieted when Edwards rose to speak. He had just begun talking when helicopters from the nearby Louisiana National Guard base temporarily drowned him out. "I don't know who ordered the flyover, but I appreciate it," he joked as the choppers' loud droning ended. The crowd laughed.

When he resumed speaking, Edwards explained why he was running—and why he would win. He stressed that Jindal's once-impregnable political façade was already beginning to show cracks. A state court had recently nullified the governor's signature education law that sought to weaken tenure for public school teachers. Equally important, if not more so, Jindal's popularity was in a state of free fall. According to annual voter surveys by Southern Media & Opinion Research, a respected Baton Rouge-based polling outfit, Jindal's approval rating among Louisiana voters had dropped from 61 percent in 2011 to just 38 percent in 2013—lower than President Barack Obama's numbers in the Bayou State, which was saying a lot. The reasons for Jindal's slide, according to pollster Bernie Pinsonat, were his frequent out-of-state travels promoting what would surely become a presidential campaign, the increasingly deep cuts to public universities and hospitals, and the governor's new plan to replace the state income tax with the nation's highest combined local and state sales taxes.

Of particular concern to voters, Pinsonat and others noted, was the growing perception that Jindal's nascent presidential ambitions—rather than what was good for Louisiana—were shaping his policies. While evangelical voters loved his positions on social issues, a growing number of other voters felt he was just "checking the boxes" that would make him appeal to voters in Iowa. One of those boxes included the governor's pledge to Grover Norquist's Americans for Tax Reform, what pundits came to call Jindal's "tax virginity," which he seemed desperate to preserve at all costs.

What Edwards and the crowd at the Jacmel Inn had no way of knowing was that Jindal's numbers would sink even further by the time the governor's race took shape in the spring of 2015—to an all-time low of 27 percent. By then, even Republicans would turn against Jindal. That low approval rating would put him among the most unpopular governors in America—and make him the man every candidate to succeed him had to run *against*.

After Edwards' talk, everyone at the fundraiser clapped and crowded around him. Better still, he learned later that evening that the guests had showered him with much more than applause: the event raised $190,000, far exceeding his goal of $75,000. That would put a lot of gas in Edwards' pickup truck —and make sure Chris Binder got paid.

The 2013 legislative session began four days later. Edwards by then was leading a solid bloc of House Democrats against Jindal's proposed sales and income tax swap, and joining the Democrats in their opposition was a group they often lined up against—the Louisiana Association of Business and Industry, the state's leading business lobby and one of the most powerful forces in the Legislature.

Most major newspapers also were lambasting Jindal's proposal, which clearly seemed intended to burnish the governor's conservative credentials as a potential presidential candidate rather than to put Louisiana on solid fiscal ground. In the face of such criticism, a large contingent of House Republicans grew skittish about raising sales taxes, even if that meant eliminating income taxes. Before the governor even delivered his Opening Day address, his plan was in trouble. Still, it came as a surprise when Jindal told lawmakers in his opening address, "I am going to park my tax plan." House Democrats were jubilant. This was Jindal's biggest legislative defeat during his six years in office.

Later in the same session, Edwards played a key role in handing Jindal yet another defeat. He had the Democrats align with the so-called Fiscal Hawks, a mostly-Republican group in the House that consistently opposed the governor's annual use of one-time money for recurring expenses, something Jindal had promised never to do when he campaigned for governor. Though the alliance might seem an odd one, the Democrat–Fiscal Hawks coalition produced a win-win for the two groups. For the Fiscal Hawks, it brought tighter controls on spending one-time money. For the Democrats, it produced more money for K–12 public education and public universities. An added bonus for the Democrats: The alliance dealt another blow to Jindal. It also taught Edwards valuable lessons and gave him the credentials of a legislative dealmaker.

After the session ended, Edwards was free to refocus on his long-shot campaign for governor. Still short of cash, he had to build a grassroots effort, piece by piece. He accepted speaking invitations from any group that would hear him and passed out copies of the eight-minute video biography Arsement had produced. Binder drove

Edwards across the state in the candidate's white 2010 GMC Sierra 1500 pickup. A fan of old-style country music, Edwards listened to "Willie's Roadhouse" on Sirius–XM radio between stops. At every opportunity, he portrayed himself as a centrist—not wedded to the left or the right—who stood with ordinary people against the establishment. Repeating the campaign slogan from the 2011 legislative elections, he promised to put Louisiana first.

Like most campaigns, this one was a roller coaster for the candidate. In mid-July, Edwards got a good turnout in Lake Charles at an event organized by Buddy Leach, a Democratic elder statesman who had served a term in Congress and later served as state party chairman. In August, Edwards attended the state Democratic Party's biggest annual confab, the Jefferson–Jackson Dinner, at the Hilton Riverside Hotel in New Orleans. Binder sat at a table outside the ballroom, offering DVDs for the taking. Although some 500 people filed past, only about 20 stopped to pick up a DVD.

There were other signs of the tough road ahead. Many people stumbled over Edwards' name—some thought his last name was Bell. No, he had to correct them, Bel was a family name. "My first name is John Bel," he said. "Edwards is the last name." Others who heard Edwards say his last name thought he was referring to a past campaign of Edwin Edwards, the former four-time governor. "No," he corrected them, "I'm a candidate for governor." The slights hurt, but Edwards just smiled and soldiered on.

Glimmers of hope sustained him. On the night of October 24, he held a fundraiser at Middendorf's, a popular restaurant renowned for its thin-fried catfish, just off Interstate 55 in the southern Tangipahoa Parish fishing village of Manchac. Several hundred people crowded onto the restaurant's sunset deck and the adjoining upstairs dining room. When it came time for him to speak, Edwards noted that the date was no accident: In exactly two years, Louisiana would hold its primary election for governor. To cheers, he said he intended to be one of the two candidates left standing to advance to the runoff. At $250 per couple, the event raised $80,000.

Edwards got more good vibes the following evening at an annual charity dinner and raffle sponsored by the New Orleans branch of the Ancient Order of Hibernians, an influential Irish–Catholic organization. The venue was St. Dominic's School in the city's heavily Irish and Italian section of town known as Lakeview.

Dan Foley, a longtime AOH member and the president-elect of the Louisiana Association for Justice, the trial lawyers' trade group, took Edwards from table to table. At each stop, Foley noted, folks stood up, shook Edwards' hand, and thanked him for his military service.

"That's a real door opener for him," Foley told his wife Angela as they left the event. But when Foley later described the crowd's response to Edwards, many of his friends said the Democrat had no shot at winning, not in Republican-dominated Louisiana.

On November 23, John Bel and Donna drove west across the state to a teacher-sponsored fundraiser in the Town of Kinder. A nice meet-and-greet at someone's home, the event produced only $3,000 after an entire day's travel. "You can't keep doing this," Donna told her husband on the way back to Amite.

Edwards' campaign wouldn't get any easier when the calendar turned to 2014. Louisiana Democrats for most of that year would focus their attention, their money, and their energies on helping Mary Landrieu seek a fourth term in the United States Senate. To them, Landrieu was more than a champion of Democratic policies and principles. She also was the last Democrat holding statewide elective office in Louisiana. They vowed to do whatever it took to secure Landrieu another term. As a result, when Edwards called potential donors, he heard time and time again that they had already maxed out on Landrieu's race and couldn't think about the governor's election until 2015.

Edwards grew discouraged but kept plugging away at raising money and raising his profile. He still liked his chances, even if so many others didn't.

6

Always Running Against the Establishment

David Vitter didn't know it yet, but a 738-foot coal freighter flying the flag of Panama was about to disrupt his morning while also presenting him with an opportunity to showcase his political prowess.

The phone call bearing news of the freighter would come in just a few moments. For now, however, the sun was beginning its ascent over Vitter's green and watery corner of southeast Louisiana, a land of stark contrasts, with dramatic changes in topography and culture evident in just a two-hour drive. Vitter knew the drive, and the contrasts. He had campaigned on the sands of semi-tropical Grand Isle on the Gulf of Mexico shore, some 70 miles due south of New Orleans. From there, he had driven up LA1 and US90 to stump in the bayou towns of Lafourche and St. Charles Parishes, where shrimp boats and alligators dot the landscape. He had campaigned door-to-door in his suburban neighborhood in Jefferson Parish, where SUVs are as common as crabgrass. And he had held forth as an idealistic young reformer at fundraisers in Uptown New Orleans, the Republican Party's main foothold in the mostly Democratic Crescent City.

This land of contrasts is where Vitter had spent most of his life, put down roots, started a family, honed his political skills, and gotten himself elected to public office.

On January 17, 2012, at 6:45 a.m., the phone belonging to the junior senator from Louisiana began ringing. Someone was about to tell him that the M/V *Rondeau* had run aground as it neared the mouth of the Mississippi River. The ringing didn't take Vitter by surprise. His work schedule knew few boundaries, so a phone call before breakfast wasn't out of the ordinary. Lately, neither was news of a grounded ship at the lower end of the mighty, muddy river, which was then beginning to fall toward its annual spring low-water stage.

The massive blue-and-beige freighter had been riding an outbound draft of 44 feet when its engine whined against the resistance of the river's bottom. In a state that relies heavily on maritime commerce, this incident triggered an urgent call to a man who could crank gears and grease skids. The *Rondeau* was stuck squarely in the middle of Cubits Gap, just a mile above Pilottown, a tiny unincorporated community situated precariously on an island in Plaquemines Parish, which straddles the last 70 miles of the Mississippi River before low-lying marshes give way to the Gulf of Mexico.

River pilots and others who work the Mississippi had seen this kind of thing with increasing frequency in recent years. Those who bore witness couldn't help but feel useless in the face of an impending maritime nightmare.

Many blamed federal budget cuts, and rightly so. That was one of many reasons the locals harbored a growing distrust for the United States Army Corps of Engineers, which had ignored their pleas for enhanced dredging in the river's lower reaches. The Corps also fielded much of the blame for south Louisiana's flooding problems. That distrust played out in press coverage, on the sides of satirical Mardi Gras floats, and in everyday conversation. In the wake of Hurricane Katrina in 2005, south Louisiana newspapers routinely called the storm's inundation of metro New Orleans "the federal flood." Vitter, for his part, never hesitated to fan the flames of distrust—or to create them.

"Mike, good morning," Vitter said, having already seen on his phone's display that the early morning call was from Michael R. Lorino Jr., the president of the Associated Branch Pilots.

"Good morning, Senator. A big ship has just run aground in the lower Mississippi and all traffic is at a stop," Lorino said rapidly before attempting to provide more detail. Vitter could talk just as fast.

"Mike, I don't mean to cut you off. I need to make a phone call. I need to do it immediately."

The senator hung up and scrolled through his contacts until he found the listing for Major General John W. Peabody, the commander of the Army Corps' Mississippi Valley Division. Vitter had been calling him as often as three times a week, pestering him to dredge the lower Mississippi. Now he had a chance to make something happen—if the chess pieces lined up right.

"General, it's David Vitter again."

"Yes, Senator," Peabody responded. "What do you need?"

"Since we've been talking about the dredging on the lower Mississippi, I just wanted to immediately touch base with you in light of this morning's events and in light of this morning's news."

The long pause on the other end of the line told Vitter that he had caught the general before he had been briefed. This was the opening the senator needed. Years in Louisiana politics had taught him that leverage is just as effective as power. He now had both. He moved his first chess piece.

"Yeah, General," Vitter continued, "I really think this underscores what we've been talking about for the last week or so."

Another pause.

"Okay, Senator," Peabody finally said. "But I'm not sure exactly what you're referring to." Another chess piece moved on the board.

"Well, General, your significant staff did not brief you that a major ship has run aground in the lower Mississippi and all traffic is at a complete halt—exactly what we feared and exactly what we predicted and exactly what we've been talking about."

A third, even longer pause. One more piece moved.

Although he didn't reveal his true endgame when recounting this exchange years later, Vitter could have hung up then and called any number of people—especially the media—to inform them that the commander of the Army Corps of Engineers' Mississippi Valley Division had no knowledge of a major ship grounding in his territory. That slight exaggeration fueled by a matter of timing would have caused quite a stir. Instead, the senator stayed on message and stressed once again the dredging needs of the lower Mississippi. He reminded Peabody that ships were running aground in the Pilottown area with increasing frequency. As much as anything Vitter said, Peabody knew that the senator had his phone number and that these calls were unlikely to stop.

Checkmate.

Roughly 12 hours later, large dredges started arriving in lower Plaquemines Parish to deepen navigation lanes. The following day, the Corps announced that it was dedicating $55 million in supplemental congressional funding to the dredging efforts. Though the *Rondeau* floated free from its grounding several hours after getting stuck in Cubits Gap and never did halt river traffic at a worrisome level, the incident—and the call from Vitter—did spur the Corps into action.

That incident, and the senator's deft handling of it, was a classic page out of David Vitter's political playbook. Since he burst onto Louisiana's electoral scene in 1991, Vitter had become one of the best known and most powerful politicians in Louisiana—and arguably one of the least understood. Metaphorically, he was a human lockbox, particularly to those who weren't close to him.

If asked to explain David Vitter, those in the public policy arena would point to instances such as the phone call to Peabody in describing him as shrewd, calculating, and uncompromising. His political opponents, and there were many, would dredge up Vitter's

2007 prostitution scandal and call him hypocritical. Staffers would say that Vitter, like most powerful men, was someone you had to get to know over time. They would add that their boss didn't like small talk and was a bit of a lone wolf.

Those who knew Vitter as a young adjunct law professor would swear that he cared deeply about Louisiana and its people, and that he began his career determined to end the state's well-deserved reputation for corruption, cronyism, and mismanagement. Even his critics acknowledged that he was a policy wonk, a tireless campaigner, a masterful political strategist, a fearsome opponent, and a champion of good government.

Nearly all who knew Vitter would have added that he was always one of the smartest guys in the room—but he was also a hyper-partisan who took no prisoners in a political fight. He often came off as cold and aloof, especially to others in the political game, and he was just as likely to burn a bridge—or even blow one up—as to build one. But Vitter also was his own best strategist. He had created his political mold in a state where you had to "go along to get along," because the Good Ole Boys Club always held enormous sway, regardless of which party was officially in power. Vitter's *modus operandi* was simple: He always ran against the establishment, even after he became part of it.

That's one reason his political colleagues grew to dislike him so profoundly: He never tired of exposing their shenanigans and holding them up to public opprobrium. If that raised his political stature, so much the better. To them, he was like a virus bent on destroying the host from the inside. That made him dangerous to the good ole boys, but popular among voters. The media ate it up, too, at least in the early days.

Throughout his public life, no matter who his opponent, no matter how intense the controversy, in the face of bad press and vengeful peers, David Vitter always leaned forward. Rewind and reverse didn't exist in the Vitter lexicon. His political style reflected the shared philosophy of Carl von Clausewitz and Vince Lombardi, both of whom preached that the best form of defense is attack. But there was more to Vitter than his steely veneer. He once said that his favorite food was ice cream and that he enjoyed watching *The Sound of Music* and *The One and Only Genuine Original Family Band.* He liked jazz, would sometimes quote Margaret Thatcher, and fancied himself an amateur architect. He even drafted the initial design of his family's home. On occasion, one could find him on the cool side of geekdom as a longtime fan of the British sitcom *Fawlty Towers.* Yet Vitter rarely showed his own sense of humor, which tended to be dry and even sarcastic.

Early in his career, he enjoyed a warm relationship with the media. Reporters found him readily accessible and always good for an insightful quote—but that was before the prostitution scandal knocked him on his heels and made him distrustful of the press. Vitter's diehard supporters came to understand his not trusting the media. They likewise didn't trust the establishment. And they totally distrusted the federal government, especially the Corps of Engineers.

The youngest of six children—four boys and two girls—Vitter grew up in Uptown New Orleans, in a conservative Catholic family that could trace its roots there to the 1880s. As is often the case with a large family's youngest child, David was the pride and joy of his parents, Audrey Malvina and Albert Leopold Vitter. His father, eventually the head of production for Chevron, took young David on helicopter rides to visit the company's offshore rigs.

Every year Audrey and Al would take a family photo for their Christmas cards, a tradition they started in the 1940s. David first appeared in the 1961 card, a few months after he was born—a smiling baby boy sitting inside an unwrapped Christmas gift box and surrounded by his brothers and sisters. Those end-of-the-year greeting cards documented life in a big family: a young David dressed in overalls one year; wearing a sailor outfit in another; then a blazer and tie; and a tiny David celebrating the holidays in an elf costume. In the card from 1967, young David held a Saints helmet for the team's inaugural season.

When he was a schoolboy at Christian Brothers middle school in New Orleans' City Park, his teachers and classmates described him as a young intellectual. He attended De La Salle High School and joined the school band before graduating as valedictorian in 1979. His favorite job growing up was working for Blaine Kern Artists, the firm that designed and built most of New Orleans' big Mardi Gras floats. His employer never allowed him to get too creative; his only task was applying the white primer coats. In his later high school years, he attended the Close Up program in Washington, D.C., which helped solidify his early interest in politics. The program annually gathered thousands of teens from around the country at the nation's capital for an immersion course in American government. There he first saw the Capitol building where he would one day report to work.

Young David had an independent streak, and it showed when the time came to pick a college. His father, brothers, and other relatives had attended Notre Dame, making that school the family tradition. He elected instead to go to Harvard. There, at America's oldest institution of higher learning—one that had a generations-old reputation for liberalism—Vitter's political views gravitated from moderate to slightly liberal. While in college, he interned in Washington for liberal Democratic Congressman Joe Moakley of Massachusetts. On the side, he bussed tables at the Republican Capitol Hill Club—more for money than political tutelage.

While Vitter excelled at Harvard, an Ivy League diploma was just the first entry on an impressive resume that ultimately would include Oxford's Rhodes scholarship program, which awarded him a master's degree in economics. In England, Vitter's politics took a U-turn. He warmed to President Ronald Reagan's message of individual responsibility and economic conservatism, then went full-tilt conservative after he attended a Labour Party rally and heard the speaker address the audience as "comrades."

After Oxford, having decided to pursue the law back home in New Orleans, Vitter enrolled at Tulane University Law School, graduated in 1988, and began to practice commercial and general civil law. He nurtured a keen interest in public policy by teaching in the public law clinics at both Tulane and Loyola law schools.

The late 1980s and early 1990s were a turbulent time in Louisiana politics, even by Pelican State standards. Just two months before Vitter graduated from law school, 44-year-old Charles E. "Buddy" Roemer III took the oath of office as Louisiana's reform-minded governor. Roemer campaigned on themes that resonated with young idealists like Vitter—fiscal reform, tighter ethics laws, and, as Roemer put it, "cleaning up our politics."

Roemer came from a political family. His father had been a top confidant and lieutenant of the skirt-chasing, gambling, roguish Governor Edwin W. Edwards. Just as Vitter had rebelled against the establishment, Roemer turned away from the politics of his father's generation and tried to reform it. The brash Roemer, however, ran into a buzz saw of opposition from entrenched political interests. Vitter, a young man who harbored political ambitions of his own, watched in dismay as the Good Ole Boys not only beat back most of Roemer's proposed reforms but also tried to humiliate him politically in the process. Vitter knew he would take up the same gauntlet at some point. It was only a matter of time.

During this same period, Vitter met a young woman whose story would become as central to his career trajectory as his own. Her name was Wendy Baldwin, and he was smitten. "We both went to Tulane Law School, and I worked at the Orleans District Attorney's Office as he was interning there," Wendy recalled later. Their first date was in fact a blind date, although David insisted they had previously met. "I don't recall that," Wendy admitted later.

Like David, Wendy was on a fast career track. She was serious, ambitious, goal-driven, and often more mature than her peers. Wendy was only six when her mother, Beatrice, died of breast cancer, but Beatrice had already instilled in her daughter a deep devotion to Catholicism. Growing up without her mom would have been tougher on young Wendy had it not been for her extended family, her siblings, and her father, Richard Baldwin, a respected attorney who never remarried. She attended Catholic elementary and high school at Mercy Academy, graduated with honors from Sam Houston State University, and earned her law degree from Tulane in 1986.

She began her law career as a prosecutor for New Orleans District Attorney Harry Connick Sr. and within three years earned the job of chief of trials, an important supervisory position in the D.A.'s office. In 1990, the year she married David Vitter, Wendy prosecuted Louisiana's first DNA-based murder case. The law was in her blood, but the decision to work as a prosecutor was a particularly good fit. "The most important thing I thought I could ever do was to be a voice for victims who could not speak for themselves," she said later.

While Wendy burnished her credentials in criminal law, David aspired to make his mark in politics. A friend introduced him to the political directors at the Louisiana Association of Business and Industry, who mentored him in state politics and the need for fiscal and governmental reform. He was a quick study. His first chance to seek public office came in 1991, with a bid for the Louisiana House of Representatives' 81st District. His target was another guy named David—David Duke, the former Ku Klux Klan grand wizard and neo-Nazi who had won the seat in a special election in 1989.

The 81st House District was 99 percent white and included the stately mansions of Old Metairie, the blue-collar former fishing village of Bucktown, and wide swaths of suburban homes nearby, all in conservative Jefferson Parish. Duke, in his widely covered 1989 campaign, supplanted the overtly racist themes of his KKK days with warnings about the "rising welfare underclass"—a dog whistle that spoke to the fears of working class whites who felt they were falling behind because of special government programs for African Americans.

Twice before, Duke had run for the state Senate—as a Democrat—but his message failed to resonate with voters until the 1989 House contest, when he ran as a newly minted Republican who publicly stoked racial fears. While Duke's win made national headlines, Vitter considered it an embarrassment. Many local observers saw Duke's victory as a fluke; still, he milked it for all it was worth, which was a lot in terms of money and press attention.

As an idealistic young conservative, Vitter was incensed that

Duke had co-opted the Republican message and turned it into a national object of shame. Vitter told friends that he loathed Duke, who was now the young attorney's own state representative. In truth, Vitter had wanted to run in the 1989 special election that Duke won, but the state's one-year residency rule barred him from qualifying. Vitter, who had been living in Uptown New Orleans, was three months shy of meeting the requirements for his new home in Old Metairie. Ironically, Duke lived *outside* the district and should have been disqualified himself—but no one challenged his residency until after the legal deadline had passed.

The year after Duke won the special election, Vitter began planning to run against him in the regular statewide elections of 1991. He started knocking on doors across the district—*every one of them*—at least four times each. By the summer of 1991, Vitter's door-to-door campaign had become a story all its own, and it was clear that he had established himself as a clean-cut Republican alternative to Duke. In contrast to Duke's thinly veiled racial code, Vitter campaigned as a mainstream conservative who would challenge the political system that Democrats had constructed. Republicans and Democrats alike eagerly anticipated Duke's demise at the hands of the fresh-faced young lawyer.

For his part, Duke had higher ambitions than re-election to the state House. The year before, in 1990, he ran for the United States Senate and garnered 44 percent of the vote against Democratic incumbent J. Bennett Johnston. By the time qualifying opened for the 1991 elections, Duke opted to run statewide—for governor.

Vitter, meanwhile, faced two unknowns in the race for the 81st, and it wasn't much of a contest. He outworked and outsmarted them.

In contrast to most states, Louisiana has a "jungle" primary system in which, if no one gets more than 50 percent of the vote, the top two finishers advance to the runoff regardless of their party affiliation. Vitter captured 68 percent of the primary vote and won his seat without having to compete in a runoff. From Day One, Vitter had run as an outsider. He entered the Louisiana Legislature intent on maintaining that status.

Meanwhile, in the governor's race that same year, Governor Roemer got squeezed out in the primary. Edwin Edwards squared off against Duke, beating the former Klansman with 61 percent of the vote in what came to be known as "the runoff from hell." Edwards' showdown against Duke was marked by a bumper sticker that read, "Vote for the Crook—It's important." The win marked Edwards' fourth election as governor, a record that was expected to stand for generations, and he quickly set about proving the words on the infamous runoff bumper sticker.

The governor's shady deals played right into the hands of Vitter, whose consistent opposition to Edwards' policies quickly elevated the freshman lawmaker's profile. In Vitter's first year as a legislator, he filed two ethics complaints against Edwards—one for a Las Vegas trip to watch heavyweight boxing champ Evander Holyfield defend his title and another involving Edwards' children doing business with riverboat casinos. Vitter loudly opposed Edwards' expansion of gambling in Louisiana, and he welcomed every opportunity to stick a pin in the governor, who returned fire by calling the young lawmaker "Bitter Vitter," a moniker coined by some of the freshman lawmaker's House colleagues and eventually picked up by the press.

When Edwards and his legislative leaders quickly shut down the House vote to pass a controversial bill authorizing a gambling casino in New Orleans, Vitter took to shouting on the House floor, "They stole the vote, pure and simple!" On multiple fronts, Vitter became the Anti-Edwards, not caring that the governor and his many House allies connived at every opportunity to bring him down. For its part, the local media loved this David-versus-Goliath story. Vitter's name soon became synonymous with "good government" and "anti-establishment," which further enhanced his popularity among voters.

As staunchly as he opposed the hijinks of Edwin Edwards and his Democratic allies in the Legislature, Vitter's list of adversaries included Republican lawmakers as well. In fact, some of the young lawmaker's GOP colleagues came to dislike him as much as Edwards and the Democrats. For starters, Vitter developed a penchant from the get-go of stealing their thunder on major issues. Veteran state Representative Charles E. "Peppi" Bruneau Jr., a New Orleans Republican who chaired the House committee that considered ethics and elections legislation, took pride in preparing "easy" bills for GOP freshmen to introduce in their first year. The bills would typically cover subjects that brought them before Bruneau's committee, where the chairman made sure they got a friendly reception. "It helped them learn the process, and it gave them credentials as reformers," Bruneau recalled years later. In Vitter's first year, he scooped up all of Bruneau's bills and filed them himself, Bruneau said.

On another occasion during Vitter's first term, the House Republican Delegation met to craft an alternative budget plan. When the plan was complete, the delegation scheduled a group announcement to the press the following afternoon—only to see Vitter call his own news conference an hour or two beforehand, grabbing the spotlight for himself and leaving his fuming colleagues to comment on "the Vitter plan." While such tactics infuriated his peers, voters saw him as an elected official who stood with hard-working taxpayers. "He did not make a lot of friends in the Louisiana Legislature," said author and independent journalist John Maginnis, who covered most of Vitter's political career. "Which some people say speaks highly of him."

Vitter ran unopposed for re-election in 1995 and entered his second four-year term as the state Capitol's undisputed irritant-in-chief. His early nemesis, Governor Edwards, was now gone, but Vitter wasted no time upping the ante against his legislative colleagues. He forced them to let voters impose legislative term limits by masterfully working the media and talk radio in support of the idea. He shamed legislators into repealing legislative retirement benefits, which earned him even more enemies inside the rails but endeared him to voters. And he exposed cronyism in the doling out of Tulane University scholarships that legislators were allowed to award thanks to a century-old, state-granted tax break to the university. Vitter was relentless in his criticism of the scholarship scandal, which headline writers quickly dubbed "Tuitiongate" and "Scholargate." Vitter ignited voter outrage at every turn, which fed weeks of white-hot talk radio fare. The angrier citizens grew over the scholarship scandal, the more Vitter turned up the heat—to the point that his House seatmate, fellow Republican state Representative Jim Donelon of Metairie, was compelled to confess that he had awarded a scholarship to his daughter. Among Vitter's legislative colleagues, that incident so defined his political tactics and persona that, even two decades later, they universally described it as Vitter throwing his own seatmate under the bus.

Jefferson Parish Sheriff Harry Lee, a close friend and ally of Edwin Edwards—and therefore an enemy of Vitter—sued Vitter three times while he was serving in the state House. Two of those lawsuits were for defamation, once after Vitter accused Lee of helping a friend with Mafia ties get into the gambling business and again when he accused the sheriff of campaigning with tax dollars. Nothing came of the suits, but Lee did convince a district court judge to force Vitter to turn over the names of his own Tulane scholarship recipients. Although Vitter's scholarships were part of a system he had earned headlines for opposing, he had wisely created an open selection process that included strict perimeters. That didn't matter to the sheriff.

"My job is to catch crooks," Lee said of the scholarship lawsuit. "My hobby is to expose hypocrites."

On that note, Vitter's critics would later take great delight in recalling an op-ed column that the second-term state legislator penned in *The Times-Picayune* in the autumn of 1998, when talk of impeaching President Bill Clinton dominated America's political discourse. Only weeks earlier, Clinton had finally admitted that his relationship with

Monica Lewinsky was "not appropriate." For Vitter, a family-values conservative who followed Huey Long's tack of raising his own stature by picking fights with politicians higher up the food chain, Clinton's sex scandal was a gift from the gods. Responding to an earlier column by a pair of Tulane law professors who argued that a sex scandal didn't rise to the level of an impeachable offense, Vitter, himself an adjunct law professor at Tulane, wrote that Clinton should be impeached "because he is morally unfit to govern."

Those words would come back to haunt Vitter, but not for almost a decade.

In the early spring of 1999, the ambitious suburban lawmaker seized an opportunity to move up the political ladder. Congressman Bob Livingston of Louisiana's 1st District, which included all of Vitter's state legislative district, announced he would resign in the wake of his own sex scandal. The large field that qualified to succeed Livingston included Vitter, former Governor David Treen, then 70, and David Duke. Treen presented himself as the only candidate with enough name ID and congressional experience—he had represented Louisiana's 3rd District from 1973 until the spring of 1980—to hit the ground running in Washington. Treen also campaigned as the only candidate who could keep Duke out of the runoff. He would be right on both counts.

For his part, Vitter took a huge gamble, but a calculated one: He announced that he was resigning his state House seat, prospectively. If he lost, he would be out of office. But his move had an up side: The special election to succeed him in the state House would be held the same day as the congressional primary, which was likely to increase voter turnout in a corner of the congressional district where Vitter was the favorite son. He would need that big turnout, because literally every one of Vitter's legislative colleagues who lived in the 1st Congressional District—including state Representative Steve Scalise, who would succeed Vitter in Congress and endorse him for governor—had endorsed someone *other* than Vitter in this contest. Vitter's gamble paid off. Treen led the primary with 25 percent, followed by Vitter with 22 percent and Duke with 19 percent.

A tight runoff followed between the top two finishers, but Treen suspended his campaign during the final week when his grandson went missing while on a hike in Oregon. Treen pulled every string available to help the search, including going to Oregon himself. Days later, a helicopter owned by a news station spotted the young man—still alive. When Treen and his grandson landed at New Orleans International Airport, Vitter showed up to welcome them home, scoring PR points in the process. The move did not impress Treen.

By then, the former governor had accused Vitter of violating an agreement between them to keep the race clean and positive. Vitter had called Treen "biologically term limited" while Treen lashed out at what he described as Vitter's questionable tactics, particularly negative fliers and attack ads. Treen's brother, John Treen, also claimed later that Vitter had cut a deal with Duke to hurt the former governor among African-American voters by having Duke endorse Treen. It was John Treen who had lost to Duke in the state House race in 1989, and both Treens detested Duke. Vitter did as well, and he rejected any suggestion that he had coordinated with the former Klansman. Vitter won—barely, with 51 percent of the vote, edging Treen by a scant 1,812 votes.

Wendy Vitter, whose interest in politics blossomed when she volunteered on the 1976 election campaign of President Gerald Ford as a high schooler, not only managed her husband's congressional campaign but also stood in for him during several debates. Politicos noted at the time how easily she could have been on the ballot instead of Vitter. "It was a crazy time and we were running the campaign out of our house," Wendy recalled later. "We trusted each other completely, but I don't think we knew at the time what kind of undertaking it was going to be."

In Washington, the new congressman moved cautiously. He hadn't made any promises about hires and actually had interns answering his phones on the Hill. That decision, which reinforced his "outsider" image, had its drawbacks. Wendy made a phone call to her husband's D.C. office one day during that transitional period.

"Can I talk to David?" she asked when an intern answered.

"There's no one here named David," the intern replied, to Wendy's amusement.

"Go around the corner and look at the congressman's first name on the door and put my husband on the line," she said with a laugh.

The evening Vitter was sworn into office in Washington, he met for the first time a young man who would quickly become his chief political architect, primary confidant, top defender, and close friend. Kyle Ruckert, who had just turned 25, was working for Texas Congressman Mac Thornberry. As a graduate of Jesuit High School in New Orleans and a former staffer for Bob Livingston, Ruckert wanted nothing more than to return to his Louisiana roots. He went to Vitter's Cannon Caucus Room reception with his sights set on landing a new job, or at least making an impression. He had heard that Vitter had overcome opposition from the Republican establishment and was a solid conservative. The two men shook hands that night and exchanged pleasantries.

Vitter had been a member of Congress for five days when Ruckert scored a job interview. He was immediately struck by Vitter's office, with its spacious floor plan and enviable view that overlooked the Capitol building. Vitter had inherited the space from Livingston, who had spent more than two decades in the House, building up the seniority to get that location. Other freshmen, by comparison, worked out of offices that resembled closets.

Apart from some friendly ribbing about Ruckert's going to Jesuit High—a rival to Vitter's De La Salle High School—both men immediately knew they would be a good fit. At six foot four, Ruckert was a towering, younger version of Vitter where it mattered most—he clung to far-right views and, more important, embraced an aggressive approach to politics. Ruckert became Vitter's second hire as the new congressman's legislative director. Chief of Staff Marty Driesler of Kentucky had received the first nod. Driesler, a hardened Washington insider who didn't mince words in rapid sentences with a bluegrass twang, became a mentor to Ruckert.

The young aide soon found love as well. Ruckert and his future wife, Lynnel, both worked in Vitter's 1st Congressional District office. He popped the question on the campaign trail, and the congressman read a Bible passage during their wedding several years later. The Ruckerts weren't the only Vitter staffers to fall in love and marry— three other couples wed while working for him. "I make people work a ton of hours," Vitter was fond of saying. "So who else are they going to marry?" Vitter also liked to joke that he was the last one to find out about these relationships, usually when he received a wedding invitation—a bit of an exaggeration, but one that drew laughs at each telling.

In 2000 and 2002 Vitter easily held onto his congressional seat while fine-tuning his ultra-conservative brand. He had begun his career in politics as an idealist, but in the partisan climate of Washington he quickly morphed into an ideologue who championed smaller government, family values, and other "red meat" conservative causes.

Wendy showed her own grit during the 2000 cycle when she told Newhouse News Service that if her husband ever cheated on her, she would act less like Hillary Clinton and more like the vengeful woman who famously sliced off her sleeping husband's penis in 1993. "I'm a lot more like Lorena Bobbitt than Hillary," Wendy said. "If he does something like that, I'm walking away with one thing, and it's not alimony, trust me. I think fear is a very good motivating factor in a marriage." Like her husband's 1998 op-ed column calling for Bill Clinton's impeachment on moral grounds, Wendy's comment would come back to haunt her years later.

Though now a congressman, Vitter resumed a familiar role back home—confronting powerful Louisiana politicians. Governor Mike Foster was one recurring target. Vitter made waves by opposing a deal Foster was pushing with the Jena Band of Choctaw Indians to establish a gambling casino in Calcasieu Parish, near the Texas border. For his part, Foster had long known something few others knew—that Vitter wanted to run for governor in 2003 and was possibly planning to use some or all of his federal campaign war chest to jump start his campaign. The grizzly, motorcycle-riding, duck-hunting governor sought the last word by getting lawmakers to pass a measure dubbed the "Bitter Vitter Bill." It prohibited the use of federal campaign money in a state election, such as a campaign for governor. Foster also used his live call-in talk radio show to accuse Vitter of slamming the Choctaw deal because Foster had refused to endorse the congressman for governor.

Vitter admitted he had asked for Foster's support but denied a quid pro quo. More important, Vitter, for the first time, had to deal with rumblings of a sex scandal, including talk that he had consorted with prostitutes in New Orleans before going to Congress. In June 2002, the *Louisiana Weekly* newspaper ran a story by Christopher Tidmore citing the rumors. Before the mainstream media could pick up the story, Vitter abruptly announced he would not run for governor in 2003, citing unspecified marital issues. "Our [marriage] counseling sessions have…led us to the rather obvious conclusion that it's not time to run for governor," he said.

Vitter suffered a devastating blow in 2003 when he lost Marty Driesler, his first chief of staff, to lung cancer. Driesler had retired about a year before her death, leaving Kyle Ruckert to take over her position. Throughout her battle with cancer, even as she had to use an oxygen tank nearly full-time, Driesler was Vitter's most trusted consultant.

One year later, Vitter once again seized an opportunity to move up. Senator John Breaux of Louisiana, a popular centrist who called himself a "Blue Dog Democrat," announced he would not seek a fourth term. Vitter promoted his candidacy far and wide, while vowing alongside Ruckert to "win this one for Marty." Vitter, who quickly cleared the field of major Republican challengers, faced three Democrats in the jungle primary. Among the Democrats, state Treasurer John Kennedy and Congressman Chris John competed with each other for the role of lead Democrat while hoping state Representative Arthur Morrell, an African-American legislator from New Orleans, never caught fire among African-American voters.

Vitter, meanwhile, ran a textbook campaign, casting himself as a loving husband and father, a supporter of cheaper imported Canadian prescription drugs, and of course a fearless reformer and family values conservative. He craftily flipped the seat red, winning 51 percent of the vote in the primary, thereby avoiding a costly and potentially dangerous runoff.

John admitted later that he had planned to use the prostitution allegations more prominently against Vitter in the runoff—but by publicly keeping that powder dry he never got the chance to ignite it.

The Democratic Senatorial Campaign Committee did shop the allegations, which landed on the pages of the left-leaning *Salon* on October 29, four days before the primary election. Very few Louisiana voters, however, got their news online in 2004. John's decision to "wait until the runoff" and the DSCC's last-minute move were classic examples of an old piece of political wisdom: You can do everything right in a campaign, but to win you still need a bit of luck. Vitter did everything right—and he got lucky when the prostitution allegations failed to catch fire during the primary.

The Senate race was the first campaign that Kyle Ruckert managed for Vitter. Declared "nearly flawless" by *The Times Picayune*, Ruckert's work on behalf of Vitter likewise earned him recognition by *Campaigns & Elections* magazine as one of 10 Republican "Rising Stars" in national politics. They were a dynamic duo, Vitter and Ruckert, and they immediately began plotting what would become the Louisiana Committee for A Republican Majority, with hopes of turning the state Legislature fire engine red.

David Vitter had never lost an election, and now he had claimed one of the top prizes in Louisiana politics. In the process, he became the first Republican in Louisiana history popularly elected to the United States Senate. More important, he was now the *de facto* boss of the Louisiana GOP, with a Republican president in the White House. The good times, however, would not last.

Vitter would find his first term in the Senate defined not only by Hurricane Katrina recovery efforts, but by news, in July 2007, that his telephone number appeared five times in the records of Deborah Jeane Palfrey, the D.C. Madam who operated an interstate prostitution ring. From then on, voters would see a much different side of David Vitter, who increasingly found himself deflecting—rather than dispensing—political fire.

7

"A Very Serious Sin"

Through the end of 2004, David Vitter had managed to avoid any prominent mention of a potentially career-ending scandal—at least in the mainstream media—since rumors had begun swirling about his alleged dalliances with prostitutes in New Orleans in the late 1990s. Other than one article in the *Louisiana Weekly* in 2002 and several subsequent mentions on talk radio programs, he had dodged a bullet and gotten himself elected to the Senate. Equally important, he was establishing himself as the Republican kingpin in Louisiana and a rising GOP firebrand in an increasingly partisan Washington. A trajectory like that could position him for a place on the national stage at some point, which admirers and critics alike assumed was his ultimate ambition. In the summer of 2007, however, Vitter's stellar trajectory would come crashing down.

Dan Moldea was a veteran investigative journalist who had partnered with *Hustler* magazine publisher Larry Flynt in 1998 to expose Republican sex scandals during the impeachment saga of President Bill Clinton. Moldea had already changed the course of history by bringing down Louisiana Congressman and presumptive House Speaker Bob Livingston for having an affair. Now he was about to set in motion the events that would topple Vitter, who was Livingston's Bayou State successor.

On the evening of Thursday, July 5, 2007, Moldea drove home from dinner bearing a compact disc imprinted with politically explosive data that he had sought for months. A file on the disc listed some 300,000 phone calls from the 10,000 to 15,000 clients of Deborah Jeane Palfrey, the D.C. Madam, now under federal indictment for running an escort service that reportedly catered to an A-List of Beltway clients. A judge earlier that day had issued an order allowing Palfrey and her attorney, Montgomery Blair Sibley, to distribute the telephone list. Because Sibley feared that prosecutors in George W. Bush's Department of Justice would immediately ask a higher court to block that ruling, he mailed CDs containing the list to 50 reporters that same day. The reporters would begin receiving the CDs the following Monday.

Moldea, who wanted a head start, had arranged to meet Sibley for dinner that night at Morty's Delicatessen, a favorite haunt, to get a jump on the competition.

Once again working for Flynt, Moldea had turned to the publisher after learning that the government was prosecuting Palfrey for running a prostitution ring out of homes and hotel rooms in metropolitan Washington. What especially got Moldea's attention: Palfrey had 46 pounds of client phone records from 1993 to 2006. Moldea was sure that he would find at least one big-name Republican in those records.

With the CD in hand, Moldea downloaded thousands of pages of telephone numbers onto his computer. One by one, he copied phone numbers into a reverse-phone database. If he received a hit, he printed the page. Then he used either a search engine or LexisNexis to find out if the number belonged to a Republican who had tried to dethrone Clinton. To simplify the time-consuming process, Moldea concentrated on phone numbers from two periods—the 1998–99 effort by Republicans to remove Clinton from office and the aftermath of the November 2000 presidential election, when Republicans and Democrats battled to determine whether George W. Bush or Al Gore had prevailed. After nearly a day of searching, Moldea had no hits. He wondered if he was engaging in a fruitless search.

Then, shortly after 6 p.m. on Friday, July 6, while poring through phone records from the Clinton–Bush transition period, Moldea arbitrarily decided he would stop searching the phone records when he got to February 27, 2001—because February 27 was his birthday. Moldea described what happened then in *Confessions of a Guerilla Journalist*, his 2013 memoir:

> *On that day at the logged-in time of 3:06 P.M., I came across a telephone number for Washington, D.C. that I had not seen before. When I ran it through the directory, the name, "David Vitter," appeared.*

> *Stunned, I ran the number again—and received the same result: David Vitter, then the U.S. congressman from Louisiana who, ironically enough, had succeeded Bob Livingston in 1999.*

Moldea called Palfrey. She said she didn't know Vitter. That was not surprising, because she operated out of a suburb of San Francisco. Moldea then called Flynt. "Larry, I got one," Moldea told him.

"Is he a hypocrite?" Flynt asked.

"Just wait until you see this guy, Larry," Moldea replied.

From his research, Moldea knew that Vitter was a family-values Republican who had campaigned to protect the sanctity of marriage by banning same-sex nuptials. He also had loudly called out Bill Clinton on the Monica Lewinsky affair. A member of the House of Representatives at the time of the 2001 call, Vitter was now a member of the Senate. To out him, Flynt agreed to Moldea's suggestion that he feed information on the phone calls to a respected reporter. Moldea chose Adam Zagorin of *Time* magazine; they met that night to discuss Vitter's use of Palfrey's escort service, and Zagorin agreed to Moldea's one request—that his article credit Flynt and *Hustler* with the discovery.

Nothing happened the next day, a Saturday, or on Sunday. By 5 p.m. Monday, July 9, *Time* had yet to publish anything about Vitter. Impatient, Flynt had a *Hustler* editor call Vitter's office and ask to speak with the senator. A secretary said he was not in. Around that time, Zagorin also called Vitter's office to ask why the senator's phone number was in the D.C. Madam's records. That was it. Vitter was cornered. No one on his staff, including the senator himself, had known that the phone records were coming out.

But instead of responding to Zagorin—or *Hustler*—the senator made a strategic decision to give the story directly to the Associated Press via a statement that he penned himself, with Chief of Staff Kyle Ruckert and longtime media consultant John Brabender getting the final read-through. Vitter also made the decision to inform his entire staff, in Louisiana and D.C., via a telephone conference call. Receiving word of the call well after regular work hours, many staffers wondered what it involved. When they were all on the line, they quickly found out.

Humbled and apologetic, Vitter said he knew that he had let them all down. When he finished, he gave his listeners the chance to speak. "We're praying for you," one staffer said. Not one quit that night, and nearly all remained on the team in subsequent years. That moment, in fact, bonded many of them, and the coming firestorm only strengthened the bond.

The AP story that night contained this statement from Vitter: "This was a very serious sin in my past for which I am, of course, completely responsible. Several years ago, I asked for and received forgiveness from God and my wife in confession and marriage counseling. Out of respect for my family, I will keep my discussion of the matter there—with God and them. But I certainly offer my deep and sincere apologies to all I have disappointed and let down in any way."

This was another page out of Vitter's political playbook:

managing bad news by trying to get in front of the story. Smart politicians (and corporations) pay big money for advice like that, but Vitter already knew instinctively what he had to do. He knew that the AP would write the story down the middle, without garnish or snark, and set the tone for other media coverage. Releasing the story was another calculated risk by a man who had spent his entire political career calibrating every word, every move. He undoubtedly knew the political fallout would be immediate and intense, but he was determined to contain it and manage it to the extent possible—and then start rebuilding his carefully crafted image. Predictably, news of a family-values Republican senator consorting with prostitutes exploded like a bombshell.

The Washington Post, The New York Times, CBS News and others immediately jumped on the story. CBS, in noting a statement of forgiveness from Vitter's wife Wendy, also recalled that she had seemed less charitable in a 2000 interview when she described herself as "a lot more like Lorena Bobbitt than Hillary." Others as well picked up on Wendy's interview, which, years earlier, had gotten her a spate of positive ink. Now, not so much. In politics, even the best quote can come back to bite you, which is why so many politicians parse their words and avoid saying anything remotely controversial—or memorable.

The story quickly shifted to Louisiana. The next day, WDSU–TV aired an interview with Jeanette Maier, known in south Louisiana as "the Canal Street Madam." An FBI raid of Maier's brothel in the Mid-City neighborhood of New Orleans had created a sensation in 2001 and 2002. Like Palfrey in Washington, Maier's clientele was an A-List of Louisiana movers and shakers—and the raid spawned a cottage industry of gossip and speculation as to who was "on the list" and who wasn't.

Maier had given the feds a handwritten list of her clients, as best she could recall them, but that list was never published. Now, however, she was saying that Vitter had visited her escort service in New Orleans beginning in the mid-1990s, when he was a state representative from Metairie. She claimed Vitter paid the customary rate—$300 an hour—but she provided few other details *and no evidence*. Moreover, her own attorney told the press that Vitter's name was not on the client list given to the FBI. Still, her claims triggered more rumors about Vitter.

A day later, on July 11, Bill Walsh of *The Times-Picayune* reported that Palfrey's phone records showed that Vitter had made five separate calls to the escort service: on October 12, 1999; on September 18, 2000; on October 26, 2000; on February 11, 2001; and on February 27, 2001—the last one the call that Moldea had found. Two days later,

CBS reported that the House was in session during four of the calls from Palfrey and that two of them occurred while the House was conducting roll call votes.

Journalists and pundits were having a field day with Vitter. *The New York Times'* Adam Nossiter reported in a news story on July 11:

> From the beginning of his political career 16 years ago, Senator David Vitter has been known for efforts to plant himself on the moral high ground, challenging the ethics of other Louisiana politicians, decrying same-sex marriage and depicting himself as a clean-as-a-whistle champion of family values.
>
> "I'm a conservative who opposes radically redefining marriage, the most important social institution in human history," Mr. Vitter, a 46-year-old Republican, wrote in a letter last year to The Times-Picayune, the New Orleans daily.

The article included a prediction from Roy Fletcher, a Baton Rouge media consultant whose clients were mostly conservative politicians: "He's got very turbulent waters ahead. This thing ain't going away."

The waters grew even more turbulent the following day, when Wendy Cortez, the prostitute who was at the center of the rumors that led to the *Louisiana Weekly* story in 2002, resurfaced. Now going by her maiden name of Wendy Yow (she later used the names Wendy Williams and Wendy Ellis), Cortez called *The Times-Picayune* after reporter Kate Moran had contacted her father. Cortez told the newspaper that Vitter had been a regular client of hers when he was a state representative. Cortez also said that she and Vitter "did not have a personal romantic relationship," although she would change that description to "very intimate" nine years later, claiming publicly for the first time then that Moran had somehow gotten parts of the story wrong.

Moran's article also noted, "She claimed to have severed ties with him after she found out he was married. Cortez said it was a part of her life she hoped to put behind her."

Moran's newspaper article gave other important details about Cortez: She had a checkered past that included other crimes besides prostitution; further, she had been arrested and charged with fraudulent use of credit cards in a Florida case that led to a jail sentence. The article also quoted Tait Cortez, who said he had been her boyfriend until she scorned him for another man. Tait Cortez identified that other man as David Vitter, whom he called a "city slicker," and said he didn't even know who Vitter was until Wendy told him. He also claimed that he had photographs of Vitter and Cortez together but had burned the photos.

By then, three days had passed since Vitter had acknowledged his unspecified "very serious sin." During those three days, the senator had not shown his face publicly, either in Washington or Louisiana. That's because he wasn't in either locale. On July 10, the day after he gave his initial statement to the AP, a staffer picked Vitter up at his apartment on Capitol Hill and took him to the airport without any reporters seeing them. Vitter and Wendy flew to Houston to stay with family. From the Lone Star state, the senator coordinated the crisis via phone.

Meanwhile, reporters staked out his office in Washington and camera crews camped outside his church in Jefferson Parish. Vitter, of course, didn't show. He missed voting on measures before the Senate that would have limited the length of troop deployments in Iraq. While the media continued to report every detail of the scandal, Vitter was already planning his comeback.

His first move was to grab the narrative by orchestrating a wave of supportive statements—all issued on the same day—from key Republicans. Most readily complied, with varying degrees of support. Thus on Thursday, July 12, just three days after Vitter leaked the story to the Associated Press, top Republicans in Louisiana issued statements of personal support for the Vitter family and praised the senator's work on Capitol Hill. The wording of each statement was crucial.

Congressman Richard Baker of Baton Rouge was effusive in his support, which surprised even the senator's staff. Baker defended Vitter's character and urged the news media to "demonstrate some restraint and professionalism." Most important, Baker said Vitter's behavior "does not define the whole of the man and it is not irredeemable." That was precisely the chord Vitter wanted his colleagues to strike.

Others who offered support included Congressman Charles Boustany of Lafayette, state GOP chair Roger Villere, and former Congressman Bob Livingston. One key Republican, however, offered only a tepid statement: Congressman Bobby Jindal, who had succeeded Vitter in the House and was about to formally announce his candidacy for governor.

Jindal struck a cautious note—and even led with a gratuitous criticism: "While we are disappointed by Senator Vitter's actions, Supriya and I continue to keep David and his family in our prayers. This is a matter for the Senator to address, and it is our hope that this is not used by others for their own political gain." That word—

"disappointed"—was definitely not part of Vitter's redemption script, and no doubt it stung. Even worse, Jindal had released his statement on his own day, not at the same time as everyone else. The redemption storyline was meant for a single 24-hour news cycle, but Jindal turned it into an ongoing story, which just invited more scrutiny. "It was just an extra story and wasn't helpful at all," Ruckert said later.

Jindal's affront did not end there. For months, Jindal's campaign website had touted news that Vitter was endorsing Jindal for governor, including a link to Vitter's letter of support. Not long after the scandal broke, however, that announcement—and the link—were scrubbed from the campaign website. Jindal was clearly distancing himself from the newly scandalized senator.

Vitter never forgot Jindal's slight. He knew his own road to redemption would be long and difficult, but paying back Jindal for the "disappointed" slap would come quickly—and easily. On Monday, July 16, news outlets got word that Vitter would appear before the press at 5:00 p.m. at the Sheraton Hotel in Metairie, not far from his home.

Vitter had been brainstorming with his staff from Houston, trying to devise the best way to conduct the press conference. A great deal of planning had gone on, a lot of back and forth. Should the senator stand on the stage and field hundreds of questions? *No way*. Instead, he would deliver a single statement. That would require discipline—not only during the press conference but also in the coming days and weeks. The inner circle, which included Ruckert, Brabender, DiGrado, and finance director Courtney Guastella, knew Vitter to be unflappable. Still, some worried about the optics, a concern that disappeared when Vitter reported that his wife, Wendy, would join him onstage and offer her own statement.

Another decision made during those conference calls was Vitter's insistence that he address the rumors about another prostitution scandal in New Orleans. That plan sent up a red flag for Ruckert, who wanted to keep it simple. He stressed that point with his boss, reminding him that people would pick over his statement for years to come. Vitter, however, was adamant. He had never had any kind of contact with a prostitute in New Orleans, he said, and he was going to tell that to the world. Ruckert already believed his boss, but at that moment Vitter convinced him absolutely that the "New Orleans stories" were untrue.

Many thought the timing of Vitter's first public appearance was not coincidental—it came at exactly the same moment as Jindal's formal announcement in New Orleans that he was running for governor. Jindal had scheduled rallies in Louisiana's major media markets that day, starting that morning and culminating in New

Orleans, the state's largest market, at 5 p.m. He no doubt had hoped local TV stations would give his announcement live coverage in their afternoon newscasts. Instead, he was all but ignored in the frenzy over Vitter's emergence from a self-imposed exile—a perceived slight Jindal would not soon forget. Vitter's staff maintained later that they had been in the bunker so long, no one had noticed the announcements would overlap.

The Times-Picayune dispatched Brendan McCarthy to the Sheraton. A crime reporter, McCarthy had found and interviewed Tait Cortez the previous week. As McCarthy arrived at the hotel, the row of satellite TV trucks outside caught his attention. The story offered the irresistible intersection of sex and politics. Inside, McCarthy bumped into several other reporters. They all wondered: *What was Vitter going to say? Would he admit to a relationship with Cortez? Might he even announce his resignation from the Senate?* McCarthy was milling outside when the doors to the meeting room swung shut without warning. He and several others were locked out. Vitter's staff held the event in a meeting room so small that McCarthy's colleague Moran would call it "no bigger than a two-car garage." Reporters, cameramen, and photographers were so jammed inside that they could barely move.

Vitter and his wife Wendy entered via a side door at 5:05 p.m. He walked to a podium amid the whir of camera clicks and immediately began speaking. Last week, he said, he and Wendy thought it was important to spend time alone with their four children. All of them were younger than 13. Vitter then thanked "the countless friends and fellow citizens" who had offered their encouragement and prayers. "Those have meant the world to us," he said. Wendy, standing to his left with a stricken look on her face, nodded briefly.

Glancing down at his notes, Vitter continued. "I want to again offer my deep, sincere apologies to all those I have let down and disappointed with these actions from my past," he said. "I am completely responsible. And I am so very, very sorry. No matter how long ago it was, I know this has hurt the relationship of trust I've enjoyed with so many of you, and that I have a lot of work to do to rebuild that. I will work every day to rebuild that trust."

He and Wendy had dealt with this difficulty several years ago, he added. "I confronted it in confession and marriage counseling. I believe I received forgiveness from God. I know I did from Wendy"— she stopped looking at the floor long enough to glance at him—"and we put it behind us." Vitter then obliquely responded to the claims by Maier and Cortez that he had been their client. "Unfortunately, my admission has encouraged some long-time political enemies and those hoping to profit from the situation to spread falsehoods, like those New Orleans stories in recent reporting," he said. "Those stories are not true."

Having expressed regret without providing specifics, Vitter next sought to begin putting the scandal behind him. "I'm not going to answer endless questions about it all over again and again and again and again," he said, even though he had yet to answer a single question about the scandal. "That might sell newspapers, but it wouldn't serve my family or my constituents well at all because we all have a lot of important work to do for Louisiana." He mentioned the "important work" he would be doing in Washington in the coming days, particularly the ongoing recovery from Hurricane Katrina. "Thank you," he said with a frown and stepped aside. Not three minutes had passed.

Wendy took two steps back, as if she were heading out, then moved to the podium. She gripped it with both hands as if to steel herself. "In most any other marriage, this would have been a private issue between a husband and wife, very private," she said. "Obviously it is not here," she added and gestured toward the cameras. "Like all marriages, ours is not perfect," she continued. "None of us are. But we chose to work together as a family. When David and I dealt with this several years ago, I forgave David. I made the decision to love him and to recommit to our marriage. To forgive is not always the easy choice, but it was and is the right choice for me. David is my best friend." Harkening back to her days as a prosecutor, Wendy maintained eye contact with everyone in the room, as if she were speaking to a jury. "Last week," she continued, "some people very sympathetically said to me, 'I wouldn't want to be in your shoes right now.' I stand before you to tell you very proudly, I am proud to be Wendy Vitter." On CNN, a graphic at the bottom of the screen boiled down the essential news. It read, "Senator won't talk about 'madam.' Wife stands by his side."

Just as her husband had done, Wendy now sought to forestall further coverage of the scandal. "Now I'm going to speak to you as a mother," she said, "and I hope you will understand. It's been terribly hard to have the media parked on our front lawn and following us every day. And yesterday the media was camped at our church—at our home and at our church every day." She paused and looked down at her notes. "As David returns to work in Washington, we're going to return to our life here. I would just ask you very respectfully to let us continue our summer and our lives as we had planned." Wendy and her husband said thanks and walked out the side door. Reporters shouted questions as the couple departed, to no avail. David and Wendy Vitter were gone five minutes after entering the room.

"He nailed it," Ruckert thought. "They both did as well as you could ever ask." It was the first time Ruckert and the rest of his staff could take a deep breath. Their playbook was simple: they would put the scandal behind them by getting back to work and, above all, not engaging with reporters. In the months and years to come, the playbook would expand to include other strategies, but for now that was enough.

Upon returning to Washington, Vitter acted as if nothing had happened, and all was business as usual. His colleagues lifted his spirits by giving him a standing ovation at a private meeting of the Senate Republican Conference when he apologized to them. Some senators kept their distance afterward, while others offered words of encouragement to the press and helped him in other ways when they could. Several well-known faith leaders defended him as well. Vitter, meanwhile, continued to duck the press.

Despite his best efforts, Vitter could control the narrative only so much. On September 11, Cortez appeared at a press conference in Beverly Hills alongside *Hustler* owner Larry Flynt. She told reporters that Vitter had been her client from July to November 1999, just after he had entered Congress. She explained why the relationship ended. "When I asked him if he would like to carry this beyond the business," she said, "I gave him my name and phone number. I said, 'My real name is Wendy,' and he said, 'Oh my God.'" That was one version of Cortez's story. It would change over time.

Flynt announced that Cortez would appear in a five-page nude photo spread in his magazine's January 2008 issue, under the headline, "SENATOR DAVID VITTER'S SECRET LOVER REVEALED." The magazine, which paid her a fee, identified Cortez as "Wendy Yow Ellis." In an interview, she described how she had been working as a stripper on Bourbon Street in 1999 when a pimp named Jonathan asked her if she would like to spread her wings, so to speak, by working for his New Orleans Escort Service. "I was young, dumb, and on drugs, so I said *Sure*," she said, adding that Jonathan called one day soon afterward to arrange a hookup with Vitter. She claimed that she had sex with Vitter two or three times a week for three or four months, for $300 per session. She gave other, more salacious details in the *Hustler* article, and the magazine reported that she passed a lie detector test when asked whether she had worked for the New Orleans Escort Service for at least four months.

The Times-Picayune received a copy of the magazine's story and photos in November and gave it a one-time treatment—printing no more details than readers would tolerate on their kitchen tables— and moved on. While the *Hustler* story revived the scandal for a day or two, in some ways the release was an early break for Vitter. The mainstream media ignored the most salacious allegations, and the article revealed nothing *new* of a scandalous nature. That made the scandal "old news" to many, a meme that Vitter's press secretary, Joel DiGrado, repeated whenever a reporter asked why the senator's phone number appeared in Palfrey's records: "The senator and his wife have addressed all of this very directly." Indeed, Vitter had already said in his July 2007 press conference that the New Orleans stories were "not true." Vitter was already headlong into his political redemption, both in Louisiana and in Washington. Then he caught other breaks.

Five weeks after Vitter's prostitution scandal made headlines, the Capitol Hill newspaper *Roll Call* reported that Senator Larry Craig, a Republican from Idaho, had been arrested for lewd conduct in June in a men's bathroom at the Minneapolis–St. Paul International Airport. Craig had already pleaded guilty to a lesser charge of disorderly conduct, when in fact he had—allegedly—solicited oral sex from an undercover police officer. The tabloids' attention shifted immediately from Vitter to Craig.

Republicans called on Craig to resign, but they had made no such demand of Vitter only weeks earlier. Why not? Possibly because Craig's accusation involved gay sex, or because Craig had pleaded guilty, albeit to a misdemeanor. Vitter had admitted to a "very serious sin" but had not named that sin—nor had he admitted breaking the law. Or maybe Vitter caught that break because Louisiana, unlike Idaho, had a Democratic governor. Republicans may have been willing to turn a blind eye to Vitter's "very serious sin" simply to keep Louisiana Governor Kathleen Blanco from appointing a Democrat to replace him, had he resigned.

Democrats held a slim 51–49 majority in the Senate at the time, thanks to two independents who caucused with the Democrats. Had Vitter resigned and been replaced by a Democrat, even temporarily, the Democrats would have tightened their grip on the Senate. Republicans could not afford to let that happen, no matter what the cost in public perception regarding Vitter's scandal.

That, too, was a big break for Vitter. At the end of the day, when sex and politics collide, sex gets more headlines—but politics ultimately trumps.

Another break came in May 2008, when the Senate Ethics Committee dismissed a complaint that Citizens for Responsibility and Ethics in Washington had filed against the senator. The group had alleged that Vitter's solicitation of prostitutes in Washington violated the law and therefore constituted "improper conduct" that the Senate should punish. The six-member Ethics Committee, however, unanimously voted to dismiss the complaint, noting in its letter of dismissal that "the conduct at issue" occurred before Vitter's run for the Senate. The letter further noted that Vitter was not charged criminally, and his conduct "did not involve use of public office or status for improper purposes." The dismissal came a week after Deborah Jeane Palfrey, the D.C. Madam, committed suicide.

Time and the shift in public attention gave Vitter some breathing space. He took full advantage. In Louisiana, he methodically rebuilt relationships with key Republicans and influential evangelical ministers. Those initial meetings were private, one-on-one sit downs, giving Vitter a chance to mend fences with his most important supporters. Eventually, he held town hall meetings, though always in tightly controlled settings, and always carefully choreographed to minimize questions while making him appear available to the general public.

Initially, the press showed up, but when questions arose about the scandal, Vitter simply noted that he had admitted his sin, apologized for it, and received his wife's forgiveness. Over time, he hosted town hall meetings in all 64 Louisiana parishes—and faced fewer and fewer questions about his "very serious sin." Time, indeed, was healing David Vitter's wounds.

In ways that would not become clear until later, Vitter caught another break in November 2008 when Barack Obama won the presidential election. Although Obama comfortably carried the national popular vote—and scored a huge Electoral College margin— he had gotten clobbered in Louisiana. Vitter quickly recognized that John McCain's 59 percent of the Bayou State vote represented his own natural constituency.

In time, the new president would provide the perfect foil for Vitter's hallmark brand of scorched-earth politics, at least in Louisiana. Meanwhile, in Washington, Vitter dove into his work. In January 2009, on the first day of the Senate's new term, he filed 34 bills that ran the gamut of social conservative "red meat" causes: abortion, illegal immigration, stem cell research, homeschooling, public prayer, drugs, the death penalty, and protecting the American flag. When President Obama nominated Vitter's Senate colleague, Hillary Clinton, to be Secretary of State, Vitter cast one of only two Senate votes against her confirmation—presciently citing potential conflicts of interest in connection with the Clintons' charitable foundation.

Although Vitter's scandal was no longer front-page news, it never completely left the media's radar screen. *The Washington Post* listed him in 2009 among the senators it deemed most likely to lose their seats. Back home and in Washington, Vitter stayed focused and on message—and he avoided the media whenever possible.

By 2010, he had regained enough political traction to announce his re-election plans. His redemption strategy was working so well, in fact, that no major Republican challenged him. His Democratic opponent was Congressman Charlie Melancon, who had won three terms representing the coastal parishes of southeast and south central Louisiana. Melancon was convinced he could beat Vitter by using the prostitution scandal as a club. In April 2010, the state Democratic Party launched a five-minute web ad called "Forgotten Crimes." It had a film noir feel, featuring interviews with three men whose faces were shadowed, as if their identities needed to be obscured for their safety. Each man expressed concern over Vitter's behavior. The ad also featured brief footage from a 2004 Vitter campaign commercial showing his two daughters holding up signs for their dad, then video of Wendy Ellis, with bare shoulders, interspersed with grainy, black-and-white footage labeled "crime scene re-enactment."

Melancon campaigned as a "pro-life, pro-gun Louisiana Democrat" who was willing to cross party lines in the tradition of former Senators J. Bennett Johnston and John Breaux. His wife Peachy's constant presence sought to remind voters that Melancon was a genuine family values candidate. Nonetheless, Vitter began the race as the favorite and stayed there. By September, Melancon trailed Vitter by nine points, giving his campaign team hope that victory was still possible. But here again, Vitter caught a break.

The Deepwater Horizon oil spill and ongoing efforts to clean up Louisiana's coast in the disaster's wake dominated news coverage across south Louisiana. The coastal economy had already taken a devastating hit when President Obama imposed a moratorium on Gulf drilling after the blowout. Melancon had trouble breaking through. It didn't help that Vitter was pounding him with ads tying the Democrat to Obama.

In one ad, a narrator said Melancon "just may be Barack Obama's biggest fan." That was nowhere near the truth, but the message resonated among anti-Obama white voters who were furious about the moratorium. Vitter, meanwhile, avoided reporters—and debates—as much as possible. He appeared mostly in friendly settings where his campaign could control both the audience and the message.

On October 28, a scant five days before the election, Melancon hit Vitter directly with an ad on the prostitution issue. "Our tax dollars paid David Vitter's salary," a narrator said, as an image of the senator flashed onto the screen. "And he used it for prostitutes," the narrator continued, as the ad flashed a comely image of Wendy Ellis. "You're welcome, Senator." The ad then showed an image of Vitter and his wife Wendy in 2007 when he emerged from hiding. "Our money paid for Vitter's 'serious sin,'" the narrator continued, as another image of Ellis appeared, "phone calls to prostitutes during official votes." The ad ended with the narrator intoning, "The real sin is that David Vitter's still a senator."

That same evening, Melancon would have one last chance to overtake Vitter by scoring big at a debate hosted by WWL–TV and other CBS affiliates across the state, including WAFB–TV in Baton Rouge. On that morning, the journalists who would appear on the panel met with WWL's producers to plan the evening. Their goal, they all agreed, was to get the two candidates off their talking points to give viewers a better feel for each man. The journalists and producers agreed that they had to address the prostitution issue with a question. That issue was the elephant in the room.

The question fell to WAFB–TV anchor Greg Meriwether. For days, he had been hearing from viewers that they wanted clearer answers from Vitter on his sexual indiscretions. Meriwether, 31, didn't relish asking the question. The matter was so personal, and Vitter's wife would undoubtedly be watching. But Meriwether knew it had to be asked. The moment came midway through the hour-long debate.

"Uh, Mr. Vitter, we've received a number of emails, uh, basically viewers questioning your involvement in the, uh, D.C., uh, prostitution ring," Meriwether began, betraying his nervousness. "You've called it a 'serious sin.' What *was* your serious sin?"

"Three years ago, when I discussed this directly with Louisiana citizens," Vitter replied in his monotone, obviously prepped for the question, "I did say in a very direct, sincere way, I committed a very bad mistake in my marriage, a very serious sin. This is going back now about 10 years." He added that he had received forgiveness from his wife, his children, and God. "Greg, I'll be honest that I think Louisiana citizens all around the state heard me. And I think they understood me. And they understood what I was saying."

Vitter kept talking. He said he had gotten an "outpouring of prayers and support and well wishes. It was truly humbling." Now he sought to turn the table on reporters. "I think it shows the gulf, quite frankly, in how Louisianans think and feel and operate and how Washington political hacks think and feel and operate."

Vitter kept talking. After two minutes, the debate's moderator, WWL–TV anchor Dennis Woltering, decided he had to intervene. "Did you violate the law when you committed this sin?" he asked.

"Dennis, again, you can look back, you can continue to write stories about it in the media. That's your decision. It's a free country."

Now it was Meriwether's turn to interrupt Vitter, "Can you look at the camera right now and talk to voters and tell them did you violate the law?" he asked.

"I did just look in the camera," Vitter replied. "I just did...."

Meriwether interrupted him again. "Did you violate the law, yes or no, sir?"

"Again, you can ask those questions back 10 years, you can stay fixated on that. My job, I believe, is to look forward on behalf of the people of Louisiana."

Meriwether tried again. "Can you offer some answers tonight, please?"

Before Vitter could answer, Woltering jumped in again. "It's a question of accountability, Mr. Vitter."

"You've asked the question," the senator said, looking at Woltering. "I've given you...."

"And we haven't heard an answer," interrupted Woltering. "We haven't gotten a yes or a no."

"You may not like the answer I've given you," Vitter said.

Meriwether tried one last time. "I'll give you the opportunity to give us a yes or a no and explain either one," he said.

"I'm not going to take that opportunity," intoned Vitter, "because I think the people of Louisiana have understood exactly what I said to them. I think they want me to focus on the key challenges we face as a state and as a country. That's what they tell me directly." He smiled. "It may not be what the media badgers me with. I can tell you that is what they tell me directly."

Nearly four minutes had passed, and Vitter had doggedly stuck to his strategy of not answering the question. Woltering gave up and moved on to the next topic.

The prostitution issue flared one more time during the debate—when the candidates were asked where they thought the other had crossed a line during an increasingly nasty campaign. "The biggest area where I think he crossed the line, quite frankly," Vitter said, "is taking and using video of my children in his two-minute, R-rated attack ad. I think that is clearly crossing the line." Vitter turned to his right to address Melancon. "If that is part of your Melancon family values, Charlie, I don't want any part of it," he said.

"David," replied Melancon tartly, "you never had family values. You've demonstrated that to America quite keenly."

After the debate ended, several reporters rushed into the studio to interview Vitter, but he beat a hasty exit before anyone could get to him. That, too, was part of his strategy. "You want to talk about discipline?" Ruckert would say later. "David nailed those questions. Every single one of them."

Five days later, on November 2, Vitter trounced Melancon, 57 percent to 38 percent. He outspent his Democratic opponent nearly three to one. With his victory, Vitter established conclusively that President Obama's unpopularity in Louisiana was a potent GOP weapon that could neutralize even a sex scandal. Simply put, Louisiana voters disliked Obama even more than they disliked sin.

To Republicans across the Bayou State, Vitter's impressive win sent a clear message about the opportunities presented by Obama's unpopularity: *Imagine what such a weapon could do in the hands of a Republican candidate not sullied by scandal.* The press took note. "(D)isenchantment with the Democratic agenda trumped concerns about the incumbent's personal character," wrote *Times-Picayune* reporter Jan Moller. "Melancon was never able to convince enough voters that he was fundamentally different than the leaders of his party in Washington."

In all, 715,415 people voted for Vitter. One of them was Greg Meriwether, the WAFB–TV anchorman who repeatedly tried and failed to get Vitter to describe his sin or say whether he had broken the law. "I felt he was right for that race," Meriwether said several years later in an interview. "I was happy with the job he had done as senator. I was not happy with his answer personally, but I had moved on." So, it seemed, had most Louisiana voters.

Vitter would move on, too. His redemption strategy was working. It suggested, not for the first time, that American politics indeed affords second acts. But he had more work to do to fully recover from the scandal, and he was eager to get to it.

The move from the House to the Senate, and the span of time marked by the long ordeal that followed news of Vitter's "very serious sin," was a transitional period for the Vitter family. Wendy had taken time away from her career while raising their four children, including twin daughters, but now was ready to practice law again. She eventually took a job as the general counsel to the Archdiocese of New Orleans and took on more serious responsibilities with the Cancer Association of Greater New Orleans, later as its president. David, meanwhile, was setting his sights on an earlier prize denied: the Governor's Mansion. Pundits back home began predicting a "reddening" of Louisiana, some even suggesting that politicians who had run as "John Breaux Democrats" in the past would soon be campaigning as "David Vitter Republicans."

Despite such flattering speculation, Vitter as a candidate for governor left something to be desired, at least in 2010, because Louisiana voters look at senators and governors quite differently. A senator goes off to Washington and is rarely seen again. A governor is someone you can actually get to know, maybe even touch—and definitely someone you had to *like* in order to support. Vitter was not that guy, not yet anyway. He was still seen as a loner, even by voters. "It's my personality translated into politics," Vitter said in an interview the year after his re-election to the Senate. "Because of that, I've really very consciously worked on trying to develop other strengths, like team building ...."

Each passing month brought new hints that Vitter was considering a run for governor. He held more town hall meetings, reached out to more ministers, and mended fences with more local Republicans. He also helped build the state party by supporting GOP candidates in key local and statewide elections. In Washington, he reached across the aisle on key issues that he knew would resonate back home. In 2012, when reporters brought up his potential run for governor, Vitter did little to stop the speculation. In March 2013, Vitter's redemption plan gelled to the point where even *The Washington Post* took notice. It reported that Vitter "is suddenly in high demand. His banishment is over, his rehabilitation almost complete."

The story praised Vitter for "teaming up" with Democratic Senator Barbara Boxer of California, the Senate's most liberal environmentalist, to push for passage of a new Water Resources Development Act, or WRDA. Boxer and Vitter got the bill out of Boxer's committee without a dissenting vote, earning him bipartisan praise. Equally important, the WRDA bill contained funds for flood protection back in Louisiana and reformed the United States Army Corps of Engineers—one of Vitter's favorite bogeymen.

In late 2013, Vitter took another big step. He emailed key supporters and expressed genuine interest in running for governor. Then, on January 21, 2014, he pulled the trigger with a video announcement that spread like wildfire on social media, in forwarded emails, and on YouTube: He was running for governor.

"I believe that as our next governor, I can have a bigger impact addressing the unique challenges and opportunities we face in Louisiana," Vitter said in the video, which had been recorded in secrecy in Washington, in front of a green screen. He continued, "This will be my last political job, elected or appointed. Period. So my only agenda will be to do what's best for all Louisianans, from our best and brightest to our most vulnerable."

That part of Vitter's announcement was meant as a jab at Bobby Jindal, who as governor repeatedly had said that he had the job he wanted—even though he was increasingly gone from the state as he geared up to run for president. The two men were still enemies, but Vitter was looking to his own political future, noting, "Although an active campaign is still a year away, I'll start preparing for it immediately by doing what I've always done, including as our U.S. senator. That's listening to you, knowing that I sure don't have all the answers."

Meanwhile, in Louisiana, Vitter's enemies—he still had plenty—weren't nearly as interested in his future as they were in his past. As much as the senator wanted to keep leaning forward and to put his past behind him, others were determined not to let that happen. Nearly seven years after Vitter's "very serious sin" burst into the headlines, many Louisiana voters had either forgotten about it or had softened on the issue. Polls showed him with an enviable 60 percent approval rating back home. His long march to redemption was nearly finished, but one last task remained—one last score had to be settled—before he could return home to Louisiana in absolute triumph.

8

"As Rare as a Snowy Day"

State Representative Paul Hollis put the air conditioner of his black Audi A8 on its highest setting—his only defense against the oppressive July heat. At that time of year, the air in south Louisiana feels even heavier and stickier than it is—a remarkable feat, as temperatures had climbed well into the 90s. Up one street and down another Hollis drove, to nowhere in particular. He was talking on his cell phone against a background score of slightly muted pop hits from the '80s on a satellite radio channel. It was smooth driving with no traffic, which is why Hollis stuck to the well-paved roads of The Sanctuary, a private subdivision in Mandeville, directly across Lake Pontchartrain from New Orleans. The Sanctuary was the kind of development that had its own logo—a pelican cruising majestically above waters bounded by pine trees. Everything about the place screamed "St. Tammany!"— the once-rural parish that hugged the lake's northern shore. Starting in the 1980s, St. Tammany changed quickly from a sleepy collection of bucolic hamlets into a bustling, often congested tangle of exurban sprawl.

The Sanctuary was aptly named, as long as one remained on campus. Its amenities included blinding white McMansions with manicured lawns, tennis courts, and hiking trails for the suburban adventurer. It also offered great cellular reception, which is what attracted Hollis.

He did this sometimes—drove around with no destination in mind while trying to clear his head, just roaming and ruminating. As a possible United States Senate candidate later that year, he had already ponied up $250,000 of his own money to send a signal that he was serious. With qualifying just weeks away, Hollis had a lot on his mind.

"Look, I need to go," Hollis spoke into the phone, his high school karate instructor listening on the other end. The two had grown close in the years since Hollis had escaped adolescence. Now, with a family, a mortgage, and a political career on the rise, he needed a sounding board—preferably sturdier than the boards he had cracked along the way to earning his black belt. His questions echoed in his mind. *Should I qualify? Should I actually run for the United States Senate?*

"They told me 4 o'clock," Hollis told his friend, glancing at the digital clock on his dashboard. "David is the kind of guy who's gonna call right at 4 o'clock. I'll follow up with you later."

Hollis placed his phone on the empty passenger seat. He knew that Senator Mary Landrieu, the 18-year incumbent from New Orleans, was vulnerable. But the field wasn't taking shape as he had hoped. His path to victory was narrowing, and he had been at it since the previous November. Now Hollis was rethinking his options. A week earlier, an aide to Senator David Vitter sent word that Vitter would call Hollis to discuss the race. That call was scheduled for today. At 4 o'clock.

A conservative Republican with slicked-back brown hair and a boyish face, Hollis came from solid political stock. His late father, Ken, had served in the state Senate for 26 years representing Jefferson Parish, the New Orleans suburb on the South shore of Lake Pontchartrain. Paul Hollis was also a successful small businessman, dealing in rare coins. In 2012 he penned *American Numismatist*, a nonfiction yarn that wove American history with the story of its coins and currency. After it was published, the Numismatic Literary Guild presented Hollis with the "Best U.S. Coin Book Award." To paraphrase the immortal words of comedian Bill Murray, *he had that going for him,* which was good.

Hollis' phone rang. It was David Vitter, calling at exactly 4 o'clock. Hollis smiled and thought to himself, "I knew it."

Despite the anticipation, Hollis already knew, in broad strokes, what was coming. Vitter had made similar calls to Congressman John Fleming, former Congressman Jeff Landry, and state Representative Alan Seabaugh. Vitter considered all of these men fine conservatives, but he thought Congressman Bill Cassidy of Baton Rouge, a physician, was the only Republican who could survive Louisiana's unique jungle primary and beat Landrieu in a runoff. Vitter was clearing the field for Cassidy, and now it was Hollis' turn to get out of the way.

"I don't want to get into your head or anything, but where are you on this?" Vitter asked Hollis.

"No," Hollis interrupted. "I want you to get into my head. I want to hear what you think about this race."

Vitter and Hollis discussed Louisiana's shifting political sands and the GOP plan for a red sweep that fall. For all the buildup, the call was relatively short. By the time both men hung up, Hollis had agreed to withdraw from the Senate race and support Cassidy. Describing the conversation as civil and evenhanded, he would later say, "David compelled me in a number of different ways."

Hollis broke the news to supporters in an email on the morning of July 14, 2014, calling for an end to "Mary Landrieu's liberal reign." By 10:04 a.m. that day, Vitter was on Twitter cheering the move: "Paul has a bright future, and I thank him for making the tough choice."

Most die-hard Republicans didn't need much convincing from Vitter to step aside. They could smell blood on the water; they knew Louisiana voters were abandoning Democrats in statewide races; and they considered Landrieu an inviting target. Still, the Cassidy–Landrieu race was shaping up to be as much about Vitter as anyone else. "He's the Michael Jordan of the Republican Party now," Hollis said two months after he dropped out. "He's not just two steps ahead. He's nine steps ahead, I think."

Vitter had been grooming Cassidy for the job. Other than President Barack Obama, who was the GOP's favorite bogeyman in conservative states like Louisiana, no one was more central to Cassidy's strategy than Vitter. The senator had long ago marked Landrieu for extinction, and now she was a Democratic domino just waiting to fall.

Taking out Landrieu would cement a foundation for Vitter's gubernatorial run the following year, but the party also needed a strong leader to keep it financially flush for rest of the 2015 ballot. Governor Bobby Jindal would normally have filled that role, but he was consumed by his presidential ambitions. Besides, the risk-averse Jindal didn't want to gamble with taking on an incumbent senator, even one aligned with Barack Obama. Moreover, he was out of the state more and more frequently as 2016 approached.

The governor thus missed all the early, pivotal moments of Cassidy's campaign, and he seemed in no rush to issue an endorsement. That was fine with Vitter. The senator and the governor couldn't stand one another anyway. If Cassidy won, the victory would be all Vitter's.

The senator crafted Cassidy's strategy and dispatched Joel DiGrado, his longtime communications director, to serve as Cassidy's campaign manager. Vitter took time away from his work to knock on doors with a national anti-abortion group that was canvassing against Landrieu. He even stood alongside Senator John McCain of Arizona during campaign stops with Cassidy—after getting the former presidential candidate to agree to visit Louisiana. In Washington, D.C., Vitter's staff kept close tabs on Landrieu and called in tips and directives to Cassidy's campaign back home.

Vitter's name did not appear on any official campaign documents or financial reports as the man calling the shots in Cassidy's campaign, but everyone around Cassidy—and the candidate himself—was well aware that Vitter was the architect and engineer of the GOP drive to unseat Landrieu. In time, the press and the public would know it, too.

In stark contrast to the colorful, sometimes carnival-like personalities that dominate Louisiana politics, Cassidy was quiet, thoughtful, buttoned-down, and sometimes even awkward. Indeed, he was an unlikely politician from the get-go. Known for his kind bedside manner, he spent years teaching at LSU Medical School and working as a low-key gastroenterologist at Earl K. Long Medical Center—treating poor patients, many of whom had no health insurance. He probably would have stayed there full-time but for a snap decision immediately after Hurricane Katrina sent a flood of patients to Baton Rouge. Cassidy led hundreds of volunteers in converting an abandoned K-Mart into a makeshift hospital in the days following the deadly storm.

Cassidy witnessed the failure of government up close, and the ordeal emboldened him to run for the Louisiana Senate in a 2006 special election as a Republican. His newfound fame for creating the temporary hospital propelled him into office. The physician's post-Katrina win would be the start of a meteoric political rise. He had not yet served two years in the state Senate when he narrowly defeated incumbent Don Cazayoux, a one-term Democrat, to represent Louisiana's 6th Congressional District. By 2014, he had served as a congressman for five years and was running for the United States Senate.

Cassidy was a prolific fundraiser but shunned exclusive, high-dollar soirees in favor of events such as "Family Fun Day" at a local bowling alley. Though he came off as somewhat slow to find his feet as a freshman on Capitol Hill, his national profile soared as media outlets drilled deep into President Obama's controversial health-care plan. Who better to lead the GOP charge against the plan than a physician, especially one who had spent virtually his entire career in public hospitals? C-SPAN. FOX News. CNN. Cassidy suddenly was everywhere. He even launched a regular feature, "Ask Dr. Cassidy," on his Website and in public meetings.

Louisiana at the time had three physicians in its House delegation—Charles Boustany from Lafayette, John Fleming from Minden, and Cassidy—but Cassidy was clearly the star of this political-medical drama. He also had the best gag line. "I'm a gastroenterologist, and gastroenterology prepared me very well for D.C.," Cassidy would say at fundraisers and other events, looking into the faces of supporters while talking about treating their nether regions. "It's incredible," he would deadpan. "Sometimes the view seems the same."

Despite Vitter's leading role in Cassidy's campaign—albeit behind the scenes—Cassidy was never asked about Vitter's involvement in the D.C. Madam scandal. He did, however, have a delicate matter he felt obliged to get out in front of. On July 3, 2014, his campaign made background calls to reporters and later released a prepared statement about his unmarried 17-year-old daughter. Entering her senior year in high school, she was pregnant. The statement included four sentences: "Earlier this year, Laura and I learned we will become grandparents this summer. Our children have been the greatest blessing of our lives and we welcome our grandchild as a joyous addition to our family. Our daughter now faces a more challenging future than her peers. She has our unconditional love and support." Unlike Vitter's sex scandal, the matter of Cassidy's daughter began and ended with the candidate's statement.

Cassidy faced two serious challenges in his Senate bid—a fractured conservative base, and the congressman's understated persona. Retired Air Force Colonel Rob Maness, who captured the "Don't Tread On Me" vestiges of the tea party movement in Louisiana, got the support of the Family Research Forum Action PAC—a key pro-life group—and 2008 vice presidential nominee Sarah Palin. These endorsements exacerbated Cassidy's problem on the right. Insider D.C. publications like *The Cook Political Report* took notice. Founder Charlie Cook, when he returned to his home state of Louisiana, noted that Cassidy had to pull the party together to join Vitter in the Senate. As for Cassidy's mild demeanor, his staffers argued that the real Dr. Cassidy didn't shine through in commercials or on stage.

Cassidy's critics were merciless. "Cassidy is as bland as this tablecloth," former Senator John Breaux told *The New York Times*. That was mild compared to what New Orleans Congressman Cedric Richmond told *Politico:* "He's weird. Dude is weird."

True believers like Jason Doré, executive director of the Louisiana Republican Party, didn't allow the insults to distract them. Doré and other Republicans believed Louisiana would have no statewide elected Democrats after the December 6 runoff. Their strategy was a three-legged stool. First, unite conservatives. That was easier said than done in the primary, especially with Maness in the race, but the Republicans could accomplish it in a runoff against Landrieu.

Second, boil all attacks against Landrieu down to a simple meme of "Obama, Obama, Obama." Guilt by association would resonate with Louisiana's rural and suburban white voters.

Third, pay attention to geography. For Doré, who went to work for the party fresh out of law school in 2007, this aspect of the plan deserved special emphasis. His goal was to concentrate on areas where Landrieu had over-performed in her 2008 campaign. That meant focusing on St. Tammany and Tangipahoa Parishes and, to a lesser extent, Washington and Livingston Parishes. Those parishes and others across Lake Pontchartrain from New Orleans form what is known in Louisiana as "The Florida Parishes," so named because two centuries earlier they made up part of the Territory of West Florida. By 2014, they were home to a large concentration of conservative white voters who did not like President Obama.

Doré and the state GOP launched an extensive field operation and hired staff in St. Tammany—the first office the party opened that year outside Baton Rouge. "This is a region where we saw a lot of people voting for John McCain for president and then also for Mary Landrieu," Doré explained as summer turned to fall. "It's all about south Louisiana and where Mary has pulled large numbers in the past."

Democratic operatives were eyeing the region as well, due largely to the suburbanization of what used to be a large swath of rural communities. The old style of retail politics there had fallen by the wayside, leaving a void in the campaign infrastructures that candidates once counted on to turn out Democratic voters. Now everyone was trying to figure out what worked. Doré and the Cassidy–Vitter team had a pretty good idea of what would work: Tether Landrieu's political brand inextricably to Barack Obama's.

With just two years left in his second term, the president was a political pariah across much of Louisiana. No one knew this better than the GOP and its super PACs, whose assault against Landrieu began early and grew louder with each passing week. Their message was honed to a simple mantra that resonated among Louisiana conservatives: "Mary Landrieu supports Obama 97 percent of the time." For months, those words shouted at voters everywhere in Louisiana—on billboards, on TV, and on radio, on push cards and door-hangers, and especially on the lips of Bill Cassidy. In every speech, press interview, and candidate forum, Cassidy began and ended his remarks by reminding folks that "Landrieu supports Obama 97 percent of the time." For Vitter, it was a familiar template. He had used Obama as a bogeyman in his 2010 campaign—his first since the D.C. Madam scandal broke. Cassidy, however, had no scandal to overcome.

Now seeking a fourth term as the last statewide Democrat standing in Louisiana, Landrieu was part of a legendary political dynasty. Her father, Moon Landrieu, had served as secretary of Housing and Urban Development under President Jimmy Carter. Before that, he had desegregated city government during two terms as New Orleans' mayor. Her brother, Mitch, was the city's sitting mayor.

The oldest of nine children, she first got into politics in 1979 when she was elected to the Louisiana House, where her father had served and her brother would one day follow in her footsteps. She served two terms in the state House before her election as state treasurer in 1987. Instead of seeking a third term in 1995, however, Landrieu ran for governor, finishing third. The loss hurt, but it positioned her for greater things.

The following year, Landrieu sought and narrowly won the United States Senate seat vacated by fellow Democrat J. Bennett Johnston—winning by 5,788 votes out of 1.7 million cast, narrowly defeating Republican arch-conservative Woody Jenkins. That race would not be her last close Senate election. In 2002, she beat Republican Suzie Terrell, the state commissioner of elections, by 42,000 votes out of more than 1.2 million cast. In her 2008 re-election bid against state Treasurer John Kennedy, who had switched to the Republican Party the year before, she gained new support in rural parishes and cut deep into the Republican strongholds of Jefferson and St. Tammany Parishes, both large suburbs of New Orleans. In that 2008 contest, she even flipped 10 parishes that former Ku Klux Klan grand wizard David Duke had carried against Johnston 18 years earlier.

Her nuanced response to Hurricane Katrina in 2005—warm and caring back home but cold and calculating in Washington to secure federal money—went a long way toward cementing her political brand as someone who delivered for her state.

With her husband, Frank Snellings, who was adopted as a young child from an orphanage in Ireland, Landrieu frequently discussed their two adopted children. Few issues were closer to her heart. She had fought to expand a federal adoption tax credit and co-chaired the Congressional Coalition on Adoption. But just as easily as Landrieu could show a vulnerable side, she also could show why she had survived in the tough political trenches of Louisiana and Washington. She would scold reporters privately if she thought they were stepping over a line, and she could cuss like a deer camp veteran if she thought it helped get her point across.

In many ways, Mary Landrieu was the Hillary Clinton of Louisiana—effective but controversial, and always a favorite GOP target. In fact, the two women became close friends when they served together in the Senate.

By August 20, the first day of qualifying, the GOP had already defined Landrieu as Barack Obama's best friend in Louisiana, and she clearly was feeling the impact of the withering attacks. Americans for Prosperity, a conservative super PAC founded by the billionaire Koch brothers, flanked her with a TV ad attacking the incumbent for her "expensive" D.C. home. The Democratic Senatorial Campaign Committee responded with a $2.4 million ad buy questioning Cassidy's votes on veterans' issues in the House.

Landrieu and Cassidy were running neck and neck financially; she had $5.5 million on hand to his $5.6 million. What separated them at that point were the amounts they had raised thus far for the runoff that awaited them. Cassidy had collected nearly $400,000 to Landrieu's measly $6,900. Until late July, Landrieu had refrained from collecting runoff money, opting instead to focus on the primary. She was putting it all into a Hail Mary pass, hoping for a touchdown in November.

Louisiana, unlike every other state, holds its jungle primary in November for federal elections, with runoffs, if needed, in December—making the Bayou State the last to choose its senators and congressmen. No southern Democrat wanted to be in a runoff against a Republican in 2014. The Landrieu campaign started accepting runoff cash in July because a number of donors had already maxed out and faced the choice of taking a refund or putting the money toward the runoff.

On that first day of qualifying, a crowd gathered outside the Secretary of State's Office as Landrieu showed up to file her papers. They were waiting just for her. An attorney associated with the Louisiana Republican Party had organized a group of young volunteers to dress as airport employees, pilots, and members of a flight crew. The name of the airline was "Air Mary," a jab at recent allegations that Landrieu had used taxpayer funds to underwrite charter flights that included campaign stops. A young man in sunglasses, an orange vest, and traffic wands waved the senator into the building. Landrieu laughed. "Well, hello," she said. She got no response, except frantic gesturing with the traffic wands to outline her recommended entry point. The state GOP also began selling $10 bumper stickers that week with an "Air Mary" logo and a slogan: "Clout Doesn't Fly Coach." The stunt underscored growing public criticism of Landrieu's expenditures. She eventually paid back $34,000 to her Senate office account and chalked it up to an accounting error.

Although under constant GOP fire, Landrieu had some fun on the 2014 campaign trail. She jumped into the middle of a line of dancers at a Southern University tailgate to skillfully do "The Wobble." While walking from one tailgate to another before an LSU football game, Landrieu helped a purple-clad young man do a keg stand—his friends holding his feet in the air as Landrieu held the tap in his mouth to facilitate upside-down consumption. The photograph instantly went viral. Cassidy didn't laugh, saying, "It's not something to celebrate." Landrieu merely huffed, "They need to get a sense of a humor, and they need to get a life. It's just the way we roll."

By mid-September Landrieu was clearly in trouble. She was getting pummeled on several fronts—particularly immigration, which was a club that Republicans were using effectively against Democrats in Senate races across America. Then, for the first time since February 2013, a major poll showed Cassidy above 50 percent in a hypothetical runoff against Landrieu. The Democratic Senatorial Campaign Committee countered by placing new ads that suggested voters could not trust Cassidy to protect Medicare. The effort proved too little, too late as the tide against Landrieu swelled over the next month.

When voter registration closed for the November primary, Louisiana counted 1.3 million Democrats on the rolls, down from 1.5 million in Landrieu's 2008 campaign. Republicans, meanwhile, had added almost 64,000 new voters over the previous six years. White voters were abandoning the Democrats in droves, and President Obama's popularity remained low.

Besides policy differences, Cassidy and Landrieu disagreed on the number of televised debates. Landrieu committed to four. Cassidy agreed to only two. The lesser-known Maness accepted virtually all invitations, to the delight of Team Landrieu. In any forum that included all three, Maness would hit Cassidy from the right, calling him part of the same establishment that embraced Landrieu and putting him on the defensive.

For her final primary push, Landrieu once again made vote-rich Orleans Parish the center of her universe. She brought in a team of hardened Big Easy gunslingers, beginning with a new campaign manager, Ryan Berni, who had run her brother Mitch's re-election campaign for mayor earlier that year. Berni was also a protégé of Democratic uber-consultant James Carville. Joining Berni was Norma Jane Sabiston, who had stood in the trenches with Landrieu in other tough elections. Sabiston had a reputation as a likable problem-solver and, more importantly, was a trusted Landrieu family friend who could run interference on any front.

While the Landrieu team was still swinging for the fences in hopes of scoring a victory on November 4, pulling in the new players allowed the campaign to begin preparing immediately for a possible runoff. National groups, from super PACs to nonprofits, were stacked on both sides of the race, causing a polling backlog in Louisiana during the final weeks of the primary. Call centers were swamped, trying frantically to serve their corporate clients while keeping pace with the surge in political activity.

"This has really taken everyone by surprise. We were caught off guard," Bernie Pinsonat, a partner in Southern Media & Opinion Research, had to tell clients. "It's the PACs. They are so big now and have so much money that they always want to be in the field [conducting polls]. Most of them need it because they don't know

Louisiana. Some of them have more money than political sense."

The only poll that mattered, though, was the one that came out late on the evening of November 4—Election Day. Landrieu barely pulled ahead of Cassidy, 42 percent to 41 percent, which meant she and Cassidy were headed to a December 6 runoff. On the right, Maness got 14 percent of the 1.4 million votes cast. Maness voters clearly would not be inclined to back Landrieu.

Equally important, Cassidy that night carried 12 parishes that Landrieu had won in 2008, and he looked poised to build on those gains in the runoff. The GOP strategy of capturing Livingston, St. Tammany, Tangipahoa, and Washington Parishes had succeeded—and everyone who followed the contest closely knew the architect of that plan was David Vitter.

Landrieu led in 25 of Louisiana's 64 parishes but received a majority in only 10. Worse, many of those parishes gave her smaller margins this time compared to 2008. The difference was particularly stark in New Orleans, with its large concentration of African-American voters. In 2008, Landrieu got roughly 120,000 votes of nearly 143,000 votes cast. In 2014, she landed only 87,000 votes out of only 103,000 votes cast. This was yet another sign that the Democrats' ground game wasn't what it used to be, especially in African-American precincts. Those who led Landrieu's voter turnout efforts in minority neighborhoods had complained that a lack of money and organization led to a shortage of vans, buses, canvassers, and sign-wavers at busy intersections in the primary's final weeks. Behind-the-scenes players also split into rival camps: state insiders versus national experts. These internal problems, plus the GOP's constant barrage of attack ads, doomed Landrieu.

November 4, 2014, was a bad day for Democrats nationally as well. Republicans tightened their hold on the House of Representatives and took the Senate from the Democrats. CNN commentator and Democratic consultant Donna Brazile, who grew up in the New Orleans suburb of Kenner, took her grief to Twitter: "In the South, now Democrats are as rare as a snowy day—without even taking climate change into account."

Bobby Jindal, well into his quest for the presidency without actually announcing, finally endorsed Cassidy on the day after the primary election in a subdued press conference that seemed more like a rehearsal for the governor's presidential talking points. Jindal's nod to Cassidy wasn't overly fervent, nor was the congressman in attendance.

With Republicans now controlling at least 52 of the 100 seats in the nation's Upper Chamber, Landrieu had lost a prime calling card—

her claim that a vote for her would allow her to continue as chair of the Senate's Energy Committee. Likewise, Republicans could no longer rally around a war cry of taking the Senate. The loss of leverage on these issues no longer mattered. Two days after the primary, the Democratic Senatorial Campaign Committee drove the final stake into Landrieu's political heart by withdrawing all financial support. Though the reason wasn't known publicly at the time, the DSCC was drowning in $20.4 million of debt, of which $15 million was in the form of loans that had been taken out shortly before the November 4 debacle. Landrieu was on her own. She vowed to soldier on, but her campaign was on life support.

The Louisiana Democratic Party went on to fire two top-level directors and more than a dozen others in the space of weeks. Those who were laid off were told money was an issue as the cycle came to a close. The Louisiana Republican Party, on the other hand, staged a "Unity Rally" on November 10 at Huey's Bar in downtown Baton Rouge. The gathering put Cassidy on the same stage as Jindal, Maness, Vitter, Paul Hollis, Jeff Landry, and a special guest: Kentucky Senator Rand Paul, a conservative favorite. Landry, with his thick Cajun accent, introduced Paul to the overheated crowd in the cramped barroom.

"What language is he speaking? Is that New Iberian?" Paul asked to laughter from the crowd as he stared at Landry after his introduction.

Cassidy was so confident of victory that he made few public appearances in the following weeks and agreed to just one televised debate before the December 6 showdown. He and his team made no flubs. Landrieu was on the ropes.

In the face of discouraging poll numbers and dire predictions, the Landrieu campaign nonetheless envisioned ways to win. Campaign manager Berni argued that "Saturday election math" was better for Democrats, as opposed to the Tuesday primary held in November. Berni and other Landrieu supporters also touted a political factoid: No Republican had come from behind against a Democrat in a statewide runoff in the last 25 years. "History is on our side," Berni told reporters privately, reminding them of Landrieu's one-point lead over Cassidy in the primary.

Team Landrieu also felt it could reverse the trend in rural parishes where Cassidy had pulled ahead, particularly among white voters, by highlighting the "clear differences between Mary's record and Congressman Cassidy's extreme votes," according to a runoff memo entitled "How And Why Mary Can Win." In addition, the number of African-American registered voters in Louisiana had never been higher than it was in November 2014.

Despite her best efforts to stave off the inevitable, however,

Landrieu could not recover from the Vitter-led onslaught in the primary. On December 6, she counted 58,192 fewer votes than in the November primary. Cassidy won convincingly, with 56 percent of the vote to Landrieu's 44 percent.

After the race was called for Cassidy on Election Night, the senator-elect and his team of supporters poured onto a small stage in the massive hallway of the Crowne Plaza Hotel in Baton Rouge. A Christmas tree was already up, about 30 feet behind the stage. In a nod to the man who had choreographed his victory march, Cassidy let Vitter speak first. While the win officially belonged to Cassidy, the night clearly belonged to a smiling Vitter, who took the microphone shortly before 9:30 p.m.

"The doctor is in the House—and now he's going to the Senate!" Vitter shouted to applause and laughter, holding the mic for at least 10 minutes, soaking up the limelight on statewide television before making way for Cassidy. When the senator-elect finally spoke, he waited only three minutes before circling back to the man who had introduced him. "Senator David Vitter and Wendy helped us from the very beginning," he said.

With Landrieu's demise, Democrats no longer held any statewide offices in Louisiana. Congressman Cedric Richmond of New Orleans was now the only non-Republican in Louisiana's congressional delegation. Editorial writers and journalists spent the following weeks writing political obituaries and predicting the fallout for the 2015 statewide elections, which would determine the next governor of Louisiana. The name "David Vitter" appeared in most of those stories, as it should have.

As Bill Cassidy began his move up to the Senate, Vitter was planning a major move of his own. Based on Cassidy's victory in 2014 and his own 2010 re-election, Vitter knew he would have a staunchly conservative electorate for the 2015 governor's race. With any luck, he also would face a little-known Democratic opponent in the runoff. Above all, he was now supremely confident he would once again have his favorite political bogeyman—Barack Obama, who had already provided such a perfect foil for him in two election cycles—to use as a political club against his eventual Democratic foe.

Indeed, the planets were aligning for David Vitter. Or so he thought.

9

"The Cheramies and the Cailliers and the Duprés and the Robérts and the Boudreauxs and the Thibodeauxs"

On a sweltering July midday in 2010 people were still walking onto the arena floor of the Cajundome in Lafayette, the economic and cultural hub of Louisiana's Cajun Triangle, as then-interim Lieutenant Governor Scott Angelle walked across the stage and took his place between Louisiana's state flag and the Stars and Stripes. Guitars and a drum set stood in a pile behind him, all beneath a massive banner declaring "Lift the Moratorium!" A diverse crowd filled the arena to its upper decks. Blue-collar workers in ragged clothes mixed with the Oil Patch suits who signed their paychecks. Men in cowboy boots lined one row. Behind them, men in button-down Oxford shirts and preppy deck shoes sat with wives decked out in silk scarves and fine jewelry. Scattered among the crowd were tattered baseball caps, frayed t-shirts, babies in strollers, and TV cameras. The scene looked more like a concert than a political rally.

"A special welcome to each and every one of you," Angelle began as he dove into his prepared remarks.

The program for the Rally for Economic Survival—92 days after the April 20, 2010, Deepwater Horizon oil spill—officially listed Angelle as the master of ceremonies. A popular, affable Cajun who got his political start in neighboring St. Martin Parish before rising to prominence in the service of two governors, Angelle was the hometown emcee responsible that day for introducing various speakers. Each speaker, including Angelle, was prepared to rail against President Barack Obama's decision to issue a drilling moratorium in the Gulf of Mexico in the wake of the offshore disaster that had claimed 11 lives.

Angelle was also prepared to introduce Governor Bobby Jindal, arguably his most important political ally. Since 2008, Jindal had carved out one important government position after another for Angelle. For his part, Angelle had filled each post faithfully and to great reviews from Democrats and Republicans alike. The two men's political arcs, in many ways, had become linked in recent years. But on that hot July day, the rally in the Cajundome was to serve as Angelle's political coming out party.

As devastating as the oil spill's death toll was to the families and friends of the deceased rig workers, Obama's subsequent moratorium on Gulf of Mexico drilling sounded an economic death knell across south Louisiana, an area whose fortunes rise and fall with drilling activity. That day, the folks who filed into the Cajundome felt as though *they* were being punished for BP's negligence, which an army of trial lawyers was already lining up to prove in New Orleans.

While the lawyers were sure to cash in on the worst environmental disaster in history, the Cajuns who worked in the industry that caused it were being laid off in droves, with no end in sight. When rigs shut down, the ripple effect is deep, widespread, and immediate. And when the shutdown can be blamed squarely on a president who is unpopular—in Louisiana at least—the response is visceral. Angelle and everyone else in the Cajundome that day could feel the anger.

"We come here clearly to send a message!" Angelle boomed, his voice reaching a crescendo as he pointed a finger in the air. "Not only from the ball field to the cane field, but from Abbeville to Capitol Hill, and from the banks of the historic Vermilion River to the powerful banks of the Potomac River!"

The audience erupted. Angelle looked down at his speech for about five seconds, preparing to recite the next sentence. Instead, glancing back at the crowd and sensing the moment, his eyes immediately drifted to the upper levels, to the cheap seats. Hundreds of people started rising to their feet. The roar grew louder as the 48-year-old Angelle, looking slightly surprised but composed, fidgeted again with the papers on the lectern and scratched his nose. He shifted his weight from one foot to the other, grabbed hold of the lectern's slanted top and stared over the crowd. The applause and cheering lasted a good half-minute, which on the political stump is a lifetime. This was the kind of moment Louisiana politicians fantasize about—a public display of mass adulation from a sea of clapping hands that would someday cast votes in a hotly contested race for governor. When such a moment comes, and it rarely does, the savvy politician recognizes it immediately—and seizes it.

"Let's keep the conversation real," Angelle said moments later, a giant monitor behind him broadcasting the face of the man who had been the interim lieutenant governor for just two months. "America is not ready to get all of its fuel from the birds and the bees and the flowers and the trees." Hearty laughter erupted from the audience. Angelle soaked up another half-minute of applause. This felt good. Better than good, it felt *right*.

Then came The Line.

"This moratorium is not hurting the stockholders of BP or Exxon or Chevron," Angelle bellowed, his voice reverberating through the standing-room-only dome. "This moratorium is hurting the Cheramies and the Cailliers and the Duprés and the Robérts and the Boudreauxs and the Thibodeauxs!"

Angelle could barely finish his sentence before his fellow Cajuns started yelling out their own last names of French lineage. More than a few in attendance let loose an "AAYEEEE!"—a Cajun cheer somewhere between a war cry and a yodel with no agreed spelling, but universally recognized across south Louisiana as a shout of approval and endearment. Sustained applause and cheering erupted again. Yes, this felt *really* good.

For a Louisiana politician on the rise, the kind of reaction the arena gave Angelle that day was more than enough to fuel ambitions. Years later, that cheer made of French surnames would function as Angelle's go-to line on the gubernatorial campaign trail, in his paid media, and at candidate forums. It would define him as a fiery orator and build the kind of Cajun brand that had stoked south Louisiana voters for generations. And there was more.

One of Angelle's favorite rhetorical devices, one he used throughout the speech he delivered that day, is as elementary as Dr. Seuss: rhyming. He loved to rhyme, and audiences loved hearing him do it. "You help pay to educate, medicate, rehabilitate and, if all else fails, incarcerate," Angelle said near the end of his seven-minute speech that day. Again he drew applause. He went on to call Jindal a "warrior" as he finally transitioned from his own speech to introducing the governor. "Our fighter, our leader," Angelle said in his most energetic tone of the rally, "our never-give-up, never-back-down governor. Let's rock the Cajundome for the coastal governor, for the oil and gas governor, the fisheries governor, your governor, my governor, America's hardest working governor, Governor Bobbyyyy Jindaaaal!"

By the time Angelle made it to "coastal governor" he was barely audible. The audience was waving handkerchiefs, hats, and pieces of paper in the air. Jindal walked onto the stage laughing and threw his arms around Angelle. The ovation drowned out part of Jindal's opening words. "Thank you very much," Jindal said to the crowd before looking stage left. "Let's give another round of applause to our great lieutenant governor, Scotty Angelle."

The headlines the next day focused on Jindal's remarks, noting that the rally was the largest event to date protesting the federal drilling moratorium. The Associated Press reported that 15,000 people had crammed into the Cajundome, which has an official capacity of 13,500. While Jindal got the mainstream media's attention, however, among the hacks and flacks who kept track of signposts along the political landscape, Angelle's speech was the birth of a regional, maybe statewide campaign. At the Rally for Economic Survival, which a coalition of business organizations had engineered, Angelle was on his home turf, where people sounded like him and looked like him. He knew the oil and gas industry. He spoke the language.

And he delivered The Line.

Angelle's approach to public service evoked a bygone political era. He had learned the trade from his father, J. Burton Angelle, a state representative from 1964 to 1972 and the state Wildlife and Fisheries secretary during the first three terms of the wily Cajun Governor Edwin Edwards. Burton Angelle was a Navy man in World War II, and he knew every man in town who had taken part in the Pacific Campaign. A salesman at heart he had owned for three decades a Ford dealership in the thoroughly Cajun town of Breaux Bridge, home of the annual Breaux Bridge Crawfish Festival. He sold pickup trucks to men in the area and eventually to their sons. It wasn't long after he opened the dealership that he was urged to run—in 1952—for the St. Martin Parish Police Jury, where he served two terms before moving to the state House. As a legislator, always aware of his ancestry, he helped establish the Council for the Development of French in Louisiana, a popular cultural touchstone for Cajuns who saw their language and way of life giving way to mainstream America. Cajuns are fiercely patriotic—to America *and* to their Acadian heritage.

Burton Angelle taught his children to take pride in their heritage and to enjoy the outdoors—from crawfishing and hunting to raising pigs and chickens. He was the rock of the family, but each of his nine children experienced the sometimes-harsh realities of life, thus learning valuable lessons as they moved into adulthood. For "Scotty," the seventh child, that day came on May 2, 1983. Scott Angelle, then 21, was attending the University of Southwestern Louisiana. He had finished his course load for the day and had decided to go fishing with a friend. He let his sister, Cathy, a nursing student, borrow his car. On her way home, some say, Cathy may have crossed the centerline. She was killed instantly in a collision with an 18-wheeler. Angelle came upon the scene of the wreck and called his father, who, after arriving, told his son, "Come on, we got to tell your mom." Reflecting on that responsibility later in life, Angelle remarked, "I was standing on the shoulders of my mom that day."

As Scott Angelle tells it, he learned everything he needed to know about life from his mother and everything he needed to know about politics from his father. His small town upbringing in Breaux Bridge, the adopted home of Longfellow's fabled Evangeline, taught him how to live as part of a larger community. Growing up alongside eight siblings also taught him a bit about human nature. Hiding behind the couch as a child in his family home, he would listen to his father interrogate his older sisters' boyfriends. That's how he picked up on the Acadiana trinity of familiarization: "Where ya from? Who's ya daddy? Are ya Catholic?"

Even as a child, Angelle was what some people might call hyper, a whirlwind of enthusiasm, jumping from one project to another—invigorated playing in the yard, thrilled dealing cards to his siblings, bubbling over anywhere doing anything. He leaned forward in all he did with a sort of controlled chaos enveloping his life. Angelle could talk barely as fast as his mind worked. His closet was always messy. Later, so was his truck and any workspace he occupied. "If there was ADD medication when I was a kid, my mother would have definitely had me on it," Angelle said later. "I am a multitasker to the extreme."

Angelle played basketball in junior high, but he wasn't much of an athlete. Instead, he would ride the bench and talk his teammates into a frenzy. He would even strike up conversations with the referees, asking how their families were doing. The adults found it comical—watching this kid approach people in authority with questions like, "How's the wife and kids?" It was Angelle aping his father on the campaign trail. Those who knew him best at the age of 13 knew that Angelle did not want to be like Walt Frazier or Pete Maravich. Like all young men raised on Louisiana politics, he wanted to be governor. In fact, later in life when he proposed to his wife Diane Bourque, he did so in the heat of the moment and without a diamond. "I told her if I ever got elected governor, I would buy her a ring," Angelle said. Roman Catholic to the core, the couple went on to have three daughters and two sons.

There was little doubt that "Scotty" was the Angelle child bit hardest by the political bug that had so consumed the family patriarch. In 1987, at age 25, he won a seat on the St. Martin Parish Policy Jury. His father, Burton, was 28 when he had claimed the same position.

Initially Angelle didn't allow politics to become his full-time business. He worked as a petroleum land manager for a while and was

vice president of the Huval Companies, an insurance conglomerate
in Lafayette. But big-time politics beckoned. Thirteen years after his
election to the police jury, he won the parish president's seat in 2000—
the first person to hold that job in St. Martin Parish. He would soon
begin anew to follow in his father's footsteps.

In January 2004, new Governor Kathleen Blanco tapped
Angelle for state Department of Natural Resources secretary—the
administration's point person for the state's oil and gas industry. In
that position, Angelle made a name for himself on a larger political
stage and was among the few holdovers who stayed on when Bobby
Jindal, a Republican, succeeded Democrat Blanco.

Jindal not only kept Angelle on to regulate oil and gas, but he
also tapped the Cajun to serve as his legislative liaison—a fancy term
for the administration's lobbyist. Each of those two jobs is full-time,
but only someone as energetic as Angelle, and perhaps as ambitious,
could juggle both jobs *and* perform both well. When Mitch Landrieu
won the New Orleans mayoral race in February 2010, Jindal tapped
Angelle to serve as interim lieutenant governor until a special election
could pick a permanent successor. The job was a plum appointment
and clearly a stepping stone that would raise Angelle's profile. He was
already highly regarded and extremely popular among oil and gas
execs and state lawmakers, but now he was poised to make his mark
among voters statewide.

On October 26, 2010, just five days after his roof-raising speech
in the Cajundome, the interim lieutenant governor switched from
Democrat to Republican in a nod both to Jindal and to the state's
changing political landscape. After promising not to run for lieutenant
governor in the special election, which Jay Dardenne, another
Republican and future candidate for governor won, Angelle returned
to his position as natural resources secretary. While Jindal created the
opportunities, Angelle crafted his political persona.

He became known for telling jokes in his thick Cajun accent,
for once cutting a high-profile levee deal with a coastal lawmaker on
the back of a cocktail napkin and for traveling to Washington, D.C.,
annually to boil crawfish for federal officials. Playing up his Acadiana
roots Angelle kept a massive glass gallon jug of Tabasco sauce in his
Baton Rouge office. He told non-Louisianans that he used it in his
coffee. Those who got to know him received an autographed copy
of *The Angelle Family Cookbook: Traditions & Feasts*. Angelle's
signature contribution to the book was "Scott's 'I'm Home Early,
Mom's In Bed With A Headache, So I Have To Cook' Spaghetti."

By August 2012, he was ready to strike out on his own. Twelve
years had passed since he last ran for office, but Angelle decided to

put his name on the ballot for the Acadiana-based seat on the five-member Louisiana Public Service Commission. Charged with regulating utility companies and common carriers, the PSC had served as a springboard for other governors, including Huey Long, Jimmie Davis, John McKeithen, and Kathleen Blanco. He resigned from the Jindal administration and told a friend, of his plans to run for office again, "It's like riding a horse or a bicycle—you just get back on, and it comes back to you." And ride Angelle did. Against a field of four opponents, including state Representative Erich Ponti, Angelle captured 57 percent of the vote in the jungle primary. No runoff was needed. His political arc was set.

Roy Fletcher had served as Angelle's media consultant for that PSC race, and he hoped the Cajun would run for governor in 2015. At the age of 61, looking out from behind his retro wayfarer eyeglasses while dissecting Louisiana politics with an unforgettable country drawl, Fletcher was a good fit for Angelle. He had helped elect a little-known state senator named Mike Foster as governor in 1995, in the process creating iconic campaign images that resonated with voters. One was a TV commercial that showed a man welding on a piece of metal, his face shielded from viewers behind the welder's helmet—until candidate Foster pushed back the mask. Fletcher was also national deputy campaign manager for Arizona Senator John McCain's 2000 presidential run. After nearly four decades of political work, he had earned as much of a reputation for his nuanced tactics as for his not-so-nuanced utterances.

Fletcher had influenced younger consultants like Timmy Teepell, who was Governor Jindal's chief strategist. During Angelle's quiet start on the PSC, Teepell took a break from lobbying the Senate floor one day to reflect on Fletcher's rugged veneer and penchant for one-liners. "If you don't hear a rumor by 10 a.m., start one," Teepell said with a guffaw. "That's one of my favorite things Roy ever told me."

In September 2014, Fletcher finally got the phone call he had been waiting for.

"I want to hire you," Angelle said as soon as Fletcher picked up the phone.

Fletcher laughed. Having moved past the hope that Angelle would run, he wasn't sure where this was going. "For what?"

The answer was short and simple and probably should have been expected: "I'm running for governor." After a pregnant pause, Angelle continued, "Well, I don't know if I'll be in it for very long. But I'm running."

"Fuck you, man," Fletcher said, egging on his friend. "You'll be there. *You will.* You can raise the money, and your politics will come together. But go get the money. You gotta get it."

Angelle had reported holding just $175,000 in his campaign account earlier in the year but had already started to gin up his fundraising operations. Reporters around the state started to catch wind of his effort and received regular updates from state Senator Fred Mills, who grew up across the street from Angelle and was known as *T-Fred* or *Freddy* to friends and family. Mills was a good salesman for Angelle. Back home in the small town of Parks, Mills was legendary for his pharmacy's television commercials, which featured the lawmaker dressed in drag portraying a down-the-bayou character he dubbed "Taunte Pills." He doubled his business with those ads and built a political career on the back of them.

On October 2, 2014, Angelle made his intentions known publicly in the political newsletter *LaPolitics Weekly*.[1] He did not immediately release a platform, and he refused to distinguish himself from the other likely gubernatorial candidates—but he promised to do both in early 2015. And he played up his Cajun persona: "I intend to campaign with a certain *joie de vivre* spirit because Louisiana deserves a positive campaign focusing on people, not just policy." He also made a subtle promise to be different from his former boss, Governor Jindal, who was starting to feel the heat for making frequent visits to Iowa and New Hampshire in his nascent quest for a role as a serious presidential candidate. "Now is the time for leadership that will be more focused on getting us across the goal line rather than grabbing the headline," Angelle intoned.

The campaign team that was coming together for Angelle viewed his relationship with Jindal, who was starting to tank in public opinion polls in Louisiana, as both a blessing and a curse. The team hired Allee Bautsch, Jindal's fundraising whiz, to bring in the money, but others from Team Jindal, like Teepell, were not given official roles. Angelle never pushed for Jindal's endorsement; how much the governor's coattails might help or hurt was a constant topic of conversation. Jindal was still popular enough among conservative Republicans to make a difference, but he was also toxic enough with the rest of the electorate to pose a liability. Fletcher developed a mantra early on and repeated it each time someone uttered the J-word. "Look guys," Fletcher would say, "Jindal can get you into the runoff—and then after that he'll get your ass beat."

The campaign truly kicked off on November 20, 2014, when Angelle booked Geno Delafose and French Rockin' Boogie to play for a "good old-fashioned party" at the Evangeline Downs Event Center. "Come as you are—boots admired but not required."

---

[1] Co-author Jeremy Alford is the publisher and editor of LaPolitics Weekly.

The Event Center stood behind the local casino and hotel, adjacent to a thoroughbred racetrack. In the distance were the grandstands and 1,000 stalls for the horses—and a large pond, about which employees liked to joke "does not have a gator…that we know of." On most Saturdays there, you'd find winners, losers, handicappers, novice bettors, college kids, retired couples, the occasional priest, and a bit of what Hunter S. Thompson described as the "whiskey gentry," all scribbling on racing forms.

On this night at Evangeline Downs, under a clear evening sky, people were hoping the political croupier would pay out with a governorship. By 6:30 p.m. the Center was electric with Zydeco music, bowls of red beans and sausage, and lines queuing at the bar, which offered Angelle-branded koozies to hug and insulate cans of cold beer. The accompanying cocktail conversations revealed a campaign in motion, albeit one taking baby steps.

One of Angelle's brothers, Glenn, introduced his wife Jennifer to a group as the campaign coordinator, which wasn't far from the truth. "We're trying to save our money," Glenn said with a smile. In another part of the room, state Representative Joe Harrison from the nearby Cajun town of Napoleonville was practically glowing as he talked with a Capitol acquaintance about Angelle. "He's one of us," Harrison said, evoking an old saying once uttered only in Cajun French—*Un de nous-autres* ("One of our own")—to connote both familiarity and tribal pride. "It reminds me of an Edwin Edwards' campaign," Harrison continued. "Back to the Cajun."

Occupying half of the far wall facing the racetrack was a line of people waiting for a photograph with Angelle, who was standing under a set of lighted umbrellas as state Senator Fred Mills directed traffic. The Friends of Scott Angelle LLC had pulled off the event in a way that was vintage southwest Louisiana: banners in French—"*Vive La Louisiane*"—and English hung throughout the Event Center and on stage, where Angelle was making his way. After a special message delivered in French by his daughter, Simone Angelle Ancelet, someone brought out a cake. It was Angelle's 53rd birthday, which came as a surprise to many in the room. The focus up to then had been on Angelle the candidate, not Scotty the birthday boy. Men in Wranglers with giant belt buckles lowered their beers to sing "Happy Birthday" as elderly couples put aside their red beans to join in. Then Angelle blew out his candles—after several attempts. "Call Acadian Ambulance!" shouted Senator T-Fred into the microphone, beginning his introduction. "He's short of breath!"

Surrounded by his five children and his wife, Angelle tried to claim center stage while Simone's twin daughters scurried around

their aunts and uncles and grandparents, with Simone in hot pursuit
hurling commands in Cajun French. "You better believe I learned to
fight every inch along the way," the candidate said after sharing his
life story, later adding, "I'm taking this fight from the Crawfish Capital
to the state Capitol!"

It was no joke that brother Glenn and wife Jennifer, along with
other family members, were serving as the heart of the campaign team.
They were the candidate's entourage, schedulers, and press flacks,
but everyone involved knew that, even with Roy Fletcher aboard, the
family-style management approach was not a sustainable model.

Roughly a month after the campaign kickoff at Evangeline
Downs, a young consultant met with Angelle to discuss both of their
futures. They had met several times before, but now Ryan Cross, age
22, was staring at a contract for campaign manager. Angelle made his
pitch. "I don't know what's going to happen," Angelle told him. "I
don't know if we'll win, but if you're willing, let's go on a journey and
let's see if we can do something good."

Despite his age, Ryan was no political novice. His father, the late
state Senator Mike Cross, was a Democrat who embraced the kind
of ultra-conservative politics that presaged the Republican wave to
come in Louisiana. Mike Cross became a well-known lobbyist before
he died in 2013. A year later, when Ryan met with Angelle, he was
just coming off a devastating loss in Louisiana's 5th Congressional
District. Ryan had managed communications for a first-time candidate,
Zach Dasher, cousin of the famous Robertson brothers from the reality
TV show *Duck Dynasty*. Dasher missed the runoff by 1,861 votes out
of 239,551 cast.

Ryan Cross was making his own way now, like Angelle
following a father's path. Driven by his faith and perhaps still a tad
impressionable, as comfortable in a church as in a duck blind, a young
man who had never even set foot in a bar, Cross signed the contract.
"Let's go," he told Angelle.

There would be no break for Cross, as Angelle told him that the
governor's race would have to take over his life. "I need you to put
aside family relationships and romantic relationships and give this
campaign everything, every hour of the day," Angelle said. The text
messages that arrived at 3:15 a.m., 2:24 a.m., and all other times in the
coming weeks convinced Cross that Angelle meant what he'd said. He
would not, however, put romantic relationships on hold—Cross met
Addie Dean the following February and by August 2015 they were
engaged.

Fletcher, Cross, and hordes of others had already sat through
Angelle's back-of-the-napkin analysis of the race. He scribbled the

names of likely opponents, adding and removing the names of some assumed candidates, such as Mitch Landrieu, in an effort to test the various lanes and off-ramps along the possible roads to victory. By the time he was finished, whatever Angelle was writing on was filled from corner to corner with ink.

The takeaway for Angelle was that Vitter was beatable, even without a second major Democrat in the race to compete with state Representative John Bel Edwards.

With a campaign team starting to come together, and Christmas giving way to the 2015 election season, Fletcher was beginning to do a campaign rain dance in hopes of Angelle pulling the trigger on an early TV buy. The campaign had $1.4 million in the bank by January, after raising $1.5 million in October, November, and December. The team knew Vitter would be its toughest competition on the right, and Fletcher was ready to pounce.

But Angelle never rushed into a decision. He reviewed every issue from a variety of angles, often using a whiteboard to map out every possible scenario. First, he firmed up his stance on the Common Core education standards, which he would eventually oppose. His team also focused its attention on the Bayou Corne sinkhole in Assumption Parish, which had developed in 2012 right before Angelle resigned as secretary of the Department of Natural Resources to run for the Public Service Commission. Around 400 feet wide and 400 feet deep, the sinkhole started swallowing swaths of land and entire trees, forcing the evacuation of the nearby community. The team knew allegations of abandonment were coming and that, if not handled correctly, the sinkhole could swallow Angelle's prospects as well.

The team commissioned an internal poll from McLaughlin & Associates of New York to get the data that the campaign—particularly Fletcher—needed. On January 15, 2015, Fletcher penned a memo about Angelle's messaging. Poll participants were 51.4 percent more likely to support a description or campaign image of Angelle as a conservative Republican, a pro-life Catholic who fights for gun rights, traditional marriage, and prayers in school. Among those who would definitely vote for Vitter, 70.9 percent said they were more likely to support Angelle after hearing this same description. "In short, this kind of candidate has the potential to gut Vitter," Fletcher wrote. "Scott does not have to out-conservative Vitter but he cannot give any ground to Vitter." As for Jay Dardenne, Fletcher repeatedly described the lieutenant governor's base as "very weak."

In a follow-up phone conference with Angelle and Cross, Fletcher unloaded on Vitter's vulnerability: "We're sitting here with all of this money, and this guy hasn't gone up on TV yet. We can beat him." That convinced Angelle to pull the trigger on his first TV shoot. On a chilly late-January day, Fletcher and Cross arrived at a farm owned by an Angelle family friend and prepared to put images on film. Eager to catch the sun at perfect light, Fletcher encouraged everyone to take their time as he scanned the landscape, locking in on a pasture. "There's something in the human subconsciousness about horses," Fletcher told Cross as he looked at a nearby herd. "It relaxes them. They don't even know it. We'll need to get some horses in the background."

Soon Angelle pulled up in a Suburban driven by his young assistant, Micah Cormier. He exited wearing a paisley shirt, a huge belt buckle, and a black Stetson cowboy hat. Cross laughed as his new boss walked up. "Where did you get that?" he asked. Angelle adjusted the hat and smiled. "Diane told me to wear it."

More discussion about the cowboy hat ensued—*Does he wear it? Does he not wear it?*—than anything else. The spot would be called "Workhorse Not A Showhorse." The cowboy hat made it into different versions, one with a message delivered in Cajun French. The horses made appearances as well. During Mardi Gras week in February, Fletcher quietly visited stations across Acadiana and the Bayou Region along the coast. He put $200,000 in campaign funds into the TV buy and tried to keep it as quiet as possible. The ads, with images of a family praying and the oil industry at work, began airing on the morning of February 20, 2015, three days after Fat Tuesday. Angelle had become the first candidate for governor to buy television ads.

Angelle's team members were so busy trying to figure out how to get to the right of Vitter that they barely saw John Bel Edwards coming. While Angelle was the first on TV, Edwards was the first to go negative less than a week later with a spot on African-American radio stations in the same Cajun area. "The bottom line is Scott Angelle is only telling half the story," the female announcer said in Edwards' radio ads. "He's a workhorse, but the wagon he is pulling is being driven by Bobby Jindal."

Edwards' first radio spots ran on February 26 and labeled Angelle "Bobby Jindal's right-hand man" for supporting hospital privatizations and cuts at Southern University. An announcer added, "Without Republican Scott Angelle, Jindal could have never done the damage he's done to Louisiana." The spots ended with a brief introduction of Edwards, describing him as a Christian and West Point grad.

Edwards' radio ads raised an intriguing question: Why would he go on the attack so early, and why against Angelle? While Angelle's $200,000 media buy sent a signal to donors and supporters that he was in it for the long haul, Democrats knew that Republicans who go up on TV early can occasionally benefit from "false positives" in polling, particularly in African-American communities that traditionally vote Democratic. In addition, Edwards was planning in part to run against Jindal's policies. As perceptions went, that meant running against Angelle. The strategy was just a hint of what was to come. Bobby Jindal still had nearly a year left in his second term and was well on his way out of the Governor's Mansion. In June, he would officially launch his campaign for president, but he was already a negative touchstone in the governor's race.

In all of 2015, Jindal would spend more and time campaigning in Iowa, which further angered voters who saw him as not focused on the Bayou State and its people. At the same time, the mini-shootout between Edwards and Angelle went largely unnoticed, except by political junkies. In fact, the governor's race at this early stage was drawing very little interest from voters.

By late summer, that and a lot more would change.

10

"We Won't Have an Inaugural Ball"

Two carloads of LSU students pulled into the driveway of the Governor's Mansion late on a Sunday afternoon in the fall of 1973. Back then, no gates or security checkpoints existed outside the home of Louisiana's most powerful politician.

After parking, the young folks slammed their doors, continued their conversations from the road, and looked around. Some, like 19-year-old Jay Dardenne, took a moment to gaze at the stately brick structure—each brick hand-molded and painted white—built 10 years earlier by then-Governor Jimmie Davis, Louisiana's famous "Singing Governor." Davis recorded "You Are My Sunshine" in 1940. The tune almost immediately established itself as one of America's best-loved melodies—and the Louisiana Legislature officially enshrined it as the official song of the Bayou State.

On that autumn afternoon in 1973, Dardenne had tried to reach a different governor by phone: Edwin Washington Edwards, who, coincidentally, had squeezed Davis out of the Democratic primary in 1971. Nearly thirty years later, at Davis' funeral in 2000, Edwards would joke to mourners, "Just imagine: He served two terms as governor of Louisiana and was never indicted. That's a genuine achievement."

The idea of reaching out to Edwards came about after Dardenne and his fellow students had wrapped up a weeklong flag football marathon, part of a student fundraiser for the Muscular Dystrophy Association. For seven days straight, teams had battled on the LSU Parade Grounds around the clock, 2 p.m. to 2 a.m. Dardenne chaired the event. His personal goal was to raise $26,000, which he believed would make the LSU fundraiser the most successful in the nation.

After the last down that Sunday afternoon, Dardenne and a small group of friends popped open a bottle of champagne and toasted their accomplishment. Surrounded by the university's storied oaks, they sat on the ground, drank their bubbly, reflected on the week, and counted the donations. The tally came to $25,500. They were $500 short.

"I can't believe this," someone said. "What are going to do?"

"We're going to call the governor," Dardenne said, eyeing the telephone they had hooked up on the parade grounds to coordinate the gridiron marathon. It was the kind of whimsical statement that young people are prone to making, but also the type of request that, in 1973, Louisianans wouldn't have thought twice about bringing to their elected officials. Whether you lived in a remote rural area or on a busy city street, favors were a form of political currency. Can't pay for your husband's funeral? Talk to your state representative. Need help finding a job? Talk to your sheriff. Politicians who doled out favors knew they could rely on folks they had helped not just for votes but also for lawn signs, bumper stickers, and, best of all, strong word-of-mouth support at election time.

A few moments later, Dardenne was on the phone. Standing there, wondering where his call would lead, Dardenne allowed his hopes to lift with each ring. A man who identified himself as a state trooper eventually answered, and Dardenne launched into his pitch: They were short of their fundraising goal by $500, which would ensure that LSU's gift to the Muscular Dystrophy Association would lead the nation.

"Wait a minute," the trooper responded, placing Dardenne briefly on hold. When he returned, the trooper said, "The governor says to come over to the Mansion. And he says to bring some sorority girls."

"I can handle that," Dardenne replied with a smile.

That's how Dardenne and seven of his friends found themselves standing on the steps of the Governor's Mansion, just four miles away from LSU. After knocking on the door and stepping inside, the students were led to the kitchen, where they would meet Louisiana's newest governor. Unlike his predecessors, Edwin Edwards was in tune with the sentiments of younger voters on such matters as civil rights and race relations. He was the first governor to acknowledge publicly and fully embrace the tremendous political influence of New Orleans' African-American political groups, which had helped him win the 1971 Democratic runoff by less than three-tenths of a percentage point. Louisiana at that time was still relying on a closed primary system, which meant that candidates first had to survive rounds of party-specific contests before their names could appear on the general election ballots.

By the autumn of 1973, Edwards was enmeshed in a rewrite of the 1921 Louisiana Constitution, which lawmakers had amended so many times that it merited the dubious distinction as the nation's longest.

Simultaneously, Edwards was earning a reputation for playing fast and loose with ethics rules, such as they were in 1973—while always keeping a keen eye for beautiful young women, including coeds.

As they waited for the governor to enter the kitchen, one minute led to another, and the collective curiosity of the students got the best of them. They opened the refrigerator and peeked inside. They opened cabinets and drawers. This was a mansion built by the people for the governor, and they were, after all, the people. Then Edwards, cutting a dashing figure at the age of 46, with a head of salt-and-pepper hair, quietly entered the kitchen wearing a jumpsuit. Dardenne and his companions went from wondering what the governor ate to wondering what he would say. Dardenne laid out the math and the backstory. They needed $500 to reach their $26,000 goal.

"We think it will be the biggest event in America," he told the governor.

"I'll be right back," Edwards said.

A few minutes later, the governor returned, pulled five $100 bills out of his pocket, and approached Dardenne.

"Why don't you give it to her," Dardenne said, stopping the governor short and pointing to a buxom sorority girl who had come along for the ride upon hearing Edwards' request.

The governor liked that idea, but played it cool. He handed her the money and she slowly pushed it into the low-cut opening of her halter top.

"That's quite a vault you got there," Edwards joked in his already legendary Cajun drawl, closely eyeing where the deposit had landed. "I'll give you another $500 for the combination."

The boys laughed and Dardenne, although he didn't realize it at the time, had just witnessed a pivotal moment in his life. It had nothing to do with Edwards or politics or the co-ed, although years later he would spend a lot more time on the governing side of politics with—and against—Edwards. It was more about his ability to generate interest and donations for the Muscular Dystrophy Association.

The following year, Dardenne went to Las Vegas as one of a handful of students from across the country to present facsimile checks on the air to comedian Jerry Lewis. He was expected to say a sentence or two and then personally hand over a giant $26,000 check. While the producers and other presenters seemed nervous about taking part in a national broadcast, Dardenne was more excited than anything else. His nerves were never an issue, even in those last few moments before the bright lights reflected in his eyes and the camera rolled. "I'm pleased to present you this check for $26,000, representing a week's worth of flag football on the campus of Louisiana State University," a smiling

Dardenne said, already a natural in front of the lens.

As it turned out, the $26,000 haul was not the biggest in the nation, but it was the second biggest of the year. Still, that caught the attention of the Muscular Dystrophy Association, which asked Dardenne to chair its youth committee. Previous chairs included celebrities like Jerry Mathers of *Leave It To Beaver*. Now the association was looking for a working chairman, and Dardenne was the ideal candidate. He accepted the gig after a meeting in New York City and went on to appear in every national telethon through 1979.

When in Las Vegas, he also picked up celebrities from the airport and drove them to the casino hosting the broadcast. He once saw every door of a casino chained and locked so Frank Sinatra could personally escort Dean Martin inside for a surprise reunion with his old comedy partner, Jerry Lewis. After his stint as MDA's youth chair, Dardenne went on to co-host the local marathons broadcast from Baton Rouge in the decades that followed. That gig made Jay Dardenne a household name in Louisiana's Capital City.

By 1987 Dardenne was practicing law, married, and ready to make a leap that surprised no one who knew him—he announced a bid for the Louisiana Senate. While he had built name recognition with his earnest efforts on behalf of the Muscular Dystrophy Association, he had also been building to this very moment since grade school. In the sixth grade at Walnut Hills Elementary, Dardenne ran for class president against his best friend, Robert Dampf. He enlisted his little brother, Richard, then in fourth grade, to introduce him before his big speech. Richard had mastered his impressions of Alfred Hitchcock and Froggy from *The Little Rascals,* and he killed it on stage before the entire student body. As a result, Richard and his magical voice helped his big brother win his first taste of elected office.

Dardenne also made a run for vice president of the student council when he was in eighth grade at Westdale Junior High. Terry Hill, a popular football player, however, claimed that win. Dardenne's first loss had followed his first victory.

His mother, Janet Lucille Abramson, had encouraged his interest in politics. She had run for a school board seat in the 1960s and gotten clobbered. She had also volunteered for the 1964 presidential campaign of Barry Goldwater. Those contests were Dardenne's earliest memories of politics, and they formed the foundation for a lifetime in the public arena. His father, John Leigh Dardenne Sr. to Jay's John Leigh Jr., was supportive as well.

Dad was a track standout who received a scholarship to LSU but had to work instead to support his family. Dardenne's grandfather served for a time as postmaster in the Town of Plaquemine, almost directly across the Mississippi River from LSU, but was removed by Senator Huey Long for reasons lost to history. Dardenne's father went to work for Standard Oil, which, in Huey's eyes, was public enemy number one. In his spare time, Dad also helped collect tickets at LSU sporting events, in his son's eyes the best job a man could have.

When Dardenne served as student council president at Baton Rouge High School, he aspired to election as governor of Louisiana Boys State, technically a summer leadership program for high school seniors but just as much a boot camp of sorts for future politicians. Unfortunately for Dardenne, after losing his voice yelling cheers and singing songs at the week-long camp, he couldn't mount much of a campaign.

Dardenne enrolled at LSU in 1972 with high hopes of making his mark on the state's flagship university. He was a serious student and a good athlete—good enough to earn a walk-on invitation from basketball Coach Dale Brown for LSU's 1972 team.

His biggest political win as a student came in March 1977, when, as a freshman in law school, he ran for president of LSU's student government association. At that time, Dardenne believed that the outgoing SGA president, Ted Schirmer, had been too confrontational with the administration. On top of that, Schirmer kept a bushy mustache, and his thinning hair flowed below his shoulders. The clean-cut Dardenne thought Schirmer was a "throwback hippie." He campaigned on the promise of a different direction.

His close friend, George Kennedy, whom Dardenne had befriended on the statewide Key Club circuit in high school, helped with strategy. When all of the votes were counted, Dardenne won with 50.8 percent of the vote. No one since Russell Long, Huey's son and a future senator, had been elected student body president at LSU on the primary ballot.

As a result of that victory, Dardenne claimed a spot as a non-voting member of the LSU Board of Supervisors, but didn't like sitting in the wings. He testified before Louisiana House and Senate committees to make the position a voting seat on the board. Lawmakers eventually agreed.

Though Dardenne had originally registered to vote as a Democrat at the age of 18, after working on Henson Moore's successful run for Congress in 1974, he switched to the Republican Party. That didn't help him much in the 1987 state Senate race. Baton Rouge Metro Councilman Larry Bankston had the Democratic side of the field cornered, and Dardenne got little help from the local Republican infrastructure, which had already endorsed a candidate by the time Dardenne announced. Still, although Bankston was a rising star in the Democratic Party, Dardenne believed he could win the race—and he almost did. Bankston claimed victory by a mere 287 votes, and Dardenne had to concede his first bid for public office.

"I'm not dissuaded by this," Dardenne told his wife Cathy, to whom he had proposed a few years earlier at Baton Rouge's Camelot Club. The two had known each other since junior high, and Cathy was certain that her husband would pursue elected office come hell or high water. She was supportive and, like her husband, not ready to give up. Dardenne felt emboldened, even in defeat. The next year he won a seat on the Baton Rouge Metro Council—besting a four-person field in the primary with 62 percent of the vote.

When he finally won his seat in the Louisiana Senate in 1991, he quickly established himself as a reform-minded public official who could work in a bipartisan fashion. While Dardenne had found Edwin Edwards humorous in 1973, however, he held a different view when Edwards served an unprecedented fourth and final term as governor from 1992 to 1996. Increasingly a thorn in Edwards' side, he opposed the governor's old-style politics and policies at nearly every turn. Then, when Mike Foster, a Republican, succeeded Edwards in 1996, Dardenne became a floor leader for the new governor, working with the administration to create a single board of ethics and to craft budgets as chairman of the Senate Finance Committee. He also earned a reputation for not bailing on tough votes on issues such as taxes and abortion.

"I learned there is a green button and a red button," Dardenne said later of his time in the Legislature. "There's not a yellow button."

During his 14 years in the Senate, Dardenne did not fit easily into any of Louisiana's prevailing political archetypes. Although Cathy was Catholic, and they raised their two boys in that faith, Dardenne was Jewish. In fact, in the history of the Louisiana Senate, Dardenne was only the fourth Jewish member. And Louisiana had never had a Jewish governor.

"It's a very private thing," Dardenne later told *Forward* magazine, explaining why he rarely mentioned his religious beliefs publicly. "Your faith is something you have yourself. I've never tried to evangelize in any kind of way. I do talk a lot about God and what the power of prayer can do."

Those who encountered Dardenne for the first time might describe him as skinny and nerdy. On the other hand, those who got to know him well would call him sincere and honest—and his sense of right and wrong compelling. Dardenne was also genuinely likable, and that's a form of political currency all its own in Bayou State politics.

At the end of each legislative session, he added to the Senate's many traditions the practice of reciting a poem, his rhymes eagerly anticipated in later years. He penned each verse himself and always touched on key issues from the preceding months, weaving in the names of his colleagues wherever possible. In fact, Dardenne's prowess as a wordsmith later earned him, to little fanfare, an award from the national Bulwer–Lytton Fiction Contest for the "Most Vile Pun" and two "dishonorable mentions" for the worst opening lines to an imaginary novel. Here is his award-winning entry:

> *Falcon was her name and she was quite the bird of prey, sashaying past her adolescent admirers from one anchor store to another, past the kiosks where earrings longed to lie upon her lobes and sunglasses hoped to nestle on her nose, seemingly the beginning of a beautiful friendship with whomsoever caught the eye of the mall tease, Falcon.*

Was it any wonder that a guy who could intentionally pen such god-awful prose would become a darling of the press corps? Dardenne delivered his final legislative poem, several pages in length, in 2006, following a failed push to ban cockfighting in Louisiana and less than a year after Hurricanes Katrina and Rita devastated the southern two-thirds of the state. Here's an excerpt:

> *An ill wind blew across our land,*
> *Leaving memorable words in her wake:*
> *Katrina, FEMA, Chocolate City*
> *LRA, levee break.*
>
> *Ever since the water ebbed*
> *We've met in endless sessions;*
> *Earning our per diem*
> *And giving voters indigestion.*
>
> *Cockfighting drew quite a crowd*
> *In the legislative debate;*
> *Art (Lentini) wanted 'em flocking to New Mexico*
> *As the only available state.*
>
> *Is it a bird? Of course, it's a bird,*
> *But one without much luck;*
> *At the end of the day we knew one thing:*
> *The bill was one dead duck.*

And on it went from there. The 2006 poem, which took several minutes to recite, was Dardenne's legislative farewell. After the sudden death in 2005 of Secretary of State Fox McKeithen, Dardenne decided to run in the special election that followed. As was the case with his very first race in 1987, however, he didn't get much help from his party. He faced Republican Party state Chairman Mike Francis of Crowley and Democratic state Senator Francis Heitmeier of New Orleans on the jungle primary ballot. Though his GOP critics tried to characterize him as a thinly veiled Democrat, voters liked Dardenne's reform message. He knocked out Mike Francis in the primary, and Heitmeier quickly withdrew from the runoff after acknowledging that Hurricane Katrina had wiped out his political base in the Crescent City. Dardenne now had a statewide political infrastructure.

In 2007, in the regularly scheduled statewide elections, Dardenne easily won a full term with only token opposition. A history buff and memorabilia collector, Dardenne found the secretary of state job a good fit. He dove into his duties overseeing the state archives as well as all Louisiana elections. He restored the desk of Winnfield's favorite son, former Governor Huey Long, and used it as his official desk. "A lot of people asked me why I was running for secretary of state and not attorney general or something," Dardenne said after his win. "But nobody thought about the fact that I would be the unofficial historian for the state. I'm loving it."

It didn't take long for donors and influencers to start looking at other offices for Dardenne. Aside from his election to a full term as secretary of state in 2007, the other big news that year came from Senator David Vitter, who was reeling from his "very serious sin." Vitter would be up for re-election in 2010, and he had many enemies. Every one of them thought—or at least hoped—he would be vulnerable.

But Dardenne's attention turned elsewhere after August 6, 2007. That's the day another vehicle forced him to change lanes while traveling east on Interstate 12 in Baton Rouge, and he overcorrected his steering. His car ran into the median and was totaled. Dardenne was rushed to intensive care, where he was treated for chest bruises, rib fractures, and other injuries to his pelvis and spinal cord. His recovery, the most challenging period in his life, allowed him time to reflect on what he had accomplished, where he was going, and where he didn't want to go: the United States Senate.

Meanwhile, reporters kept him in the mix of potential candidates for the 2010 Senate race and donors kept knocking on his door. That was enough for Vitter to pick up the phone and request a meeting. The two men met in Dardenne's law office in downtown Baton Rouge. The encounter was brief, with only minimal small talk.

"Are you going to run?" Vitter asked, getting right to the point.

"You will not see me raising money or advancing my candidacy, but at this point I'm not going to say I'm not running," Dardenne told Vitter.

The truth was that Dardenne never had any intention of running for the Senate. He enjoyed his life in Baton Rouge, and, like all boys raised on Louisiana politics, his heart was in the state Capitol, and his sights were on the Governor's Mansion. He didn't have to wait long, however, to run for higher office.

On Dardenne's 56th birthday, February 6, 2010, Lieutenant Governor Mitch Landrieu was elected mayor of New Orleans, leaving the state's number two spot open. Dardenne officially announced for the job less than a week after Landrieu's victory. Running for statewide office is never a cakewalk, but this was going to be a dog fight.

Dardenne had raised only $1,100 the year before, and his war chest held only what was left from his first full year in office. The October 2 jungle primary for lieutenant governor was a memorable contest that saw Dardenne running against another GOP chairman, Roger Villere of Jefferson Parish. Country music star Sammy Kershaw also qualified as a Republican, as did St. Tammany Parish President Kevin Davis, who was quite popular in the Florida Parishes across Lake Pontchartrain from New Orleans. Democratic candidates included state Senator Butch Gautreaux of Morgan City and Caroline Fayard, an attorney and daughter of big-time trial lawyer Calvin Fayard of Denham Springs, a suburb of Baton Rouge.

Thanks to her father's long-standing political connections, Fayard had the support of former President Bill Clinton, who helped her raise a pile of campaign cash. Dardenne led them all in the October jungle primary and faced Fayard in the November runoff—which, coincidentally, was also the general election for David Vitter's Senate seat. For his part, Vitter easily won the GOP nomination in August, then cruised past Democratic Congressman Charlie Melancon in November by using a tactic that Dardenne likewise deployed against Fayard: loudly and constantly tying the Democrat to President Barack Obama.

Dardenne beat Fayard 57 to 43 percent. He was now just a heartbeat away from the office of governor—a position that friends and family had always predicted he would one day seek and win.

A year later, Dardenne's 2011 re-election campaign for lieutenant governor would mark his fourth statewide run since 2006. It was also to be his most agonizing on several levels, beginning with a challenge from fellow Republican Billy Nungesser, the president of Plaquemines

Parish and the son of yet another former GOP chair, William A. Nungesser. The parish president was an aggressive fundraiser and a political brawler with a common touch that the more reserved and erudite Dardenne lacked.

Dardenne, meanwhile, received some disturbing news from his doctor that summer: the lieutenant governor had prostate cancer. It was slow-growing but had advanced enough in certain areas that Dardenne would have to decide soon between radiation treatments or removal of the prostate. The doctor agreed that Dardenne could wait until after the election, and the lieutenant governor decided not to tell a soul except his wife. "Billy will have me in a grave if he knew I had cancer," Dardenne told Cathy.

Nungesser instead had the next best thing for a Republican running statewide—the support of a freshly re-elected David Vitter. Dardenne, after a bruising campaign that saw him yet again painted as a moderate "RINO" (Republican In Name Only), turned back the challenge and won with 53 percent of the vote. After the election, surgeons at Tulane University Hospital in New Orleans removed his prostate.

The following years saw Dardenne grow into his role as Louisiana's cultural ambassador. Years earlier, he had poured his love for Louisiana and its history into a lengthy and thoroughly entertaining PowerPoint presentation that he delivered to groups all over the state. He called it "Why Louisiana Ain't Mississippi." As with the secretary of state's job, Dardenne was a good fit for the lieutenant governor's office, which oversaw museums and the state's Department of Culture, Recreation and Tourism. When Napoleon's death mask was moved from the Cabildo in New Orleans to the Louisiana State Museum in Baton Rouge, Dardenne couldn't pass up the opportunity to showcase his sense of humor. "A lot of people called for Napoleon's head but it never happened," he said. "We've at least delivered his face."

By February 2013 Dardenne made it clear but not official that he was gearing up to run for governor in 2015. A formal announcement could wait until much later. At that time, the only other candidates making moves were Vitter and Democratic state Representative John Bel Edwards, who paid a visit to Dardenne on February 20, 2013, in the lieutenant governor's office.

"I'm going to run," Edwards told Dardenne. "I'm not trying to dissuade you, but I am going to run. I wanted you to hear it from me."

"I'm going to run too," Dardenne said.

The men shook hands, promising to see each other on the campaign trail once they officially announced, which they agreed would likely be months away. That afternoon, however, Edwards appeared on The Jim Engster Show and inadvertently—awkwardly, even—announced his candidacy. Few took notice, but Dardenne, who had met with Edwards just hours earlier, knew that the contest had begun. The lieutenant governor got to fundraising like never before and prepared for a multi-candidate race. He raked in $118,000 on one May evening at the Uptown New Orleans home of national Republican campaign consultant Mary Matalin. He had already held five other major fundraisers around the state that year, all organized by his fundraising consultant Sally Nungesser, a cousin of Dardenne's erstwhile opponent Billy Nungesser.

In November 2013, Southern Media & Opinion Research released a poll, two years out from Election Day. It showed Vitter atop a field of mostly Republicans with 30 percent. Treasurer John Kennedy, who wasn't serious about running, got 19 percent, followed by Dardenne with 18 percent. Edwards was at 8 percent, despite his distinction as the only Democrat in the trial heat, and Public Service Commissioner Scott Angelle was at 2 percent. Speculation likewise began to mount that Mitch Landrieu, still in his first term as New Orleans' mayor, would run as a higher-profile Democrat, easily eclipsing Edwards. Landrieu did little to discourage such talk.

The following month, in December, Dardenne shifted further into high gear. He launched a campaign website and released an internal poll from Wilson Perkins Allen Opinion Research that showed him running well. George Kennedy continued as senior consultant, a long-held role that dated to Dardenne's run for student body president at LSU. Kennedy told reporters that many of Dardenne's supporters were encouraged that Vitter wasn't polling at around 50 percent in trial runs. "He should be the *de facto* water-walker right now," barked Kennedy, a mad scientist of Louisiana politics and the brother of Treasurer John Kennedy. A month later, Kennedy said of polls and candidates in general, "If you look at a client and the research, the surveys and all the math, you can make their greatest weakness their strength."

Actually, as a potential candidate for governor, Dardenne's strengths were his weaknesses. Voters and the media perceived him as a good guy, a do-gooder, and no one could ever accuse of him of twisting arms for donations. But that also meant he couldn't raise a lot of money. Moreover, far-right Republicans pummeled him for not being conservative enough. On the other hand, Dardenne's moderate streak gave him appeal among fellow GOP moderates as well as independents and, very likely, Democrats, if he were to make the runoff against Vitter. Everyone, Republicans and Democrats alike, figured Vitter had a lock on one of the runoff spots.

In all of 2014, Dardenne raised only $690,000—far less than Vitter, who raised $4 million and Angelle, who raised $1.5 million—prompting speculation that Dardenne might run again for lieutenant governor instead of governor. That option never crossed his mind.

On March 20, 2015, Dardenne officially announced his candidacy for governor in front of some 200 people at Westdale Middle School in Baton Rouge. His announcement included new material that reporters and headline writers loved, such as this promise: "We won't have an inaugural ball." That pronouncement sent a clear signal—Dardenne was not going to dance around the state's growing budget hole, even if that meant canceling Louisiana's favorite quadrennial political bash.

Soon thereafter, Dardenne made a key campaign hire: communications director Marsanne Golsby, who had served as press secretary to Mike Foster when he was governor. In recent years, Golsby had worked in public relations for corporate clients in the Baton Rouge area. A former Capitol reporter and lifelong Democrat, Golsby was known for her loyalty and willingness to take a hit for the team.

In March 1999, for example, when Greenpeace activists were shadowing Mike Foster's every move and complaining about polluted waters along the Mississippi River, protesters prepared and delivered a "toxic lunch" for the governor: a meal of pan-fried catfish harvested from an allegedly tainted bayou. As they waited inside the governor's office to give the meal to Foster, Golsby deflated the moment by chowing down on two mouthfuls of the supposedly toxic fish while staring down the protesters.

She could be confrontational when she thought it necessary but otherwise was enthusiastically chatty. When Foster left public office after two terms as governor, Golsby exited the state Capitol thinking, and perhaps hoping, "I will never set foot in that building again."

Golsby found in Dardenne a reason to revisit that notion. She wanted him to win, and she planned to help him get crossover votes among Democrats. She was also eager to see him stay in the middle lane in this race. But more than anything else, she believed he would offer a counter to what she perceived as the damage done by Bobby Jindal. That's what convinced her to go back to work flacking for another Republican. She felt Louisiana would be best served by moderate politicians, and Dardenne was the perfect case study.

"Look, I really respect you and I'm going to support you," Golsby told him after he hired her. "But if you're going to have to run to the right of LGBT issues or religious issues down the line, I need to know now."

Dardenne told Golsby he wasn't one to flip-flop, that he intended to campaign as the same Jay Dardenne who had first run for public office in 1987. Since his early days in the Louisiana Senate, Dardenne had been reliably moderate on social issues—including abortion and LGBT—while just as reliably conservative on taxes and spending. He hadn't changed for anyone or anything over the past two and a half decades, he told her, and he wasn't going to change now.

Here again, Dardenne showed a trait that George Kennedy would see as both a strength and a weakness. While he refused to change his brand and beliefs, Louisiana's political landscape was changing— radically—all around him. Dardenne would learn that soon enough, particularly when it came to outside money and super PACS.

He paid little mind to those new players at the outset of 2015. That would prove to be a costly mistake.

Part Two

"People never lie so much as after a hunt,
during a war or before an election."
—*Otto von Bismarck*

11

"The Largest Gathering of Sociopathy in the Nation"

From his perch on a curved bench near the entrance of The District Line Restaurant, just off the Washington Hilton Hotel's lobby, Austin Stukins could have thrown a carnival doubloon in any direction and hit either a Louisiana elected official, his or her spouse, one of their offspring, an aide, a lobbyist, a donor, or a consultant. Stukins, taking it all in at the age of 31, had spent the morning trying not to miss a moment of the political parade passing before him. That was, in a way, his job. He was working on former Congressman Jeff Landry's campaign for Louisiana attorney general as Landry's political and digital director.

When not dishing with other campaign workers near the hotel's north entrance, Stukins sipped his Bloody Mary and scanned the lobby. On that Saturday morning in January 2015, he was close to surviving his first Washington Mardi Gras—*close* because Saturday was still just the morning of the third and final day of Louisiana's decades-old political carnival, held annually at the same hotel in the nation's capital. For rookies like Stukins, it was as much a bacchanalian marathon as a gathering of political movers, shakers, and wannabes.

Officially, the festivities culminate with Saturday evening's Mardi Gras Ball, hosted by the Mystick Krewe of Louisianans— unofficially the Bayou State's political and economic politburo. But the real goings-on—the scheming, deal-making, and fundraising— had already reached a fever pitch, particularly in this year of statewide elections. Even after the ball concluded around midnight, the partying and plotting continued into the wee hours of the morning, fueled by gin, gossip, and a governor's race in the making.

Nearly 3,000 people, almost all of them from Louisiana, had made the trek to the Hilton over the preceding days. They came for the parties hosted by members of the congressional delegation in their hotel suites and for the private soirees in Washington's iconic restaurants.

On Thursday night, they came for the over-the-top "Louisiana Alive!" event, which required a wristband, the color of which determined your access either to the main floor or to the raised and sponsored VIP level. Oysters and other fresh seafood from coastal Louisiana, along with musical talent from Acadiana and New Orleans, had been flown up for the occasion. The entertainment included circus performers on stilts and uber-lobbyist John Breaux, the former senator from Louisiana, playing a washboard onstage with a Zydeco band.

On Friday night, men in tuxedos and women in shimmering evening gowns returned for the black-tie dinner dance, where festival queens were presented like debutantes along with "princesses"—the daughters of the state's ruling class.

The Saturday evening ball was the grand finale. Real Mardi Gras floats were going to roll through the hotel's ballroom, the largest in D.C. and the only one that can accommodate the annual event, while Krewes of revelers paraded behind, tossing trinkets to the tuxedoed and sequined onlookers. Unlike the real Mardi Gras in New Orleans, which bills itself as the biggest free show on earth, Washington Mardi Gras was invitation only and required tickets—$200 each for the dinner dance and ball, made payable to the nonprofit Mystick Krewe.

Stukins, a native of Lafayette and a former Marine, took a deep breath and looked thoughtfully at the red, icy surface of his drink. Washington Mardi Gras made for late nights and tough mornings, even for those accustomed to living out of a suitcase and passing time in hotel bars. Stukins had worked his way up through the Louisiana Republican Party directing digital efforts and overseeing the field staff that was unleashed during Mary Landrieu's Senate defeat a few months earlier. Now he was with Landry, a tea party Republican who was about to run well to the right of incumbent Attorney General Buddy Caldwell, whose switch from Democrat to Republican in 2011 did little to impress the conservative core of the state GOP. Landry and Caldwell had both visited the lobby and would probably resurface soon. So would practically every other statewide elected official and candidate by day's end.

Except for Governor Bobby Jindal.

The governor, busy running for president as an unannounced candidate, had thus forsaken Washington Mardi Gras in recent years. Jindal was instead on the campus of LSU that morning, hosting a prayer rally that promoted religious freedom and drew protesters from around the country. He was getting the headlines he wanted out of his Baton Rouge rally while, some 1,100 miles away, several thousand of his constituents were already busy trying to figure out who would take his place. While he prayed and proselytized, they schmoozed and boozed.

Looking dapper in a dark suit and bowtie, his brown beard trimmed close, Stukins sat on the curved bench and draped one leg over the other. People milled around everywhere. "I do believe, right now at least," Stukins said matter of factly to those closest to him, gesturing with his Bloody Mary, "that this may be the largest gathering of sociopathy in the nation."

Light laughter filled the air as rays of sunshine spilled in from the nearby glass doors. Ambition also spilled out onto the floor of the Hilton lobby, a holding room of sorts during Washington Mardi Gras, where politicos huddled before and after parties and leaned over their drinks late into the night. Only the meetings that were meant to be seen took place in the lobby; those not intended to stoke fires or impress were confined to private suites.

Some folks never even bought a ticket to the official festivities. Instead, for the cost of lodging and airfare, they took up positions in the lobby and soaked up the benefits of Louisiana's premier political networking event. A good spot was always McClellan's Sports Bar, one of the hotel lobby's two watering holes, which long ago had acquired legendary status among Washington Mardi Gras veterans. If you were to ask revelers where to find McClellan's, many of them would have no idea. That's because, during the festivities, McClellan's replaces its sign with another declaring the bar "The 65th Parish"—a jocular reference to Louisiana's 64 parishes (counties) back home.

Getting a drink order filled there often took forever, and the room was often overflowing, but there was always plenty of interesting gossip and someone with an expense account to pick up the check. If you needed a new room, a restaurant reservation, tickets to anything, or even a cell phone number, The 65th Parish was where you could find someone with enough juice to fulfill your request. To avoid the pestering for such favors, senior Krewe lieutenants avoided the bar at all costs.

The major candidates for governor, including the four frontrunners—Scott Angelle, Jay Dardenne, John Bel Edwards, and David Vitter—had already rolled through the bar or worked its edges. Vitter, the only one among them with an official role at the Washington Mardi Gras, was the captain of the Krewe, an honorary title that rotated among members of the state's delegation every four years, according to seniority, past involvement, and general interest in getting involved with the inner workings, including ticket sales. Delegation members often lobby for the gig and write letters to senior Krewe lieutenants seeking the nod. Vitter had taken over from Mary Landrieu in 2012.

The captain, in consultation with the Krewe lieutenants, awards the ball chairmanship, which rotates annually. This year the honor went to Congressman Charles Boustany, which meant that he had selected the ball's theme and royalty.

As captain, Vitter served as the point man between the delegation and the lieutenants and as honorary host. His children were said to be more impressed by the title of captain than by that of senator, and Vitter seemed to enjoy it as well.

The senior senator's team was riding high. Communications director Luke Bolar couldn't stop laughing about the custom-made Mardi Gras beads emblazoned with "FOCK," which stood for "Friends Of the Captain of the Krewe." Vitter's team deserved a laugh or two. Bolar and several others had stuck with their boss during the toughest of times, when hordes of reporters were knocking down their doors after Vitter's prostitution scandal became public in 2007. Bolar thought the beads were humorous, but he also felt they sent a message: *He's our guy.*

Bolar thought about John Bel Edwards—between bites of king cake and rounds of bourbon. If the state representative from Amite managed to clear the field of other Democrats, especially New Orleans Mayor Mitch Landrieu, Bolar was confident Edwards would face Vitter in the runoff. Many others agreed with his assessment. As Vitter again took the reins of Krewe captain, his campaign for governor clearly was gaining steam.

The now-senior senator hosted an oyster party in his suite on Saturday afternoon, where his official duty was toasting the court's princesses. A large crowed was expected—not because of the oysters or princesses, but because so many politicos and hangers on wanted to kiss the ring of the early fundraising leader and clear frontrunner in the race for governor.

Vitter, who had officially been running for governor for a year, had managed to navigate the state's political waters ably enough to expect smooth sailing ahead. His "very serious sin" was a liability in Louisiana, but not so much in Washington. In discussions with lobbyists during the festivities, Vitter made it clear that he didn't want to see anyone playing both sides of the fence. It was Team Vitter or nothing at all.

As a second-term senator, he could solicit donations for his federal campaign account *and* raise money for the governor's race through a separate state account. While he couldn't use his federal money on a state race, at least not directly, that was no hurdle. An independent super PAC called The Fund for Louisiana's Future had been created to support Vitter's bid for governor, and thanks to a favorable federal court ruling his lawyers had obtained, he could legally transfer oodles of cash from his federal campaign war chest to the super PAC.

Consequently, during the previous October and November, Vitter's federal campaign account was the super PAC's largest donor, cutting a check for $740,000 and bringing the super PAC's total donations to date to $840,000.

At The 65th Parish that afternoon, revelers couldn't avoid mentioning the cash that was expected to swell the coffers of the super PACs. This special breed of political action committee could raise unlimited amounts of money thanks to the United States Supreme Court's 2010 ruling in *Citizens United*, which held that certain types of political donations were a protected form of speech. While Louisiana got a good taste of the super PAC landscape during the 2014 Senate race, this would be the first time a super PAC would figure in a governor's race.

Many at the bar had awakened on Friday morning to find a copy of the political newsletter *LaPolitics Weekly* shoved under their doors. One of its stories reported the creation of Now or Never, a new super PAC backing Dardenne's gubernatorial campaign and spearheaded by Axiom Strategies, whose principal partner, Jeff Roe, was also working on the presidential campaign of Texas Senator Ted Cruz. Vitter's supporters had already broken new ground with The Fund for Louisiana's Future. Now Dardenne had become the second candidate poised to take advantage of the spending spree to come.

All of the candidates, save Dardenne, seemed impressed by the prospects of the super PAC era. Deep down and publicly, the lieutenant governor didn't like outside spending, and he opposed the loopholes that allowed candidates to play fast and loose with political action committees that were supposed to be independent. Campaign finance case law had strictly prohibited most forms of communication between super PACs and the candidates they were supporting, but in terms of fundraising the law allowed some leeway. Dardenne, for instance, could encourage his donors to write checks to Now or Never, but he couldn't accept donations on its behalf. True to his reform roots, Dardenne said later he had "no interest" in going down that road.

Similarly, Joel DiGrado, executive director of the Fund for Louisiana's Future, avoided Washington Mardi Gras. The farther away he was from Vitter's team the better, but that didn't mean he wasn't focused on the campaign. The Byzantine rules that flowed from *Citizens United* created a strange dynamic in which campaigns sometimes tried to suggest strategies to super PACs via unknowing reporters. While campaign managers and candidates couldn't phone or meet with a super PAC director and say which opponent to attack, they could suggest as much to a journalist in the hope that a friendly super PAC strategist would see the message in a story or column. DiGrado watched for such signals from the Vitter camp. "I'd rather them tell the press, and I find out from there," he said.

Some campaigns even considered posting their video b-roll, or unused footage from TV commercials, on public sites such as YouTube, which would allow super PACs or anyone else to use the video however they wanted. Ryan Cross, Angelle's campaign manager, was already holding active conversations on the subject with his staff, should a super PAC surface to support his candidate. One was already quietly in the works.

Back at Washington Mardi Gras, a record crowd checked into the Hilton for the three-day political mosh pit. The Friday night dinner dance had sold out before Christmas, and the Saturday evening ball had tapped out not long after. Smart lobbyists and various campaigns had squirreled away extra tickets for last-minute requests from key clients and supporters. For ball veterans like lobbyist Tyron Picard, one of the five senior Krewe lieutenants who manage the host organization, behind-the-scenes machinations could get stressful before the party even started. Almost everyone in attendance, for example, wanted seats front and center at every event. These were people accustomed to privileged treatment back home, where each was a big shot; now they found themselves in the same room in Washington.

As was usually the case, this year's crowd skewed heavily towards the region of the ball's chairman, Congressman Boustany of Lafayette. The Cajun contingent was so large that this year's king, oil executive Charlie Goodson, had leased an entire Airbus. Picard's advice to his friends from Lafayette: "Hydrate, hydrate, hydrate."

That was no joking matter. The liquor store across the street from the Hilton, Martin's, boasted that Washington Mardi Gras provided its most lucrative three days of the year. Longtime enthusiasts, like Picard, even had standing accounts there. A few ball organizers also swore by Pedialyte for morning-after hangovers—and kept cases of the children's hydration formula in their suites.

On another front, this was the first Washington Mardi Gras in 18 years when Mary Landrieu, now out of office, did not host a hospitality suite as part of the delegation. That meant no reprise of her now-infamous karaoke parties. A year earlier, someone had released a cellphone video of Attorney General Buddy Caldwell serenading Landrieu in his near-legendary Elvis impersonation. Though at the time all was good fun—and good politics—the footage found its way into a campaign commercial by one of the many third-party groups targeting Landrieu in her re-election. That video was another sign that politicking in Louisiana, Washington, and everywhere else would look and sound different from now. Henceforth, no one wanted to be caught having too much fun in public.

Long gone were the days of the late Senator Russell Long singing with a jazz band at 3 a.m. Even behind closed doors, the Washington Mardi Gras began shedding some of its frat-house ways. One mainstay, offered for saints and sinners alike, however, remained: Loyola University's vigil Mass on Saturday afternoon.

John Bel Edwards made his presence known as volunteers hung his campaign's branded Mardi Gras beads on every door handle in the hotel. His skeleton staff was well aware of the lobby crowd's general thinking: Edwards' candidacy was a long shot at best. Edwards media consultant Jared Arsement had gotten an earful the night before in the suite of a prominent businessman who was weighing how heavily he'd get behind Edwards. As the crowd thinned, he expressed his concerns about Edwards' prospects—and how his relevance would disappear with Mitch Landrieu on the ballot.

"Jared," the businessman said, "do you honestly think that John Bel has a chance to win this thing?"

"I really do," Arsement replied. "If we have a decent amount of resources, this guy is going to turn some heads. I'm telling you, he's going to contrast well against Vitter in a runoff."

"You're crazy if you believe that John Bel can win," the businessman said.

The response to Edwards' candidacy hadn't gone much better earlier that Saturday at a Democratic Governors Association meeting, where Arsement and Edwards made a joint appeal for help. Mary Landrieu's defeat barely a month earlier was still fresh on the minds of the DGA's political architects, who, for all practical purposes, showed Arsement and Edwards the door as soon as they began outlining their path to victory.

Getting into an elevator on their way back to the Hilton, Arsement looked at Edwards and shook his head. "I don't think they're sold," he said, stating the obvious. Coincidentally, Mitch Landrieu had also discussed the Louisiana governor's race with DGA officials earlier in the week.

Republicans, meanwhile, weren't sold on Dardenne. He wasn't getting the high-powered meetings that his GOP opponents were lining up, and some potential supporters were distancing themselves from his campaign as Vitter's shadow grew longer over Washington Mardi Gras.

Although Dardenne hadn't officially announced his candidacy by the time he arrived in Washington, he was telling donors and influencers that he would be on the ballot no matter what. For many, that wasn't enough. For starters, Dardenne wasn't as flashy as others in the field, and he was unlikely to raise anywhere near Vitter's money. But he was dependable and steady—in contrast to Jindal, who often left Louisiana to gin up a presidential campaign while Dardenne remained on the job.

"I was acting governor for 144 days last year and have probably been acting governor most of this year too," Dardenne told anyone who broached the topic during Washington Mardi Gras.

For his part, Angelle was perhaps the only candidate actually enjoying the party. Given his Cajun heritage, that should have come as no surprise. Though he had announced just four months earlier, he had more control over his narrative than the other candidates, mostly because he had only a relative handful of recorded votes on the Public Service Commission and LSU Board of Supervisors his opponents could use against him. Meanwhile, they had logged hundreds if not thousands of votes, some of them potentially controversial. Angelle thus took his time staking out positions on big issues, moving as deliberately through them as he worked the crowds at Washington Mardi Gras. Many concluded that Angelle might actually have the money to compete.

With Saturday evening approaching, the Hilton lobby began to take on a glitzier look. Men in tuxedos and women in slinky gowns began heading downstairs to the ballroom. Outside The 65th Parish, Angelle had shed his boots and jeans for a tuxedo, while his sister-in-law Jennifer, his campaign's first manager, made sure supporters and friends were all set up. "Y'all need any tickets?" she shouted to someone lost in the herd of people moving downstairs.

Historians note that Washington Mardi Gras was founded as an excuse for Louisiana natives who were stuck, often by choice, in the District of Columbia during the real Carnival season back home. That's why the Louisiana State Society of Washington, D.C., had been formed in 1856—to recreate occasionally a way of life its members missed dearly and daily.

Society members tried to organize the first Washington Mardi Gras in 1938, though in the years that followed, during World War II, when even New Orleans had to cancel its Mardi Gras festivities, that dream proved difficult.

The first Washington Mardi Gras ball wasn't actually held until 1944, on George Washington's birthday, at the Statler Hotel. Hale Boggs, who was about to make a comeback run for Congress—long before he took over as the House majority leader—portrayed George Washington at the ball. Lieutenant Colonel Leonce Legendre of New Orleans was supposed to serve as the first king, but the costume that had been purchased didn't fit him. It did, however, fit New Orleans

Congressman F. Edward Hebert, a former newspaperman who had made a name for himself by exposing the "Louisiana Hayride" scandals of 1939. Members of Congress from Louisiana have donned tights ever since.

Over the years, the ball took on an identity all its own. Whereas the traditional New Orleans Mardi Gras reinforces the social status of the city's *ancien régime* and, to a lesser extent, its business and professional class, Washington Mardi Gras is all about political clout and the next election.

That's not to say Washington Mardi Gras has never attracted attention outside the political bounds of the Bayou State. *Time* magazine covered the ball in 1975, when then-President Gerald Ford and the First Lady attended. The *Time* write-up noted that then-Krewe captain Russell Long, who chaired the powerful Senate Finance Committee, had imposed a rule that any member who removed his mask had to pay a fine of $50—but then got busted himself for breaking the rule:

> *"There he was, swaggering along in the mask of captain emeritus of the Louisiana State Society's annual Mardi Gras Ball in Washington.... When Long approached Honored Guest [First Lady] Betty Ford to claim a dance, a Secret Service man barred his way, saying, 'You can't dance with Mrs. Ford until we know who you are.' Russell identified himself, but Mrs. Ford's protector persisted, 'You will have to take off your mask.' So Long dropped his mask and $50 for a dance with Betty (Ford)."*

Long had taken over the annual Washington event back in the late 1950s, pulling control away from the Louisiana State Society. Both lobbyist Ted Jones, at one time viewed as a master of the Senate Finance Committee, and Long's chief of staff Bob Hunter played a big role in that takeover. But it was Long who ruled the event as his own and made the Washington Hilton its official home. Then, beginning in 1977, the Washington Mardi Gras Association, created to act as the official sponsoring organization, reigned until 1981, when the Mystick Krewe of Louisianans incorporated as a nonprofit organization—quite possibly as a result of tax legislation passed out of Long's Senate committee—and replaced it.

On this enchanted Saturday evening in 2015, the Mystick Krewe was still in charge, its masked senior members roaming the ballroom floor, making sure everyone stayed in their seats for the royal procession. Another 300 or so Krewe members waited backstage while preparing their throws for the foot parade to come. The event was running smoothly and as planned—or so the Krewe thought. Some of the revelers who were sitting in box seats to the right of the main stage, however, caught whiffs of what smelled like smoke. A few people in the stands jokingly guessed that someone was sneaking a cigarette backstage. Others, well into a night of wine and spirits, noticed nothing at all. No one panicked. No one did anything at all, in fact.

The ball proceeded at an excruciatingly slow pace, as usual. As their names were announced, princesses in elaborate gowns and large rhinestone tiaras appeared on the arms of their fathers, who escorted them along a circular route. The young women who took their bow that night were mostly high school seniors or college freshmen whose parents had connections to members of Louisiana's congressional delegation. Festival queens from across Louisiana—from the Cameron Parish fur queen to the Washington Parish paper queen—were introduced as well. One. By. One. The alcohol flowed freely; drinking heavily was the only way to endure the slow pace of the formal event.

As Picard and Vitter, leading the procession in full costume, finally reached the front of the stage, they came to a dead stop and looked around.

"I smell something burning," Vitter said.

"I do, too," Picard replied.

At that point Picard and other lieutenants checked every corner of the room, finding nothing. That's because the fire wasn't on the floor. It was in a production room at stage right, the source a small smoldering wire someone had placed under a rug. The decision to throw a pitcher of water doused the small flame but created a much bigger problem: huge clouds of smoke entering the ballroom.

State Representatives Stephen Ortego and Robert Johnson, sitting in box seats a few rows off the floor near the stage, turned their heads away from the pomp and pageantry when they heard a commotion. "The ballroom's on fire," Johnson said, nodding his head toward the billowing smoke. His statement seemed stuck between a question rooted in shock and a declaration of disbelief. "There's a fire!" a woman screeched, echoing similar outbursts that spread through that section of the ballroom.

Baton Rouge lobbyist Randy Haynie, a Krewe member dressed in a silver-and-black sequined costume, attempted to make his voice heard through his mask. "It's a fire," he said, offering an outstretched hand to his wife and daughter. Other guests were already walking down the main aisle to escape the approaching haze. "Come on, y'all," Haynie said, helping more people reach the floor.

As confusion mixed with the sounds of coughing, Ortego stayed in his box to usher the women out. As Krewe lieutenants evaluated the threat and made hurried evacuation plans, several revelers casually walked to one of the many self-serve bars on the floor. If they were going to be evacuated with a few thousand others already imbued with the spirit of Mardi Gras, they would certainly need fresh drinks. Like-minded attendees gathered almost immediately in a haphazard line behind them, waiting for their turn with the ice and bottles. Something about filling a to-go cup before facing the heat and flames of a crisis was very much Louisiana.

Picard's own thoughts went to a dark corner. "If we have to evacuate this ballroom, with 120 girls and their families and the king and queen, all having probably together spent $1 million, we're never going to get everyone back in here," he worried to himself.

The crisis, however, never came to that.

"There was a small electrical fire in the rear of the ballroom but it has been contained," emcee Jim Reeder Jr. announced over the public address system, as organizers turned on suction fans. "Please return to your seats, and we'll carry on with the ball."

Carry on they did, until the time came for the after-parties and the after-after-parties. By sunrise the next morning, revelers Austin Stukins, Tyron Picard, Luke Bolar, and Jared Arsement could say they had survived the 2015 Washington Mardi Gras.

Hangovers notwithstanding, important connections had been made, and the ballroom had not caught fire. Nor had any of Vitter's major challengers, at least not yet.

Plans were already underway for the 2016 gala, but organizers knew they had to get past another major event: the race for governor, still months away from taking center stage in the grand ballroom of Louisiana politics. Meanwhile, one of the burning campaign questions of 2015—whether Mitch Landrieu's name would appear on the gubernatorial ballot—still had to be answered.

12

"I Hope in November to Be Eating Crow"

For all their differences, political and otherwise, David Vitter and John Bel Edwards shared one common goal in the wake of Bill Cassidy's victory over Mary Landrieu in December 2014: Both wanted Edwards to be the only major Democrat in the race for governor. The reason was simple—each man wanted to face the other in the runoff, because each man saw the other as the easiest candidate to beat. Were either man to face one of the other major Republican candidates— Scott Angelle or Jay Dardenne—he would almost certainly lose.

So it was that since his first days as a candidate, Edwards constantly dealt with rumors of this or that Democrat mulling his chances as a potential candidate for governor. Most of them decided not to run as soon as their names surfaced. One potential Democratic candidate took his time deciding, however, and his delay cast a pall over Edwards' early fundraising efforts. That Democrat was Mitch Landrieu, the mayor of New Orleans, who freely told close friends and confidants that he would love to serve as governor some day. This made for an uneasy relationship between Edwards and Landrieu.

When the two men greeted each other at the dedication of the Whitney Plantation slave museum in December 2014, the mayor told Edwards that he had to cancel the meeting they had planned for the following day at New Orleans City Hall to discuss their mutual interest in running for governor. This was but one of the snubs and one-ups that the two men would deal each other in the coming months.

The state's top elected Democrat following his sister's defeat, Landrieu had served 16 years in the state House before winning election as lieutenant governor in 2003 and re-election in 2007. In 2010, he was easily elected mayor of New Orleans, and he won re-election four years later without breaking a sweat. Under his leadership, most New Orleans residents—African Americans and whites alike—thought the city was finally rebounding from Hurricane Katrina and the disastrous tenure of Landrieu's predecessor, the recently jailed Ray Nagin. Property values were rising, murders were down, school test scores were up, and parks, recreation centers, and buildings Katrina had shuttered were reopening.

Landrieu had keen political instincts, but what set him apart as a potential candidate for governor was his ability to hold a crowd while speaking. He also had three major weaknesses. First, Mary's decisive loss in the 2014 Senate election had damaged the family brand. Second, Landrieu was a Democrat. Third, he was from New Orleans. No New Orleans mayor had been elected governor in more than 100 years, and, with his sister's defeat, no Democrat held statewide office going into the 2015 election cycle. In addition, Mitch Landrieu had a legislative voting record and had made decisions as mayor that could easily allow Republicans to tag him as a tax-and-spend liberal. Still, running for governor in 2015 would be a free shot for him, because he wouldn't have to relinquish the mayor's office to run.

Edwards had always eyed Landrieu as his biggest potential rival. Shortly after Landrieu canceled their meeting in December, Edwards' campaign secured a billboard promoting his candidacy in New Orleans, near the Mercedes–Benz Superdome—and within several blocks of City Hall. It was a shot across Landrieu's bow, even if most of Edwards' supporters knew the mayor's entrance into the race would have scuttled Edwards' chances. The state representative from Amite had earlier tweaked Landrieu, on February 3, 2014, two days after the mayor swept to re-election, by noting in a statement that the mayor had promised during the final campaign debate to serve all four years of his second term. Edwards congratulated Landrieu on his victory, then added archly, "I can tell you that when I make a promise, I keep it." The statement infuriated Raymond Blanco, who thought it an unnecessary swipe at Landrieu that could prompt retribution later. Indeed, it irked Landrieu, who notoriously never forgot a slight.

At this point in the campaign, Edwards' small team of advisers was worried more about Landrieu than Vitter. These Edwards insiders, Sam Jones and Mary-Patricia Wray, had different reactions to Mary Landrieu's defeat and what it meant for her brother. Jones, the politically astute state representative who was Edwards' seatmate and closest friend in the House, was frustrated by Mary Landrieu's loss. He believed it would underscore the notion that a Democrat could not win the governor's race. Big donors, Jones feared, would point to her loss as a reason not to give to his friend's campaign. That's what a number of trial attorneys had told Rémy Starns, a Metairie-based trial attorney who had already maxed out with a $5,000 contribution to

Edwards. Some even suggested he get Edwards to quit the race.

Wray, the campaign's communications strategist, had a different view. She suggested that Mary's loss allowed Edwards to differentiate himself from the former Democratic senator and her reputation as a pro-Obama, national Democrat. Clearly, Edwards could not win by relying solely on registered Democrats, who comprised 46 percent of voters. Unlike Mary, however, he could appeal to conservatives and right-leaning independents because he was pro-life, pro-gun, and anti-gay marriage. Daniel Edwards, the Tangipahoa sheriff, also saw a silver lining in Mary Landrieu's defeat. "There's no way Mitch is running," Daniel told his older brother. "His sister just lost badly. Her ties to Obama killed her. Mitch can't do it." John Bel agreed.

But Jones was also right: Raising money after Mary's defeat continued to drag, particularly with Mitch Landrieu still mulling his options.

Good news came in late January 2015, from Florida, of all places. Nearly two years after Edwards had announced his candidacy, he had finally authorized Jim Kitchens to conduct his first poll. From his home in Orlando, Kitchens was anxious to see what the survey showed. As he awaited the results, he was not optimistic. Frontrunner David Vitter had won big in his 2010 Senate re-election race, and the "D" after Edwards' name seemed likely to weigh him down. Kitchens was sitting in the den at his townhouse when the data popped up on his computer. He grabbed a pen and a highlighter, printed out the crosstabs, double-checked the demographics and dove in.

The so-called topline, or horserace numbers, showed Vitter leading a four-man race. No surprise there. What did surprise Kitchens—pleasantly—was that Vitter led Edwards by only three points, 30 percent to 27 percent, in a head-to-head matchup—and Lieutenant Governor Jay Dardenne by only four points, 32 percent to 28 percent. Vitter had garnered more than 50 percent in head-to-head matchups in 2014. Now the data confirmed Vitter's weakness: Only 32 percent of voters said they could envision voting for him, while 27 percent said they could not do so under any circumstance.

The poll also tested voters' reaction to Edwards' profile as a West Point graduate and Army Ranger who was pro-life, had an "A" grade from the National Rifle Association, and opposed Jindal's budget cuts to higher education and health care. Given that information, a stunning 45 percent said they would be more likely to support Edwards, while only 11 percent said they were less likely to back him. The poll also tested potential lines of attack against Vitter. Told that he had recently said he agreed with all of Jindal's political values, only 19 percent said they would be more likely to support Vitter, while 43 percent said they would be less likely. Voters clearly didn't want Vitter if they thought he represented a third term for Jindal.

The poll likewise asked about Vitter's taking calls from the D.C. Madam on his cell phone while on the floor of the House of Representatives and then refusing to provide anything more than a cursory explanation. Only 9 percent said they would be more likely to support Vitter after knowing this information while 54 percent said they would be less likely to do so. These were promising results, Kitchens thought. Although Vitter had won re-election in 2010—three years after the prostitution scandal went public—Kitchens concluded that voters still didn't know that much about it.

Kitchens recalled his 1974 doctoral dissertation. In it, he tested voter reaction to two hypothetical candidates. One had the support of voters on the issues but had character flaws. The other was on the wrong side of issues with voters but had a strong positive character. The candidate with the positive character won handily. Kitchens also remembered an adage from his former client, House Speaker Jim Wright of Texas: "There's never been a horse that couldn't be rode." That was only half of what Wright used to tell him. Here was the other half: "There's never been a cowboy who couldn't be throwed."

Vitter had never lost a race—and he was the heavy favorite in 2015—but Kitchens was now convinced the senator could be "throwed." To accomplish that, Edwards had to make sure the race focused on Vitter's character, not on Edwards' Democratic voting record in the state House.

Vitter had nearly 100 percent name recognition, but he didn't have more than 50 percent of the vote. "David Vitter cannot run a positive campaign and win a majority of the vote," Kitchens wrote in an analysis of the poll. "His image is too well defined." He added, "The only strategy for David Vitter's campaign is to attack the opponent early and attempt to define him as an unacceptable person from the beginning of the campaign."

Vitter was sitting on a pile of money. If he believed that Edwards presented a threat, he could sink the Democrat's campaign. "This is a very winnable race, but to beat David Vitter will require sufficient financial resources," Kitchens concluded. "It is unlikely that anyone will be able to match his financing from outside groups, but there must be sufficient money to keep his campaign from defining John Bel Edwards from the beginning."

Within a day, Kitchens called Edwards and passed along what he had found. "Good," Edwards replied. "Maybe this will help me raise money."

On January 26, 2015, the day before Kitchens got the poll, Mitch

Landrieu finally had time to meet with Edwards. The underdog's message to the mayor was clear: He was running for governor no matter what. Mitch's message to Edwards was muddled: He probably wouldn't run, but he wasn't ruling it out.

By the time the Police Jury Association of Louisiana held its annual convention at the New Orleans Marriott four days later, the friction between Edwards and Landrieu was well known to political insiders. Whispers filled the meeting room when the two men were seated next to each other on stage during the luncheon, as attendees waited for the mayor to give his keynote address.

As local elected officials took their seats, Landrieu looked every bit the candidate. During his hour-long speech, he waxed eloquent—without notes. He got the crowd laughing, pulled at their emotions, and offered nuanced policy positions. Although he was a mayor, Landrieu discussed statewide issues, often turning directly to his right and making eye contact with Edwards. Without ever mentioning a possible candidacy for governor, he was fanning the flames of speculation.

Before Landrieu's speech, members of the association had heard from three candidates for governor—Scott Angelle, Jay Dardenne, and Edwards. Vitter, who was in D.C. on official business, had sent a recorded video message. While Vitter had made it a point to attend the association's convention in past years, speaking via video was an approach he sometimes favored during the governor's race. That tack would backfire with the police jurors. As Vitter's video was being readied, Angelle looked at his opponents and asked, "Do we have to stay for this?" Dardenne was already scheduled to visit another part of the state, and Edwards had no desire to listen to Vitter.

The three men stood up and collectively made for the door. Association president Lisa Nelson of St. Martin Parish slowed them down long enough to give them gift bags, but they soon exited. Several local elected officials followed them out, eager to get a word in with the candidates.

As soon as the video started, the chatter from those remaining grew to a roar as more people said a few words to their seatmates and left. Nelson intervened. "Excuse me," she asked, as an enlarged Vitter spoke on the projection screen. "Could we get your attention?" No, they couldn't. Nor could Vitter. The local elected officials kept chatting and mostly missed the part where Vitter gave out his personal cell phone number. Had Vitter been there in the flesh, it's doubtful any of them would have moved. Still, many viewed him as the eventual winner, the walkout notwithstanding.

That evening, Democrats in the state House convened for a retreat at the L'Auberge Casino in Lake Charles. Upon arriving, Edwards ran into state Representative Walt Leger III, a supportive Democrat from New Orleans who served as the House speaker pro tem. Leger asked him about the City Hall meeting with Landrieu. Edwards' face dropped. He said that the mayor had been noncommittal about running but had said that if he didn't run, he might even support a Republican. Landrieu at that time still doubted that a Democrat could win—and he was *really* peeved at Edwards. At that point, Leger hadn't contributed any money to Edwards. To buck up his friend, he pulled out his checkbook and wrote out a $2,500 contribution.

Mitch Landrieu was not the only potential spoiler for Edwards. Foster Campbell, a veteran member of the Public Service Commission who had finished fourth in the 2007 governor's race, was telling reporters that he was thinking about it and that he didn't hear any of the candidates talking about the right issues.

Another potential spoiler was retired Army General Russel Honoré, the man who took charge of federal troops in New Orleans in the immediate aftermath of Hurricane Katrina. With his three-starred black beret, aviator sunglasses, camouflage uniform, and military bearing, Honoré cut an imposing figure and quickly calmed a nervous city. By 2015, he had retired and become an active presence in the state Capitol as the head of what he called The Green Army. Honoré lost no opportunities to lambaste oil and gas companies for polluting Louisiana's land and water and for allowing their drilling activities to wash away parts of Louisiana's coast. As he traveled the state, people constantly told him that he ought to run for governor. Honoré was not wild about the idea. He had already provided more than three decades of public service in the Army and hated having to ask people for contributions. Then again, he thought someone needed to stand up to oil and gas.

On February 2, Honoré appeared before the Press Club of Baton Rouge to drive home his green message. During the question and answer period, he acknowledged his interest in running for governor. "I spent 37 years serving our country as a public servant," he said. "I like this space I'm operating in, but I'm still thinking. Last time I checked, we've got several months left, and I'm thinking. But I'm going to have to do some hard convincing where I live and sleep." Honoré would obviously have no chance—What candidate had won in recent memory by running against the oil and gas industry?—but as an African American who took on Big Oil, he sure could take away votes from John Bel Edwards.

Meanwhile, the names of other African-American political leaders surfaced as potential candidates. Donald Cravins Sr., a former mayor of Opelousas and state senator, had resisted overtures from

Scott Angelle that he get in the race. "All I would have been was a pawn in a game to pull the black votes to create a division within the Democratic Party that would have certainly enhanced the chance of a Republican," Cravins said later. Baton Rouge Mayor Kip Holden said at the time he was being encouraged to run as well, but he was more interested in a bid for lieutenant governor. State Senator Rick Gallot of Ruston also was approached, but he had quickly read the politics behind such a move though he couldn't pinpoint the source. "Any candidates who would engage in that sort of tactic right now would give a signal of the kind of leadership they would provide as governor, and it would be an extension of what we're getting from the current administration," Gallot said. "It's a divide-and-conquer technique."

Honoré's potential candidacy added to the litany of doubts about Edwards as a viable candidate. The Democratic Governors Association clearly believed Edwards had no chance. On February 21, its chairman, Montana Governor Steve Bullock, told *The National Journal* that Landrieu was still considering the race. The mayor would make a "strong candidate," Bullock said, and "would give (Democrats) a fighting chance" in a "structurally tough state." Edwards apparently wouldn't give them that chance, DGA officials believed.

To get the DGA and others to his side, Edwards came to an inescapable conclusion: He needed Landrieu out of the race as early as possible. Edwards, who had studied military tactics at West Point, decided to outflank the mayor. The first step was getting the state AFL–CIO to endorse him. This would give him instant credibility, he thought. With the AFL–CIO's support, the various union locals could trumpet Edwards in monthly newsletters to their members, write checks, and provide volunteers to make phone calls, accompany the candidate at weekend festivals, and go door to door for him. The statewide union was scheduled to hold its annual convention on March 9 and 10 at the Hilton in downtown Baton Rouge.

The AFL–CIO generally didn't endorse a candidate until after qualifying, which was not until September. But Steve Monaghan, president of the Louisiana Federation of Teachers and Edwards' biggest union supporter, thought Edwards could get the endorsement early. The LFT was the biggest union within the AFL–CIO, and Edwards had an A+ voting record with LFT. As Edwards liked to note, he had a personal connection to the union: Donna was a public school teacher and a longtime union member. After the Legislature did Jindal's bidding in 2012 and passed the education measures opposed by LFT, "Rep. Edwards was one of the heroes who actually read the legislation, did his own homework, and stood tall in defense of our constitution, our kids, teachers, and communities," Monaghan wrote later.

On February 3, Monaghan turned for help to Louis Reine, the AFL–CIO state president. Reine, who had come up through the carpenters' union, had been the son-in-law of Victor Bussie, head of the state AFL–CIO when it wielded significant political clout. Now, like the union movement nationwide, Reine was frequently defending union members' interests against business initiatives in Baton Rouge.

Reine didn't think Jindal even knew how to pronounce his last name (it sounds like "wren"). Reine also knew that David Vitter would make sport of crushing unions. He had seen Edwards stand up for working families in the Legislature during the Jindal years, and he wanted a guy like Edwards to win. Reine had even attended Edwards' first fundraiser, organized two years earlier by unions in New Orleans. For all those reasons, Reine was receptive when Monaghan asked him to allow a special order of business to endorse Edwards at the convention. Reine also wanted to make sure Edwards had broad support within the AFL–CIO before committing to push for a statewide endorsement.

That affirmation came soon enough. While the convention gathered in a closed session on March 10 at the Hilton, one of the delegates made a motion for the AFL–CIO to endorse Edwards. It passed unanimously. Reine gave a rousing speech in Edwards' favor. Afterward, the candidate gave a less-than-rousing speech, but he heartened the union delegates nonetheless. After Edwards departed, Reine realized that the candidate had left behind a notebook. Reine took it to him at his Baton Rouge house on North Eighth Street, half a block from the federal courthouse downtown. "What are you going to do now that you have the endorsement of the unions and the Republicans start attacking you about it?" Reine asked as they stood on Edwards' small porch.

"I'm going to tell them I've never had a problem standing with working men and women," Edwards replied. "If I'm asked, I'll say I'm proud to stand with them." Reine liked what he heard, but he thought Edwards was a little naïve and would catch hell for that view.

The AFL–CIO's endorsement didn't impress Mitch Landrieu. Six days afterward, former Governor Kathleen Blanco was at City Hall in New Orleans for the pre-planning to mark the 10th anniversary of Hurricane Katrina later that year, in August. After the formal meeting, when she visited with Mitch and his sister Mary, talk naturally turned to the governor' race. "John Bel cannot win," Mitch told them. "Louisiana has to elect a moderate Republican—Jay or Scott."

"You're wrong," Blanco told Mitch Landrieu. "He can beat David Vitter. You're absolutely wrong."

The second maneuver for Edwards to outflank Landrieu was to

get the state Democratic Party's endorsement. The party also did not normally issue early endorsements for governor, but Edwards traveled from parish to parish, meeting with key Democrats and asking them to get the party behind a single candidate soon. He and his top advisers also called all the members of the party's state central committee. By late February, Stephen Handwerk, the party's executive director, was hearing from party activists throughout Louisiana that Democrats ought to endorse Edwards.

The Democrats met on March 28 at the Capitol. Edwards was confident he could get the nomination, but first he had to pass a test: The two dozen members of the party's executive committee wanted to hear from the candidate before the full state central committee met to consider an endorsement. The executive committee members gathered in House Committee Room 5, seated in the high-backed chairs where legislators normally sat, while Edwards stood in front of them, alone. He began by seeking common ground. It was time to have a governor who put Louisiana first, he said. Jindal was leaving the state in a financial ditch and cared more about running for president than serving the needs of Louisiana citizens. The party officials liked what they heard, but they tilted left. Where exactly did Edwards stand on key social issues? Arthur Morrell, a former state representative who was now the clerk of the Orleans Criminal District Court, asked Edwards to clarify his views on abortion. In asking the question, Morrell made it clear that he believed in a woman's right to choose. Edwards thanked him for the question and said he respected Morrell's views. But, he added, citing his Catholic religious beliefs, he was pro-life.

Kyle Gautreau, a political consultant and activist with Equality Louisiana who lived in Gonzales, asked Edwards if he understood the full complement of constituencies that made up the Democratic Party. Gautreau was being coy. He really wanted to know whether Edwards supported the LGBT community and its issues. Edwards smiled, because he understood exactly where Gautreau was going. He brought up gay marriage. "You and I disagree on that," he said. "But we agree more than we disagree," and he segued to his support for equal pay for women, a higher minimum wage, and an expansion of the earned income tax credit that benefitted the poor. His stance on key statewide issues—and his West Point and military background— positioned him to beat David Vitter, he emphasized. Gautreau liked how Edwards, while marking his disagreement, didn't waffle on the issues. When the session ended a few minutes later, Edwards sought out Gautreau to thank him for his question. Gautreau liked that, too. After the candidate left the room, the executive committee agreed that Edwards should be the party's nominee—that day.

Edwards went upstairs to the House Chamber, where the full state central committee would discuss the nomination. He felt good about his chances, but just to be sure, he moved about the chamber, shaking hands, visiting with folks he didn't know and posing for photos. The meeting began at 12:30 p.m. About 100 party members were there. Someone nominated Edwards as the party's candidate for governor, and moments later someone else moved to close the nominations. Applause broke out. Edwards faced no opposition.

He gave a short speech blaming Jindal for cutting higher education by $700 million over the past seven years and closing the only emergency room serving Mid-City and downtown Baton Rouge. "Louisiana has lost its way," Edwards said, to nods of approval.

The party officials voted unanimously to endorse his nomination and then stood to applaud their candidate. Edwards shook hands and hugged the committee members. "It's a good sign for me," he told reporters afterward. "Too often in the past, the party has been divided." The endorsement buoyed Mary-Patricia Wray, Edwards' communications strategist. "You know, he's going to win the race," she told Mark Ballard, *The Advocate's* Capitol News bureau chief. Ballard only laughed.

Julia O'Donoghue, who covered the event for *The Times-Picayune*, explained in an article why the endorsement would help Edwards. "An official party endorsement means the Democrats can devote staff and financial resources to Edwards' campaign this month, instead of waiting until the summer," she wrote. "It also makes it more likely national groups—like the Democratic Governors Association—will start supporting Edwards' efforts."

O'Donoghue's story also captured the skepticism that so many felt. "Edwards needs all the financial help he can get," she added. "All three major GOP gubernatorial candidates—U.S. Sen. David Vitter, Lt. Gov. Jay Dardenne, and Public Service Commissioner Scott Angelle—raised more campaign cash individually than he did last year, even though the Republicans were presumably fighting over the same donor pool."

Nonetheless, Edwards had now crowded out Mitch Landrieu among state party leaders and unions, whose members comprised Democrats' largest and most reliable pool of volunteers. A month later, on April 27, the mayor used an appearance before the Press Club of Baton Rouge to end the speculation. He would not run for governor.

Landrieu told the crowd that he had given the race careful consideration, especially since polls showed him as the leading Democrat. "I'd be fibbing to you if I said it didn't make me feel good that when my name is put in polls, when my name is mentioned, that

I'm at the top of that list," he said. Ever the politician, Landrieu said that remaining mayor was the main factor in his decision. "We have made tremendous progress that was admirable of the city, but we have a very long way to go," he said.

The mayor pointedly declined to endorse Edwards—or anyone else. Of course, he couldn't back Vitter. "They all have their strengths; they all have their weaknesses," he said.

The mayor made one additional ominous comment for Edwards: "I intend to play a role in this election, and I will do what I think is in the best interest of Louisiana," Landrieu said, adding, "Party affiliation is not my top priority." What the mayor previously said only privately, he now signaled publicly: He might support Dardenne or Angelle. For now, Edwards took comfort that the mayor had said he wouldn't run.

By this time, Edwards was sharing Kitchens' January poll with potential donors at every opportunity. It showed him nearly running even with a weak—and potentially vulnerable—Vitter in a head-to-head matchup. More often than not, Edwards returned from such meetings empty-handed, or with less money than he had hoped to get. "They're just not buying it," he told state Representative Sam Jones after one foray.

Edwards was asking donors to go against everything they were hearing—that a Democrat had no chance. Pollsters (other than Kitchens), pundits, political scientists, and other "experts" almost universally cited "the fundamentals" in declaring that no Democrat could win the Louisiana governor's race. By "fundamentals" they meant political party, which they believed was the overriding factor for most voters—especially in the increasingly Republican South.

In addition to fighting entrenched conventional wisdom, Edwards was particularly disappointed that he wasn't getting more help from trial lawyers. He had always figured they would shower him with money. After all, since 2002 he had been a board member of the Louisiana Association for Justice, the new name for the trial attorneys association. Trial lawyers more than anyone else feared seeing Vitter as governor. Some trial lawyers were key supporters, including Glenn Armentor in Lafayette, Phil Cossich in Belle Chasse, and Dan Foley and Steve Herman in New Orleans. Armentor threw a lavish fundraiser on March 25 at his opulent home. The event, at $250 per couple, raised $170,000, but it cost Armentor many hours of calling friends to raise that much.

Indeed, Robert Travis Scott, president of the Louisiana Public Affairs Research Council, a nonprofit think tank, was struck by the bare-bones structure of the Edwards campaign when he moderated a candidate forum on April 25, during PAR's annual meeting at the

Crowne Plaza Hotel in Baton Rouge. Edwards had no entourage. During the forum, Scott noticed that Edwards was scrawling notes in small print on a single sheet of paper. Vitter, on the other hand, appearing by video from Washington, waved a thick booklet chock-full of his positions on the key issues. Scott, who had been *The Times-Picayune*'s bureau chief in Baton Rouge before taking over at PAR, noted that Vitter gave deeply reasoned answers to the questions. The senator was obviously the product of a highly professional campaign machine with a lot of resources. Edwards gave good answers, too, Scott thought, but he didn't seem as thoroughly prepped as Vitter.

If only Scott had seen the Edwards campaign's new headquarters in Baton Rouge at 423 North Eighth Street, directly across the street from Edwards' shotgun house at 428 North Eighth. Edwards' staff—at this point he had only one paid campaign employee, Mary-Patricia Wray, in addition to volunteers and family members—called the campaign headquarters *the Yellow House* for the color of its exterior. A real estate agent might have called it a fixer-upper. The walls between the four office-space rooms were paper thin. The environment was so loud that Wray and the volunteer staffers had to shout to be heard when others were talking. Meanwhile, the house's foundation had shifted, creating holes in the hardwood floor in several rooms. Everyone shared a single bathroom that had no hot water.

In the coming weeks, the Edwards campaign continued to take one step forward, one backward. On May 12, Southern Media & Opinion Research released its latest survey, of 600 likely voters. The results did not help Edwards' case:

Vitter 38.1 percent
Edwards 24.6 percent
Dardenne 16.5 percent
Angelle 5.4 percent

More ominous for Edwards, when asked whether they would support a Republican or a Democrat for governor, 46.8 percent chose a Republican, while only 38.8 percent favored a Democrat. Even more ominously, fewer than 1 percent of Republican voters said they would vote for a Democrat. This fed the so-called experts' mantra about "fundamentals" and party affiliation.

Bob Mann made note of the results. A former press aide to Senator John Breaux and then to Governor Kathleen Blanco, both Democrats, Mann, who now taught at LSU's Manship School of Mass Communication, had written well-received history books, beginning with an authorized biography of former Senator Russell Long. Mann also wrote a Sunday column for *The Times-Picayune* from a decidedly liberal point of view. In fact, he had been one of the few people in

Louisiana who had openly challenged Jindal—repeatedly on his blog and in his columns—when Jindal was still riding high in the polls. Three days before the Southern Media poll was released, Mann wrote in his *Times-Pic* column that Vitter shouldn't feel too confident of winning. Conventional wisdom called for a Vitter victory, Mann wrote, "and over the past 36 years and possibly longer—the conventional wisdom has usually been wrong in contested governor's races. In fact, being the leading candidate in a campaign for an open governor's seat is often a highly perilous position. Conversely, dwelling near or at the back of the pack with about six months to go is sometimes not a bad spot."

But the Southern Media poll results got Mann to thinking. How in the world could Edwards win? How could he emerge as the one who upset conventional wisdom? Mann began to consider writing a column with that thesis. First, though, he tested it with a dozen political insiders who were not working for any of the four campaigns. Not one thought Edwards could win. In fact, no one made even a half-hearted argument on how he could pull it off. Mann decided to lay out his thoughts in his May 15 column.

"A Democrat—even one as effective, honest, and politically moderate as Edwards—cannot win a Louisiana statewide election," he wrote. "Twenty years ago, someone like Edwards would have been unbeatable. Today, however, a vote for the Amite Democrat is, for all practical purposes, a vote for Vitter."

Mann went on to express the conventional wisdom that Louisiana had turned irreversibly red with Mary Landrieu's defeat in 2014 and that, at least for now, "Louisiana is hostile territory for Democrats." Mann's bottom line: "Democrats have a clear choice: send Edwards into a runoff that he almost certainly cannot win—or back a moderate Republican, who could defeat Vitter. If Democrats have any power left in Louisiana politics, it is electing moderate Republicans. That's not a goal that will launch Democratic activists out of bed each morning, but it's about all the power the party has left (in statewide elections, at least)."

Mann's column sent shivers through the Edwards campaign. This was not *The Hayride*, Jeffrey Sadow, or some other arch-conservative making the argument, but Bob Mann, the state's preeminent liberal pundit. If enough Democrats bought Mann's argument, either Dardenne or Angelle could edge Edwards out of the runoff and in all probability serve as the next governor. Edwards' team was outraged.

"Motherfucker!" thought Jared Arsement, Edwards' media consultant. To him, Mann was refusing to look at the evidence that clearly showed his boss had a path to victory, albeit a narrow one.

The strongest reaction from the Edwards team came in a tart text message to Mann a couple of days later.

Bob,

Do you realize you could very well damage the only possibility that we have to change the direction of our state by just the title of your article. Too many people read and respect your articles.

Shame on you! You should really be careful in how you use the talent of your pen.
Let's all pray people don't take you too seriously.
Shame on you!

Donna Edwards

John Bel Edwards called Mann a day or so later. The pundit was expecting a tongue-lashing. Instead, Edwards was genial, telling Mann that he wanted to explain why his analysis was wrong. For 30 minutes, Edwards made his case, as if he were presenting a legal brief. One point stuck out for Mann. Edwards said political insiders knew about the prostitution scandal in detail, but the general public was not as well informed as Mann might think. When voters learned more about it and about Vitter's character, Edwards said, they would be turned off. Mann found that the candidate made a persuasive argument, and he was struck by Edwards' calm demeanor. Mann had heard of many people getting nasty telephone calls or texts from David Vitter after displeasing him. In contrast, Edwards saw Mann as an ally who had simply erred, and he wanted to keep open the lines of communication.

"John Bel, I really hope I'm wrong," Mann said. "I wrote it because I think it's the facts. I hope in November to be eating crow."

"I'll serve it any way you want it cooked," Edwards replied.

Three days after Mann's column, Edwards got the chance to lay out his path to victory in a column by *The Advocate's* Stephanie Grace.

As the only major Democrat in a gubernatorial race that's singularly focused on dissatisfaction with the outgoing Republican incumbent," Grace wrote, *"Edwards wants voters to know that he was criticizing Gov. Bobby Jindal before it was cool.*

His Republican rivals, he insists, were 'enablers' who didn't *fight policies that contributed to the current $1.6 billion budget shortfall 'when it would have made a difference.' He even has nicknames for Lt. Gov. Jay Dardenne, Public Service Commissioner Scott Angelle and U.S. Sen. David Vitter: 'Jindal Lite,' 'Jindal Incarnate' and 'Jindal on Steroids.' Edwin Edwards, of course, would have come up with much better nicknames, but this was about the best the West Pointer could do.*

Days later, John Bel Edwards was facing a potential challenge from another flank: Tony Clayton, a prominent African-American attorney, was considering getting in the race. A member of the Southern University Board of Supervisors, the New Roads resident was known in metro Baton Rouge for having prosecuted serial killer Derrick Todd Lee. "I'm a conservative Democrat," Clayton told a reporter. "I believe in smaller government, I'm pro-life, and I'm for traditional marriage. I hunt, and I believe in the Second Amendment. I also think our oil companies play an important role in Louisiana and I don't think we should be trying to run them out of the state." It was clear whom Clayton would undercut.

"For Clayton, a run for governor would likely not get him far in the race, but it certainly has the potential to upset Edwards' chances," wrote *The Hayride*, a conservative blog in Louisiana. *The Daily Kos*, a leftist blog, took an inadvertent dig at Edwards with its reporting: "The Louisiana gubernatorial race may get interesting after all." In other words, if Edwards was the only Democrat, Vitter was going to win easily.

After seeing the news coverage, Edwards holed up with two of his top advisers, Sam Jones and Mary-Patricia Wray, in the House Democratic Caucus room in the basement of the state Capitol to plot a response. A bit of quick research told them that Clayton had ties to both Vitter and Bobby Jindal. They concluded that Clayton was a Vitter plant. No Louisiana governor's race would be complete without at least one major candidate surreptitiously putting forth a straw-man candidate to take away a rival's votes. Chances are that wasn't the case with Clayton, however, because Vitter *wanted* to face Edwards in the runoff. In fact, Vitter had to request a meeting with Clayton to ask the prosecutor the same question: *"Why are you running?"* Clayton, who was a mover and shaker on many political levels, may simply have been playing his own angles.

Fortunately for both Vitter and Edwards, other prominent African-American leaders convinced Clayton to get out. On June 9, Clayton went on Jim Engster's radio show and announced his intentions. "I will not be bringing my talents to the Governor's Mansion," Clayton told Engster, who laughed and said, "You sound like LeBron James." Engster asked for an explanation.

"I don't want to hurt John Bel Edwards, David Vitter, or any of the other guys. I just don't see me being a spoiler for any of these guys." Clayton also told Engster that none of the candidates had tried to get him in or out of the race—an improbable claim, to be sure. Either way, Clayton's quick exit left the Edwards campaign breathing easier. A little more than three weeks later, Russel Honoré likewise made it official that he would not run. With just 10 weeks left before qualifying, and with Landrieu, Honoré, and Clayton out of contention, Edwards was confident that he would have the Democratic field all to himself.

That left one potential spoiler: New Orleans businessman John Georges. He had run for governor in 2007 as an independent, spent $11 million of his own money, and finished third as Bobby Jindal won the election in the primary. Georges later ran for mayor of New Orleans in 2010 as a Democrat, spent $4 million of his own money, and once again finished third, this time as Mitch Landrieu won the election in the primary.

Georges had taken over the family business, Imperial Trading Company, and grown it into one of the country's 25 largest wholesale distributors for convenience stores. He had also jumped into the video poker business after it was legalized in 1991 and become the largest owner and distributor of video poker machines in the state. During his 2007 and 2010 races, critics harped on the nature of his businesses, but Edwin Edwards put it best in a 2007 interview with the *Baton Rouge Business Report*. "I like Georges," Edwards said. "He's running as a businessman, which could be a good thing, except that his business is selling cigarettes, alcohol, and gambling machines."

Even before the mayor's race, Georges began to diversify into higher-profile activities. In 2009, he and a partner bought Galatoire's, one of New Orleans' grand dame restaurants. In 2013, he bought *The Advocate* newspaper from the Manship family, after the owners of *The Times-Picayune* had alienated its readers in New Orleans by ending daily home delivery of the newspaper.

Given his desire to keep out any other major Democrats, Edwards met with Georges several times. Each time, Georges made it clear that he was interested in running *if Edwards got out*. Georges had the money to self-finance a campaign and make sure the Democratic Party had enough cash to boost turnout for its down-ballot candidates. But that didn't matter, because Edwards firmly told Georges at each meeting that he wasn't getting out. Why should he? He was confident of victory, even if political insiders didn't believe him.

13

"Only If I Die"

As the weather in Louisiana turned hot and humid during the summer of 2015, the major candidates for governor juggled their time between trying to impress key constituencies in public forums and raising money from supporters in private meetings. On both fronts, the results were mixed for David Vitter and John Bel Edwards. Their campaigns were barely underway but there were already signs of trouble. Vitter was facing significant opposition in his home parish of Jefferson—and questions about his character in high-profile public forums. Edwards was gaining traction with traditional Democratic stakeholders in Louisiana, but still had difficulty convincing national influencers.

Vitter's problems in Jefferson Parish surfaced for everyone to see at a forum on June 17 at the Alario Center in Westwego, a suburb of New Orleans on the West Bank of the Mississippi River. There, the candidates paid fealty to issues important to the West Bank business organizations that had sponsored the forum. Each of the men promised more money for a local industrial rail spur, for example, even though some had no idea of where it would be located.

Edwards, Jay Dardenne, and Scott Angelle showed up, as promised. Vitter, after initially agreeing to attend, begged off less than 48 hours before the forum began. The senator instead offered an eight-minute videotaped address that he recorded in Washington. The sponsors reluctantly agreed to play the tape—at the end of the forum. As the tape rolled, a contingent from the City of Gretna, the parish seat in Jefferson whose leaders were, like Sheriff Newell Normand, no fans of Vitter, walked out in silent protest. The exodus was a repeat of what had happened at the Police Jury Association meeting in late January.

Nine days later, Vitter exhibited two more potential weaknesses: his legendary temper, which he rarely showed in public, and his avoidance of forums at which he might have to answer *The Question*— that is, anything related to his 2007 "very serious sin."

On June 26, the senator joined the three other major contenders at the Louisiana Farm Bureau Federation's gubernatorial forum at the Marriott Hotel in New Orleans. Jim Engster, the Baton Rouge-based radio talk show host, moderated the event. Before the forum began, Engster received a stack of questions for the candidates from the audience. Two of the questions dealt directly with Vitter's sex scandal. Engster didn't think they were appropriate, but he didn't want to avoid the issue entirely. Instead, midway through the event, he posed an open-ended question to all of the candidates, beginning with Vitter: "What has been the greatest personal challenge in your life, and how did you work to resolve it?"

"The greatest personal challenge in my life is issues I had in my marriage many years ago," Vitter said. "I worked very hard and did resolve that before that ever became a public issue, and it made our family and our marriage stronger." He immediately pivoted to the work he did as a senator to help Louisiana recover after the devastation of Hurricane Katrina in 2005. "We pulled together as a state," Vitter said. "We pulled together certainly as a federal delegation and met the challenge head-on. We're better for it. We're literally better for it. Nobody would wish Katrina and Rita on anyone. But in so many ways, we're better for it because we did rebuild bigger and stronger and better. That certainly was the greatest professional challenge."

Vitter's answer impressed Engster. "He hit it out of the park," the moderator thought, and he said as much on his statewide radio show shortly after the forum ended. Although the senator didn't betray it on stage, he was furious with the talk radio host for asking what most would consider a softball version of *The Question*. When the forum ended, Vitter made a beeline for Ronnie Anderson, the longtime head of the Farm Bureau, to express his feelings. An unsuspecting Anderson stood just behind the stage and reached out his hand to greet Vitter. Carey Martin, the federation's PR director, stood nearby with a camera. Anderson wanted to ask the senator to pose with him in a photo with the three other candidates. Vitter didn't give him the chance. "Ronnie, Engster blindsided me," Vitter said, his voice rising. "It was a set-up. We were not supposed to allow those kinds of questions."

"I thought you handled it well," said a surprised Anderson.

That only made Vitter angrier. He shook his finger in Anderson's face and unleashed a 20-second tirade. It would have gone on longer, but when Vitter spied Engster walking up to greet him, he turned and headed straight into the nearest elevator. A minute later, he realized it was a freight elevator taking him nowhere. Vitter stormed out. An hour later, a text popped up on Anderson's cell phone. "Thanks again, ronnie, for not following the rules, allowing engster to write most of the questions, allowing him to ambush me, and going 45 minutes late (destroying the rest of my schedule today). I really, really appreciate it—David Vitter."

Less than three weeks later, on Bastille Day, John Bel Edwards and his wife Donna found themselves a long way from Amite as they sat inside the posh 116 Club several blocks east of Capitol Hill. The private club is best known for its crab cakes, discretion, and a membership list that reads like a "Who's Who" of Beltway insiders. Sponsoring the Edwardses that day was a Louisiana political legend, attorney and lobbyist Ted Jones.

From his offices in Baton Rouge and Washington, Jones knew everybody who mattered in Bayou State politics, dating back to when he was a teenager playing guitar in the warm-up band for Earl Long's 1948 gubernatorial campaign. Jones had also played for years in the band of Louisiana's two-term singing governor, Jimmie Davis. He worked officially for Governors John McKeithen and Edwin Edwards and unofficially for an array of senators and representatives. Jones also knew Trent Lott, the former Republican Senate Majority Leader, from their days together at the University of Mississippi in the 1960s. When Lott spotted Jones at lunch in the 116 Club that day, he came over to say hello.

Jones introduced Lott to his guests, telling him that Edwards was a Democrat running for governor of Louisiana. "You can't win," Lott said, looking at Edwards. "David Vitter will be the next governor."

"Senator, you know a lot," Edwards smiled, "but you're wrong on this one."

Edwards and his core group of supporters were convinced he would move into the Governor's Mansion come January 2016, but getting others to share that view remained a tough sell. This trip to Washington underscored Edwards' predicament.

He had planned to meet with various power brokers whose backing could give him credibility and, he hoped, real money for his campaign. A day earlier, on July 13, before departing New Orleans, his challenge came into sharp focus when Elisabeth Pearson, the executive director of the Democratic Governors Association, emailed Edwards to cancel her meeting with him. Instead, she offered him a get-together with the association's political director. The cancellation disappointed Edwards, even angered him a little. Officials at the DGA were supposed to be helping him, he thought. They had only two competitive governor's races in 2015, and Edwards believed they had been stiff-arming him since their initial meeting during the Washington Mardi Gras in January.

He emailed back a thanks-but-no-thanks to visiting with DGA's political director, and, to further show his displeasure, he canceled a meeting with the CEO of the Democratic National Committee. When he arrived in Washington that night, Pearson had emailed back to say she would be available after all—but by then Edwards had made other plans. It would be rude, he said, to change them now.

In addition to his sit-down with Jones and brief encounter with Trent Lott, Edwards met the next day with a number of political directors at various AFL–CIO national unions. Though he thought the meetings went well, in the end he got no commitments of support.

From there, he visited with J. Bennett Johnston, who had represented Louisiana in the United States Senate from 1972 to 1997. Edwards had a special regard for Johnston because he had provided one of the two congressional recommendations that Edwards needed to get into West Point. They reminisced about the institution—Johnston had attended the military academy for a year before deciding he was better off transferring to Washington and Lee to pursue a career in law. They also talked about the 1971 governor's race, which Johnston narrowly lost.

"Early on, it was Bennett Who?" Johnston recounted. "There were whole parishes where I didn't have a single supporter. I had to go out and win votes person by person, parish by parish."

Johnston had hoped that he would build enough support to catch fire late in the race, and that's what happened. Edwin Edwards ran first and Johnston second. The two met in the Democratic runoff, as the state held separate party primaries at that time. Edwards defeated Johnston by less than 1 percent before going on to trounce David Treen, the Republican nominee, in the general election. Johnston ended up winning by losing, as his narrow defeat positioned him to capture the United States Senate seat the following year, after the death of longtime Senator Allen Ellender.

Johnston, noting that John Bel Edwards was similarly attempting to build enough support to make the runoff, said he was optimistic about Edwards' chances, because he thought Edwards' military service would be a real asset. "You're the right guy," Johnston said as they concluded their meeting.

The next day, July 15, Edwards and Donna met with the political director of the National Education Association. Same deal—no commitment. The trip wasn't going well. The couple had one final meeting, with Randi Weingarten, the president of the other major teachers' union, the American Federation of Teachers. Edwards was optimistic. This time he was not meeting with a political director but with someone who could actually decide to help his campaign.

Edwards knew that Weingarten had received glowing reports

from the union's Louisiana president, Steve Monaghan, who joined Edwards on this stop. When the meeting began, Weingarten and Edwards recalled seeing each other the preceding November when she attended the annual convention of the Louisiana Federation of Teachers, which had awarded him its highest honor by designating him "a friend of education."

In Weingarten's office, Edwards made his pitch—he was the one Democrat who had the background and the training to beat David Vitter. He also had been a reliable ally of the teachers against Bobby Jindal's top-down changes in K–12 public education, which weakened teacher tenure and expanded the state's voucher program. Besides, he noted, Donna had been a member of the teachers' union for years.

Weingarten asked a series of questions, and she must have liked his answers, because as the meeting ended, she smiled and said, "We're with you. We know you. We know the work you've done." She promised that the union would make a contribution, though she wouldn't know the amount until she talked to her political people.

"But we'll be with you and see how much is possible," she added.

Edwards, Donna, and Monaghan were pumped as they walked out. They had finally gotten concrete support. A short time later, AFT sent $100,000 to Louisiana Families First, Edwards' super PAC.

Back in Louisiana on July 18, Edwards went to the Airport Hilton in Kenner to meet with state Senator Karen Carter Peterson of New Orleans, former Senator Mary Landrieu, and Congressman Cedric Richmond of New Orleans. Each was a heavyweight Democrat in Louisiana. In addition to her work as a state senator, Peterson headed the Louisiana Democratic Party, which had officially endorsed him. Landrieu had served three terms in the Senate before her loss the year before. Edwards had supported her during that race. Richmond was serving his third term in the House of Representatives. Besides New Orleans, his district included the River Parishes that straddled the Mississippi River between New Orleans and Baton Rouge, and part of the Capital City itself. Richmond had served with Edwards in the state House before winning election to Congress. All three had been supporting Edwards for governor, so the candidate assumed he was meeting with friends when he walked into the hotel. In fact, he was still on a high from Weingarten's pledge of significant financial support a few days earlier.

Edwards' mood quickly soured when Peterson and Landrieu surprised him by saying he ought to get out of the governor's race. While Richmond mostly remained silent, the two women made many of the same arguments *Times-Picayune* columnist Bob Mann had raised in his op-ed two months earlier—that Edwards couldn't raise enough money to win, would very likely lose to Vitter, and should stand aside so that a moderate Republican could win.

Edwards countered by laying out his path to victory. Unmoved, the two women suggested he run instead for attorney general, a race without a major Democratic contender.

After more than a half-hour, Edwards had enough. "The only way I don't run is if I die between now and when I would qualify," he told them. Edwards spoke so emphatically that Landrieu and Peterson backed off. "What can we do to help?" they finally asked.

Edwards was unimpressed, believing them insincere, given everything they had said during the preceding 40 minutes. As he walked out, he could scarcely believe what had transpired. He would later call it the lowest moment of his campaign. He stewed about the meeting during the entire one-hour drive north to a fundraiser at the home of Britney Spears' mother in Kentwood.

Edwards had faced rejection during the campaign more times than he could count, but this was different. Landrieu and Peterson had been supporters and exerted widespread influence in the Democratic Party. Now they wanted him out. He felt as though he had been punched in the gut. He even began to wonder if he had misjudged his chances, a rare wavering in his confidence. During the drive, he decided that they wanted him to drop out in favor of John Georges, the wealthy businessman who had run for governor in 2007 and for mayor of New Orleans in 2010. Georges wanted to run for governor again if the conditions were right.

Campaign manager Linda Day could hear the pain in Edwards' voice when they spoke the next day. After discussing what had happened, they both expressed concern that Mary Landrieu and Karen Carter Peterson might pass along their negative message to key supporters. Day suggested circling the wagons posthaste.

They called a meeting two days later at Ted Jones' law office on the 7th floor of the City Plaza Building in downtown Baton Rouge. Among the 15 to 20 people attending were Louis Reine, the statewide AFL–CIO president; Dan Robin Sr., a major fundraiser and lobbyist; Ronnie Goux, the president of the Louisiana Nursing Home Association; former Governor Edwin Edwards; and Glenn Armentor, a Lafayette trial attorney and fundraiser. John Bel Edwards sat at the head of a conference table. The others could tell he was upset. Day thought he was going to cry. Edwards recounted what had happened. Everyone in the room immediately voiced their support for him and expressed outrage at what they saw as Landrieu's and Peterson's treachery.

"John Bel, listen," Jones said, "You don't have to kowtow to anybody. Run your own race. You're going to win." The others chimed in their support. By the time the meeting ended an hour later, Edwards had regained his confidence. No one was going to unhitch his wagon.

A day or so after the Airport Hilton meeting, Edwards called his pollster, Jim Kitchens. "Do you still think that if I'm the only Democrat, I can win?" Edwards asked.

"Absolutely," replied Kitchens. "We can beat this guy. It will be tougher, though, if Vitter is not the nominee."

To win, Edwards needed to raise more money—lots more money—to begin airing TV ads at qualifying time in September and remain on the air through the primary election six weeks later. For two years, Edwards had been calling potential donors. Most candidates admit that raising money is their least favorite part of campaigning. Edwards was no exception. For months, he had cut corners on call time. Then, in mid-July, the campaign brought in a professional fundraiser by the name of LA Harris. To anyone who asked—and plenty did—he said that LA didn't stand for anything; that was his name.

Harris, who came to Baton Rouge from Kentucky, quickly set up shop in Edwards' house on North Eighth Street, directly across from his ramshackle campaign headquarters. He instilled into "call time" a level of professionalism and discipline that had been missing. To keep track of Edwards' progress, someone from the campaign bought whiteboards and anchored them to a wall. The boards showed the specific dollar targets in commitments that Edwards met each day. To meet his goals, Edwards had to call and call and call.

He took to Harris' regimen. Going back to his West Point days, Edwards knew how to follow a disciplined course of action. He was elated one day when Harris told him that the percentage of people Edwards called who actually gave was the highest he had ever seen in a candidate. Though it's possible that Harris said this to all his clients, his words had a salutary effect on Edwards.

The next big event on the political calendar was the Louisiana Sheriffs' Association annual meeting, where candidates presented their bona fides and jockeyed for support. The sheriffs' endorsement was a big deal—as the state's leading retail politicians, they could deliver votes *and* credibility. In fact, the battle for their endorsement had begun a year earlier, at the sheriffs' 2014 gathering at the Hilton Sandestin Beach Golf Resort and Spa in the Florida Panhandle. At that 2014 meeting, Vitter had organized a party on opening night to begin courting the influential group, but Edwards had an inside track. His father Frank had served three terms as sheriff for Tangipahoa Parish, and his youngest brother, Daniel, had held the job since 2004. Edwards wanted to hold his own soiree, but he didn't have the cash.

That's when trial attorney Glenn Armentor of Lafayette stepped up.

Armentor, a charter member of the nearby Sandestin Golf and Beach Resort, was not one to do things halfway. He made a point of holding his party for Edwards at the same time as Vitter's—with the goal of outclassing the senator.

Vitter knew that securing the group's endorsement was going to be an uphill climb because of Edwards' connections. Instead of casting a wide net, he took individual sheriffs out for meals and cocktails during the convention, cherry-picking those he thought he could convert or those who were already with him. Those who hadn't been courted individually, however, scratched their heads when they arrived at Vitter's event. They found themselves standing in line to greet the senator—and then having to pay for their own drinks at the bar. That rubbed many sheriffs the wrong way, not just because they were accustomed to being wined and dined, but also because they knew Vitter was sitting on millions of dollars in campaign cash.

It didn't take long for word to spread among their ranks to ditch Vitter's stodgy meet-and-greet for Armentor's splashy poolside shindig on behalf of Edwards. The wealthy trial attorney didn't skimp on anything. The drinks were free, the bar well stocked, and the food plentiful. Edwards made a point of speaking to sheriffs individually, and he also addressed the throng. He had won the first round in the fight for this critical endorsement.

A year later, when the sheriffs met in Shreveport, Vitter was determined to get the endorsement right then—not after qualifying. That was going to be a tough sell. To issue an "early" endorsement, before anyone was *officially* a candidate, the sheriffs would have to suspend a new association rule prohibiting endorsements prior to qualifying. The sheriffs had historically endorsed in statewide races during their summer conclaves, or, in some instances, earlier, when the choice was obvious. But after 2014's contentious backing of Mary Landrieu in the Senate race, which divided the sheriffs, they had implemented the new rule. Now Vitter was pushing them to ignore it before they even applied it for the first time.

Edwards had made a personal appeal to each of the sheriffs by then. Vitter met with many of them as well and had given each a custom-made map of his parish. He also relied on group text messages, the same message to all of them. One text that he had sent four days earlier caught their attention, but for all the wrong reasons. Vitter texted that he had been a reliable friend of the sheriffs and would continue to be one as governor. Then he cut to the chase.

"It makes sense for the sheriffs to invest in and build our relationship now through an early endorsement," he wrote, adding, "(A later endorsement would be much, much less significant and helpful.)" Many of the sheriffs thought he was trying to strong-arm them.

On July 20, each of the four candidates made a brief pitch behind closed doors, in alphabetical order. Scott Angelle oozed Cajun charm. Jay Dardenne was matter-of-fact if not wonkish. John Bel Edwards pledged not to repeal the inventory tax—a popular position among the sheriffs because the tax produced significant revenue for them. Vitter went last.

He was blunt: "I'm the senator," he told the sheriffs and handed out a campaign booklet. He encouraged them to go to his website to get more information. "I'm going to win," he said. "This train is leaving, and the time to get on board is now."

As Vitter left, many sheriffs shook their heads in dismay at the senator's heavy-handed tactics. "I feel like he just threatened us if we don't endorse him," one sheriff said to another. "It's like he's saying if we don't do that, it will be too late. He won't need us." Several others stopped to make their feelings known to Newell Normand, the Jefferson Parish sheriff who had long made it known that he disliked Vitter. "Now we know what you mean," they said.

The sheriffs issued no endorsement, which insiders took as a repudiation of Vitter.

Shortly after the sheriff's July conference, veteran pollster Verne Kennedy conducted a statewide survey for a group of 20 businessmen who wanted their own independent survey results. Kennedy had polled Louisiana elections for the group since 1995. Over the years, while the members of the polling group changed, one man remained a key fixture—John Georges. Recruiting new members to replace those who left from year to year fell to him.

Each person in the group paid $10,000 for the privilege of seeing Kennedy's polls, which often included Georges' name as a potential candidate. Given Georges' past political ambitions, Kennedy faced questions from time to time about the accuracy of his numbers. The pollster always assured doubters that he was a professional and showed no favoritism, though Georges' insistence on including his own name in the survey occasionally caused some members to quit the group. For his part, Kennedy noted that by 2015 he had conducted more than 5,000 surveys for more than 1,000 political campaigns and for Democrats and Republicans alike.

Kennedy first polled the 2015 governor's race in May but for some reason excluded Angelle. As he would in subsequent surveys, he polled 600 likely voters, and the survey had a margin of error of plus or minus 4 percent. Here's what Kennedy found in May:

Vitter 38 percent

Edwards 27 percent
Dardenne 20 percent
Undecided 15 percent
At first glance, those results tracked what Southern Media & Opinion Research had found in April. But Kennedy then did something different. He redistributed the African-American vote based on the group's history of voting 90 percent for Democrats. Kennedy's redistributed numbers looked like this:
Vitter 36 percent
Edwards 35 percent
Dardenne 16 percent
Undecided 12 percent
That analysis shuffled the deck dramatically, because it attempted to predict, based on voter attitudes five months out, the actual vote in October. With the change, Edwards appeared to be running much stronger than the public perceived, and he looked like a lock for the runoff against Vitter.

In Kennedy's June survey, Vitter's support declined even in the unadjusted numbers:
Vitter 28 percent
Edwards 26 percent
Angelle 15 percent
Dardenne 10 percent
Undecided 21 percent
The notable change from May to June was Angelle's rise and Vitter's 10-point decline—a significant drop. Angelle had made a strategic decision in June to draw down his campaign treasury to spend heavily on TV ads and to run to the right of the two other GOP candidates, betting that he would jump enough in the polls to bring in more money. Campaign manager Ryan Cross also worked hard to get newspaper, radio, and television coverage for his candidate. The ploy worked, according to Kennedy's poll, as Angelle pulled conservative white voters—especially evangelical Christians and seniors—from Vitter.

As before, Kennedy redistributed the June tally by allocating 90 percent of the African-American vote to Edwards, the lone Democrat. Here's what he found:
Edwards 38 percent
Vitter 27 percent
Angelle 13 percent
Dardenne 9 percent
Undecided 14 percent
That was the shocker. With the redistributed vote, Edwards now

enjoyed a healthy lead over Vitter and the others.

Kennedy polled again in late July. Here are his unadjusted numbers:

Angelle 25 percent

Vitter 22 percent

Edwards 20 percent

Dardenne 12 percent

Undecided 21 percent

Kennedy once again redistributed the African-American vote, with the following results:

Edwards 34 percent

Angelle 21 percent

Vitter 21 percent

Dardenne 12 percent

Undecided 12 percent

These results revealed several problems for Vitter. First, they showed him potentially not making the runoff because he was now trending—for three straight months—in the wrong direction. In effect, the more that voters saw of Vitter, the less they liked of him. Second, someone leaked the poll to the media, and several outlets gave it prominent attention and analysis. Third, whether the African-American vote was redistributed or not, Angelle's rise was a threat to Team Vitter. Fourth, Vitter's "favorability" numbers were tanking. In Kennedy's May survey, for every voter who rated the senator unfavorably, 1.8 voters gave him a favorable rating—a decent ratio.

But in July, only 1.2 voters viewed him favorably for every one that rated him unfavorably. Worse, 92 percent of voters said they knew enough about Vitter to have an opinion of him. That meant, as Edwards' pollster Jim Kitchens had found in January, Vitter had little room to grow. All in all, Louisiana's senior senator was in deep trouble, according to Kennedy's surveys.

When Vitter got Kennedy's poll results, he wanted an explanation. At John Georges' behest, Kennedy had issued a standing offer to meet with any of the campaigns to discuss his findings. On August 5, Kennedy traveled to Metairie to meet with Kyle Ruckert, Vitter's campaign manager, and presented a slide show of his latest results. Vitter's unfavorable rating had risen dramatically among white voters, he said. Vitter depended on die-hard Republicans, evangelical Christians, and seniors, but he was losing each category of voters in worrisome numbers to Angelle.

"David might not even make the runoff," Kennedy said. "You ought to seriously consider whether he should even qualify for the election. Don't make your decision based just on my survey. Do your own survey a week before qualifying."

Ruckert was aghast. "You can't believe that David is not going to win or make the runoff," he said.

"Unless something happens between now and then to stop Angelle from making the runoff, he might not," Kennedy replied. He added that he would not release the poll results but said that it was quite likely that someone in the group would. That was the safest prediction of all, given Georges' history of talking freely to political writers across the state.

The next day, August 6, Ruckert sent an email blast around the state that challenged what he called Kennedy's "fantasy-land polling." Kennedy, wrote Ruckert, had conducted polls in three previous races where he was 30 to 40 percent off the final result. "Bottom line: it's silly season, and desperate candidates try desperate things," concluded Ruckert, all but saying that Kennedy was goosing the numbers to help Angelle. Ruckert's response to the poll had questioned Kennedy's competence and independence. Angered, the pollster threatened to sue the Vitter campaign for libel. Kennedy also issued a point by point rebuttal to Ruckert's broadside, saying that Ruckert had deliberately misquoted if not misrepresented the findings of Kennedy's earlier polls. Angelle's campaign, meanwhile, reached out to reporters to brag about the results and to donors in hopes of getting a fundraising boost.

By then, Vitter had enough. With nearly $10 million on hand, the senator moved to begin making his case to voters statewide—and to put distance between himself and his two Republican rivals. On August 19, he launched his first television commercial, which signaled several themes of his campaign. As he had in his past races, he would run against the establishment, in this case the Baton Rouge political establishment (even though by now he had helped create it). The ad toggled back and forth between Vitter in a suit standing in front of the state Capitol decrying Louisiana's problems (a budget mess, not enough folks working, failing schools) and Vitter in a checkered, button down shirt and blue jeans touting a brighter future (eliminating thousands of unnecessary state government cars, creating a program to put workers in good-paying jobs, spending less on the education bureaucracy and more in the classroom). "Join me, in a much brighter tomorrow," Vitter said as the ad ended.

His second spot on August 27 continued the same themes. "The politicians in Baton Rouge have handed us a massive budget mess," he said, without noting that many of those "politicians" were his Republican allies. "Their plan" called for "raising your taxes," Vitter added, completely ignoring that, if elected, he would have to work with "them." He called for eliminating state cars, politicians' pet projects, and consulting contracts. "And I've already given them term limits," he said. "They say I'm annoying the politicians." He smiled and then offered the clincher: "Must be doing something right."

His third spot aired on August 31 and took dead aim at Common Core, the controversial education standards, which he had previously supported. Now he stood in an empty classroom and decried a "dangerous plan" by Washington "to take over how we educate our kids." Viewers saw scenes of kids in classrooms as Vitter in a voiceover said he would cut the education bureaucracy and put the savings into the classroom. "And I'll put parents back in charge," he said. "That's not Common Core. That's common sense."

Angelle, who was the only other candidate on television, sought to counter Vitter, although the Cajun didn't have the money to match the senator ad for ad. That was part of Vitter's strategy. He could have waited until after qualifying to go on TV, but by going up now he forced Angelle to spend his limited money sooner. Angelle's late August spot—which followed ads that ran in February and June—interspersed shots of him in blue jeans in front of a bayou with video of workers. "Everybody needs to work, including the able-bodied on welfare," Angelle said, targeting a favorite Republican bogeyman. "When you're working, you're pulling the wagon, not riding in it. Don't you think it's time for more pullers? I'm ready. Aren't you?"

Dardenne didn't have the money to compete with Vitter's ad buys, but he did take a free shot at Vitter on August 29, during a forum sponsored by WRKF radio. He was the only candidate in attendance. When asked how he differed from the senator, Dardenne replied, "I have not frequented prostitution, especially not while on the floor of the U.S. Congress." That was the first time any of Vitter's opponents had raised the senator's "very serious sin" at a forum. It would not be the last.

By the end of August, two potential African-American candidates—retired Army General Russel Honoré and attorney Tony Clayton—had surfaced publicly but only to announce that they wouldn't run. Now, Edwards had to contend with one final scare from an African-American candidate. Jason Williams, an at-large member of the New Orleans City Council, confirmed rumors that he was considering the race. He then told *The Advocate's* Jeff Adelson that important issues such as mental health care, environmental concerns, and women's issues weren't getting their due on the campaign trail. "I feel like these are some serious issues that will directly affect the health of this state," Williams said.

Williams couldn't win, but, with a wealthy benefactor, he could knock enough points off Edwards to keep him out of the runoff and put a moderate Republican in against Vitter—making him a double threat. Edwards, however, had a card to play on Williams. Edwards' media consultant, Jared Arsement, had crafted Williams' TV ads during his 2014 City Council campaign. Arsement called Williams, who assured him that he was not seriously considering the race. More than anything, Williams wanted to make sure that New Orleans' needs got the attention they deserved. On August 20, Williams officially ended his two-week flirtation with running.

By then, Edwards had gotten more good polling news but was still having trouble getting traction from it. On August 11, Jim Kitchens got the results from the campaign's first poll since January. Kitchens liked the results:

Vitter 30 percent
Edwards 27 percent
Dardenne 16 percent
Angelle 11 percent
Undecided 16 percent

Like Kennedy, Kitchens redistributed 90 percent of the African-American vote to Edwards. With the change, his candidate got a significant jump:

Edwards 41 percent
Vitter 28 percent
Dardenne 14 percent
Angelle 10 percent
Undecided 7 percent

Digging into the poll, Kitchens noted that while Vitter's favorable-to-unfavorable rating was 50 percent to 37 percent, Edwards' was 35 percent to 16 percent. In a head-up race, Vitter led Edwards, 46 percent to 41 percent. Kitchens then asked voters a question putting each candidate in his most favorable light—Vitter: conservative, family values, Christian; Edwards: West Point, commanded a rifle company, wants to put Louisiana first—and in his darkest possible light—Vitter: has never passed a bill in the Senate, consorted with prostitutes; Edwards: a Democrat who voted for Obama twice, is a trial lawyer. After hearing positive and negative information about each candidate, voters shifted their views dramatically, favoring Edwards, 50 percent to 33 percent. The data told Kitchens that the negatives of being a Democrat who had voted for Obama were not nearly as devastating as Vitter's sex scandal, despite the senator's impressive re-election victory in 2010, just three years after the scandal broke.

Looking at the data from another vantage point, it showed the difference between a "national" election such as a Senate race and a "local" election for governor. No matter what state they represent, senators go off to Washington after they get elected. Governors, on the other hand, remain close to home. Voters actually have a chance to see and touch their governor; their senator, not so much. That put Vitter's sex scandal in a whole new light. Voters didn't much care about it as long as Vitter was "gone," but electing him governor had the effect of bringing it "home" and putting it on the family table. "As long as we make character the issue, we will win," Kitchens told Edwards and his team.

In a strategy memo, Kitchens wrote that only half of the electorate had enough information about Edwards to have a definite opinion about him. Either the Edwards campaign would fully define his public image or the Republicans would do it for him. What Edwards needed, wrote Kitchens, was for Angelle and Dardenne to mount strong enough campaigns to keep Vitter's attention focused on *them* and not on Edwards. "If Vitter becomes convinced that he will be the leading Republican and make the run-off, either his campaign or an independent campaign will immediately attack John Bel Edwards," wrote Kitchens. The pollster now turned to his final point, which he made in bold-faced text: **The biggest danger for the John Bel Edwards campaign is a lack of financial resources.** Basically, John Bel Edwards needs to spend 90 % of his time raising money. The only reasons he should make an appearance is if there is press coverage or there is a debate with all the candidates that he cannot miss. Efficiency with the candidate's time is critical for the remainder of this campaign. John Bel Edwards has a potentially very powerful story and message to present to the Louisiana voters. This message can only reach sufficient numbers of voters through mass media."

Edwards took the message to heart. On August 20, he flew to Washington to present the good poll news to the Democratic Governors Association and the Democratic National Committee one last time. Accompanying him were Congressman Cedric Richmond and state Senator Karen Carter Peterson. Edwards hadn't forgotten that Peterson, with Mary Landrieu, had asked him to get out of the race a month earlier, but she had to accompany him on the trip since she chaired the state Democratic Party. At the DGA, they met with Elisabeth Pearson, the executive director, and Corey Platt, the political director. Edwards presented Kitchens' poll. He was a stronger candidate than people realized, while Vitter was deeply flawed, he said. Edwards was convinced that the results showed he had a clear path to victory, and he wanted them to understand that and loosen their purse strings. Pearson and Platt complimented Edwards and praised his campaign, but they remained noncommittal. In fact, they seemed not to believe Kitchens' numbers.

Richmond intervened. He told Pearson and Platt that the Congressional Black Caucus wanted the DGA's strong support for Edwards. He reminded them that he had campaigned for Democratic gubernatorial candidates elsewhere. Now it was the DGA's turn to step up in Louisiana. Pearson, however, continued to string them along. "You're not giving us a commitment," interjected Peterson. They talked some more. Finally, Edwards looked at Pearson and said, "I'm going to be the next governor of Louisiana; whether I do it or not with your help is entirely up to you." The visit ended. The meeting at the Democratic National Committee went better, but Edwards left it empty-handed too. That made him 0-for-3 on visits with his own party leadership in D.C. since January.

As August ended, Edwards had achieved his goal: He was the only major Democrat in the contest. Yet he remained a decided underdog in the eyes of the public, political insiders, and potential donors, despite what his instincts and his own polling told him.

For his part, Vitter remained the odds-on favorite to win in November—at least, according to the "experts." Team Vitter knew the senator's numbers had weakened, but Vitter oozed confidence, even cockiness, because he knew what millions of dollars in TV advertising could do to his opponents—particularly Angelle and Dardenne.

Only one thing was clear as the official qualifying period approached: The candidates were headed for a wild ride.

14

"This is an election, not an auction"

An early riser who preferred the top starting position in any race, David Vitter was the first candidate to arrive at the Secretary of State's Office for the first day of qualifying on September 8, 2015. He passed through the doors moments after 8 a.m. and made his way into an interior office, where he sat across from Secretary of State Tom Schedler. The fee was $750 to qualify as a candidate for governor, plus another $375 for the state central committee of a candidate's political party.

Vitter placed $1,125 in cash on the glossy surface of the wooden table that separated them. It was a large stack of money, mostly $20 bills. "We want to put all of that on red," Vitter said with a smile as he arched his eyebrows and pointed at the cash, knowing full well that every Louisiana election was a gamble. Schedler laughed and nodded to a staffer, who in turn started counting the bills. They were inside the deputy secretary's office, which was the only space large enough to accommodate the reporters and photographers who wanted to witness the big wager firsthand. "If we both win we should get a photo of us together for De La Salle," Schedler told Vitter, as the staffer made sure the stack wasn't short. "And Young, too."

Both men had attended the same private Catholic high school in New Orleans, as had Jefferson Parish President John Young, who was running for lieutenant governor. In terms of New Orleans' social structure, a person's high school was an important distinction. Whereas politicos in the Cajun heartland of south Louisiana always asked who your daddy was, those in New Orleans inquired most about where you went to high school—and it was never, "Where'd you go to high school?" It was always just, "Where'd you go to school?" It was *understood* among New Orleanians that the question meant high school, not college. The answer to that question fostered assumptions about where you lived, whom you knew, and what your life was like growing up in The City That Care Forgot.

Over the course of the three-day qualifying period, others seeking statewide office would also trek to the Secretary of State's Office. It was, in theory, a solemn rite of democracy. After months of preliminary campaigning, candidates like Vitter were beginning to line up to sign documents—under oath—officially declaring their intentions to run and attesting that they had filed all state and federal income tax returns and owed no unpaid ethics fines. This ritual took place in an ordinary-looking three-story office building on Essen Lane in Baton Rouge, tucked behind the more imposing State Archives building. For the next three days, Schedler's office would be the center ring of Louisiana's political circus.

Vitter arrived hand-in-hand with his wife Wendy, who wore a dark blue dress and, in her heels, stood half a head taller than he. When they entered the lobby, about a dozen supporters greeted them with campaign signs and encouraging words. His opponents were waiting as well, ready to add a circus-like flavor to a governor's race that had been low key up to this point. A young man who would identify himself only as "Brian" stood in the middle of the lobby. Brian was shirtless and wearing a green bath towel over running shorts that were looped between his legs and wrapped around his waist like a diaper. He carried a hand-lettered sign —"I ♥ Diaper Dave!"—for the photographers and TV cameras. For those who hadn't trafficked in the wild, unsubstantiated stories about Vitter's dalliances with prostitutes in New Orleans and Washington, Julia O'Donoghue of *The Times-Picayune* provided an explanation. "Rumors have swirled—though they have not been confirmed—that the Senator apparently asked a prostitute to incorporate diapers into her services," she wrote in her account of the day's activities.

This was the kind of coverage that drove Vitter's campaign team mad. They believed that reporters would never dare cast such aspersions about Scott Angelle, Jay Dardenne, or John Bel Edwards. But Vitter had brought all this on himself. By admitting to a "very serious sin" in 2007—and then ducking the press and the controversy for years— Vitter invited lines of questioning that no other candidate would have to endure.

For their part, David and Wendy Vitter gave Brian and his diaper nary a second glance on that morning of qualifying. Once they finished meeting with Schedler, the Vitters made their way into the front office, where a microphone and podium had been set up for the candidates to address the press. "We're very excited that Wendy signed up for governor," Vitter joked before turning to his prepared remarks. More than a few people, however, thought she would have been the better candidate.

When asked if he could work with Democrats in the state Legislature after posting a staunchly Republican voting record, Louisiana's senior senator sought immediately to distinguish himself from the current occupant of the Governor's Mansion. "I'll get up every day to be focused and do right," Vitter said. "Of all the candidates in the race, I have the strongest and most concrete record of bipartisan accomplishment."

Over the course of the preceding year or two, while reporters fixated on Vitter's undeniably partisan history, the senator had grown more open to working with those across the aisle in the Senate. *Politico's* Burgess Everett would point out as much later in the election: "In public, David Vitter is the face of Senate gridlock, a master of holding up the entire chamber if he doesn't get what he wants. But in the backrooms of Congress, Vitter has worked seamlessly with Democratic colleagues to advance their priorities—as long it allows him to bring home the bacon to Louisiana."

Next to qualify at the Secretary of State's Office came Scott Angelle, holding his twin granddaughters in what was clearly meant as an unspoken statement of his family values. Angelle's assistant, Micah Cormier, swapped stories with reporters about what had transpired so far that morning. "It's kind of like the draft," Cormier remarked, likening Louisiana politicians to professional athletes. During Angelle's turn with Schedler, the secretary of state told Angelle that he had met his own wife while in college in Lafayette; Angelle had also gone to college there. "Was it at The Keg or in the classroom?" Angelle asked, referring to the legendary Lafayette college bar. Schedler replied with only a chuckle. Earlier, when a staffer asked for Angelle's address to input it in his paperwork, the Cajun responded, "God's Country."

John Bel Edwards entered on Angelle's heels. Edwards had forcefully linked Angelle with unpopular Governor Bobby Jindal in the first attack ad of the race, on African-American-oriented radio stations across God's Country. Nevertheless, the two men had developed a camaraderie after appearing at numerous candidate forums together—almost all of them *sans* Vitter. They introduced their wives to each other, and Donna Edwards, in a cute moment, playfully tickled one of the giggling twins Angelle was holding in his arms.

When Angelle spoke to reporters, he said he was "excited to be introducing my brand of politics to Louisiana." Asked about Vitter's fundraising advantage, Angelle shot back, "This is an election, not an auction."

What about his ties to Jindal?

"I got elected before Bobby Jindal even had a driver's license,"

Angelle retorted.

As he walked back through the lobby, two young women in yellow construction helmets and job-site vests held up a cardboard sign: "The Angelle Pipeline," read black lettering over an orange map of Louisiana, covered in part by a pipeline with the words "Sunoco" and "574K to Scott Angelle." Images of dollar bills were flowing out of the pipeline from Sunoco. This was a bit of guerrilla theater, just like Brian and his "Diaper Dave" sign, this one courtesy of Vitter supporters—not that anyone would admit to it at the time. The aim was to highlight payments that Angelle had received for sitting on the board of Sunoco Logistics Partners, a Dallas-based pipeline company; the payments had yet to make the news. Angelle brushed past as if he hadn't noticed the sign.

No one asked Edwards if he was too close to the governor. In fact, he *wanted* to talk about Jindal, to make sure everyone knew they weren't pals. "It's time to turn the page on the Jindal era," he said. "We have to put Louisiana first. That's not just the theme of the campaign but what I'll do as governor." Edwards added, "I've always stood up to Bobby Jindal."

Then came *the* question: "How are you going to win in a red state?"

"People in Louisiana won't be voting the party," Edwards replied. "They'll be voting the person."

No protesters met Edwards as he left—a telling sign of what would happen in the coming weeks, or rather, what wouldn't happen. For now, each of the three major Republicans would leave Edwards alone.

Dardenne was the last of the candidates to qualify, arriving with his wife Cathy. Like Vitter, he promised that voters would get a full-time governor. "I'll be in there getting my hands dirty," Dardenne said.

"The fun begins," he said with a smile as he ended the brief press conference.

In fact, the fun was awaiting him in the lobby. Two young women wore black berets, red neck scarves and black-and-white striped shirts—like sailors in the French Navy—and held up a giant mock copy of Dardenne's passport...except that in this passport photo, Dardenne wore a birthday hat and carried balloons, and his name was "TAX AND SPEND LIBERAL," his nationality was "RINO" (as in "Republican In Name Only"), and the Date of Issue was "2014 BIRTHDAY & VALENTINE'S DAY IN EUROPE." Instead of a passport number the sum $15,809.79 appeared.

If no one understood the message at the time, the pro-Vitter Fund for Louisiana's Future would make sure everyone understood in the next few weeks. On this day, Dardenne just smiled as he glanced at the two women. Ever-gracious, Cathy Dardenne stopped to tell them that they looked cute and then asked with a mischievous grin if they would give her the sign. They wouldn't.

One other incident enlivened the first morning of qualifying. It involved a 23-year-old television reporter named Derek Myers, who worked for WVLA–NBC 33/Fox 44 in Baton Rouge. Originally from a small town in Ohio, Myers had arrived at the station three weeks earlier, eager to make a name, an agenda that wouldn't surprise anyone who had seen his Twitter profile. His nickname in the newsroom, it said, was "bulldog." Myers had quickly picked up Vitter's scent and learned of an exchange of tweets in 2012 between Vitter's official Twitter account and that of a 20-year-old student whose handle was @ LuvMy_Kisses.

Both *Gawker* and *The Huffington Post* had reported the exchange, seeing it as an opportunity to resurrect Vitter's prostitution scandal. A Vitter spokesman said at the time that his boss hadn't actually sent out the tweet. Vitter didn't *ever* tweet, in fact. But the spokesman couldn't say who had sent out the tweet or why.

That was enough for Myers to go to the chain restaurant where the young woman worked in Baton Rouge in an attempt to find out more. She had no interest in talking to him.

Undeterred, Myers aimed to get Vitter to talk after he qualified. As Vitter and Wendy left the building and walked toward a gray family van in the parking lot, Myers followed in hot pursuit, a microphone in one hand and his cell phone in the other. His cameraman tried to keep up. "This woman says she knows you, Senator Vitter," Myers half-shouted, making a misstatement in an attempt to provoke a response from the senator. Vitter ignored the question and walked around the back of the van as Myers tried to show Vitter a photograph of the woman on his cell phone.

With the TV reporter one step behind Vitter, one of the senator's sign-holding supporters—a young woman in a white campaign t-shirt and shorts—indifferently tried to block him.

"Don't touch me!" Myers shouted, and the woman stepped aside. Myers followed the senator to the passenger side of the van. As Vitter laid his suit jacket on the front seat, Myers caught up and threw another question at him: "Senator Vitter, when's the last time you cheated on your wife?"

Showing impressive restraint, Vitter remained mute while he waited for the van's sliding door to open so he could climb in. Myers fired another question. "Senator Vitter, do you know this woman?" he demanded. "She claims she knows you. Do you still frequent prostitutes, Senator Vitter?"

Myers didn't let up as Vitter climbed into the backseat. "This woman says she knows you," Myers said. "Do you know her, Senator Vitter? When's the last time you cheated on your wife, Senator Vitter?"

Vitter closed the door. Myers reached in the open window with his microphone.

"Anything else?" Myers asked in a last stab. "Don't you think people deserve to hear answers?"

The van drove off and the Vitter supporters melted away, leaving Myers empty-handed. When he returned to the station, Myers got a telephone call from Luke Bolar, Vitter's aggressive communications director. "Who put you up to this?" Bolar demanded. "Which candidate put you up to this?"

"I'm insulted that you think I'd be a mouthpiece for any candidate," Myers replied.

Fifteen minutes later, the station news director asked Myers about an accusation that he had assaulted a Vitter staffer. He said it wasn't true.

At 2:30 p.m., the news director called Myers into his office. "We're going to part company," the news director said.

"What does that mean?" Myers asked.

"It means that today is your last day."

"Why? I was just doing my job."

The following day, *The Advocate* learned about the incident and called Myers for the story. Myers explained what had happened and said that he had overheard the reason he was fired: the Vitter campaign had threatened to pull its campaign ads from the station.

It was an explosive allegation. Both the Vitter campaign and the station's general manager said it wasn't true, and Myers couldn't support his claim with any hard evidence. The station's general manager said at the time that he was "surprised" the incident had even become a story, and decision-makers in the newsroom later said privately that Myers was already on his way out, although he didn't know it, after complaints about other stories he had reported.

Candidates still had two more days to qualify for governor and hundreds of other offices on the ballot, but the field for governor appeared to be set. Or was it? Rumors flew on Wednesday and Thursday morning: *Democratic power brokers were going to force Edwards out of the race because he couldn't win. Wendy Vitter was telling her husband that she had had enough and that he had to get out of the race. Dardenne and Angelle had met secretly, and one of them was going to cede the race to the other. Mitch Landrieu had changed his mind and was going to jump in.* No one could be sure if any of this was true, but one thing was clear: No one could run for governor who had not qualified by 4:30 p.m. on Thursday.

In the meantime, one big-name potential candidate still loomed: John Georges. On Wednesday, Georges flew to France with his wife Dathel to celebrate her birthday. One of Georges' attorneys, asked about the possibility of his getting in the race, said it wouldn't happen, since he had traveled to France. Georges, however, was gaming all of the possibilities from France—just in case, because he knew he could qualify by proxy. He also knew he hadn't taken the steps required to position himself to mount a formidable campaign. He hadn't toured the state lining up support or tried to raise any money. But how could he stay out if Edwards or Vitter chose at the last hour to step aside?

Georges, who had run for governor in 2007 and for mayor of New Orleans in 2010—and who had self-funded most of those unsuccessful campaigns—was hearing encouragement from some big political players to get in the race. Some genuinely wanted him to win. Others wanted him to be a spoiler to help their own candidate. Georges was smart enough to know which was which. At a minimum, he enjoyed being the center of attention at such a critical moment in the campaign.

On Thursday morning, from Bordeaux in the southwest of France, Georges called Jack Capella, a close friend and fellow political player. Capella was nominally the president of Georges Enterprises but in reality served as Georges' chief troubleshooter. Capella's legal and political background served Georges well. He was a longtime power broker in Jefferson Parish, the epicenter of Georges' business empire. Now, on the final day of qualifying, Georges asked Capella to drive to the Secretary of State's Office that afternoon with cash and qualifying papers—just in case someone got in or out of the governor's race and changed the dynamics in the businessman-politician's favor.

In fact, the previous weekend Georges had quietly mounted an effort to convince Dardenne to leave the race, based on Verne Kennedy's poll results. Georges argued that Dardenne's exit would weaken Vitter's ultimate chances of victory—but Dardenne's pulling out would also have presented an opportunity for Georges to get into the race. Dardenne had no interest in getting out.

Stephanie Riegel had been dogging Georges' possible entry into the race for weeks by checking regularly with him and Verne Kennedy, who polled for the group of businessmen Georges had organized. A former reporter with WWL–TV in New Orleans, Riegel now worked for *The Baton Rouge Business Report*. She wanted to be the first to report Georges' plans, thus scooping Georges' own reporters at *The Advocate* as well as those at the paper's arch-rival, *The Times-Picayune*. In August, she had reported that Georges' decision to step down as *Advocate* publisher fueled speculation that he might run, notwithstanding his frequent disavowals.

Now, on Thursday, following her morning workout, Riegel called Kennedy a final time to make sure that Georges was not running. Instead, to her surprise, the pollster told her that Georges might make a last-minute entry and that his attorney was heading to Baton Rouge with the necessary paperwork. Riegel texted Capella, whom she knew from her days at WWL. "Think it's worth my time to hang out at the Secretary of State's Office?" she asked. "Might I have the pleasure of seeing you today??"

"You just might," he texted back a half hour later, "but as of 8 am, I am not heading to Baton Rouge."

Riegel quickly wrote a story with the news about Georges and posted it on the *Business Report's* website. With the political world now abuzz, she drove to the Secretary of State's Office in case Capella showed up. At 11:47 a.m., Lamar White Jr., a liberal blogger, sent out a tweet: "Hearing unconfirmed rumors that John Georges will qualify for LA Gov by proxy at 3PM."

TV reporter Mark Armstrong got a call from his station, WBRZ in Baton Rouge. A source said Georges was about to land at Baton Rouge Airport and rush over in time to qualify in person. Could it be true? Armstrong doubted it, but he was waiting at the Secretary of State's Office, just in case.

Shortly before noon, with no sign of Georges or Capella, Riegel left to record her radio show, "Out to Lunch." Afterward, she reached Capella on the phone. "So he's going to file?" she asked.

"I'm not saying that, sweetheart," Capella replied, declining to say anything else.

"I'll see you when you get there," she said.

Riegel's article that morning had sent shivers through Mark Ballard, who headed *The Advocate*'s Capitol News Bureau. A pro's pro, Ballard did not relish having to cover the paper's owner running for governor. He emailed Riegel's article to *Advocate* editor Peter Kovacs and to new publisher Dan Shea. "What's up?" he asked them. Both men assured Ballard that Georges would not be a candidate. When Riegel returned to the Secretary of State's Office in the afternoon, however, Ballard grew worried that Georges might run after all.

After Capella left his office on Causeway Boulevard in Metairie and turned onto Interstate 10, he noticed a sedan following him. Just to be sure, he exited at LaPlace and stopped at a convenience store to buy something. Back on I-10, Capella saw the same sedan trailing him. It followed him all the way to the Secretary of State's Office, where he arrived at about 3:30 p.m., slowly passed by the entrance, and parked nearby. Riegel, maintaining a stakeout with Ballard and several other reporters, spotted him. They rushed up to Capella's white Land Cruiser and tapped on the window. With a cellphone pressed to his ear, he rolled down the window. "I'm on the phone," he said with a smile, and rolled the window back up. It began to rain.

The reporters retreated to the lobby of the Secretary of State's Office.

The 4:30 p.m. filing deadline was quickly approaching. Would Georges qualify? Ballard emailed Shea and Kovacs again to report Capella's arrival. They again told him not to worry. Secretary of State Tom Schedler and Meg Casper, his press secretary, came to the lobby to observe the last-minute drama. "We're going to have to shut the door at 4:30 p.m.," Schedler said aloud to no one in particular.

Just about then, Capella texted Riegel: "Come out to my car."

"I'm going outside," Riegel told the others. "I want to find out what's going on." Two TV cameramen followed her into the rain. Capella had just gotten off the phone with Georges. Riegel knocked on Capella's window. He rolled it down. "He's not going to do it," the attorney said. No one else had entered the race, and none of the four who had qualified two days earlier had gotten out, so Georges had no political space to run and win.

"What the hell?" asked Riegel. "Why did you come?"

Capella shrugged, rolled up his window and drove off. Riegel posted an updated article reporting that Georges was staying out. Ballard had gotten the news in an email from Georges while Riegel was at Capella's car. Ballard had prepared two ledes for his news story. He went with the one that said the final day of qualifying contained no surprises and filed his story.

Georges was not the only one waiting in the wings. Longtime Angola State Penitentiary Warden Burl Cain made last-minute moves as well. A warden at various prisons for the past 34 years, Cain gained national renown soon after taking over Angola in 1995, thanks to his faith-driven changes at the historically violent prison. He was the hero of a 1998 documentary titled *The Farm: Angola USA* and a 2005 biography, *Cain's Redemption: A Story of Hope and Transformation in America's Bloodiest Prison.* Had he qualified, Cain probably would not have been considered a major candidate, but he could have created a distraction for fellow Democrat Edwards.

A poll paid for by his supporters showed Cain with only 1 percent. Nonetheless, he made a last-ditch effort to get donations pledged for a possible campaign and claimed he "was very close" to qualifying. "I was sitting over there at TJ Ribs in the parking lot," Cain said later that evening, referencing the Baton Rouge restaurant just down Interstate

10 from the Secretary of State's Office. At the end of the day, Cain chose the ribs over the race.

The field was now set: The four major candidates, David Vitter, John Bel Edwards, Scott Angelle, and Jay Dardenne—along with five minor candidates—would battle for the two runoff spots.

Just as he had cleared the field for Bill Cassidy to take out Mary Landrieu in the Senate race a year earlier, Vitter now had the field he wanted in the governor's race. So did Edwards.

One of them had to be wrong.

15

"That was a gut shot"

One day in May 2015, Don Carmouche, his son John, and their law partner Vic Marcello were sitting around a conference table at their law firm in Baton Rouge discussing the governor's race. Don Carmouche, in particular, had been stewing for weeks about the election, and now he felt pressed to make a decision. Which candidate should they back? A lot was at stake.

The three men were trial attorneys at the Talbot, Carmouche & Marcello law firm. They did not handle the kinds of personal injury or mass tort cases that their fellow trial lawyers typically filed. Instead, they focused on a very specific type of case known as *legacy lawsuits*. After the firm won several big judgments in the 1990s, landowners throughout Louisiana hired the group to sue oil companies for polluting their aquifers and soil. The lawsuits were known as "legacy" cases because, although the original exploration and development—and resulting environmental damage—had oftentimes occurred years earlier, sometimes decades earlier, all companies that had conducted operations on the damaged land shared, under Louisiana law, the liability for damages.

By 2015, the Carmouche law firm had filed 182 of the 385 legacy cases identified by the Louisiana Department of Natural Resources. The Carmouches liked to say their goal was restoring Louisiana's environment and coast for their children and grandchildren, but the cases they brought also made them plenty of money—and some powerful enemies. Their success spawned anti-trial lawyer groups, such as Louisiana Lawsuit Abuse Watch, that considered their lawsuits harmful to the state's business climate.

When they sat down in May, the Carmouches realized that their firm's business model was at risk. On March 13, David Vitter had appeared with the other three leading candidates for governor at a forum in Lake Charles sponsored by the Louisiana Oil and Gas Association. From the get-go, Vitter was a favorite of the Oil Patch crowd. With a smile, he noted that his father had been a petroleum engineer at Chevron in charge of local oil production. He recalled how his dad had taken him as a child on repeated helicopter inspection trips in the Gulf of Mexico.

"I'm sure Chevron owners will never allow that anymore for children, but thank God they did in 1973 when I was 12," Vitter said. "It was a great part of my upbringing and education."

From there, Vitter left no doubt that he stood squarely with the oil and gas industry—and against the Carmouches, although he didn't mention them by name. He didn't have to; the crowd knew whom he meant. The senator noted that in 2012 he had weighed in on a legislative effort to clamp down on legacy lawsuits—but Governor Bobby Jindal wouldn't support the move. As a result, the two sides— the Carmouches and large landowners on one side and the oil and gas industry on the other—forged a shaky compromise that left the lawsuits intact. The oil and gas companies tried again in 2014 to limit the lawsuits, again with Vitter's support, but they failed when Jindal withheld his backing.

Now Vitter was promising that oil and gas wouldn't have a namby-pamby governor on this issue. "I am the only candidate for governor that is here that has made tort reform, litigation reform, major components of my platform," he told the appreciative crowd. "I'm the only candidate for governor this year who has said flat-out the biggest problem we have for our business climate is the litigation environment. We have to change it." He went on to cite a favorite figure from the industry—the United States Chamber of Commerce Institute for Legal Reform ranked Louisiana 49th among the 50 states, next to last, for its litigation climate.

Vitter also cited a conversation he had with the CEO of Hilcorp, a Houston-based oil and gas exploration company, who, according to Vitter, said that 70 of the 75 lawsuits against his company were filed in Louisiana. As a result, he no longer planned to invest in the state.

"That's why I'm going to take action," Vitter said.

He added that he had convened what he called "a tort working group" to devise a plan to stop the legacy lawsuits. In fact, the group at its next meeting would bring in the folks from Texas who had pushed through changes in the law that made it harder to sue there.

"And I'll be fully committed to that as governor, including taking a leadership role, including making sure the right committees of the Legislature have the right members on them," Vitter said. No one there doubted him.

Vitter took dead aim at the Carmouches on another front as well. "A strong governor certainly can make clear that our strategy for coastal restoration has to be a team effort statewide," he said. "If a parish wants to go its own way in litigation, it may have to go its own way in funding restoration, too." That was a clear threat, which was Vitter's style, because the Carmouches also represented coastal parishes in lawsuits against Big Oil over alleged damages to wetlands caused by pipelines and other oil-and-gas operations. There was nothing nuanced about Vitter when it came to intimidation: He wanted to put big-time trial lawyers out of business. For the Carmouches, watching the forum on videotape later was a sobering experience.

The Carmouches and Vic Marcello knew they had to respond. Besides, Don Carmouche, 74, liked a good political fight. He came from a political family. His grandfather Aubert Talbot had been the district attorney of the 23rd Judicial District—covering Ascension, Assumption, and St. James parishes—for 34 years before dying in office in 1954. Aubert's son Bert—Don Carmouche's uncle—succeeded him and held the job for another 31 years.

After Uncle Bert announced he would retire in 1985, Don Carmouche ran for the seat and won it. But he lacked his uncle's and grandfather's political skills and was defeated after a single six-year term. He returned to practicing law full time, made a lot of money, and raised even more for favored candidates. In time, Carmouche moved to Baton Rouge, where his son John later joined the firm.

In 2012, the Carmouches got involved big-time in a heated race to elect a Louisiana Supreme Court justice. They created a super PAC called the Clean Water and Land PAC to support Jeff Hughes, a Republican who had served as an appellate court judge on the Louisiana First Circuit Court of Appeal for eight years. Prior to that, Hughes had been a district court judge for 14 years and a private attorney for 12 years before that. "He has more experience as a judge than any of the other candidates," according to the Clean Water PAC's website. "Judge Hughes is known for his fiscal and social conservative agenda, with a pro-life, pro-gun, and pro-traditional marriage philosophy." The website said the PAC had selected Hughes "based on his conservative approach to protecting landowner rights and restoring our land and water to its natural state." That message resonated in the conservative Supreme Court district—God, guns, and freedom were typically a winning combination in Louisiana—but the real issue for the Carmouches was Hughes' position on legacy lawsuits.

The Clean Water and Land PAC spent $486,124 in support of Hughes during the election, paying for polling, direct mailers, and TV ads that portrayed Hughes as a "rock solid conservative." Attorneys in the Carmouche firm contributed roughly 75 percent of the super PAC's money. Hughes won handily.

Their success in electing Hughes created a template for the Carmouches as they discussed what to do about Vitter in their law office in May 2015. "We have to make a financial decision," someone said. "Either we give to the candidate we support, or we can put up a lot of money and make sure it's *not* Vitter." They decided to create another super PAC. This time the goal would be "ABV"—Anybody But Vitter. "I think it's a good business decision," John Carmouche told his father and Marcello as they ended the meeting.

Don Carmouche began calling trial attorney friends. "I know you have the same goal—to beat David Vitter," he said. "Do you want to help?" The answer, time and time again, was *no*. One reason for the early rejections was the Carmouches' reputation as mavericks among trial lawyers. They had dropped out of the trial lawyers' trade group, the Louisiana Association for Justice, after John Carmouche questioned how the association spent money. Another reason Don Carmouche struck out was that most trial lawyers, like a good many voters and pundits, considered Vitter unstoppable. Besides, another ABV group had just been formed.

It was called Gumbo PAC, the brainchild of Trey Ourso, a Democratic campaign operative who was steeped in Louisiana politics. As a boy, Ourso frequently lived with his grandparents in the neighborhood behind the Governor's Mansion. One of his grandparents' neighbors was Jimmie Davis, and young Trey often joined the former governor as he took his daily walk in the neighborhood. Ourso's stepfather was Joe Sevario, elected in 1975 to the state Senate from the Town of Prairieville, about 20 miles downriver from Baton Rouge. Sevario won re-election four more times. Ourso worked as a page in the Louisiana Senate beginning at age 12 and then, during his studies at Millsaps College, served as Sevario's legislative assistant.

During and after his time at LSU's law school, Ourso worked as a special counsel to Attorney General Richard Ieyoub. In 1997, Ourso became the executive director of the state Democratic Party. He stayed at his post until resigning in 2001 to form a consulting firm that specialized in direct mail for Democratic candidates and issues. His business partner was Michael Beychok, whose father Shelly had been a legendary lawyer and political fixer for Governor Edwin Edwards.

Ourso billed Gumbo PAC as a nonpartisan group that simply wanted "anybody but Vitter" as the next governor. Gumbo PAC's main goal was "to tackle and erode the aura of inevitability surrounding Vitter's ascension to the Governor's Mansion," as Ourso wrote later. For starters, he resurrected the senator's prostitution scandal. At that point in the campaign, it hadn't surfaced—and Ourso wasn't sure if anyone would *ever* raise it. When he launched Gumbo PAC on May

13, its website featured an anti-Vitter video from Charlie Melancon's 2010 Senate campaign entitled, "Forgotten Crimes." Though it got limited play in the media, it at least started chatter about Vitter's scandal.

Vitter spokesman Luke Bolar was quick to dismiss Gumbo PAC. "Sadly, this is more politics as usual from liberal Obama Democrats and their allies," Bolar said. "When you fight to really reform things—like taking away politicians' automatic pay raises and special Obamacare exemptions—this crowd is gonna come after you. But David Vitter is undeterred. He'll continue to lead, to lay out his plan to build a brighter future for all Louisianans." That exchange presaged the campaign showdown to come—anti-Vitter forces focusing on his character, and Vitter tying his foes to Obama.

Ourso wanted the website to give comfort to the anti-Vitter crowd—*You aren't alone!*—and provide a place where they could pass along anti-Vitter tips. By assisting political reporters and posting ads on Facebook, Ourso sought to chip away at Vitter. Down the road, he hoped, Gumbo PAC could serve as a vehicle for larger attacks against Vitter—if enough money became available. Because Ourso also lobbied for the Louisiana Association for Justice, he knew he could count on trial lawyers to pony up. Indeed, three such firms— Herman Herman & Katz in New Orleans, Gordon McKernan Injury Attorneys in Baton Rouge, and Cossich, Sumich, Parisola & Taylor in Belle Chasse—seeded Gumbo PAC with $50,000 apiece. That gave Ourso enough money to begin anti-Vitter ads on Facebook and to use a Facebook page to amplify news articles critical of the senator.

In early June, Gumbo PAC also rented a huge billboard alongside Interstate 10 near the Mercedes–Benz Superdome in New Orleans. Its message, in stark letters, was right to the point: "ABV—Anybody But Vitter." At that time and later during the campaign, the billboard generated media coverage for Gumbo PAC. Ourso later called it "our most public show of defiance."

Soon after launching Gumbo PAC, at a time when Vitter still looked invincible—and inevitable—the 44-year-old Ourso realized he had embarked on a lonely path in challenging the senator. One day at the Capitol, as he walked from the basement of the Senate side to Alario Hall on the House side, he noticed that people "turned away and pretended like I wasn't there," he recalled later. "It was hard to get anyone to talk to me. Remember, Vitter had a reputation for being vindictive."

Meanwhile, Ourso tried several times to get Don Carmouche to abandon his go-it-alone effort and join forces with Gumbo PAC. On August 26, they met once again at Carmouche's law office. Joining

Ourso were two trial attorneys from Opelousas, Pat and Craig Morrow, whose law firm had donated $25,000 to Gumbo PAC. As soon as they sat down, Carmouche told them, "Guys, I'm going to disappoint you. We're going to do our own thing." Carmouche was certain they could duplicate the success of the Hughes race and defeat Vitter. The Carmouche law firm would create its own super PAC the next day and call it the Louisiana Water Coalition.

By then, the Carmouches had hired the same pollster they used for the Hughes race in 2012. His name was Robert Green, and he worked for the Democratic firm of Penn Schoen in Washington. "Can Vitter be beat?" Don Carmouche asked Green when they first discussed the governor's race. "Are we just wasting our money?" chimed in his son John.

"Let's run a poll," replied Green. He firmly believed that numbers, not hunches, should dictate strategy.

Going in, Green thought Vitter was vulnerable to being tagged as a career Washington politician. But when he got the poll back on August 19, the results showed that voters were more concerned about Vitter's lack of judgment relating to the 2007 prostitution scandal. When Green oversampled Republicans to test various negative messages against Vitter, his approach showed deep concern about the behavior of a former Vitter aide named Brent Furer—and Vitter's response to that behavior. Furer was listed in some Capitol Hill directories as Vitter's director of women's issues, but the senator said later that he had never assigned him to that policy area—a distinction that became all the more important when Furer was arrested for domestic violence after slashing his girlfriend with a knife in 2008.

Furer, who had served in the First Gulf War, pleaded guilty to a lesser offense. Vitter suspended his pay for roughly two weeks, but kept him on staff until the slashing incident and earlier charges, including driving while intoxicated, became public in June 2010. Furer resigned shortly thereafter amid widespread media reports of his conduct—and equally widespread criticism of Vitter for keeping him on staff. Years later, one Vitter staff member confided that although the senator's office knew Furer suffered from post traumatic stress disorder, it had not done enough "due diligence" regarding his arrests.

Overall, Green's poll for the Carmouches showed that while voters thought Vitter had a solid conservative voting record, he had a favorable job rating of just 44 percent—and an unfavorable rating of 43 percent. That was not good at all for an incumbent senator seeking to win the state's highest office.

"Vitter was winning only 42 percent of his base," remembered Adam Rosenblatt, an associate of Green's. "We thought there was a chance to take this guy down."

For Hughes' 2012 Supreme Court race, the Carmouches had hired Roy Fletcher to craft their message. At the time of the 2015 governor's race, as Fletcher was already working for Scott Angelle, Green suggested they hire a Republican ad man, since their goal was pulling Republicans off Vitter. To get ideas, Green called Marty Wilson, a former collaborator who handled political campaigns for the Chamber of Commerce of California. This was not an easy proposition. Most potential Republican consultants had conflicts. Besides, who wanted to take on a sitting Republican senator who had a reputation for punishing those who crossed him?

Wilson in turn contacted Rob Stutzman, who had done work for the chamber's PAC. Stutzman *was* up for the job. He had served as communications director for California's attorney general and later as deputy communications director for California's then-celebrity Republican governor, Arnold Schwarzenegger, before creating his own consulting firm in Sacramento.

Stutzman said later of Vitter, "My view is the herd should be thinned of our bad candidates, and he might be one of the worst candidates we had anywhere in the country as an incumbent."

He got to work on an ad based on Green's polling data. "The voters knew about prostitutes," Stutzman recalled later. "Vitter tried to move on from it by saying *it was an indiscretion, my wife has forgiven me.* We wanted voters to think about it in a broader way—law-breaking— and add additional pieces of information, the employee who stabbed the girlfriend, and Vitter kept him on the payroll. We wanted voters to consider this in a way they hadn't considered it before. This also emboldened the other candidates—we were trying to define the issues in the race, what would come up in the debates."

Stutzman's first 30-second TV spot for the Carmouches' super PAC aired on September 9, the day after the four candidates qualified for governor. The ad was put together under tight wraps, with the super PAC's status as a so-called 527 political action committee allowing for minimal public disclosure of its donors and organizers. Less than a day after the spot aired, word leaked that the team behind the Clean Water PAC, including the Carmouche firm, had underwritten it. Media buy reports at the time showed as much as $627,000 behind the broadcast and cable TV campaign.

Entitled, "The People vs. David Vitter," the ad unfolded like a legal brief against the senator. It began with images of two newspaper articles—a 2007 story by the Associated Press headlined "Senator caught in 'DC Madam' scandal" followed by a quick shot of a 2015 Bob Mann column in *The Times-Picayune* headlined "Sen. Vitter has an image problem." Then came a brief clip of prostitute Wendy Ellis from her 2007 press conference with *Hustler* owner Larry Flynt.

"It was purely a sexual relationship," Ellis said matter-of-factly (although that was nothing more than a claim). The ad then shifted to an ABC News announcer reporting, "A guilty plea for a violent attack on an ex-girlfriend with a knife," referring to Furer, who had actually pled to a much lesser misdemeanor charge. The female narrator added, with an exaggerated air, "And Vitter kept his aide on staff years after he pled guilty to stabbing his girlfriend." The ad then showed a photo of the woman displaying the stab wound just below her chin. The closing argument came from Bill O'Reilly, the Fox News favorite, who said in a clip, "I don't think Vitter should be there, absolutely not."

The ad ended with the female narrator intoning, "We can do better than Vitter."

Kyle Ruckert, Vitter's campaign manager, almost missed the ad when it first appeared. He caught only the ending line. Ruckert hit the rewind button on his cable remote as his heart raced. For some time, he had expected something like this. He called John Brabender, the campaign's Virginia-based media consultant.

"How big is it?" Ruckert asked. "How big is the buy?"

"It's big," replied Brabender. "They're on radio, too."

"That was a gut shot," Ruckert said later.

Team Vitter did not take the hit lying down. The campaign's lawyers sprang into action, convincing television stations in Alexandria, Baton Rouge, Lafayette, and Monroe to pull the ad almost immediately. Rocky Daboval, general manager of WBRZ–TV in Baton Rouge, called the spot "misleading" and forced the anti-Vitter PAC to cut a revised spot. The fallout did not end there. Attorneys Alesia Ardoin and Gray Sexton, both former employees of the state Ethics Administration, stepped aside as the attorneys for the super PAC after the first ad aired. Vitter supporters in the media and elsewhere claimed the Sexton law firm had a conflict of interest because it had handled legal work for Vitter as well as for the entity that was now attacking him.

Ardoin and Sexton did not disclose the conflict to the Vitter campaign, which referred to their failure to do so as a "serious violation." Nonetheless, the attorneys were never publicly disciplined or sanctioned for their roles with the super PAC.

Four days after the Water Coalition ad ran—on September 13— *The Advocate* published a lengthy piece that didn't break any new ground but summarized in detail what was known about the senator and the scandal. It noted that the race had been tame above the surface but "in the shadows, a parallel, and much less polite, campaign has been unfolding" over Vitter's history with prostitutes. The article noted that "a small army of journalists, bloggers, private eyes, and opposition research specialists" had been chasing rumors about Vitter's "murky actions." The article also identified several members of that army—Ourso, the liberal blogger Lamar White Jr., and Jason Brad Berry, a New Orleans videographer and investigative blogger who published *The American Zombie* blog.

Vitter still held a wide lead in fundraising and had a large statewide profile, but, as University of Louisiana at Lafayette political scientist Pearson Cross told *The Advocate*, "Any new revelations could hurt him deeply with women voters, if not all voters. The stakes are high."

A day later, the prostitution issue flared once again. This time it came at an Alliance for Good Government forum at Loyola University's School of Law. Vitter and Dardenne were the only two candidates in attendance. It was a ho-hum affair until the final question: "Have you ever violated Title 14 under Louisiana statutes as an elected official?" To a layman, the query seemed innocent enough. But the real intent behind it became apparent when Dardenne answered the question.

Title 14 is the entire Criminal Code in Louisiana law, so the question actually was whether the candidates had ever committed a crime while in office.

"It's a question that ought to be asked," Dardenne told the small crowd. "I have never violated Title 14, and I never will."

Then it was Vitter's turn. "Off the top of my head," he said defensively, "I couldn't cite you Title 14. I don't know exactly what it says. But given that Jay Dardenne knows exactly what it's about, this question was obviously planted as a 'gotcha' question at me."

He repeated the accusation: "It's a gotcha question, not a good public debate question for a discussion about the future of Louisiana. So let's all recognize what's going on here and what it's all about. I've spoken about my past and how my family has dealt with that, actions from 15 years ago, and how me and my family have dealt with that. I'm very happy and very proud to say we've dealt with it just fine. If that's not good enough for you, then that's not good enough for you. But it is for Wendy [Vitter's wife], and it is for our family. It is for us. I really don't appreciate the games and the gotcha question planted on behalf of my opponents."

Vitter made a hallmark speedy exit. Afterward, the lieutenant governor expressed surprise that the senator—an attorney, like Dardenne—couldn't identify Title 14 as the Criminal Code. "It's the whole Criminal Code," Dardenne said. "Every lawyer knows that." As he walked away, Dardenne added, "I didn't even know the lady would ask the question."

Vitter's prostitution scandal had now broken perilously into the open, with more than five long weeks remaining until the October 24 primary. News of Vitter's awkward denial completely overshadowed the fact that Dardenne won the Alliance's coveted endorsement.

On September 22, two weeks after the Water Coalition launched its first ad and eight days after Vitter's Title 14 "gotcha" soliloquy at the Alliance forum, Green polled again for Carmouche's group. From a 44–43 percent favorable-to-unfavorable rating on August 19, Vitter had dropped to 37–53 percent barely a month later. Those were bad numbers for anyone, let alone for the early frontrunner and presumptive favorite. The senator was now clearly in trouble, though only a handful of insiders fully understood the depth of his problems.

16

"Release the Kraken"

Wars are won on the ground, not in the air—or so the old military saying goes. The caveat to that maxim is that in modern warfare, "air support" is critical to success on the ground.

So it is in politics, where the ground game is turnout on Election Day, also known as GOTV, or Get Out The Vote efforts. Much like a military invasion or maneuver, GOTV requires extraordinary planning and organization, as well as carefully coordinated logistics. The air game in politics is television advertising, which precedes GOTV by weeks or months, much like air strikes typically precede a ground invasion. Political TV ads are less targeted than GOTV, but just as in warfare, technology has made it possible to conduct surgical air strikes when the need arises.

The 2015 campaign for governor of Louisiana would be fought on the airwaves with an entirely new element: super PACs, which could now raise unlimited amounts of money from donors. The Fund for Louisiana's Future, a super PAC that was supporting Vitter, paved the way for the change by challenging Louisiana's statutory $100,000 cap for donor contributions to certain campaign committees. In its legal challenge, the Vitter-allied Fund cited the Supreme Court's 2010 *Citizens United* decision, which equated independent campaign expenditures with freedom of speech. In May 2014, a federal judge in New Orleans struck down the state's $100,000 cap, giving Team Vitter what it wanted.

The senator's national base of large corporate interests and wealthy businessmen could now pour millions into his supportive super PAC. The court ruling, however, came with one catch: Super PACs had to operate "independently" of the candidates they supported. As it turned out, that wasn't much of a hurdle, because candidates could still *attend* super PAC fundraising events as special guests. Thus, the Fund for Louisiana's Future would employ its own pollster, its own media consultant, and its own director, Joel DiGrado. Vitter and DiGrado could no longer communicate on strategy, which would present a major change, but DiGrado knew the thought patterns of Vitter and campaign manager Kyle Ruckert. He had worked for years as Vitter's communications director, a post he vacated in 2014 to run Senator Bill Cassidy's campaign. Instead of returning to Vitter's stable, he took over the super PAC. It was a perfect fit, with DiGrado believing he could read Vitter's needs without communicating and Vitter hoping he was right.

The Fund for Louisiana's Future kicked off the "independent" advertising campaign in late August with a positive spot that called Vitter a "reformer with results." Whether or not deliberate, that was the same tag line George W. Bush had used in one of his presidential campaign commercials in 2000.

Although the rise of super PACs was seen as a boon to Vitter, another super PAC, one supporting Scott Angelle, actually kicked off the negative super PAC war on September 8 with an attack on the senior senator. The ad, sponsored by a group called Louisiana Rising, aired on the same day that the four candidates qualified for governor.

"In Louisiana, David Vitter wants you to think he opposes Common Core," a female narrator said, referring to the new education standards that conservatives hated. The ad then played a clip from a Vitter ad that had begun to air nine days earlier, in which Vitter stood in a classroom and declared his opposition to the program. The ad then cut to a 2014 clip of Vitter in Washington, stating, "I strongly support the Common Core standards." Just in case that hadn't fully registered, the ad then replayed his statement of support.

"We all know David Vitter breaks his word," the narrator said. "You can't trust Vitter." The ad then switched to video of an animated Angelle and told viewers that he opposed Common Core. "Scott Angelle is a man you can trust," the ad concluded.

Vitter's flip-flop on the issue of Common Core had angered some of his long-time supporters. Lane Grigsby, a rough-cut businessman who had built a construction empire from the ground up, was among them. Grigsby asked the pro-Vitter super PAC to refund his $100,000 check. The donation came back. "I will not support his candidacy," Grigsby growled at the time.

Not long after, Vitter and Grigsby were slated to hunt together at Grigsby's ranch, and the businessman honored the invitation. The two mended fences during the hunt, and Grigsby eventually offered financial support anew.

"I think he's probably going to be governor," Grigsby said several months later, "and there might be areas where he'll need my help in the future, and I'm willing to do that."

Vitter would indeed need the help. On September 9, a day after

Louisiana Rising aired its first spot, the Louisiana Water Coalition suddenly appeared with its attack ad darkly painting Vitter as a scandalized politician who kept on staff an aide who had been arrested for stabbing his girlfriend.

Less than a week later, the Vitter campaign aired its latest positive spot—which had actually run during Vitter's 2010 Senate campaign. It featured a woman from the town of Geismar, south of Baton Rouge, crediting Vitter with helping her secure a liver transplant that saved her life. "I was dying. I was at death's door stop," Deborah Cazalot said, tugging at viewers' emotions. She told *The Advocate*, "I know he's made mistakes in the past. We've all made mistakes. He's the kind of person we ought to have in public office."

On September 15, Dardenne became the last candidate to take to the air. His ad sought to draw a clear distinction between him and Vitter, although it did so in a decidedly understated fashion, with awkward and jerky scenes featuring a form of stop-motion imagery that drew snarky comments from the other campaigns. As a low-key narrator said Dardenne "talks straight, because he's not a Washington politician," viewers saw images of the lieutenant governor speaking to a crowd at the Bayou Country Superfest in Baton Rouge. "He doesn't drive a wedge through our heart with partisan politics," the narrator intoned. Like the other candidates in their introductory ads, Dardenne wore blue jeans. Apparently focus groups had convinced consultants that wearing blue jeans made candidates seem in tune with the needs and desires of regular folks.

The day before, the pro-Vitter super PAC unleashed negative ads against both Angelle and Dardenne. One began with the announcer warning, "Jay Dardenne and Scott Angelle really have a lot in common. They both like tax increases." The other ended with the voiceover "Dardenne and Angelle, a pair of used car salesmen trying to sell Louisiana a clunker."

DiGrado went after both men, because he couldn't be sure which one presented a bigger threat to Vitter. While Angelle was the one moving up in the polls, attacking him alone could give Dardenne the votes the Cajun might lose. Likewise, Angelle was in a position to gain the votes that Dardenne might lose. DiGrado described his strategy as a game of "Whack-A-Mole"—hitting whichever candidate was moving up.

The whacks outraged Angelle, Dardenne, and their supporters, because the ads stretched the truth. Dardenne started referring to the super PAC as "The Fund for Making Stuff Up."

Vitter's negative spots aired only in Shreveport and Monroe, whereas the "reformer with results" commercial ran only in Baton

Rouge and Lafayette. Laying down negatives in north Louisiana served two purposes. The Vitter camp viewed Angelle and Dardenne as regional candidates, from Acadiana and Baton Rouge, respectively. Dardenne, in particular, had an LSU-focused campaign and had just been endorsed during an "All-American Fundraiser" by LSU greats Dale Brown, Skip Bertman, Billy Cannon, and Tommy Casanova.

Hitting both Dardenne and Angelle—especially Angelle—in north Louisiana, where they were trying to gain ground, was an effort to identify them as regional candidates. The move also helped shore up Vitter's electoral stronghold in south Louisiana.

Edwards had his own super PAC, but it had far less money—at this point, not even enough to go on television. It was named Louisiana Families First and had been created by Laura Veazey, a Democratic campaign operative, with state Senator Ben Nevers, a populist Democrat from Bogalusa serving as its chairman. The super PAC had been the best kept secret of the election cycle. While news coverage repeatedly cited Edwards as the only candidate without a supportive super PAC waiting in the wings, Veazey and Nevers had managed to register it with the state in May. The press found out only several months later, in early October, after the fund had begun advertising on African-American radio stations and social media sites. In all, Louisiana Families First would spend about $400,000 during the primary.

On September 19, Vitter went negative—or, as one of his aides had whispered to a reporter several weeks prior, "We're going to release the Kraken." Vitter's first attack ad tagged Dardenne as a liberal who, when he was a state senator, voted against the anti-abortion position six times and for taxes 21 times. As ominous images flashed on the screen, the ad said Dardenne had even voted to allow illegal aliens to keep coming to Louisiana. "And now there are 55,000 illegals in Louisiana," the announcer said in dark tones. "Jay Dardenne's ideas aren't just liberal," concluded the announcer. "They're dangerous."

Without a full campaign war chest, the best Dardenne could do was respond with a written statement. "These are the same false attacks that opponents have used against me for a decade, and the voters of Louisiana have elected me statewide four times," he said. "I am pro-life and my record clearly shows that, as does the 100 percent record from Louisiana Right to Life. This is typical Washington politics, playing fast and loose with the facts. David Vitter says I'm dangerous, and he's right. I'm dangerous because I'm the man who will beat him in a runoff and keep him in Washington." It was a good statement, but it couldn't match Vitter's air campaign of saturation bombing.

On September 19, Team Vitter also launched a TV broadside

against Angelle, claiming he had a lot in common with President Obama. Noting that Angelle had been a Democrat for 31 years—he switched to the Republican Party in 2010—the ad featured several photos of Obama and Angelle on a split screen. The spot also said that while on the Public Service Commission, Angelle took positions that the Obama administration favored. "Obama and Angelle," the ad concluded, "both wrong for Louisiana."

The irony here was not lost on Team Edwards. The Vitter forces were carpet-bombing their Republican opponents—lobbing the same grenades that Vitter had used against Democrats in previous campaigns.

On the same day, the Fund for Louisiana's Future unloaded on Angelle its most devastating attack spot of the primary campaign. The focus was the August 2012 collapse of a massive salt dome deep below a bayou in Assumption Parish, a collapse that soon evolved into a massive sinkhole threatening the entire community of Bayou Corne. The site was operated by Texas Brine and regulated by the Office of Conservation—a branch of the Department of Natural Resources, which Angelle headed at the time the sinkhole first appeared.

"Scott's Sinkhole," began the announcer, as viewers saw an overview of the site. Then came video of the ground and water swallowing a whole tree, like something from a horror movie. "Bayou Corne, an environmental disaster that forced more than 100 families from their homes," the announcer continued. The ad then showed Angelle and said that, as DNR secretary, "he never disclosed a failed integrity test. Then just five days later, Angelle suddenly resigned. Angelle took no responsibility."

Viewers saw more images of trees getting gobbled up as the announcer concluded, "First, Angelle failed Louisiana families. Then he quit on them. Scott's Sinkhole." The ad ended with a final image of another tree being swallowed whole, a fitting metaphor for what happened to the gains Angelle had made against Vitter over the summer.

The Angelle campaign responded by saying that he had resigned his post to run for the Public Service Commission, a plan that had been in the works for months, but as with Dardenne's reply to Vitter's first attack, Vitter's non-stop TV barrage drowned out Angelle's attempt to fight back.

Vitter, however, wasn't the only aggressor. The Louisiana Water Coalition, which had first hit Vitter in early September, slammed him again on September 22. This time, the ad focused exclusively on Brent Furer, the Vitter aide who had pled guilty to a lesser misdemeanor offense after his arrest for attacking his girlfriend with a knife. The ad noted that Vitter had kept Furer on his staff for two years afterward, and that Furer had resigned only after ABC News in 2010 reported the stabbing. At the time, the Vitter campaign claimed it had fired Furer.

"David Vitter?" the ad asked in conclusion. "He won't be a governor we can trust. We can do better than Vitter."

A day later, on September 23, it was Angelle's turn to hit back at Vitter. Angelle's 30-second spot said that Vitter had started "a false smear attack" against him, as Angelle had led the fight against President Obama's oil drilling moratorium and the EPA's "job-killing" rules. The ad showed warm images of Angelle, one hugging supporters while wearing casual clothes and another looking decisive in a coat and tie. The ad included a photo of Vitter grinning awkwardly. "David Vitter—he just can't tell the truth," the ad concluded.

Dardenne remained on the sidelines during the back and forth. He still didn't have the money to slam Vitter.

Within days, the pro-Vitter Fund for Louisiana's Future turned its attention to Dardenne with a spot entitled, "Jay's Birthday Bash." As viewers saw a birthday cake, a cork popping out of a champagne bottle, and Buckingham Palace, a female announcer said Dardenne had gone to Europe on his 60th birthday with his wife and major donors—and stuck taxpayers with a $34,011.02 tab. The ad infuriated Dardenne. He said he had met with German airline executives to promote a direct flight to New Orleans, which later materialized. He had also met with travel industry officials in Germany and England to promote tourism in Louisiana and had brought tourism officials to the state. Taxpayers had *not* paid for his wife or friends, he said. Dardenne also said he spent only $11,382.09 on both this and a similar tourism promotion trip two years earlier to France.

The air war had clearly driven a wedge between the leading Republican candidates for governor—with Vitter on one side, and Dardenne and Angelle on the other. The level of spending and the intensity of the attacks called to mind a Cold War military doctrine regarding the *ultimate* air war, one in which nuclear missiles come flying out of silos: "mutually assured destruction." Ironically, when Team Vitter challenged Louisiana's campaign contribution limit, an all-out war, in which Vitter might also present a target, was not on its radar. In addition to letting Vitter dump $950,000 from his federal campaign account into a state-based super PAC supporting him for governor, however, the court victory also opened the way for others to create super PACs that would take aim at him.

After the election, Kathleen Blanco, who had felt the sting of Vitter's barbs many times, would look back and call Vitter's plan a classic example of Shakespearean "hoist on his own petard" justice.

At a minimum, the outcome proved the wisdom of a more recent adage: Be careful what you wish for—you may get it.

In response to criticism about the intensity of his attacks against Dardenne and Angelle, Vitter argued that he was merely standing up for himself and responding to allegations lobbed at him, but the senator's attacks rubbed publisher Rolfe McCollister Jr. the wrong way. McCollister had founded and now served as the chief executive officer of Louisiana Business Inc., which published the *Greater Baton Rouge Business Report*, *225* magazine and several other niche publications. He had served on just about every important civic board in Baton Rouge and took a keen interest in politics—running twice for mayor-president of East Baton Rouge Parish.

McCollister had been part of Buddy Roemer's inner circle when Roemer was governor from 1988 to 1992, and he served as Bobby Jindal's campaign treasurer and transition chair when Jindal was elected governor in 2007. Jindal gave McCollister, an LSU grad, a patronage plum by naming him to the LSU Board of Supervisors, just as Roemer had. Along with overseeing his media publications, he wrote a weekly column for the *Business Report* from a decidedly conservative point of view. On September 30, he weighed in on Vitter's attacks against the two Republicans.

"Vitter may be forgiven for his past 'sins,' but he is still mean-spirited, vindictive, and threatening to people—not your 'humble servant leader,'" wrote McCollister. "Vitter cares about Vitter, and he knows if he doesn't win, he could even lose his Senate seat next year. He is scary, and many are afraid to speak out. Does that sound like the governor we want leading our state?…Vitter running sleazy attack ads only reinforces his mean and nasty reputation."

While it was true that many Vitter critics in the political arena found him "scary," that did not stop them from circulating McCollister's column far and wide via social media.

Meanwhile, John Bel Edwards and his campaign team cheered the Republicans' internecine air war. As the three Republicans blasted each other, Edwards remained unscathed—just as he had planned. A poll taken by Rob Green for the Louisiana Water Coalition from September 20 to 22 showed the damage to Vitter—and the benefits to Edwards. Compared to a month earlier, Edwards' favorability rate had risen by eight percentage points while Vitter's had dropped by seven points. The September poll showed Edwards, Dardenne, and Angelle all with about 25 percent unfavorable ratings, while Vitter's was sky high at 53 percent. Another ominous sign for Vitter showed up when voters were asked to list their second choice for governor. This would matter to whoever made the runoff. Among Dardenne voters, Edwards led Vitter 33 percent to 18 percent as their second choice. Among Angelle supporters, Vitter led Edwards—but by only 29 percent to 26 percent. On another question, 40 percent of voters said they would absolutely not vote for Vitter.

Edwards launched his first TV ad on September 8, the day that he and the three other candidates qualified for governor. His 33-year-old media consultant, Jared Arsement, had grown up at the knees of Coach and Kathleen Blanco—literally. Arsement's mother had been Coach's secretary for years at the University of Louisiana at Lafayette when Coach was the dean of student affairs. In 1995, when he was 14, Arsement was an extra in a campaign ad for Kathleen Blanco when she was elected lieutenant governor. He was an extra in another ad four years later when she won re-election. Her media consultant at the time was Ray Teddlie, who was based in New Orleans.

The Blancos got Teddlie to bring Arsement aboard after he completed his degree in film studies from the University of New Orleans. He assisted Teddlie when Teddlie served as the media consultant for John Georges' failed 2010 campaign for mayor of New Orleans. By then, Teddlie was dying of Parkinson's disease. In early 2011, Arsement created the media campaign for Jonathan Perry when he won a special election to the state Senate—the race that gave Republicans their first majority in the Senate since Reconstruction. Later that year, Arsement met Edwards, who hired him to produce TV and radio ads for House Democrats in the legislative campaigns Edwards was coordinating. In 2012, the year Teddlie died, Arsement did the TV ads for Scott Angelle, another Republican, when Angelle won a seat on the Public Service Commission. Unlike national political consultants, Arsement worked for candidates in both parties.

Edwards hired Arsement for his gubernatorial campaign in January 2013, when Angelle still wasn't sure whether he would run.

Two days after Edwards had inadvertently announced his candidacy on Jim Engster's radio talk show in February 2013, he asked Arsement to produce a video biography that would introduce him to voters. Arsement said he liked the idea but told Edwards that he needed to spend time with him to get to know his story.

Arsement drove to Amite on March 1, and the two men climbed into Edwards' pickup truck for a tour that took them onto East Mulberry Street in downtown past Edwards' boyhood home, now the Hitching Post restaurant. They stopped several blocks away outside Amite High School, and again outside St. Helena Catholic Church, where Edwards related how his family filled an entire pew when he was a boy, and how he was now a Eucharistic minister, altar server, and reader. Edwards also talked about his time at West Point and his adherence to its Honor Code. Arsement was impressed.

They returned to Amite two weeks later to tape the biopic. Viewers around the state got their first glimpse of Edwards' personal story in a September 8 TV ad. "John Bel Edwards is a born leader," it began. The spot showed him as a high school quarterback and as an honors graduate at West Point. It noted he had led paratroopers in the 82nd Airborne Division and then returned home to raise a family. It identified him as pro-Second Amendment while showing him in hunting camo with his son, John Miller. "A fighter for education, health care, and working families," the ad continued, "who puts Louisiana first."

The next Edwards ad aired on September 21 and emphasized issues important to Democratic voters. The spot said he had voted for equal pay for women, had supported giving working families increased access to health care, had stood up for teachers, and had voted to increase the minimum wage. "And I'm the only one [of the gubernatorial candidates] who fought against Bobby Jindal's disastrous policies," Edwards said in the ad, which closed with the campaign's tagline: Edwards would *put Louisiana first*, a clear dig at Jindal.

The third Edwards ad also had its origins in Jared Arsement's March 2013 visit to Amite. During their drive around town, Edwards began offhandedly telling Arsement a story as they approached the railroad tracks. "I don't know if this is appropriate in a campaign," Edwards said, "but one of the big criticisms of Democrats is not being pro-life. Not only am I pro-life, but we had a situation with our first daughter, Samantha." He then told Arsement about the decision that he and Donna faced when they learned that she was pregnant in Hawaii with a child who would have spina bifida. Their doctor recommended to Donna that they abort the fetus, but they decided to give birth to Samantha.

"What do you think?" Edwards asked. "Is that a story people would respond to?"

"John Bel," replied Arsement, "if you lose this election and we don't tell this story, Ray Teddlie will rise from the dead and strangle me."

Edwards said he couldn't air the story without Samantha's permission. Over the years, as Samantha had struggled, Donna had told her daughter that one day she would share her story with others. Now was the time, Samantha agreed.

Arsement filmed the spot at their home in Roseland in June 2015. They needed several takes because Donna kept choking up as she told the story. At one point, Samantha, a 23-year-old master's degree

John Bel Edwards and his high school sweetheart Donna on their wedding day

John Bel Edwards, an Army Ranger, with his parents Frank and Dora Jean

LSU student body president Jay Dardenne with Governor Edwin Edwards in 1977

David Vitter and Bobby Jindal, while the two men were allies and on the political upswing, during Vitter's 2004 Senate campaign

Photo by: Amy Mikler

State Representative John Bel Edwards and his son John Miller watch "Mo" dive into a pond in a photo shoot from his 2011 re-election campaign

Photo by: Jeremy Alford

Senator David Vitter and Lieutenant Governor Jay Dardenne answer questions following an early campaign forum hosted by the Louisiana Oil and Gas Association

Photo by: Ryan Cross

Scott Angelle got an enthusiastic response at a rally in his hometown of Breaux Brid

New Orleans Mayor
Mitch Landrieu
seemed likely to
be the strongest
Democrat in the
race, if he ran

Photo by: Patrick Dennis/The Advocate

Photo by: Mary-Patricia Wray

John Bel Edwards, standing, led legislative Democrats from his seat
in the back corner of the state House of Representatives

Photo by: Mary-Patricia Wray

Edwards rallied traditional Democratic groups behind his candidacy,
including at this event on the steps of the State Capitol

Scott Angelle showed off his twin granddaughters when he qualified for governor in September 2015

Jay Dardenne signed the papers to qualify for governor

David Vitter had plenty of support at this campaign rally in Kenner

to by: Tyler Bridges

David Vitter and Scott Angelle leave the stage following a televised debate at WDSU, which came under fire for its focus on social questions

Roy Fletcher, who produced TV ads for Scott Angelle, preferred a bird's eye view on his sets

Jay Dardenne was the only candidate to attend a forum at the Old Governor's Mansion, and what he said about David Vitter made news

Photo by: Ryan Cross

Scott Angelle gave his take to reporters after one of the televised gubernatorial debates

Photo by: Mary-Patricia Wray

John Bel Edwards had few moments to himself during the later stages of the governor's race

Blogger Jason Brad Berry was determined to report the full extent of David Vitter's sex scandal

Photo: Courtesy of Jason Brad Berry

Berry found Wendy Ellis, but could her explosive allegations be believed?

Photo: Courtesy of Jason Brad Berry

Photo by: Tyler Bridges

Josh the Tracker, right, was a ubiquitous but usually unwelcome presence at campaign events for the three candidates not named David Vitter

John Bel Edwards, Jay Dardenne, and Scott Angelle became accustomed to appearing at campaign forums that David Vitter skipped

"We have a stench that is getting ready to come over Louisiana," Scott Angelle told a statewide televised audience during the primary campaign's final debate, at LSU's Manship School of Mass Communication

Private Investigator
Robert Frenzel
bungled a visit to the
Royal Blend coffee
shop in Metairie

Photo: Courtesy of Danny DeNoux

Jefferson Parish
Sheriff Newell
Normand was not
amused by Frenzel's
visit and wanted to
make David Vitter
pay the political
price for it

Photo by: Matthew Hinton/The Advocate

The Royal Blend might be
the last place you would
expect David Vitter to visit,
but he held meetings there
one morning during the
runoff election

Photo by: Tyler Bridges

David and Wendy Vitter marked his showing on the night of the
gubernatorial primary with a kiss

Cartoon by: Walt Handelsman

Pulitzer-Prize winning cartoonist Walt Handelsman had this take on what David Vitter would face in the runoff

Photo by: Jeremy Alford

Ironically, David Vitter stopped playing hide-and-seek with reporters during the runoff

Photo by: Hilary Scheinuk/The Advocate

The two remaining candidates did not enjoy warm relations when they met in this televised debate during the runoff

Photo by: Mary-Patricia Wray

When the four-time Governor Edwards spoke, the would-be Governor Edwards listened

After the votes were counted, on November 21, 2015,
at the Monteleone Hotel in New Orleans

student at Southeastern Louisiana University in Hammond, poked her head into the room where they were filming. Donna choked up again upon seeing her daughter.

When Arsement had written a rough draft of the script, he sent it to Sam Jones and the Blancos. All three expressed concern that it was too personal, too dramatic. Jones noted that 15 to 18 percent of voters said that having a pro-choice candidate was very important to them. Would the pro-life decision turn them off? "This is a huge part of this man's life," Arsement replied. "This is telling people who he is. You just have to see the final product. Then you can judge whether it will turn people off."

Jones previewed the final version on his cell phone to 30 different women, several of whom teared up watching it. Jones was now convinced. The Edwardses' decision to have Samantha was living proof of their pro-life bona fides, but the ad also showed that they had freely made the decision, which could appeal to the pro-choice crowd as well.

Edwards and Donna showed it one evening to a group of lawyers and businessmen from Lake Charles at a hunting lodge in Cameron Parish called Grosse Savanne. The owner was Buddy Leach, a wealthy businessman who had formerly chaired the state Democratic Party. A hardened trial lawyer named Rock Palermo inhaled after watching the ad. "Wow!" he said and immediately joined others in calling out, "Show it again." Edwards showed it a second time, a third time, and a fourth time. The ad mesmerized Palermo. Edwards also showed the ad to a group of trial attorneys during their annual conference at the Windsor Court Hotel in New Orleans. Afterward, you could hear a pin drop. "God, that will make you cry," an attorney sitting in the back of the room called out.

The ad aired statewide on October 5, less than three weeks before the primary—and at a time while Vitter was still saturation bombing his fellow Republicans. In the spot, Donna Edwards sat alongside her husband and related how, when she was 20 weeks pregnant, a doctor told them that the child would have spina bifida, a serious problem of the spinal cord, and encouraged her to get an abortion.

"But John Bel never flinched," Donna told viewers. "He just said no." The couple glanced at each other. "'We're going to love this baby no matter what,'" she added. "And at that moment, I watched the boy I fell in love with become the man I'm still in love with today." Donna added—as the ad showed Samantha and her fiancée holding hands— that their daughter was going to get married that spring. "She's living proof," Donna concluded, "that John Bel Edwards lives his values every day."

The ad particularly resonated with white women, a key group for Edwards. Before it aired, Edwards was trailing Vitter by four points among all voters in a four-candidate field, according to Jim Kitchens' internal poll. Afterward, Edwards had a nine-point advantage, 31 percent to 22 percent.

The ad also benefitted Edwards by taking the abortion issue off the table, a huge benefit for a Democrat in a state that the National Right to Life Federation reported year after year was the most pro-life in the union. Only the year before, Bill Cassidy had bludgeoned Mary Landrieu during their Senate election for her pro-choice stance.

So much was going Edwards' way, but he still hadn't nailed down the support of New Orleans Mayor Mitch Landrieu and his major campaign donors. For months, Mitch had been actively discouraging them from giving to Edwards, telling them that the state representative from Amite had no chance against Vitter. Mary Landrieu, after all, had spent roughly $18 million and lost. Edwards hadn't raised even $2 million in the governor's race. Sam Jones and other members of Edwards' inner circle believed that Mitch wanted Dardenne or Angelle to make the runoff against Vitter. Because Mitch was talking to political insiders, his doubts got back to Edwards. At one meeting with Mitch, Edwards told him that he had a request. "What's that?" Mitch asked.

"You could stop telling people that I can't win," Edwards said.

On September 10, some of Landrieu's key supporters met at the Rib Room Restaurant in the Omni Hotel in the heart of the French Quarter to try to decide where to put their money in the coming weeks. Among those attending were Blair Boutte, a bail bondsman and New Orleans political operative; Norma Jane Sabiston, an outside political advisor; Ryan Berni, a top political aide to Landrieu; and Emily Arata, another top Landrieu aide. The group heard pitches for support from people who ran three different political action committees: Ravi Sangisetty, a New Orleans trial attorney who ran the Blue Bayou PAC, which gave money to Democratic House candidates; Eva Kemp, the director of the pro-charter school Democrats for Education Reform LA PAC; and Trey Ourso, who headed Gumbo PAC, the "Anybody But Vitter" super PAC. Landrieu's advisers and the PAC directors discussed strategies through dinner, but the meeting ended inconclusively.

Landrieu would soon have another chance to settle the question of whom to support financially. On September 21, Hillary Clinton made a morning campaign appearance in Baton Rouge and then appeared at a fundraiser at the home of Jim Bernhard, the Shaw Group founder who now owned a private equity firm after selling Shaw two years earlier. Bernhard had briefly served as state Democratic Party chair while Kathleen Blanco was governor, and had expressed interest in running for governor himself at one point but had not followed through. Several dozen people attended the daytime fundraiser for Clinton. When it was over, several members of Landrieu's team, at his invitation, repaired to a private room at Ruffino's, an Italian-Creole restaurant near Bernhard's home, for a late lunch.

Berni began by telling everyone that the purpose of the meeting was to help the mayor and key supporters settle on whom to back for governor over the next several weeks. The primary election, on October 24, was just around the corner. Berni then ceded the floor to the mayor, who gave an impassioned plea for the gathering to come together to defeat Vitter, who, he said, would be a disaster for the state. But, Landrieu noted, Vitter had millions of dollars more than Edwards. The mayor said it wasn't difficult for a Democrat to get 40 percent of the vote in the governor's race. It was harder to get 45 percent. And it was even harder to get 50 percent plus 1. Landrieu said he didn't think Edwards could reach 50 percent plus 1 against Vitter and then asked, "What do you want to do? What do you want me to do?"

Sangisetty stood up and explained the benefits of trying to stop Vitter by electing Democratic legislators who would oppose him. Kemp next gave a similar pitch—backing Democratic legislators who would support access to quality childcare and other education issues. Ourso followed and told everyone why they ought to give money to Gumbo PAC. "How much are you hoping to raise to defeat Vitter?" asked Bernhard.

"One million dollars," replied Ourso.

"This guy will chew you up and spit you out," Bernhard said. "Unless you're going to put up $6 or $7 million, you won't have an impact on the race."

Ourso countered that they had to start somewhere and do something. Landrieu stood up again and defended giving their money to Gumbo PAC. That was a much better bet than Edwards, he said.

Several others spoke up, including Sean Reilly, a Baton Rouge businessman and former Democratic state House member who said he favored Dardenne. Someone else opined in favor of Angelle. By then, Russ Herman could stay silent no longer. A veteran trial attorney, Herman was accustomed to commanding attention from a judge or a jury in court, and he had been close to the mayor for years. Landrieu had clerked for Herman's law firm not long after graduating from law school. Now Herman had an unwanted message. "Mr. Mayor, I understand what you've said," Herman began. "But there is only one candidate to support, and that is John Bel. He can win. He will win. John Bel is a fighter, and he and Donna are tireless. There will be a runoff, and John Bel, an honorable warrior with a many-generation pedigree as a Democrat, will defeat Vitter. Look at Vitter's negatives! Nobody likes him!"

Herman's wife Sandra followed immediately. With a long career as a business woman and senior state government official—she was previously known as Sandra Thompson, having married Russ late in life—she had no qualms about challenging a powerful man, tactfully. Fearing that Landrieu had been swaying the crowd against Edwards, she wanted to build on her husband's argument. "If everybody would stand up and support John Bel, he'll win," she said. "Mitch, Mary's election was a totally different campaign."

The mayor interrupted her to disagree. "Once Vitter begins to attack John Bel...."

It was Sandra Herman's turn to cut in. "What can he say?" she asked, noting Edwards' Boy Scout background.

"They'll find something," Landrieu said.

"Mitch, we know what you went through with Mary's race," she said. "But it's a totally different race. John Bel is going to win."

Sandra Herman looked around the room and made eye contact with some of the most powerful Democrats in the state. "If the people in this room would stand up here today and support John Bel Edwards," she said, "he would win."

She turned to Ourso. "You're a strong Democrat," she said. "What are you going to do?"

"I'll be voting for John Bel," he replied.

Sandra Herman said she had worked for the DNR when Scott Angelle was the secretary and was not a fan of how he managed the agency. Then she added, "Russ and I are friends of Jay Dardenne, but he's running fourth."

She turned to the mayor. "Okay, Mitch, if you support Angelle or Dardenne and one of them wins, what do you do in four years, as a loyal Democrat?" she asked. "Do you support him for re-election or do you run against him—and how do you justify the flip-flop?"

Congressman Cedric Richmond stepped in. "My supporters," he said, "will be with John Bel Edwards, and I predict that if and when the tide starts to turn toward John Bel, the dominoes will fall, because then people who really don't like Vitter will see that it's okay to vote against him." This meeting, like the one in the Rib Room, ended inconclusively.

Any momentum for Landrieu to swing the group behind Angelle, Dardenne, or the Anybody But Vitter movement had died.

That was a victory for Edwards, but most pundits, like Landrieu, still believed Vitter would triumph. "If John Bel Edwards is in the runoff he will get the shock of his life," Bernie Pinsonat, a campaign consultant and pollster for Southern Media & Opinion Research, told Lafayette's KATC-TV at the end of September. "He hasn't run statewide before. The Republicans will identify him as a Barack-Obama-left-leaning liberal. He will have trouble raising money."

Pinsonat obviously subscribed to the theory that wars could be won solely in the air. He also was not one to mince words, especially when giving a soundbite to a reporter—and he was never in doubt. Pinsonat's theory of political warfare, like that of so many other experts, was about to be tested as the primary campaign entered the home stretch.

17

"Answer *The Question*"

In hotly contested elections, suspicion and paranoia sometimes function as a form of currency. For months, John Bel Edwards, Jay Dardenne, and Scott Angelle had appeared at campaign forums across the state while David Vitter skipped most of them, citing the press of Senate business in Washington. Vitter also missed the campaign's first televised debate on September 2 at Southeastern Louisiana University in Hammond, but he agreed to attend the next debate, an hour-long event on October 1 at WDSU-TV, the NBC affiliate in New Orleans. Two of the minor candidates would also be there.

Vitter's decision to appear at that debate triggered speculation and rumors. *He got the questions in advance! The station's producers promised not to ask him* The Question*! Vitter insisted on including minor candidates to give less air time to his main foes!* The rumor mill was in overdrive.

Yes, viewers would get the benefit of hearing from the four major candidates—and also from Jeremy Odom, a United States Army veteran, tax consultant, and Baptist minister from Natchitoches; and from Cary Deaton, a long-time intellectual property rights attorney from Metairie who had run for governor in 2011, when Bobby Jindal cruised to victory over Tara Hollis, a little-known Democrat. Deaton won only 5 percent in that race.

Jonathan Shelley, the news director at WDSU, denied any favoritism for Vitter and said he invited Odom and Deaton because the station had included minor candidates in the previous year's mayoral debate. Still, including the two men would take valuable air time from the main combatants. Besides, Odom and Deaton were barely campaigning and didn't register in polls, including the most recent independent survey, the first for a media outlet. Ron Faucheux had conducted it for WWL-TV, the CBS affiliate and the dominant news station in the state, and for *The Advocate*. Faucheux, a former state representative and former editor of *Campaigns & Elections* magazine, had run for mayor of New Orleans in 1982. He then operated his own polling firm, Clarus Research Group.

Surveying 800 voters statewide from September 20 to 23, Faucheux found that Vitter's formidable lead had vanished. Whereas Vitter had had 38 percent of the vote in Southern Media's April poll, now Vitter and Edwards were tied at 24 percent, with Angelle and Dardenne each trailing by about 10 points.

Especially worrying for Vitter, Faucheux's poll showed that each of the senator's three opponents—including Edwards—beating him by four to seven points in a head-to-head runoff-style matchup. Faucheux was the first media pollster to say that Edwards had a visible path to victory over Vitter.

Gambit, the New Orleans alt-weekly,[2] summed up the race in its political column: "On top of all that bad news for Vitter, consider this: Because he has virtually universal name recognition, unlike his three major opponents, Vitter has little if any room to improve his 24 percent share of the vote. That may explain why his 'independent' Super PACs are attacking Angelle and Dardenne. Those two Republicans and Edwards all have significant room to grow because they are known well by only about half the state's voters. Vitter's attacks are intended to keep them from creeping up on him as his support dwindles—but that has occurred anyway, according to the WWL/*Advocate* poll."

Neither Angelle nor Dardenne could defeat Vitter, however, without first securing a spot in the runoff. Each man had three weeks, beginning with the WDSU debate, to overtake Vitter and face Edwards, who, as the only Democrat, seemed to have already locked up a runoff spot. For his part, Edwards wanted Vitter for his runoff opponent, and Vitter likewise wanted the Democrat. "Edwards needs to avoid partisan rhetoric and run on a theme of change, contrasting with Jindal's governing style and policies," Faucheux told Elizabeth Crisp for *The Advocate's* article on the poll. "If Vitter wins a runoff spot on the basis of a polarized partisan coalition and doesn't improve his positive ratings in the process, he risks winning the primary and losing the runoff."

Dardenne and Angelle, reported Crisp, were splitting voters who wanted a Republican alternative to Vitter. Dardenne and Angelle, Faucheux said, "have the same task: Become the Republican alternative to Vitter and become the candidate who is perceived by Democrats and anti-Vitter independents as having the best chance to beat Vitter in a runoff."

---

[2] *Gambit* is co-owned by Clancy DuBos, who edited this book. DuBos is also the *Gambit* political editor and columnist quoted here.

Larry J. Sabato's Crystal Ball, a national prediction site for big races, took notice of the changing landscape when it changed the status of the race in its October 1 summary: "Overall, there does seem to be at least a small twinkling of daylight for Democrats in the Pelican State, which leads us to shift this race from Safe Republican to Likely Republican. At the end of the day, though, a Republican hold on Baton Rouge remains the most likely outcome in late November."

At 6 p.m. on October 1, WDSU cut to news anchor Scott Walker, the station's debate moderator, standing in Studio B. He faced the six candidates, who were standing on a raised stage, each one behind a glass lectern, with blue curtains as a backdrop. Vitter came out swinging. Walker's first question concerned Kim Davis, a clerk of court in rural Kentucky who had been jailed four weeks earlier for refusing to issue marriage licenses to gay couples after a Supreme Court ruling made marriage equality the law of the land. The question was not central to the future of Louisiana, but it had dominated cable television coverage in recent days.

After the six candidates offered their views, Vitter jumped in to suggest that Edwards didn't support religious freedom because he had said Davis was not free to ignore the Supreme Court ruling. "I'll be a leader on this, standing up for those Louisiana values," Vitter said. Edwards was left to defend his initial answer with a legal explanation.

"He was surprised by that," thought Kyle Ruckert, Vitter's campaign manager, as he watched Edwards react to his candidate's punch. The calculated jab at Edwards was a good start for the senator. The Vitter campaign had decided to go after Edwards to shift the dynamic of the race, which the Louisiana Water Coalition PAC was increasingly defining with anti-Vitter attacks.

Walker's next two questions also focused on a hot-button social issue, guns. The candidates mostly voiced agreement on their support for the Second Amendment and the need to provide treatment for the mentally disturbed before they might try to use a weapon. Walker's fourth question kept the focus on a cable news-type issue—whether Louisiana should defund Planned Parenthood after the recent airing of videos by a conservative group that aimed to discredit the organization. Vitter, Dardenne, and Angelle all denounced Planned Parenthood, while the Democrat called the videos "disturbing" but said he wanted all the facts before condemning the group. That led Vitter to jump in again, this time to take a shot at both Dardenne and Edwards. Dardenne, Vitter said, had voted for six measures as a state senator that ran afoul of the anti-abortion group, the Louisiana Right to Life Federation. Edwards, Vitter added, had twice voted for President Obama, and that surely put him out of step with Louisiana voters, because the president was a Planned Parenthood supporter. "If that is consistent with a pro-life voting record, God help us," Vitter said.

Edwards retorted that as a legislator he had a 100 percent voting record with the Louisiana Right to Life Federation. "While I did vote for the president," he added, "I have never voted for David Vitter." The studio audience laughed.

Next it was the lieutenant governor's turn to respond to Vitter. "He is lying on the votes," Dardenne said, raising the temperature a notch. Dardenne then sought to quash the allegation by the pro-Vitter super PAC that taxpayers had picked up the tab for his wife and friends when he went to Europe to promote tourism in Louisiana. "It's the kind of misleading things you're hearing from Senator Vitter," Dardenne said. "He's now getting desperate in this campaign."

Walker kept up his focus on social issues. He did not ask *The Question*—or any other question that would differentiate the candidates or address any major policy issue that would come before the Legislature. Instead, he noted that Oregon had recently legalized marijuana and asked how many of the candidates had ever gotten high. Only Odom raised his hand.

By now, Walker's attention to minor issues from other states and his failure to ask about the most important issues facing Louisiana— the budget mess and cuts to health care and public colleges and universities—was lighting up Twitter.

The "WDSU debate spends 1 minute on higher education, but 10 minutes on Kim Davis … Oh, 0 minutes on budget," tweeted Joshua Stockley, a University of Louisiana at Monroe political science professor.

"All social issues, 30 minutes in, nothing Louisiana specific," tweeted Andrew Tuozzolo, a campaign consultant and Democratic legislative aide. Many other Tweets were aimed right at Walker, savaging him for asking questions that many considered irrelevant.

Walker next asked if legalizing marijuana could help the state's budget woes. Dardenne used his answer to make a sly attack on Vitter. "Some may want to legalize prostitution in Louisiana," he said. "That's not what we ought to be doing."

Angelle had been waiting for a chance to cut Vitter on the prostitution issue, but *The Question* never got asked. With only about 15 minutes left in the hour-long debate, Angelle answered a question about Common Core by noting that he was the only Republican candidate who had consistently opposed the new education standards. Dardenne supported them, while Vitter, a one-time supporter, now opposed them. Vitter couldn't be trusted, Angelle said, and then slammed down a line he had practiced beforehand. "He has not only been wrong on fornication, he's been wrong on taxation and he's been wrong on education," Angelle said.

Walker noted to Vitter that he had been called a liar, desperate, and untrustworthy. Did he have a response?

Vitter chose to tar Angelle by reminding viewers that the Cajun had served as Jindal's chief legislative lobbyist. "He was in the middle of that inner, inner circle to pass legislation to implement and further Common Core," Vitter said.

That only prompted Walker to give Angelle another shot.

"Again," Angelle said, "let me take this opportunity to call out Senator Pinocchio. I'm surprised he showed up for this forum. He has the sixth worst voting record [in the Senate]. He's not here. He's not there. He just simply does not care."

In what had become standard practice for Vitter, as soon as the debate ended, he hurriedly left the stage and the studio without speaking to reporters, although he had visited with journalists for several minutes that evening before the cameras started rolling. Edwards, Angelle, and Dardenne all stuck around after the debate to answer questions and mingle with the studio crowd.

Afterward, the focus was less on what the candidates had said and more on the performance by WDSU and Walker. Commentators on both the left and the right were unsparing in their remarks about the station and the anchor. "This debate was a complete farce," wrote Kevin Boyd, a contributor to *The Hayride*, an arch-conservative blog. "It was so bad that I really could not give grades to the candidates and that's not their fault. The fault lies with the moderator and WDSU."

Bob Mann, the LSU professor and liberal columnist, called the debate "journalistic malpractice."

"Learning that Reverend Odom may have smoked pot once is not useful to voters," said Martin Johnson, a professor of mass communication and political science at LSU.

Meanwhile, several days before the debate, Don and John Carmouche, the father-and-son team of trial lawyers behind the anti-Vitter Louisiana Water Coalition, had faced a decision. They thought their first two television ads had hit the mark. But now their super PAC was out of money, and the money they had spent was mostly their own. "What do we do?" John Carmouche asked his father.

"We need to keep going," Don Carmouche replied.

The younger Carmouche was reluctant to spend more. "I'm sick of taking all the heat," he said.

"We got to do it," Don said. "We've gone this far. I know we're alone. But we don't have a choice."

They decided to have Rob Green run another poll. Afterward, they would listen to advice from him and Rob Stutzman, their ad consultant. After analyzing the poll results, the two Robs—one a Democrat based in Washington, the other a Republican based in Sacramento—told the Carmouches that while the first two spots had done their job and pulled voters away from Vitter, he was spending so much money on his own ad blitz, and doing it so effectively, that he might regain the support he had lost. The Carmouches gave the go-ahead for one more ad. They would buy another $450,000 of air time.

For the third ad, Stutzman wanted to dispense with the video clips and quick cuts used in the first two spots. He wanted someone to speak into the camera with a message that would connect with women in a visceral and emotional way. Green's polling showed that Vitter's dalliance with prostitutes had made him especially vulnerable with women voters, and the two men expected Vitter to counteract that weakness with his ace in the hole, his wife Wendy. They needed a woman to deliver the message. As for the message itself, Stutzman wanted to go beyond the issue of prostitution and ask the voters to ponder whether they wanted a governor who had broken the law and engaged in risky behavior. Stutzman also wanted the message to reinforce the point to Republicans that they could vote for someone other than Vitter. The actress couldn't be from California. In fact, she ought to be from Louisiana.

Stutzman held a casting call and settled on a brunette 40-something actress with green eyes who went by the stage name PJ Clarke. A one-time computer programmer, Clarke had relocated to Prairieville with her husband and two sons after Katrina. She then trained as an actress and had appeared on stage and in numerous television commercials and films. Clarke played the part perfectly for her latest role. The ad aired on October 6.

"David Vitter wants to be our governor," Clarke said, talking directly to viewers. "But how can we trust him?" A soft piano played in the background.

"Louisiana can't have a governor with such secrets," she continued. "Our future needs to be in safer hands." She paused half a beat. "Truthful hands.

"Come on, David Vitter," she said, her eyes narrowing. "*Answer the question:* Did you break the law?"

The ad ended with a brief clip of Vitter from the 2010 TV debate with Charlie Melancon when he ducked questions about prostitution. "We have not heard an answer," viewers heard the debate's moderator, Dennis Woltering, tell Vitter. "You may not like the answer...." Vitter was heard saying when Stutzman's ad ended. Vitter's words had been abbreviated to suit the attack ad.

The ad was devastating. "The dynamics between Mary Landrieu's Senate race last year and David Vitter's race this year are eerily similar," offered John Couvillon, a Baton Rouge-based pollster and demographer. "The money in neither race has translated into a positive narrative. It's drip, drip, drip against his candidacy." In a separate interview, Couvillon noted Edwin Edwards had also faced sex scandals. "But Edwards had considerable charm," Couvillon said. "Vitter has not run a likable campaign. It's been more slash and burn."

Two days later, on October 8, the Vitter campaign responded with a testimonial from Kevin Wise, a former Army Ranger. Wise, who lived in St. Tammany Parish, had been injured in a helicopter accident during training stateside. With his wife sitting to his right, Wise identified himself as a disabled veteran and said, "When I had a bone infection due to a hip replacement, I was either going to lose my leg or lose my life." He said he called the Veterans Administration for help, "and they absolutely didn't care. Then I called David Vitter. Literally within 24 hours, my operation was approved. David and his team didn't rest until they knew I would be taken care of. That's how you know he'll be a great leader." This and the ad three weeks earlier featuring Deborah Cazalot—in which she talked about Vitter's helping her get a liver transplant—were Vitter's strongest spots. They provided a rare opportunity to show that he cared about others. The fact that Wise was a veteran had the added benefit of taking the fight to Edwards on his turf.

On October 13, the Vitter campaign turned to Wendy Vitter, its best asset, to shore up her husband's support. "I know David Vitter better than anyone," she said from what appeared to be her living room, against a backdrop of soft music. "And I can tell you he'll make a great governor." As viewers watched images of a casual Vitter with his children and then with voters, Wendy continued, "David has the courage to stand up to the Baton Rouge politicians. He's proven it." The camera returned to Wendy. "David is the one who gave them term limits!" she said. Viewers next saw Vitter and Wendy with their four children at the breakfast table. "And David has refused to take his Congressional pension," Wendy added. "That's right. He returned it to the taxpayers. How many politicians do you know willing to do that?"

Then she delivered the close: "Do I think David has the courage and vision we need to turn Louisiana around? I don't think it. I *know* it!"

Wendy Vitter did not talk about love or their relationship, and certainly not about *The Question*. Instead, she made a straight-on political pitch for her husband. The images in the spot focused more on the senator and his children than on the senator and his wife. A warm-and-fuzzy spot would come later. Campaign manager Kyle Ruckert believed that warm and fuzzy would work only once. Now was not the time, Ruckert told campaign supporters who wanted it immediately.

Bill Cassidy, who won his Senate seat a year earlier thanks to Vitter's political stewardship, also came to Vitter's defense. "His wife loves him," Cassidy said in an interview. "They've worked that through. Shouldn't that be significant to us all? I think it is. Secondly, he or she who is without sin should cast the first stone. His wife and he have worked through it. At some point, that's probably what's most important of all, isn't it? It isn't a marriage of convenience. You see them together. They care for each other. They love each other. They're committed to their families. It's not a European marriage where they are living apart."

In the meantime, the Republican Governors Association had been weighing whether to become a force in the Louisiana governor's race. In mid-September, Timmy Teepell contacted the RGA and warned them that Vitter was in trouble. Teepell, Bobby Jindal's political guru, also worked for Jindal's national Republican consulting group, OnMessage. Teepell had a theory about primary elections: Voters go into the voting booth with two candidates in mind, their first choice, for whom they will vote, and their anybody-but choice, the candidate for whom they will *not* vote under any circumstances. Teepell advised the RGA in September that he believed Vitter was becoming the anybody-but choice and would have only four weeks during the runoff to shed that label.

Teepell encouraged RGA officials to engage quickly with negative ads against Edwards. If they wanted a Republican to win the governor's race, he argued, they couldn't let the sole Democrat go untouched in the primary. They needed *him* to become the anybody-but choice.

Vitter made the counter argument that they needed to stay out and save their money. Louisiana was a Republican state, he said, echoing "the fundamentals" cited by so many pundits and political scientists. Without a doubt, Vitter predicted, he would defeat Edwards in the runoff. Vitter probably was still thinking that roughing up Edwards too soon might allow Angelle or Dardenne to slip past the Democrat into the runoff—and polls showed that either man would likely defeat Vitter. The RGA initially deferred to the state's senior senator.

Several weeks later, at the end of September, the RGA ran a poll and saw that Edwards was running stronger than expected. The group decided that it had no choice but to soften him up.

The first of three RGA ads aired on October 9—just 15 days

before the primary election. No one was surprised when all three ads took a page from the Republican Party's favorite playbook—claiming Edwards wanted to raise taxes and tying him to President Obama. One ad took a clip from the WDSU-TV debate where Edwards had said of Obama's two campaigns for the White House, "I supported the president" and then repeated the statement three times. As the ads were running, the question loomed among political insiders: Were the RGA ads too late to halt a surging Edwards?

On October 15, nine days before the primary, Edwards responded to the barrage by Vitter and his surrogates with an ad that kept the focus on his personal story with testimonials from West Point buddies. "John Bel doesn't just talk about his values," said one of them, classmate Murray Starkel, "he lives them every day." The ad echoed the Edwards campaign's key themes while, without mentioning Vitter, underscoring the senator's shortcomings. Coach Blanco loved the spot and played it on his cell phone for visitors to his room at Lafayette General Hospital, where he was being treated for a staph infection.

Dardenne's gubernatorial campaign sought to demonize Vitter with its own negative ad, in part by linking him to Jindal. The spot featured Dardenne speaking directly to the camera while he stood in front of an interior brick wall. "Bobby Jindal put political ambition and power ahead of what's right for Louisiana," he began. "Now David Vitter brings in Washington outsiders to do the same. They're dangerous. They spend millions on ads, say or do anything to get what they want." Tieless, Dardenne had been leaning casually against the exposed brick wall. Now he moved slightly toward the camera. "It's their money and power versus us," he said. "They don't own you, because they don't own me. There will not be a second Louisiana Purchase."

Five days before the West Point ad aired, Edwards and Angelle went to Abbeville for the Cattle Festival parade. One of many weekend festivals attended by the candidates, it offered a barn dance, a trail ride and a *fais do-do* dance party with zydeco and Cajun music. But the highlight was the parade, where voters who were starting to make up their minds about the race lined the route. Mike Simon, a retired firefighter, said he would vote for Vitter. "He knows how screwed up Washington is," Simon said underneath a canopy on the hot and humid afternoon. "Maybe he can un-screw-up things here."

A few yards away, Eddie McKenzie, a retired policeman, said Vitter's prostitution scandal didn't bother him. "Everybody's got skeletons," he said.

Ruth Boudreaux, a retired school bus driver, held a different view. "The cheating scandal bothers me," she said and recalled a scene from

2007. "It was pitiful that his wife had to stand alongside him."

Most everybody got excited when the floats began to pass. Those aboard tossed Mardi Gras beads, Tootsie Rolls, and bubble gum, and that got kids scrambling to scoop the candy from the ground. Angelle passed by first, on the back of a flatbed truck. Edwards, too, stood on the back of a flatbed. His float featured American and Louisiana state flags and a host of teachers volunteering from the Louisiana Federation of Teachers. Wearing blue jeans, a work shirt and cowboy boots, Edwards tossed blue to-go cups, seeming to enjoy seeing how far he could throw them. When the parade was over, he clambered down and shook hands with folks. One voter asked Edwards whether he was related to Edwin Edwards. "I am, if you really like him," Edwards replied with a smile.

At a fundraiser earlier in the cycle, the scandalized former governor had offered John Bel a piece of advice on how to handle that question. "Everyone is going to ask you if you're related to the former governor," he told John Bel. "This is what you do: If you're around Republicans or people who don't like me, just say, 'I don't know the son-of-a-bitch.'"

Vitter didn't attend the Cattle Festival. That fit with a growing narrative by journalists and other critics, a narrative that made the senator look worse with each passing day. They tied his repeated absences from campaign debates to the character issue—to the prostitution scandal at the heart of that question. On the eve of an October 14 televised debate, the other three candidates blasted Vitter's decision to skip the event. "He doesn't want to answer the question he's been asked a couple of times that he's refused to answer, whether or not he broke the law," Dardenne said in an interview, echoing the thrust of the Water Coalition ad.

"He doesn't want to answer that question," added Angelle, picking up the meme. The campaign forums and debates are, Angelle said "a job interview. Showing up for the job interview is important and taking the unscripted questions is important."

Vitter did attend a debate the following night, on October 15, at Louisiana Tech University—but event organizers kept the public from watching the debate in person, even though a public university was holding it. Rival campaigns cried foul, accusing debate sponsors of caving to what they suspected were Vitter's demands, if not outright helping him dodge *The Question*. Vitter's campaign called such claims ridiculous—four journalists comprised the panel that grilled the candidates during the debate.

Nonetheless, Mary-Patricia Wray, Edwards' communications director, initially was denied entry into her candidate's green room to scout it out before the debate. When the organizers relented, they insisted that an armed guard accompany her—and then they wouldn't let her leave. With the guard within earshot, she called Campbell Robertson, the New Orleans-based correspondent for *The New York Times*. She got his voicemail but pretended he had answered. "Hello, Campbell Robertson with *The New York Times*? I have been escorted by an armed police officer at the gubernatorial debate in Ruston. They're guarding the door. They've told me I cannot leave." Minutes later, someone let her go.

Journalists covering the event were greeted by law enforcement and escorted through screening areas, then sequestered in a room where the football team watched films and held meetings. University officials offered no explanation for this unusual treatment, prompting some reporters to joke that administrators apparently considered them a threat. At the beginning of the debate, the video and audio feed cut out. When the sound and picture returned, the candidates competed against the cacophony of the university band practicing on the nearby football field. At the end of the debate, Vitter departed without giving reporters a chance to interview him.

Amidst the hullabaloo over the debate's many anomalies, Vitter's campaign message—that his opponents represented a "broken and dysfunctional" Baton Rouge—got overlooked in the post-debate coverage. Julia O'Donoghue's article in *The Times-Picayune* noted that Vitter's opponents met with reporters after the debate ended. "Vitter didn't make himself available to media," she reported. "His campaign said he opted to go get something to eat and watch the Saints game instead."

Elizabeth Crisp's account of the debate for *The Advocate* followed the same narrative. Her story noted that Vitter's three opponents told reporters that the senator's campaign was behind the lack of a live audience and the sequestered media viewing room.

"I was very disturbed by it," Edwards said of the setup.

"[Vitter] doesn't want to answer the tough questions," Crisp quoted Angelle as telling reporters.

Dardenne, who visited with student protesters prior to the debate, afterwards called the arrangement "ridiculous." He told reporters: "It was an attempt so that you would not have immediate access to him."

It fell to Vitter's spokesman, Luke Bolar, to deflect blame for the debate restrictions. He emailed O'Donoghue a memorable take for her story: "Are they going to blame Sen. Vitter if the Falcons score on the Saints' defense tonight too?"

Later, after the campaign ended, Bolar said that media coverage of the Ruston debate was a "classic example" of what Vitter faced during the entire campaign. "Their first instinct was to blame, or, in most other cases, attack David," he said of the press. "They didn't even write about the debate."

The other big takeaway from Ruston was the souring relationship between Angelle and Dardenne. During the debate, Dardenne had dismissed Angelle's idea about a commission to review tax exemptions as "impractical." After the debate, Angelle responded, "*He's* impractical. He's the one who helped create these problems."

"I happen to be very practical," Dardenne said, responding to the response. "He's Bobby Jindal's chosen one.

When a reporter asked Dardenne about water reserves in north Louisiana, he quickly replied, "That's Scott's fault. He was at [the Department of Natural Resources]."

During the next televised debate, on October 19, in the front parlor at the Governor's Mansion, Dardenne saddled Angelle with Jindal, before Angelle reminded the lieutenant governor that he too had once endorsed the governor.

While Angelle had called Vitter *"Senator Pinocchio,"* he put a twist on it that night and called Dardenne *"Senator Pinocchio 2.0."*

The bad blood had been slowly brewing for some time, with repeated suggestions over the summer that one man's dropping out would boost the other's chances. Neither liked that idea, and each, when asked directly in another public forum, declined to say whether he would endorse the other. Dardenne bluntly said, "No," while Angelle dodged the question.

Through all of this sparring, the spotlight remained on Vitter, especially when he skipped the debate at the Governor's Mansion. "We have a candidate for governor who has no courage to come here," Angelle told viewers.

David Vitter was in trouble, with only a few days before the October 24 primary. He wanted the race to showcase his conservative values and record. Instead, it was pointing again and again to the prostitution scandal and to his character—all variants of *The Question*.

18

"Little Green Pieces of Paper With Dead Presidents on Them"

At 1:03 p.m. on Saturday, October 17, just a week before Louisiana's statewide jungle primary, a New Orleans blogger named Jason Brad Berry took one last look at the post he had been working on and hit the "Publish" button.[3] That sent a horde of journalists and four gubernatorial campaigns scrambling. Berry's post, uploaded to his website, *The American Zombie*, contained bombshell allegations about David Vitter by a woman who appeared in a series of videos Berry had filmed. She had straight black hair and wore a black blouse and large black-framed glasses. Her name was Wendy Ellis, formerly Wendy Cortez. She had last surfaced in the January 2008 issue of *Hustler* magazine under the headline: "SENATOR DAVID VITTER'S SECRET LOVER REVEALED."

In a salacious *Hustler* question-and-answer article, Ellis claimed she had serviced Vitter as a prostitute for three or four months when he was a state representative. When the article—which contained five nude photographs—made news in late 2007, however, it rated only a one-day story. At that time, the media had heard plenty about Vitter and prostitutes, and the senator's refusal to talk about his "very serious sin"—coupled with his denial of everything Ellis claimed—made keeping the story alive difficult. Besides, few journalists considered *Hustler* a credible source. That was just what Vitter wanted. Berry, however, remained convinced that there was more to the story.

Originally from Kentucky and a videographer by profession,

---

[3] Berry shared the contents of his blog post with several news reporters before publishing his story, hoping it would foster media coverage. Among them were Tyler Bridges of *The Advocate* and Clancy DuBos of *Gambit*, the co-author and editor, respectively, of this book. Because this chapter deals extensively with events covered by DuBos and Bridges, the authors submitted the entire manuscript to LSU Manship School of Mass Communication Dean Jerry Ceppos, a former newspaper editor in Miami and San Jose, for his review and advice.

Berry, 46, moved to New Orleans in the 1990s. Exposing politicians' dirty deeds through *The American Zombie* was his hobby. He called himself an "independent investigative journalist." He said he published his findings as a public service and never paid sources for information or took money to publish a story. Like other bloggers, Berry operated by publishing standards different from the mainstream media, including sometimes posting rumors to see if they generated additional information. His postings thus ranged from thoroughly researched exposés of political corruption to salacious rumors. Some campaign operatives readily shared opposition research with him, hoping he would publish their findings after newspaper and television reporters had passed on the information.

Berry was credited by *Gambit*, New Orleans alt-weekly, with breaking several important stories about New Orleans Mayor Ray Nagin's illicit activities. Berry's exposés of Nagin figured prominently into the former mayor's conviction on federal corruption charges in February 2014. Later that year, in the waning days of Louisiana's heated Senate campaign, Berry posted a story raising questions about payments that the Republican candidate, Dr. Bill Cassidy, had received from the LSU Health Sciences Center for part-time medical work while he served in Congress. An internal review by LSU later found no wrongdoing by Cassidy, but Berry dismissed that inquiry as a whitewash.

Along with political corruption and cronyism, Berry was obsessed with the fallout from the 2010 BP oil spill, which caused massive damage to Louisiana's coast. By 2015, he had written an estimated 360,000 words on that topic, dedicating much of his efforts to buttressing his view that some of the lead plaintiff lawyers in the class action lawsuit had put their desire for large legal fees ahead of the interests of ordinary coastal residents hurt by the spill.

In 2010, Berry began chasing rumors about prostitutes Vitter allegedly had hired. The blogger got his start with a tip from the Democratic Party's press secretary during that year's Senate campaign between Vitter and Democratic Congressman Charlie Melancon. Berry believed the senator had an obligation to give more definitive answers, given his self-righteous embrace of "family values." By September 2015, as the governor's race heated up, Berry continued to pursue the story but was growing frustrated—and skeptical—after hitting so many dead-ends. "Ninety-five percent of the leads have not come to fruition," he said. "There's a lot of misinformation out there."

Nonetheless, because of Wendy Ellis' 2007 allegations, Berry didn't give up searching for her. Through a New Orleans madam, he found a former prostitute who had been a friend and coworker of Ellis in the sex trade. The woman told Berry that Vitter had impregnated Ellis and that Ellis had put the child up for adoption. This caused Berry to redouble his efforts to find her. He got promising telephone numbers but couldn't reach her. Next, he visited the workplace of Ellis' grown daughter, but she wasn't there.

Berry wasn't alone trying to find dirt on Vitter. A reporter for *The Advocate* spent a week chasing stories about the Republican frontrunner.[4] Stories swirled that Gumbo PAC, the Water Coalition PAC, Vitter's opposing candidates, and God-knows-who-else had hired private investigators to find a silver bullet that would take down the senator. John Cummings, a retired New Orleans trial attorney and Edwards campaign donor, was among those rumored to have hired someone to expose Vitter. No one would cop to it.

In the end, one gumshoe, Danny DeNoux, did locate Ellis. "I can find just about anyone," DeNoux was known to say, and over the years he proved many times that his was not an idle boast. DeNoux had served in the Army near the end of the Vietnam era, then returned home to join the New Orleans Police Department. In 1982, after a decade as a cop, he left the force to work as a bounty hunter for insurance companies and bail bondsmen. He was good at it, though his methods were sometimes unconventional.

In one instance, DeNoux corralled a drug dealer who had skipped bail and fled to Miami. DeNoux flew there, bought a Catholic priest's shirt and collar at a costume shop, and surprised the man at his home. In another case, he brought home a drug dealer who had absconded to Guatemala after posting bail. DeNoux chartered a jet to fly the dealer back to New Orleans. Another time he tracked a drug dealer to Detroit—and caught him working behind the counter at a drugstore.

DeNoux later became the chief investigator for the Louisiana Insurance Department. After the statewide elections of 1987, he discovered that the incoming insurance commissioner, Doug Green, had promised to keep open an insolvent auto insurance company in exchange for bribes disguised as campaign contributions. DeNoux alerted federal prosecutors, and Green was convicted and sentenced to 25 years in prison before completing a single term as commissioner. DeNoux went on to become a private investigator whose services ranged from busting adulterous husbands to recovering money for victims of Ponzi schemes.

As a P.I., DeNoux acquired a variety of high-tech surveillance tools and had access to computer databases that allowed him to pick up trails that had gone cold. He could also tap into a network of law enforcement friends, as well as people who lived on the fringes of the

---

[4] The reporter in question was co-author Tyler Bridges.

law. "I live in the gutter," he liked to say. "I have a lot of connections."

In the spring of 2015, a businessman—whom DeNoux refused to identify to anyone (except to say that the man was *not* Cummings)—hired him to dig up dirt on Vitter. DeNoux said the assignment was just like any other: What mattered was that he would get paid. At 62, with glasses, thinning hair, and thick forearms, he was the father of twin 2-year-olds from his third marriage—and he had five older children. "I don't have a dog in this hunt," he would say of the governor's race. "It's not personal. I'm not doing this for God and country. I'm doing this for little green pieces of paper with dead presidents on them."

DeNoux ran down leads, collaborating at times with Berry before concluding, as did the blogger, that Wendy Ellis offered the most potential as a source of information. According to DeNoux, the businessman who hired him had instructed the P.I. to deliver Ellis—if he could find the elusive former hooker—to Berry. DeNoux tracked down one of Ellis' former husbands and passed the word through him and other family members that he wanted to speak with her. She called him on the night of October 12—just 12 days before the primary election. She was willing to meet. DeNoux immediately called the blogger.

The following morning, DeNoux and Berry, each man paying for his own ticket, flew from New Orleans to San Antonio to meet with Ellis. Berry added later that he paid for *all* of his own expenses related to the trip and his research. The two of them picked her up at what Berry would later describe only as a "medical facility" and took her to a nearby hotel, where DeNoux had rented a conference room. As a preliminary matter, the two men needed to confirm her identity. She handed over her driver's license and a bus pass from Hawaii, where she had been living. She also showed them an insurance card that contained her photo. The men were satisfied.

Ellis, 42, said that she was ill from lupus. She added that she believed she was dying and wanted to set the record straight while she could. According to the Lupus Foundation of America, lupus is a chronic disease that keeps the body's autoimmune system from doing its normal work of fighting off bacteria, viruses, and the like. The foundation estimates 80 percent to 90 percent of the people with lupus can expect to "live a normal life span."

Berry set up his video camera and began taping her as she talked about Vitter. The interview lasted about 60 minutes. As they left, DeNoux and Berry agreed that they had struck gold. They flew back to New Orleans that night.

Berry believed Ellis' account. She came across as credible to him, and her story tracked what her friend, the former prostitute, had told him the previous month. Too excited to sleep, Berry stayed up all night at his Algiers home editing the interview. He decided to break it up into segments of no more than four minutes each. Before he would post anything online, however, Berry knew he had to verify Ellis' details, including some apparent discrepancies. He was in the process of doing just that when he got a phone call from James Garner, an attorney working for Vitter at the white-shoe law firm of Sher Garner Cahill Richter Klein & Hilbert in New Orleans. Though diminutive in stature, Garner was a bulldog of a lawyer. He suggested that Berry ought to come to his office and share what he had. Berry felt as though Garner was pressuring him.

"You need to stop telling me what to do," retorted Berry.

Garner tried another tack. Berry ought to be very careful about what he posted, the attorney said, insinuating that he was ready to file a lawsuit. Instead of backing down, Berry asked to interview Vitter over the phone about Ellis' claims. Garner replied that his client was too busy.

By asking to interview Vitter, Berry had insulated himself—at least somewhat—from a potential defamation suit. Because Berry had expressly sought Vitter's version of the story, it would be difficult for Vitter to claim that the blogger had recklessly disregarded the truth, an essential element in any claim of defamation. Nonetheless, Berry's conversation with Garner was sobering. Berry published *The American Zombie* as a side project and certainly didn't have the deep pockets of a newspaper to defend himself against a defamation case brought by a big law firm on behalf of a United States senator.

Berry spoke with Scott Sternberg, a New Orleans First Amendment attorney and general counsel for the Louisiana Press Association, about his conversation with Garner.[5] Sternberg agreed to advise Berry *pro bono*. The young attorney had to duck into a closet at his in-laws' home—where he and his wife were staying during their own home renovation—so no one could hear his privileged conversations with Berry. Sternberg's initial advice left the blogger with mixed feelings. On one hand, Vitter was a public official and Berry was a member of the media, albeit "new media." In addition, Berry's posts concerned a topic of great political importance. That meant the courts would give his reporting the highest level of First Amendment protection. On the other hand, if Vitter were to sue—even unsuccessfully—the costs of litigation alone would likely far exceed what Berry could afford. Sternberg's advice gave Berry pause. Ultimately, the blogger decided that what mattered most was whether Ellis was telling the truth.

---

[5] Book editor DuBos, a member of the Louisiana Press Association's board of directors, informed Berry that Sternberg might be willing to advise him.

He checked every detail that he could and concluded that she had in fact been truthful. Berry then rolled the dice, betting that Vitter would not sue. It seemed like a safe bet. If the senator did file a lawsuit, he would have to answer *The Question*—and a lot more questions—under oath. Considering how Vitter had skipped most campaign forums, the chances of his subjecting himself to an attorney's probing questions *under oath* were slim and none. Satisfied that he had nailed down everything that he could about Ellis' allegations, Berry published eight segments of his videotaped interview with her on Saturday, October 17, just after 1 p.m.

In the posted segments, Berry could be heard but not seen off-camera. He began by asking Ellis when she met Vitter. She told the same story published in the *Hustler* interview seven years earlier: She was dancing at a strip club on Bourbon Street when a pimp named Jonathan asked her if she wanted to work for his escort service. When Jonathan told her that her initial customer had been David Vitter, a state representative, she said she didn't care. "He and I became very intimate," she told Berry, a description that had changed over time. She initially told *The Times-Picayune* in July 2007 that she and Vitter "did not have a personal romantic relationship."

The blogger pointed out the discrepancy in his interview with Ellis. *Times-Picayune* reporter Kate Moran had gotten that wrong, Ellis said now. "She wrote what she wanted to write," she said. "She didn't write my words." That comment sent up a red flag because Moran was a respected reporter. "It's always been that he and I had a personal romantic relationship," Ellis insisted. That was not the only inconsistency that would prove troubling.

She went on to tell Berry that Vitter set her up in her own apartment across the street from where the paid sex had occurred, near the corner of Dumaine and Dauphine streets in the French Quarter. Vitter had his own set of keys, she said. "That's where he could come and see me whenever he wanted to," Ellis said. "He knew he could come at 2 o'clock in the morning, and there would be nobody else there."

Ellis added that *Hustler* also had gotten its facts wrong by reporting that the sexual relationship had lasted three to four months. "Our relationship lasted much longer," she said now.

"How long?" asked Berry.

"I was six months pregnant whenever we ended our relationship," Ellis said, dropping a bombshell accusation. As she said this, she pulled her lips together tight, looked off to the side, and the first segment ended.

"He was the only person I was sleeping with," Ellis said at the beginning of the next video segment, explaining her confidence that the baby was Vitter's. She then said that Vitter had asked her to have an abortion. That allegation was even more explosive than the first, because Vitter had a 100 percent pro-life voting record as a lawmaker. Such a revelation, if proved, would expose him as a hypocrite of the first order.

Ellis said she was impregnated after she moved into her own apartment and they began having unprotected sex. This statement was another red flag because she had told *Hustler* that Vitter was so careful that he always used a condom—and that he took the evidence with him when he left. In 2007, in interviews with *The Times-Picayune* and *Hustler,* she never mentioned having a child with Vitter, and she also had claimed to have practiced safe sex with Vitter. If Larry Flynt was out to expose Vitter, Berry asked, why wouldn't he have published her claim that Vitter had impregnated her and asked her to have an abortion? That would have only ratcheted up interest in her story. Ellis could not explain why *Hustler* had not printed the information in 2007.

Berry asked what happened after Ellis told Vitter that she was pregnant.

"I knew that if I had the baby, that the life for the child and myself would be completely unmanageable," she said. "We would never live a normal life. So at eight months, I decided to give the baby up for adoption."

She said she told Vitter about the child.

"It's not mine," Vitter replied, according to Ellis.

Why didn't she have an abortion?

"I believe I'm woman enough to lay down and spread my legs," she said. "I'm woman enough to make the right decision."

In the third segment, Ellis said she became Vitter's kept woman after moving into her own apartment. "I guess in my own fantasy world, that was my boyfriend," she said, adding that Vitter gave her $5,000 cash each month to cover her rent and living expenses. He also bought her the ring, she said, that she was wearing the day of the interview.

In the final segment, Ellis said that she had the baby in 2000 and that Vitter called her again just after she was released from prison in mid-2003. She had served time on a probation violation. Ellis said she initially resisted reestablishing the relationship but that they eventually resumed it. The sexual relationship continued until just before the D.C. Madam scandal broke in July 2007, she said.

In the videotapes, Ellis provided no evidence of her paternity claim, such as a birth certificate, or any documents from the hospital or the adoption agency.

When Berry posted the videos, his blog immediately began ricocheting around the Internet, thanks to emails, Twitter, and Facebook. This forced the mainstream media and the other three candidates for governor to decide how to respond. The candidates reacted cautiously, hoping to stoke the flames while trying to make it appear as though they weren't.

"Cathy and I continue to pray for David and his family," Jay Dardenne said in a statement. "Miss Ellis' courageous decision to give her child a chance at life should be commended. My focus is on Louisiana's future and not Senator Vitter's past."

"These allegations are deeply troubling," was Scott Angelle's take. "The people of Louisiana deserve the truth and answers from David Vitter. That being said, this race isn't about David's character, it's about Louisiana's future and that's what Scott Angelle will remain focused on."

John Bel Edwards invoked his military background. "I live my life by the Honor Code I pledged at West Point: 'A cadet will not lie, cheat, steal, or tolerate those who do.' That's how I will govern Louisiana," Edwards said.

In the meantime, the media—from the Associated Press to the state's largest newspapers and television stations to the blogosphere—weighed the same question: whether to publish Ellis' incendiary account. Within minutes after Berry posted the videos, *Gambit* posted a story on its news blog outlining Ellis' accusations and analyzing the political repercussions for Vitter.[6]

Baton Rouge-based blogger Lamar White Jr. published next. Though White wore his Democratic loyalties on his sleeve, he was skeptical of the new revelations about Vitter. "Unless and until there is more evidence provided, it appears as if Ms. Ellis is not telling the truth," White wrote. He pointed to her criminal record, her dishonesty, and the contradictions between her latest account and her earlier ones.

"I respect Mr. Berry and have worked with him in the past," White added, "but I am compelled to note that, until additional information is provided, I believe this particular story is deeply problematic." A day later, White went even further. "Ellis' story," he wrote, "in my humble opinion, is destructive, because it is riddled with huge holes; it is flawed; and with all due respect to the reporter [Berry], it was not properly vetted."

Another media outlet that published a news story about Berry's blog post was WDSU-TV in New Orleans. Its news director, Jonathan Shelley, reported Ellis' claims on the station's website and later, after its initial reporting, pointed out inconsistencies within her story.

The next morning, Sunday, October 18, attorney James Garner was called by the *Gambit* editor who had written the alt-weekly's initial story and had just seen the discrepancies in Ellis' account on WDSU's website. Garner admitted to the editor that he had given dossiers

---

[6] The initial *Gambit* analysis, and the shorter update posted the following morning, were written by Clancy DuBos, who also edited this book.

on Ellis to other media but that the Vitter campaign had blacklisted *Gambit* because of its critical coverage of the senator's "very serious sin" in the past. Garner then conferenced in Vitter spokesman Luke Bolar and offered to send the same dossier to *Gambit*, but he asked that the story be taken down while the paper reviewed the information. The editor agreed, but only *after* he got the dossier. Several hours later, *Gambit* posted an updated—and much shorter—version of the story, referring to "court documents that conflict with parts" of Ellis' account.

The update concluded, "The bottom line is this: There are holes in parts of the woman's story, but this remains largely a 'she said/he said' tale that may never be proved totally true or totally false."

As of Sunday afternoon, one full day after Berry first posted the Ellis interview, media coverage of her accusations had been limited to online posts by *Gambit*, White, and WDSU—all three of which by then had noted discrepancies in Ellis' story. The mainstream media, particularly the state's and the nation's largest newspapers, networks, and online publishers, had yet to touch it. Many journalists questioned the source, the credibility of the website, and the timing of the posts, one week before the election. In addition, by having Garner preemptively send dossiers on Ellis' criminal history to selected media, Team Vitter cast further doubts on her credibility.

The Times-Picayune did not report the story. Neither did Gannett's Louisiana papers in Monroe, Shreveport, Alexandria, Opelousas, and Lafayette. The locally owned Lake Charles *American Press* likewise passed on it. The decision-making matrix at all those papers—and in any major media newsroom that had seen Berry's posts—was likely very similar to that of *The Advocate*, which published editions in New Orleans, Baton Rouge, and Acadiana. *The Advocate*'s decision rested with its editor, Peter Kovacs.

Even before Berry posted the videotapes on Saturday, *The Advocate* had a story in the works. A reporter from the newspaper had been talking to Berry for weeks, and three days earlier, Berry had invited the reporter to his home to screen the videos.[7] The newspaper also had obtained information from the Vitter campaign—via campaign attorney Garner—casting doubt on Ellis' story. Kovacs had already decided the newspaper would not publish an article on Ellis' claims *before* Berry posted the videos, because such an article would have to rely almost solely on information that was not yet public. Once Berry posted the videos, the newspaper could weigh whether to publish an article. Every day closer to Election Day, however, the bar for publishing explosive new material got a little higher. It was now

---

[7] That *Advocate* reporter was Tyler Bridges, co-author of this book. He also joined the discussions at *The Advocate* regarding whether to publish a story on Ellis' allegations as presented on Berry's blog.

only a week before the primary.

On Saturday afternoon, after Berry posted the interview, Kovacs faced a difficult decision. He knew that publishing an article on Ellis' allegations would lend credence to her claims, but she had not provided proof that she had had a child with Vitter—or any child at all. Her story raised as many questions as it answered, and Ellis had changed her story in significant ways since 2007. The paper also had to consider other problems with Ellis' credibility, thanks to documents on her criminal record obtained by the newspaper in Arkansas that supplemented what it had received from Garner.

In addition to inconsistencies in the stories she had told about Vitter over the years, Ellis had a long rap sheet that went beyond prostitution arrests. She pleaded guilty in 1995 in Arkansas to writing 11 bad checks, and she was convicted of writing eight bad checks in Louisiana in 1996. She had also been arrested for credit card fraud, forged checks, and theft. She served a stint in prison in Arkansas for violating parole, pleading guilty on September 20, 2001, according to court records, before being paroled on June 3, 2003.

One threshold that Kovacs established in deciding whether to publish the article was getting access to Ellis and vetting her allegations directly. "We would ask her questions about why she was changing her story in so many significant ways," he explained more than a month later, at an LSU forum on media coverage of the election.

Seeking direct access to Ellis was a reasonable request, but DeNoux, who had become a gatekeeper to Ellis, would not make her available to the newspaper. That raised a red flag for Kovacs. He decided not to publish a story on Ellis' claims on Saturday, after Berry posted the videos, but he told the crowd at the LSU forum that he would have been willing to change his mind later if one of the *candidates* had accused Vitter of fathering a child with a prostitute. "That changes the news threshold of it." Kovacs said. "We're not putting our credibility on the line. We're not saying *The Advocate* says there is a love child. We're saying Scott Angelle says there is a love child. In that instance, we went as far as Scott Angelle went with it." (The authors of this book attempted to locate and interview Ellis, but were unsuccessful.)

All three candidates had hoped that at least one mainstream media outlet would pick up the story and give them the chance to comment on it—and potentially air TV attack ads about it. At the same time, the media were waiting to see if Vitter's opponents used Ellis' allegations in debates or TV commercials, allowing them to cite the candidates rather than Berry's blog. The machinations thus became a cat-and-mouse game, with the candidates waiting on the media and the media waiting on the candidates. This game of wait-and-see continued through Sunday and Monday. On Monday night, Vitter's three major opponents engaged in an hour-long, statewide, televised debate at the Governor's Mansion, but none mentioned Ellis' claims, which continued to go unreported by the mainstream media.

That left one more opportunity at the final debate of the primary on the evening of Wednesday, October 21, at LSU's Manship School of Mass Communication. LSU students hosted and moderated the debate, which was broadcast statewide. Dardenne, Angelle, and Edwards participated. Vitter was again a no-show.

Before the debate began, Angelle sat with his campaign manager, Ryan Cross, to discuss exactly how to address Ellis' claims. They agreed that with Angelle in third place in the polls, this would be his last chance to land a blow that might get him past Vitter and into the runoff against Edwards. Cross and Angelle agreed that Angelle had to look for an opportunity to strike, and strike hard. Before heading over to LSU, Angelle rehearsed the words he would use.

The early questions focused on how to tackle the budget deficit, reduce poverty, and fix the state's deplorable roads, leaving Angelle no opening to attack. With only 10 minutes left in the hour-long debate, candidates were asked about Louisiana's popular TOPS college scholarship program, which was threatened with cuts in the face of another Bobby Jindal budget crunch. Angelle decided it was now or never. He began by saying that he would absolutely protect TOPS as governor. Then, looking directly into the camera, he shifted gears. "Now having said that, one of the ways we make sure we always fund TOPS is having an economy that creates jobs," he began.

Then came the zinger. "We have a stench that is getting ready to come over Louisiana if we elect David Vitter as governor," Angelle said, gesturing repeatedly with both hands for emphasis. He encouraged viewers to go to *The American Zombie* website and review Ellis' allegations. "There is a shadow that has been cast over Senator Vitter, a shadow that if it continues, will follow Louisiana," he added, continuing to gesture with his hands. "When that follows Louisiana, it hurts our ability to create jobs. It hurts our ability to grow our economy. We can't have a cavalier attitude about this. I understand a serious sin. It is now perhaps a *lifestyle* that we need to examine, a lifestyle that Louisiana cannot afford."

Angelle had commented on the videos in a public forum, broadcast statewide, but Kovacs still didn't feel comfortable running a full-blown article on Berry's videos. It was a touchy subject, and *The Advocate* was hardly alone in its approach. The Associated Press, Gannett Newspapers, and *The Times-Picayune* all steered clear of mentioning Ellis by name in their debate accounts, although some did mention Angelle's attack.

The Advocate ran an article by Elizabeth Crisp headlined, "Scott Angelle launches most pointed attack yet on David Vitter's prostitution scandal in final debate before Saturday election." Crisp's story specifically mentioned *The American Zombie* website but did not name Ellis or describe her allegations. The story also quoted Luke Bolar, Vitter's spokesman, who said, "Desperate candidates in last place do desperate things. Grasping at a story on a shady blog that's been proven completely untrue is pathetic."

Crisp also quoted Dardenne afterward. "People ought to be aware of all of that," he said. Crisp noted that Vitter "has repeatedly declined to elaborate on his 2007 prostitution scandal," and she quoted Edwards as saying he had not watched the videos. "I know all I need to know about David Vitter," he said.

It was now less than three days before the October 24 primary. Thanks to Vitter's resurrected prostitution scandal, voters were witnessing an epic governor's race—and one final, crazy twist would unfold before Election Day.

19

"Are You Taping Us?"

Robert Frenzel, all of 30 years old and 500 miles away from his home in Dallas, sat quietly inside the Royal Blend coffee shop in Old Metairie, a couple of blocks across the parish line from New Orleans. It was 8:45 a.m. on October 23, the day before the primary election. Frenzel blended into the morning coffeehouse scene seamlessly, wearing a gray polo shirt and jeans, keeping to himself. More important, he had finally spotted what he had been looking for—and it wasn't on the menu. The smell of fresh-brewed coffee filled the air as Frenzel, a private investigator, spied his target: the man with a white beard.

That man was a septuagenarian trial lawyer and real estate developer named John Cummings. Frenzel had followed Cummings into the coffee shop and had deliberately sat at an adjoining table to watch and listen. Five other men were seated with Cummings for their usual morning klatch conducted over two tables they had pushed together. The topics ranged from Donald Trump's unbelievable run for the presidency to—and this is when Frenzel's ears perked up—David Vitter's alleged dalliances with a former escort named Wendy Ellis. The salacious accusations had appeared on Jason Brad Berry's website, *TheAmericanZombie.com*, on October 17 but had drawn little coverage in the mainstream media. On social media, however, Ellis' claims had garnered a lot of attention. Team Vitter wanted to know who was footing the bill for it all. Frenzel was there to find out.

The young P.I. texted his boss back in Dallas: "Holy shit. The guy is here, and they are talking about Vitter and Jason's blog."

He received a one-word reply: "Video."

Among those at the table with Cummings were Danny DeNoux, a former New Orleans homicide detective-turned-private investigator who had found the ex-hooker and had taken Berry to meet her in Texas; and Jefferson Parish Sheriff Newell Normand, the most powerful elected official in the state's second most-populated parish—and a longtime political foe of Vitter. At one point during the table's banter, Normand turned to his left to speak to the 78-year-old Cummings, who wasn't wearing his hearing aids that day. The sheriff had to lean in close to whisper in Cummings' ear, which is when he noticed the young man in the gray polo shirt extending his cell phone toward their table. Frenzel was following his boss' instructions—and hoping to get audio as well. When Normand pulled back from Cummings, the young man also pulled back his cell phone.

"Are you taping us?" Normand said, swinging around to look at Frenzel and, in the process, noticing a recording app on his phone.

"No," Frenzel quickly replied, sputtering about having a job at a bank, which was his cover story.

"Are you taping us?" Normand repeated. "It sure looks like you were."

"No," Frenzel said again, growing visibly nervous and fumbling with what appeared to be two cell phones.

Of all the tables in all of the coffee shops in Louisiana, Frenzel had eavesdropped on the one where the local sheriff was sitting— along with the veteran P.I., DeNoux. Also at the table, as usual, was state Senator Danny Martiny, a Republican and outside lawyer for the sheriff's office who was also one of Normand's closest friends and political allies.

"Can I see your phone?" asked the sheriff, who was also a lawyer.

"No," Frenzel said, adding a word or two about private property to a man who knew the Fourth Amendment's protections and limitations as well as anyone. Trying to play it cool, Frenzel picked up one of his phones and pretended to talk to someone on the other end.

Normand turned back to the group and rejoined the conversation.

Cummings, the man with the white beard, was too suspicious to let it drop. He walked around the table, planted himself in front of the young stranger and, with his own phone, snapped Frenzel's photo.

Frenzel nervously grabbed his two cell phones and, according to a Jefferson Parish Sheriff's Office report, "fled" the coffee shop. His sudden departure aroused suspicion at Normand's table. "Let's see what kind of car he gets in," Martiny told the others. He and Cummings rushed outside.

Frenzel approached his car but didn't open the door. Instead, he began walking briskly up Metairie Road as DeNoux, who had already left the coffee shop, navigated his mini-van around to the entrance of Royal Blend and saw Martiny and Cummings looking agitated. When they quickly explained what had happened, DeNoux took off in a low-speed pursuit. Now it was P.I. versus P.I., spy versus spy. DeNoux saw Frenzel turn a corner into the quiet, toney Metairie Club Gardens neighborhood and round another corner. Martiny, meanwhile, gave chase from another direction. An increasingly frantic Frenzel turned yet another corner, then dashed up a private driveway at 227 Vincent Avenue and through the empty home's backyard gate. He climbed over a rear fence into the private backyard of 112 Stella Avenue, where he took cover behind an air conditioning condenser.

Back in the driveway of 227 Vincent Avenue, the sheriff surveyed the scene. Normand was not amused. He parked his vehicle and requested backup. Five deputies showed up within minutes. It didn't take them long to find Frenzel crouched behind the air conditioning unit. They cuffed him and brought his driver's license to Normand. The arresting deputy also handed the sheriff a card identifying Frenzel as a private investigator from Dallas. Normand knew a P.I. in Dallas named Wes Bearden. Married to a New Orleans woman whose father was friends with Normand and the others, Bearden had previously joined the breakfast club at the Royal Blend. The sheriff also recalled that Bearden was working for the Vitter campaign.

Normand reached for his cell phone and called Bearden. "Wes, I have one of your investigators here," the sheriff said. "What's going on? He was trying to video and audio-tape me. I'm not happy."

"I don't know what you're talking about," Bearden said. "Let me find out what's going on. I'll call you right back." He called back several minutes later and said, "It's my guy."

"I'm just letting you know out of courtesy that we're going to arrest him," Normand said.

"Please don't do that," Bearden said.

"If you think that I'm going to tell five deputies who have been jumping fences with guns drawn, who are sweating bullets right now, to let this guy go, you're sadly mistaken," Normand said. "That's not the way I conduct business. I'm calling you as a courtesy so you can go get him out of jail."

Frenzel was booked on one count of criminal mischief, a misdemeanor.

While conducting opposition research and hiring private investigators to tail opponents is common practice—and perfectly legal—in political campaigns, videotaping a sheriff at a coffee shop and then fleeing from deputies stands out from the norm. When Kyle Ruckert, Vitter's campaign manager, found out about the incident, he was furious. "This is amateur hour stuff," he thought to himself. "This is not what we paid for."

Frenzel refused to talk at first but eventually confirmed that he had been sent to conduct surveillance on a man with a white beard. He also revealed that Cummings, not Normand, was the target. To insiders, this news came as a surprise, because the sheriff and Vitter had become political enemies over the years, dating from the era of Normand's predecessor and mentor, the late Sheriff Harry Lee. Normand, in fact, was supporting Lieutenant Governor Jay Dardenne over Vitter, even though the senator was the sheriff's neighbor.

Still, why the interest in Cummings? He had won big settlements for his clients in class action lawsuits, but in recent years Cummings concentrated on developing real estate throughout metro New Orleans. Months earlier, he had reopened the Whitney Plantation, some 30 miles upriver from the city, as a slave museum. Sure, Cummings was a trial lawyer who had long used his wealth and contacts to help Mary Landrieu and other Democrats. More recently, he and his wife Donna, as well as their businesses, had given John Bel Edwards a total of $25,000. But why would that merit a P.I. tailing him? Several weeks would pass before the Vitter campaign explained its interest in Cummings.

As Normand's deputies were taking Frenzel to the parish lockup, DeNoux had located Frenzel's car in the parking lot outside the Royal Blend. On the passenger seat of a silver Ford Focus hatchback with a commercial license plate, DeNoux saw a stack of LexisNexis reports— the same kind of reports he typically compiled when backgrounding a target. On the back seat, DeNoux saw boxes that contained recording equipment—similar to what he used to videotape or audiotape someone while working as a private eye.

As he examined the car, DeNoux remembered a phone call two nights earlier from Jason Brad Berry. The blogger related how he had been sitting on his porch in Algiers early that evening when he noticed a silver hatchback passing by slowly for a second or third time. Berry thought it odd, as he lived on a quiet street that gets little or no through traffic. He walked toward the front sidewalk and, sure enough, the car passed again. He and the driver made eye contact. The hatchback did not return.

Spooked, Berry canceled plans to go out that evening. He didn't want to leave his family alone. Then he phoned DeNoux. Suspicious by nature, the blogger was certain the vehicle was somehow related to his having posted the Wendy Ellis videos. It had to be someone from the Vitter campaign, he told DeNoux, adding that he was glad he had installed a security camera outside his home. That gave him the model and make of the car. DeNoux told him to make sure he kept the video.

Now, two days later at the Royal Blend, DeNoux took a picture of the silver hatchback and texted it to Berry. "Holy shit, that's the car in front of my house," Berry replied.

Records would soon reveal that the Vitter campaign had paid Bearden & Associates at least $135,000 for what the campaign described as "legal fees." It soon became apparent that the Vitter campaign had hired Bearden & Associates not only to tail Cummings but also to spy on Berry. Even before Frenzel bungled his encounter with Normand and Cummings at the Royal Blend, the Vitter campaign was worrying about the impact of Berry's video interviews on the race. Reporters and editors at key mainstream new outlets—including *The New York Times* and *Politico*, not to mention the local *Times-Picayune* and *The Advocate*—had received thick dossiers from Vitter's New Orleans lawyers outlining Ellis' criminal record in Florida, Louisiana, and Arkansas. That kind of research did not come cheap.

As sensational as Frenzel's arrest was, Jefferson Parish District Attorney Paul Connick Jr., who had supported Vitter for governor, would refuse, some eight months later, to pursue criminal charges against the young investigator. Team Vitter would cite Connick's decision as proof that Normand had abused his power as sheriff, that is, had attempted to torpedo the senator's campaign by making a big deal of Frenzel's amateurish attempt at sleuthing. For his part, the sheriff was nonchalant about the ultimate disposition of the case. "It doesn't rock my world in the least bit," he said. "We don't need to be wasting the time of the criminal justice system on this."

Frenzel's arrest, however, would not be the only bad news for Team Vitter on October 23 in Jefferson Parish. Early that afternoon, just hours after the Royal Blend incident, Normand got a phone call from John Fortunato, who handles media relations for the Jefferson Parish Sheriff's Office. "You're going to love this," Fortunato told his boss. "Vitter just left the scene of an accident."

It happened at 12:05 p.m., at the corner of Veterans Boulevard and Carrollton Avenue in Metairie—like the Royal Blend, just two blocks from the Orleans Parish line. Vitter was the passenger in a car that struck another vehicle in an otherwise minor fender bender. The press found out about the incident shortly, thanks to a few well placed phone calls from DeNoux, who was still in contact with Normand after the events of that morning. Fortunato sent out a statement that identified the driver as Courtney Guastella, who served as the fundraiser for both the Vitter campaign and his supporting super PAC, the Fund for Louisiana's Future. Fortunato's statement also noted that Vitter had no obligation to remain at the scene.

Despite this bit of information, some headlines placed Vitter inside of a car with an unnamed woman, not a paid staffer, and most of the original coverage and real-time social media updates stated he had fled the scene. In truth, after speaking to a law enforcement officer, Vitter had merely crossed the street for a pre-scheduled lunch. To political insiders, the funniest part of the auto accident was that it occurred right outside a Wendy's restaurant—Wendy being the first name of both Vitter's wife and the former prostitute who was now his accuser.

The Advocate had reporter Jim Mustian call Normand about Frenzel's arrest. The sheriff said he wasn't ready to confirm details. In the meantime, word having spread about Frenzel, operatives from the other campaigns tried to advance the story themselves. They called reporters and editors across the state, offering their own take and urging journalists to publish the story as soon as possible. Mustian didn't get Normand's confirmation until after 6 p.m. He posted his story three hours later.

"The arrest could have been ripped from a Hollywood script, playing out on the eve of a statewide election," read Mustian's lede. "But was it a drama or a comedy? Either way, it left one of the most powerful officials in Jefferson Parish pointing a finger at the leading Republican candidate for governor over alleged—if somewhat clumsy—spying."

As word of both the Royal Blend incident—quickly dubbed "Spygate"—and the fender bender went viral on social media, Team Vitter realized it had lost control of the primary campaign's narrative in the final stretch. The man who had so painstakingly orchestrated his every political word and deed after the scandal of his "very serious sin" came to light in 2007—and who just as thoroughly deconstructed most of his adversaries—was now tasting his own brand of political karma.

About 30 minutes after *The Advocate* news story posted, the Angelle campaign released a statement: "This is shocking and beyond troubling. It reeks of old-school politics. The questions about David Vitter continue and he refuses to provide any answers. This is yet another reason why Louisiana can't afford to elect David Vitter governor."

Dardenne followed with his own broadside 45 minutes later. "He's been caught cheating, lying, and now spying. Voters have seen enough from David Vitter to know two things. He is corrupt and can't be elected in a runoff."

The primary campaign had ended on a bizarre note. Polls would open at 7 a.m. the next morning. Vitter, Edwards, Angelle, and Dardenne had poured everything they had into the race. Now Louisiana voters would decide which two would advance to the runoff—and which two would wonder where they had gone wrong.

20

"We're Going to Kick Their Ass"

A gray family van pulled up in front of Jefferson Parish Fire Station #15 in the New Orleans suburb of Metairie, on a service road alongside Interstate 10. Out spilled David Vitter, his wife Wendy, and their four children. It was about 9:45 a.m. on October 24, Election Day. As the senator and Wendy held hands, the family walked up a circular driveway to the rear of the fire station, which doubled as the polling place in Vitter's home precinct. At long last, the voters of Louisiana were deciding which two candidates would advance to the gubernatorial runoff. It was time for American democracy, Louisiana style, to strut its stuff.

At that same time, John Bel Edwards was making stops in New Orleans, trying to pump up supporters. He had voted in Amite eight days earlier. Now he was all about the ground game—turning out his vote.

Jay Dardenne, who also had early-voted, met with campaign volunteers at his Baton Rouge headquarters on Perkins Road. They would make sure his supporters got to the polls that day.

Angelle spent Election Day morning touring his Acadiana home region in a caravan. His team ultimately headed north, making stops along the way, including one at Lea's Lunchroom on Highway 71 in Lecompte (pronounced "le-COUNT"), which was named after LeComte, a legendary thoroughbred racehorse whose owners had lived nearby. Lea's was equally legendary; folks were known to drive many miles for a slice of Lea's fresh-baked pie. On this day, Angelle was in search of votes. Not shy about discussing Spygate, he told one voter who asked about it, "From Vladimir to Vitter, nobody puts up with the KGB."

Each of the candidates had closed the campaign on a positive note, at least personally. In the last couple of days, Angelle had campaigned at a fish fry in Shreveport and at events in Acadiana, while broadcasting a television ad in which he wore a suit and tie, looked straight into the camera, and said, "I want your vote, and I won't ever embarrass you."

The pro-Angelle super PAC Louisiana Rising, meanwhile, fueled by more than $1 million in contributions from a Houston-based oil and gas executive named James Flores, had been broadcasting an ad that showed people holding their nose at the prospect of voting for Vitter. The ad pivoted to say they should instead vote for Angelle.

Vitter continued to broadcast the spot in which his wife Wendy said she knew that her husband would be the best choice. On the morning of the election, the senator gave his staff a pep talk at their campaign headquarters, waved signs with volunteers on West Esplanade in Metairie, met with elderly supporters in St. Tammany Parish, and spent time with his family.

Dardenne kept to his base in Baton Rouge on the final two days of the campaign while airing the ad in which he warned against the "Washington insiders" backing Vitter. Dardenne also spent Election Eve, well past midnight, in a studio recording a last-minute web video that sought to alert voters to the Spygate incident before they headed out to vote. "So we know this about David Vitter," Dardenne said in the video. "He's cheated, he's lied, and now he's been caught spying. We're no stranger to political corruption, but they usually wait until after they're elected to betray our trust."

Edwards closed with his earlier ad featuring West Point buddies attesting to his honor and courage. On Thursday afternoon, Edwards had appeared at the grand opening of the Louisiana Carpenters' Union headquarters along Interstate 10 in Metairie. His visit received such a rousing response that the union's national president, who had come from Washington for the event, pledged $100,000 on the spot to the pro-Edwards super PAC, Louisiana Families First. From the carpenters' HQ, Edwards drove to the Plumbers and Steamfitters Union Hall in Metairie. There, well-wishers greeting him and his wife Donna also enjoyed jambalaya and white beans in white plastic bowls, served from two giant black iron kettles. The AFL-CIO's top two union leaders, Louis Reine and Tiger Hammond, gave stem-winding speeches to introduce Edwards. As he walked to the podium, Donna leaned to Reine and said, "Oh, Louis, you got him riled up."

Indeed, Edwards was fired up. In the middle of his speech, he recited the litany of Republican attacks against him, then punctuated it with a bold prediction: "If that's the best they got, we're going to kick their ass!"

Edwards had reason to feel confident. Most of the final polls had shown him leading Vitter by a healthy margin. Angelle and Dardenne trailed the top two, but each man thought he could sneak past Vitter to face the Democrat.

A key factor deciding the fate of Angelle or Dardenne was whether most of the 15 percent to 20 percent of undecided white voters would break for either man or spread out among all three Republican candidates—the outcome Vitter wanted. Affording Angelle and Dardenne some hope: Undecided voters favored them more than Vitter, according to a poll, widely circulated two days before Election Day, that Verne Kennedy had conducted for the independent group of businessmen and women

For Edwards, the key question was whether African Americans, who formed the core of the Democratic Party, would comprise at least 25 percent of the overall turnout. If so, he would stand on very solid ground, especially if Jim Kitchens' poll for Edwards two days earlier was on target. It gave Edwards 40 percent of the vote in the primary versus 22 percent for Vitter. Of course, no one could be certain how the election would turn out. The University of New Orleans released an opt-in Internet poll on Thursday that had Vitter leading the race with 27 percent, followed by Edwards with 25 percent, Angelle with 15, and Dardenne with 11.

"Is this a joke?" tweeted a skeptical Ryan Cross, Angelle's campaign manager. The contradictory results were enough to prompt Jeremy White, the publisher of *Red Shtick*, a news parody magazine in Baton Rouge, to tweet that the various polls "remind me of this," and he attached a photo of hurricane forecasting models going in a spray of directions.

As Vitter and his family entered the rear of Fire Station #15, poll watchers sat at two folding tables near several voting machines. Vitter and Wendy presented their IDs and signed in. Making pleasantries with the poll watchers, Vitter noted that his twin teenage daughters were excited. They would be voting for the first time. Vitter entered the polling booth with his teenage son Jack and closed the plastic curtain. He gave a thumbs up as he emerged.

Other voters took the place of Vitter's family in the line at the fire station, and many of them didn't mind telling a reporter afterward that they were in the senator's corner. Lindsey Vindel said he backed Vitter because of the one-time frontrunner's "experience and connections"—echoing at least one of Vitter's TV ads. Vindel added, "His time in office allows him to know who to call to get help. That's important."

A woman named Rose said she lived in Vitter's neighborhood, and her reason for supporting the senator likewise reflected one of his campaign messages on a key issue: "Yes, I know he was messed up in a little scandal, but hell, I'm not perfect. He's a family man."

William Twitty, who described his own politics as "somewhere to the right of Attila the Hun," voted for Vitter because he "stands for the things I stand for. He's a conservative."

Edwards had his supporters, too. "I like his character," said a woman named Mary Windmeyer. "He appears to be honest."

A man named Joe called Edwards "a nice guy" but said more than anything his was a vote against Vitter. "The prostitution scandal was uncalled for. How can you trust somebody who does that?"

Vitter would hold his election party at the Airport Hilton in Kenner that evening. Edwards would appear at the Lyceum Dean Ballroom in downtown Baton Rouge, with Dardenne nearby at the Capitol Park Museum, and Angelle at the Acadiana Center for the Arts in downtown Lafayette.

The polls closed at 8 p.m. At 8:15 p.m., early returns gave Edwards the lead with 34,000 votes, followed by Angelle with 21,000, Vitter 19,000, and Dardenne 12,000. Angelle supporters were ecstatic. Maybe, just maybe they could knock off the long-time favorite. But only five minutes later, Vitter passed Angelle and took a 1,000-vote lead over him, while Edwards continued to pace the field.

By 8:30 p.m., Vitter's advantage over Angelle stretched to 7,000 votes and by 8:45 p.m., it was 8,000.

At 8:59 p.m., WWL-TV in New Orleans reported that Edwards was assured of a spot in the runoff. But which Republican would he face?

At 9:21 p.m., Angelle trailed Vitter by only 1 percent.

At 9:24 p.m., with just over half the precincts reporting, returns showed Edwards far in the lead with 39 percent, followed by Vitter with 23 percent, Angelle 21 percent, and Dardenne 14 percent.

At 9:36 p.m., *The Advocate's* Elizabeth Crisp tweeted that Edwards would not address the crowd until he knew the identity of his runoff opponent.

At 9:39 p.m., *The Advocate's* Marsha Shuler tweeted that Dardenne's supporters at his election night party were beginning to realize that they wouldn't have anything to celebrate.

At 9:41 p.m., The Associated Press called the race: It would be an Edwards–Vitter runoff.

Troopers from Louisiana State Police immediately offered both men protection and started providing transportation in State Police SUVs for Edwards. Vitter, hoping to draw further distinctions between himself and Governor Bobby Jindal, declined the protection. He had accused Jindal of using a "caravan" just to get his children to school and suggested that four troopers per candidate was overkill. Vitter even promised to cut all such protective details for state officials if elected.

At the Capitol Park Museum, Dardenne conceded to his downcast gathering. He offered his best wishes to only one of the two men in the runoff, and anybody closely following the race could guess which one he disfavored. Around the same time Dardenne was speaking to his election night party, Angelle took the stage at the Acadiana Center for the Arts against the backdrop of the Sister Sledge anthem, "We Are Family." He waited for the applause to die down. "We came up a little short," he said. "Don't cry for me. Don't weep for me. You will hear from me again." Cheers again. Angelle did not endorse Vitter, his fellow Republican.

Just after Angelle finished, at 10 p.m., Edwards took the stage at the crowded Lyceum Ballroom. For many long and lonely months, he had been an Army of One fighting to gain relevance. During that time, only he and a handful of people believed he had a path to victory. He needed no other big name Democrat to enter the race, and, indeed, Mitch Landrieu and several potential African-American candidates had opted not to run. That had allowed Edwards to unite the Democratic base in the primary, beginning with the unions that represented industrial workers, teachers, and government employees. His pro-life, pro-gun, and anti-gay marriage voting record allowed him to make inroads among social conservatives who had voted for Republicans in recent elections but were willing to look at a Democrat, given Vitter's scandals. Now he stood among a cheering throng, surrounded by his family and key supporters, basking in returns that few could have foreseen and even fewer would have predicted just a few months earlier:

	Votes	Percentage
John Bel Edwards (D)	444,517	39.89
David Vitter (R)	256,300	23.00
Scott Angelle (R)	214,982	19.29
Jay Dardenne (R)	166,656	14.96
Cary Deaton (D)	11,763	1.06
S.L. Simpson (D)	7,420	0.67
Beryl Billiot (NP)	5,694	0.51
Jeremy "JW" Odom (NP)	4,756	0.43
Eric Paul Orgeron (NP)	2,248	0.20

"On Saturday night," *The Washington Post* reported, "many Democrats began to see hope in an unfamiliar place: Louisiana." Vitter, added the newspaper, "seen as the frontrunner in this year's gubernatorial election since the day he announced, wheezed over the finish line to secure a runoff spot."

A look at the six largest parishes showed that Edwards won big majorities in East Baton Rouge, New Orleans, and Shreveport. He carried his home parish of Tangipahoa, while Vitter won Jefferson Parish by only 4,600 votes. Edwards limited the senator's advantage in the Republican stronghold of St. Tammany to a 9,000-vote lead, and nearly equaled Angelle in Lafayette. In all, Edwards led in 45 parishes, Vitter in 10, Angelle in nine, and Dardenne in none. One figure no one celebrated: Turnout was only 39.2 percent of registered voters.

The election results provided more numbers to parse: Edwards led the pack in 23 rural parishes that Mary Landrieu had lost a year earlier. He would have to make further inroads with conservatives, however, to get above the magic 50 percent threshold in the runoff.

In 31 parishes, or nearly half the state, Edwards' share of the vote was higher than Angelle's and Dardenne's combined. In two other parishes, he tied their collective tally.

Edwards had said only a few words to the crowd at the Lyceum Ballroom before he delivered his most important message of the night. "I want to tell you, I have developed a true affection for Jay Dardenne and Scott Angelle," he said. "They both ran tremendous races. They are good public servants, decent men, and I like them a lot. I know it's got to be tough on them and their families and their supporters. I want to reach out to them right now and tell them we have room for them." The ballroom erupted into cheers. Edwards returned to his tone of inclusion minutes later. "I want to invite all the voters out there who didn't vote for me tonight, whether they voted for Scott or Jay or quite frankly whether they voted for David Vitter," he said. "I want to invite them to come to our campaign, to join our effort, so together we can put Louisiana first. The stakes are too high. We cannot afford to get this one wrong." The crowd roared again.

Edwards then drew a bead on his favorite bogeyman. "For eight years, our people have been sacrificed on the altar of Bobby Jindal's ambition," he said.

"No more," a man cried out.

Edwards immediately picked up on that. "No more," he said. "No more. We're going to correct that. We need a committed, disciplined governor with the leadership ability to bring people together, regardless of race, gender, party, geography—bring people together to pursue the common interest, the kind of leadership I learned at West Point, the kind of leadership I further developed commanding troops at the 82nd Airborne Division, my leadership in the Legislature, standing up to Bobby Jindal when he was at the height of his power, but he was wrong." More cheers.

Edwards gave shout-outs to teachers, to investing in higher education, to raising the minimum wage, to providing equal pay for women, and to expanding Medicaid—all hallmarks of his campaign. Now he was excited. "We're going to kick their butts," he told the live TV audience. "We're going to kick their butts." The crowd erupted once again. Amidst the cheers, Donna turned to her left, to her daughter Sarah Ellen, and gave her a yes-he-did-say-that look.

"Go, John Bel!" yelled a woman.

Edwards now trained his fire on his opponent. "Over the next few weeks, David Vitter is going to spend millions of dollars lying about my record, lying about my values, lying about my service to our country and to our state," he said. "He's desperate. He's desperate. All he offers are lies and hypocrisy. But I'm not going to sell my soul to win this election. I will not do that. I live by the Honor Code: A cadet will not lie, cheat, steal, or tolerate those who do." He raised his left hand for emphasis. "David Vitter would not last five minutes at West Point!" The crowd yelled its support. "He wouldn't last five minutes at West Point!" Edwards yelled again above the raucous cheers.

Now Edwards sought to define the upcoming election on his terms. "Let me tell you, Senator Vitter is going to make this race about everything but what's important to us here in Louisiana," Edwards said. "He's not going to have his focus on you, or this state, or on Baton Rouge. He's going to try to distract you. He's going to try to divert your attention. Let me tell you something, I studied the art of war. I know all about diversionary tactics. That ain't gonna work. This isn't going to work. But you can't let it work. The people of Louisiana are better than that. They are smarter than that. He's going to try to divide us. He wants to prey on our fears. He wants to relate to certain people's bigotry. That's what's going to come in this race. I want you to brace yourself.

"This is going to be a real tough runoff to watch unfold on TV. It's just going to be that way. And I'm sorry about that. I'm not going to be the one doing it. I haven't run a single negative spot in the two years I've been running this campaign." The crowded applauded. "Let's just talk about it," Edwards continued. "David Vitter's going to try to put the focus on the president in Washington, D.C. If he believes those are our biggest problems in Louisiana, he needs to stay in Washington. He needs to stay in Washington." Edwards paused and ad-libbed, "By the way, I intend to make sure that that happens." The crowd cheered again.

Edwards returned to a theme of inclusion. "My pledge to you is this: I will always put Louisiana first," he said. "Make no mistake about it. Make no mistake about it. I will gladly stand up with the men and women of either party when they want to do something that's right for Louisiana. And I will proudly stand up and fight against anyone of any party when they want to do something against Louisiana. That's what it means to put Louisiana first."

Edwards then returned to the task of defining his opponent. "The simple fact of the matter is that David Vitter doesn't want the people to know who he really is and what he thinks," he said. "What is he hiding? Why is it that he doesn't want to go to debates? Why is it that he doesn't face the press? That he doesn't answer questions? Or *The Question*, perhaps?" The crowd laughed. Edwards said he looked forward to the two debates scheduled during the runoff and said he hoped Vitter would show up.

Even before Edwards had finished at the Lyceum, Vitter—and his wife Wendy, their children, and key supporters—walked onto the stage at the Airport Hilton. They were all smiles, as if Vitter were running a strong first instead of a disappointing second. In fact, the Vitter camp knew it would be Edwards' big night, and they knew that appearances on live TV matter. "Wendy! Wendy! Wendy!" chanted the crowd when she stood behind the microphone to introduce her husband. It would be the loudest ovation of the evening. The crowd supported David, but they *loved* Wendy. "Twenty five years ago, I made the decision to marry my best friend," she said. The crowd cheered.

"David! David David!" went the chants as her husband stepped up to the podium. Like Edwards, Vitter knew that winning over the votes of his Republican rivals was paramount going forward. "I want to thank Scott Angelle and Jay Dardenne for their dedicated service and competitive service," he said. "I've always respected their accomplishments." Notwithstanding, of course, how both he and the pro-Vitter super PAC had savagely attacked the two men.

Vitter quickly turned to his us-versus-them campaign message. "The politicians in Baton Rouge have created one helluva mess," he said. "We're going to take our future back."

Then Vitter turned to the familiar template, the one that worked so well for him in 2010 and for Bill Cassidy 2014. "We have a stark difference in the runoff," he said, adding that Edwards was backed by "national liberals and Barack Obama. John Bel Edwards is not a casual supporter of Barack Obama. He is a true believer. Voting for John Bel Edwards would be the same as a voting to make Barack Obama governor of Louisiana. The good news is that we can chart a different path." It hadn't taken long for Edwards' prediction to come true.

Throughout the race, John Bel Edwards and David Vitter had wanted to face each other. Now they had that matchup. On this night, Edwards had won more votes than practically anyone had predicted even a few weeks ago. Moreover, he and his team believed that his reaching the 40 percent mark would loosen purse strings enough to allow him to match Vitter's fundraising prowess over the coming four weeks. Still, most analysts that night gave the senator the advantage, heading toward November 21.

Vitter had had a bigger campaign treasury and had found a way to win every race that he had run. He would remain the heavyweight champion in Louisiana politics until he was defeated, and on this election night Republicans had kept all the other statewide elected offices—and had kept their majority in both the state House and Senate. Vitter seemingly had another advantage: nearly 60 percent of the electorate had voted in the primary for one of the three Republican candidates. Could those conservatives really turn against Vitter in deep-red Louisiana?

Edwards and his team saw it another way. In the Southern Media & Opinion Research poll in April, Vitter had roughly 45 percent of the decided vote (38 percent in the "raw" numbers). Tonight he had won barely half that total. His campaign was in a nose dive, and he had only four weeks to pull out of it.

Both views made sense, but only one could be right. The key was to snatch the runoff narrative and not let go. On October 24, 2015, the narrative was up for grabs.

Part Three

"Hell, I never vote for anybody. I always vote against."
—*W.C. Fields*

21

The First Rule of a Knife Fight

On the afternoon following his stunning primary lead, John Bel Edwards stood at the right hand of a Louisiana political legend—a massive photograph of Huey Long that covered the entire wall of a meeting room inside the Hotel Indigo. Edwards was in Baton Rouge, holding his first press conference of the runoff. There was an easiness to this encounter. Reporters cracked jokes with Edwards throughout, a sure sign that he had an "in" with the political press. David Vitter had focused his messaging the previous night on the similarities between Edwards and Barack Obama. Today, Edwards stood before reporters with a different set of talking points that would appear in coverage across the state within hours. "My message is squarely in the mainstream of the political spectrum," Edwards said, later adding, "If Senator Vitter insists on making this election about associations, I will engage him about his associations, and I believe the voters will be more concerned about his associations than mine."

The first rule of a knife fight, and of a political showdown: There are no rules. This runoff was going to be a brawl between the one-time Army Ranger from Amite and the take-no-prisoners senator from Metairie.

After his press conference, Edwards joined the reporters who had made their way to the hotel bar to watch the final plays as the New Orleans Saints held off the Indianapolis Colts to notch a badly needed victory. Although Vitter was known to friends and family as a die-hard Saints fan, he would never have watched a game with a gaggle of campaign reporters at a bar. In fact, Vitter did not have an open press availability that day. He instead spoke to pre-selected reporters one-on-one. He otherwise focused on raising money for the runoff by meeting donors for brunch at Andrea's Restaurant in Metairie. Between Andrea's and calls to other potential donors, Vitter was on his way to collecting $1 million in new donations that day.

The primary over, the dynamics of the race began changing

quickly. Marsanne Golsby, Jay Dardenne's communications director, endorsed Edwards on Twitter and Facebook, and the Democratic Governors Association finally decided to begin sending resources to Louisiana. Word had also leaked that Edwards would secure the endorsement of the Louisiana Sheriffs' Association, which had scheduled an official vote the following day.

In another positive sign for Edwards, Bob Mann came around on the Democratic candidate's chances against Vitter. The LSU professor and *Times-Picayune* columnist had written in May that Edwards could not win, and he had received a pointed text message from Donna Edwards as a result. After attending church on the morning after the primary, Mann wrote an opinion piece for his blog that had a markedly different tone. "I was wrong: John Bel Edwards can win the Louisiana governor's race," read his headline. "I'm not prepared to say that Edwards will be Louisiana's next governor (let's see a poll in about ten days, after Vitter, his super PAC and the Republican Governors Association dump a million or two in negative spots on him). But as of Sunday night, it is not hard to see how Edwards can defeat Vitter."

Before Mann finished his column, Edwards was meeting with about two dozen of his key donors at the Lod Cook Hotel on LSU's campus. For Edwards, fundraising in the runoff was a whole new game. Until the late summer of 2015, he drove clear across the state to raise $5,000. Now, four weeks before the November 21 runoff, Edwards and his team were giddy. Even without their asking, pledges for campaign contributions were pouring in like Niagara Falls at flood stage. "You can count on me," texted one person to Daniel Edwards, the candidate's younger brother and Tangipahoa Parish sheriff, late on election night. "Let me know when the next fundraiser is," texted another.

At Lod Cook, Andrew Edwards, a distant cousin who was the campaign's treasurer, handed out copies of the proposed budget, broken into 11 categories of spending. John Bel Edwards had spent $1.7 million during the entire primary. Now he was proposing to spend $4.4 million during the four-week runoff. No one blinked at the amount. "I have commitments for $100,000," called out one person.

"I can raise $500,000 in two weeks," shouted another.

What a difference a big primary vote makes. Edwards stood before the group and smiled confidently. "I'd much rather be in my shoes than his," he told the donors. "The only way we can lose the race is if we take it for granted and are outworked. That will not happen."

Still, Edwards faced a short-term cash flow problem. He needed to start paying for television ads immediately, and accessing the big money would take his campaign at least a week. Cousin

Andrew's budget called for spending $650,000 a week on TV. John Bel Edwards was a man who tended to move cautiously, but he had learned to improvise—and take risks when necessary—throughout the campaign. He realized he would have to take a big personal risk right then. Edwards authorized cousin Andrew to seek a line of credit from the First Guaranty Bank of Hammond, using his Rosedale home as collateral. Alton Lewis, the bank's chief executive officer who knew both John Bel and Andrew, quickly understood the situation they faced. Andrew walked out of the bank with a $750,000 line of credit for the campaign.

In the compressed time frame of a runoff campaign, everything has to move faster. Both candidates wasted no time launching new television campaign ads on Monday, October 26, to grab the early narrative. Edwards wanted the focus squarely on Vitter's character. The senator wanted it all about *Obama! Obama! Obama!* Both men got their wish.

In his first runoff ad, Edwards stood in an office setting, wearing a coat but no tie, and he spoke directly into the camera. "For the next few weeks, David Vitter will spend millions of dollars lying about my record, my values, and my service to our country and our state," he said. "He's desperate. All he offers is deception and hypocrisy. I won't sell my soul to win an election." He then half-smiled.

"I live by the West Point Honor Code: I will not lie, cheat, steal, or tolerate those who do." Edwards smiled more broadly now as he reprised the attention-getting line from his election night victory speech: "David Vitter wouldn't last a day at West Point." The ad would run for the first week to 10 days of the runoff, defining the Democrat and his message—and contrasting him with Vitter's scorched-earth campaign.

As if on cue, Vitter's first ad was dark and foreboding. "Voting for John Bel Edwards is like voting to make Obama Louisiana's next governor," an announcer intoned over shots of the two men as if they were together. *Obama wants to release 6,000 dangerous convicts from prison,* the ad said. "Edwards joined Obama, promising at Southern University that he'll release 5,500 alone," the announcer said as viewers saw a slow motion clip of Edwards speaking at Southern, shot by a pro-Vitter super PAC's campaign tracker. "Fifty-five hundred dangerous thugs," the announcer said ominously. More scary black-and-white images flashed on the screen—of convicts, cocaine, a woman anxiously looking out her window through blinds. "Obama and Edwards—wrong for Louisiana," the ad concluded.

The Edwards campaign immediately cried foul. "In fact, Edwards has never suggested 'releasing prisoners,'" the campaign said in a statement sent to reporters. "He has suggested a comprehensive plan to address Louisiana's ranking as the number one state when it comes to incarceration per capita by addressing treatment of non-violent offenders."

The ad also offended *Times-Picayune* columnist Jarvis DeBerry, who put Edwards' statement in a September 22 speech at Southern into context. "We will be number two in the nation in incarceration rates when I'm finished because it's going to require us to take 5,500 inmates out of our prisons," DeBerry quoted Edwards as saying. "We will get to number two behind Mississippi."

DeBerry went on to add: "There's the stench of Willie Horton in Vitter's ad. If you can't smell it, then you're ignoring the race of the people who pop into your mind when you hear the word 'thugs.' They're the same race as Horton, the black Massachusetts prisoner who didn't return from a weekend furlough and later raped a woman. Michael Dukakis, the Bay State governor when Horton was furloughed, ran for president in 1988, and Lee Atwater, campaign manager for Republican George H.W. Bush, said, 'By the time we're finished, they're going to wonder whether Willie Horton is Dukakis' running mate.'"

While the campaigns were releasing their ads on Monday, sheriffs from throughout the state were deciding which candidate to endorse. At the group's annual conference in July, Vitter had pressed for an early endorsement—but he had pushed too hard. The sheriffs had met again on September 16 to see if they wanted to issue an endorsement during the primary. In a straw poll, Edwards had led with about 25 votes while Dardenne and Angelle had 12 and 15. Vitter pulled up the rear with only five votes. The sheriffs didn't endorse that day because no candidate had won a majority, but the tally nonetheless was an ominous sign for Vitter. Now that the primary was over, the sheriffs' endorsement, a key part of the early runoff narrative, was sure to get a lot of attention.

On the night before the sheriffs' meeting, Vitter used a softer approach. He texted that he would be "a strong law enforcement-supporting governor; I sincerely want to be your friend. I'll do everything possible to see that we forge that great relationship."

The sheriffs met the next morning at 10 a.m. in the auditorium at the Louisiana Sheriffs' Association headquarters in Baton Rouge. Edwards handed out red lapel pins with his name on them for the sheriffs in attendance to wear. Holding the small bag of pins in his hand, all the team color of the opposing party, he laughed and asked himself, "Why the hell didn't we get these in blue?"

The color didn't matter. With his brother Daniel and Newell

Normand in Edwards' corner, the vote for the Democrat was a formality, and the candidate knew it. Sheriff after sheriff stood up to voice his support for Edwards, while only one or two championed Vitter. When the secret vote concluded, Edwards had won the endorsement handily. More important, on the first weekday of the runoff campaign, a day on which Vitter began trying to paint the Democrat as soft on crime, the state's top law enforcement officials had overwhelmingly said Edwards was their guy. The Democrat had not lost his momentum from the primary. In fact, he was gaining momentum—and the narrative was his, for now.

The Republican Governors Association came to Vitter's aid again, quickly. On October 27, one day after the sheriffs' endorsement of Edwards—and three days after the primary—the RGA ran its first runoff ad attacking Edwards. The opening line got right to the point: "John Bel Edwards wants to raise taxes just like Obama." The spot noted his vote to increase his legislative salary and labeled him "just another Obama liberal."

That same day, the Democratic Governors Association made its move and announced a partnership with the anti-Vitter Gumbo PAC run by Trey Ourso. The Baton Rouge consultant, known nationally for his work with direct mail, had formed Gumbo PAC in mid-May and believed its existence had helped puncture Vitter's perceived inevitability. But Ourso had had trouble raising money and mostly confined his anti-Vitter message during the primary to Facebook posts and social media ads. Meanwhile, the DGA had repeatedly rebuffed Edwards' requests to pony up cash for his campaign. By early October, however, DGA officials had had second thoughts. They commissioned a survey by Gumbo PAC's pollsters, Anzalone Liszt Grove, based in Montgomery, Alabama.

From October 15 to 20, the polling firm interviewed 500 likely voters, all of them white. Why only whites? Because as John Anzalone explained later, they knew that white voters' support would be critical if, as expected, Edwards faced Vitter in the runoff. Among other encouraging results for Edwards, the poll showed Vitter's unfavorable rating among whites at 51 percent, while Edwards' was only 29 percent. One more finding stood out: Dardenne and Angelle voters didn't like Vitter. That created an opening for the Democrat.

The DGA liked the numbers enough to put its weight behind Edwards in the runoff by joining forces with Gumbo PAC. The association sent Ourso an initial $350,000. He got to work immediately.

On October 27, the same day that the RGA launched its "John Bel Edwards wants to raise taxes just like Obama" ad, viewers saw Gumbo PAC's 30-second ad featuring clips of Dardenne and Angelle from the televised primary debates. Each sound bite thoroughly thrashed Vitter. The spot began with Angelle at the LSU debate 11 days earlier: "We have a stench that is getting ready to come over Louisiana if we elect David Vitter as governor." It then jumped back and forth between Dardenne and Angelle hurling barbs at their fellow Republican— "vicious" and "ineffective"—before giving the lieutenant governor the last word: "It's not going to go away, and it's a stain on Louisiana." The ad spoke directly to Dardenne and Angelle voters, and expressed concerns about Vitter. "The goal of that first commercial was basically to 'freeze' the Angelle and Dardenne voters in their current posture of not voting for Vitter," Ourso would write later.

The ad had another target audience: the two Republican candidates themselves. Ourso wanted to remind Dardenne and Angelle of Vitter's harsh treatment of them in the primary and make it tougher for them to endorse him in the runoff. The two men hadn't forgotten. Vitter called each the day after the primary. Angelle refused to take his calls and didn't respond to emissaries asking him to call the senator. Dardenne took the call but told Vitter that he wouldn't endorse him. When they met on Wednesday, October 28, at the lieutenant governor's apartment in the Pentagon Barracks near the Capitol, Dardenne again said no.

Edwards, meanwhile, was bringing aboard his biggest potential Democratic rival from the primary, New Orleans Mayor Mitch Landrieu—who had frustrated Edwards by telling his political circle that Edwards had no chance. As recently as a month before the primary, Landrieu had pressed his team to support either Dardenne or Angelle—or Gumbo PAC's "ABV" campaign—to block Vitter. After Edwards' strong primary vote, Landrieu joined six other mayors who endorsed him on October 30. That afternoon Landrieu flew with John Bel and Donna Edwards to a fundraiser in the nation's capital. Business executive Jim Bernhard, himself a would-be Democratic candidate for governor at one time, provided the plane and accompanied them.

The party was hosted by James Carville at his D.C.-area home, a former art gallery across the Potomac River from Washington. Carville, one of the most recognizable Democrats in America, split his time between his homes in Old Town Alexandria and Uptown New Orleans. A confidante of Mitch Landrieu, he, too, had kept his distance from Edwards for most of the primary, doubting the Democrat's chances. "You really didn't want to have Vitter, and we could live with Dardenne," Carville explained after the election. He became an Edwards supporter in late September—several weeks before Landrieu got on board—and agreed to host the fundraiser.

About 50 people showed up, including former Louisiana Democratic Senators John Breaux and J. Bennett Johnston; Donna

Brazile, the Kenner native and party leader who regularly appeared on national TV talk shows; and Virginia's Democratic governor, Terry McAuliffe, a longtime friend of Carville's. The money raised went to the Democratic Governors Association, which was in the midst of pouring $2.25 million into Gumbo PAC to defeat Vitter.

The night before Carville's big-dollar gathering for Edwards, a 43-year-old Republican state representative from Bossier City named Mike Johnson set his laptop on his kitchen table and began typing. For weeks, Johnson had been stewing about the governor's race. He knew and liked Edwards, going back to when they overlapped at LSU's law school for two years, with Johnson one year ahead. They had gotten reacquainted after Johnson won a special election to the state House in 2014. The freshman legislator's grasp of the law and House procedure immediately stood out.

Johnson, who had spent years traveling the country, speaking on behalf of conservative causes, had become a sought-after attorney to represent the right-to-life movement. His dogmatic views against abortion and gay rights were polarizing. During the 2015 session, he sponsored a so-called religious freedom bill that Christian conservatives championed as protecting the rights of people who didn't want to be "forced" to violate their religious beliefs by, say, having to make a wedding cake for a gay couple. Leftists vilified Johnson, calling him a bigot. In person, he came across as a friendly, neighborly sort.

Johnson had gotten to know Vitter when Vitter was elected to the Senate in 2004, as Johnson frequently accompanied him to Sunday services at the Christian churches in his area. Afterward, they worked together on pro-life legislation, and Johnson always came away impressed. "I always felt like David Vitter was playing chess and everyone else checkers," Johnson said later. "In every setting I was in, David was always affable and magnanimous. I regarded him as a guy with high ethics."

Immediately after Vitter admitted his "very serious sin" in 2007, Johnson was among those he called. Vitter was contrite and soft-spoken as he apologized. At the senator's request, they met a short time later at his Shreveport office. As they talked, Johnson saw a side that Vitter had not shown publicly, certainly not to the reporters who had concluded that the senator's statements about the affair were contrived to get him past the scandal. Johnson believed that Vitter genuinely regretted his behavior, had changed his ways, and had made right with his wife Wendy and four children.

"Senator, we all fail," Johnson told him. "I believe in redemption. I believe in forgiveness. If you've made it right with your God and your family, who am I to judge you?" Johnson's understanding of scriptures told him that contrition and a broken heart—which he was seeing in Vitter—were how you got right with God.

Yet eight years later, as he traveled in conservative circles during the gubernatorial campaign, Johnson was struck repeatedly by the ill will toward Vitter. "Oh, I could never vote for him," people would say. Johnson would ask why. "Oh, he was a sinner," they would say.

"Who doesn't have sin in their past?" Johnson would ask. "Don't we believe in redemption? The Bible says we forgive and move on and give people a second chance. You judge people by the fruits of their life." In Johnson's view, Vitter's fruits were bountiful. Johnson made this argument with every Vitter naysayer he encountered, but finally decided he needed to express his views to a wider audience. That's why he spent several hours typing away at his kitchen table on October 29, 2015. By 10 p.m., after his wife Kelly had put their four kids to bed, Johnson had completed a nearly 3,000-word epistle in which he spelled out why Christian conservatives ought to support Vitter. Satisfied with his work, Johnson posted it on his Facebook page.

He divided the piece into two parts. The first focused on policy, akin to a legal brief, citing legislative bills and website links as exhibits. "David Vitter is a PROVEN conservative who has CONSISTENTLY stood and voted over the years for less government, lower taxes, and traditional American values like religious liberty, the sanctity of human life, and traditional marriage," wrote Johnson. In sharp contrast, Edwards "is the Louisiana leader of the Democratic Party, which openly advocates for bigger government, higher taxes, and radically liberal social stances on abortion, the redefinition of marriage, amnesty for illegal immigrants, and all sorts of other leftist policies."

In the second part, Johnson answered the question that troubled many conservatives: "Can you vote for an imperfect candidate?"

"He had asked for forgiveness, worked towards restoration, and sought reconciliation," Johnson wrote. "He was forgiven by God and his extraordinary wife, they saved their marriage, and they are faithful believers. They have a truly inspiring Christian testimony."

Johnson then turned to the Bible to make his case. "Adultery is a serious sin, indeed, but it is not unforgivable," he wrote. "Jesus said so repeatedly."

He added, "Sometimes, a baptism of fire is necessary preparation for leadership. Indeed, I am a bit wary of any aspiring leader who has never endured great trial. There is a depth of insight and authenticity that can only be known by one who has limped through the darkest of valleys and emerged with an iron embrace of the love and sovereignty of God. Dark valleys help us to develop the kind of eternal perspective that sustains and satisfies the human heart—and keeps us humble and useful to our Creator."

Johnson's piece resonated with believers. When he checked his computer in the morning, he saw that the Facebook post was spreading like wildlife. "Very humbling," Vitter tweeted out to his 30,000 followers that morning, and many of them retweeted Vitter's comment and Johnson's piece. The news journal for Louisiana's Baptists wrote it up. *The Hayride* blog reprinted it. The state Republican Party and the Vitter campaign sent it out. State Representative Lance Harris, a Republican from Alexandria, reprinted it in full-page ads that he bought in *The Town Talk*.

Edwards was not happy. He called Johnson at 6:30 a.m. on Monday, November 2. "What are you doing"? Edwards asked angrily.

"What do you mean?" responded Johnson.

"You made it personal," Edwards told him, adding that Johnson had failed to note Edwards' pro-life voting record, his pro-NRA record, and his opposition to gay marriage. Johnson had made Edwards seem to support the national Democratic agenda, he complained. "You know I don't believe in all that stuff," Edwards said.

Johnson said that he was simply making a clear policy distinction.

Edwards wasn't buying that argument. "Look, he said, "I'm going to tell you one thing. I am going to win this race. I am going to win it by a wide margin. I am going to be your governor. And I will never forget this."

"That's very disappointing to hear," Johnson replied. "This is not personal. It's a policy distinction. I thought that was fair game in a political race."

"I'm just telling you that I'll never forget this," Edwards repeated and hung up.

The Democrat had a busy day of campaigning ahead of him. He ended the evening at Ruth's Chris Steak House in Baton Rouge with a bevy of video poker device owners and truck stop casino owners. Though few were aware of the connection, Edwards was close to the video poker industry and its nattily attired chief lobbyist, Alton Ashy. He had, in fact, a 100 percent voting record with the industry. One of his first contributions during the campaign for governor, in 2013, had come from Minnie Hughes, a truck stop owner in Amite.

During the primary, Ashy had met with Vitter, who tried to reassure him that he would be open to their interests, unlike Bobby Jindal, who for eight years had heeded the requests of the anti-gambling Louisiana Family Forum. Because Christian conservatives were a key part of Vitter's political base, Ashy was not convinced that the senator's actions would be any different from Jindal's. The upshot was that device and truck stop owners gave money to Edwards throughout the primary. When the Ruth's Chris fundraiser on November 2 ended, the Edwards campaign kitty was $200,000 richer, and within a week, Ashy had secured another $150,000 from video poker interests.

The Democrat had come out of the primary with the political wind at his back, and events during the first week of runoff seemed only to strengthen his position. The latest independent poll reflected this dynamic. Conducted for WVLA-TV in Baton Rouge by pollster John Couvillon and released on November 2, it showed Edwards leading in every Louisiana market except Alexandria. The poll had Edwards over Vitter, 52 percent to 32 percent, with 16 percent undecided. In the runoff, Couvillon said in an interview, Vitter needed to get 80 percent of the people who voted for Dardenne and Angelle in the primary. In Couvillon's poll, however, the senator was drawing only 60 percent. "Vitter is not getting the votes of Republicans that he needs to win," the pollster said. "Vitter ran a negative campaign against Dardenne and Angelle in the primary. It's difficult for voters to flip the switch."

As for Edwards, everything was going his way, which, for a campaign, can signal the calm before the storm. Outside factors no one can foresee or control have a way of suddenly casting the world in a different light. That happened on Tuesday, November 3, in Kentucky, of all places. There, Matt Bevin, the conservative Republican candidate, won the governor's race despite late polls showing him trailing his Democratic opponent. Team Vitter immediately seized on Bevin's victory to question the Louisiana polls that showed he would lose to Edwards. The senator's point made sense to a lot of voters in Louisiana, and to some pundits. Not many people were ready to believe that a Democrat in ruby-red Louisiana could beat the longstanding Republican frontrunner. An undercurrent of doubt began to swirl.

For his part, Edwards reminded himself and others that he was very different from Mary Landrieu, Charlie Melancon, and others the Republicans had crushed by tying them to President Obama. Voters got another reminder of that difference on November 4, when they saw a new Edwards ad. It featured four sheriffs telling viewers to dismiss stories that Edwards wanted to release dangerous prisoners. The men who oversaw many of the state's prisoners said, in the words of Calcasieu Parish Sheriff Tony Mancuso, that such claims were "false" and "irresponsible."

A day later, the news got worse for Vitter: Jay Dardenne officially endorsed Edwards for governor. That news couldn't have come as a surprise to Team Vitter. The senator had tried to end Dardenne's political career in 2011 by backing Billy Nungesser in the lieutenant governor's race, and his own months-long campaign against Dardenne for governor had only deepened the Republican's disdain for the erstwhile frontrunner. A Vitter victory would be "catastrophic" for Louisiana, Dardenne said privately, a week after finishing fourth in the primary with 15 percent of the vote. He said he was hearing from a majority of his supporters that they planned to vote for Edwards.

Standing behind a podium decked with a blue-and-white "Edwards For Governor" sign at LSU's student union, the Republican lieutenant governor spoke confidently, without any hesitation. "He knows that fear, intimidation, and vindictiveness are the enemies of building the coalition to move Louisiana forward," Dardenne said of Edwards, echoing the Democrat's campaign theme against Vitter. "He will govern in a bipartisan manner, based upon what's best for Louisiana, without regard to how it plays to a national audience. The Republican brand has been damaged by the failed leadership of Bobby Jindal during this last term. A David Vitter governorship will further damage that brand, as I and others have pointed out during the campaign. I cannot and will not sit idly by and refuse to speak truth to power. I will support an honorable pro-life, pro-gun Democrat who can build coalitions."

Dardenne's decision outraged many conservatives. Rob Maness, the former Air Force colonel who had run third in the 2014 Senate race, called Dardenne "Benedict Arnold." State GOP Chair Roger Villere reached for a more contemporary insult, comparing him to the football coach who had forsaken LSU for the hated Alabama Crimson Tide. Dardenne, according to Villere, was the "Nick Saban of Louisiana Politics." Villere, a florist by trade, apparently took little notice that Saban was at the time leading Alabama to yet another national title.

After the Dardenne endorsement, Edwards drove to Alexandria. Jay Luneau, an attorney who had just been elected to the state Senate, hosted a fundraiser at his home that evening for the Democrat. Edwards had originally told Luneau that he hoped to raise $100,000 at the event. A few days later, Luneau told him he thought he could raise $150,000. They talked a day or two later, and Luneau upped the expected haul to $175,000. Edwards' supporters ended up turning out in droves, and the campaign raised $350,000. The event left Luneau shaking his head, as he had raised a total of only $125,000 during his own successful campaign.

Edwards' big night was yet another sign of the changing political tide. *The Cook Political Report*, a respected national newsletter published by Louisiana native Charlie Cook, had already taken notice and reclassified the race as a "toss-up," noting that Vitter's vulnerabilities were carrying more weight "than we would have anticipated."

Other political "experts" remained skeptical that Edwards could win. On the same day as Luneau's fundraiser, *Roll Call* reported that the Rothenberg & Gonzales Political Report in Washington rated the race "Favored Republican."

For its part, Team Edwards remained convinced that its strikes had left Vitter barely standing. Now they were ready to deliver what they believed would be a knockout punch.

22

Patriots, Prostitutes, and the Purple Party Bus

The image stuck in his mind, and it wouldn't go away. Throughout the governor's race, John Bel Edwards' adman, Jared Arsement, remembered a July 2007 CBS News story when David Vitter's sex scandal burst into the national headlines. The piece reported that Vitter, not yet in the Senate, had received five phone calls from 1999 to 2001 from Deborah Jeane Palfrey, the so-called D.C. Madam, on days when the House of Representatives was taking roll call votes. The article listed the exact dates and times of the calls to Vitter's cell phone. Arsement wondered: *What exactly was the House doing on those days? Could its members have taken a vote on a pro-family-values bill?* That would be some juxtaposition for a TV ad, Arsement thought.

In mid-January 2015, he had a conversation with Mary-Patricia Wray, who had been volunteering for the Edwards campaign while working as a political strategist and lobbyist for the Louisiana Federation of Teachers. Wray was about to join the Edwards campaign as its full-time communications director. Arsement had a request: Could she match the date of Vitter's five phone calls from Palfrey with the House of Representatives' activities each day?

Already caught up in the campaign whirlwind, Wray put off the assignment for several weeks. Early on the morning of January 30, unable to sleep, she decided to see what she could find. She curled up on a couch in her Baton Rouge home with her laptop and Coltrane, her Weimaraner. Wray found the CBS News story easily enough via Google. Then she went to the Library of Congress website and reviewed the House actions. One after another, for the first four phone calls, she had no luck and told herself that she really ought to return to bed. Then she checked the last call, on February 27, 2001. The House took only one roll call vote that day—a resolution honoring 28 American soldiers killed by an Iraqi missile 10 years earlier during

Operation Desert Storm. Wray checked to see if Vitter had voted.

Barely able to contain her excitement at 5:30 a.m., Wray fired off an email to Arsement, Edwards and state Representative Sam Jones. It began, "Good morning everyone! Check out the last one!!!! :)"

Wray provided five headings, each one with the date of the call, a link to what the House did that day, and a brief description of Vitter's votes. For the first four, she found nothing noteworthy to report. Her final heading concerned the last call from Palfrey, when the House voted to honor the soldiers killed a decade earlier. Wray excitedly noted: "VITTER WAS ABSENT!!!!"

The call that Vitter got from Palfrey on February 27, 2001, came only 39 minutes after the unanimous approval of House Concurrent Resolution 39 at 5:27 p.m. It honored "the ultimate sacrifice" of 28 soldiers killed by an Iraqi Scud missile attack on February 25, 1991, during Operation Desert Storm. Vitter was among 35 House members who did not vote.

For months, Wray's discovery was a closely held secret within the Edwards campaign. The team wanted to hit Vitter with it at just the right time.

A week into the runoff, everything was set. The only question was when to run the ad that Arsement had prepared. Then Edwards faced another question: Should it even run? He and his top aides had previewed it to Donna and other family members. Nearly all of them disliked it. "If I were in your shoes, as tempting as it is, I wouldn't run the ad," Daniel Edwards told his brother during a quiet moment at Ruth's Chris Steak House during the video poker industry's fundraiser on November 2. John Bel had a healthy lead, Daniel noted. Why run an ad that will stir up controversy? Raymond Blanco, with his decades of experience in Louisiana politics, also thought the ad unnecessary. "When you're ahead, you ride the pony on in," he advised.

Arsement, however, argued that the ad packed such a wallop that they *had* to run it. He cited Jim Kitchens' tracking poll, which showed that by November 6—just 13 days into the 28-day runoff—Vitter's favorable-to-unfavorable ratio was improving. Arsement predicted the ad would not only stop Vitter's rise but also dominate news coverage for several days and, with Vitter on the defensive, give him less time to mount a comeback. Arsement thought this strategy was especially important in case some unexpected issue exploded in the final days.

"My friends are concerned," Edwards told Kitchens in a phone call. "They don't want me to go negative. But my inclination is to hit him and hit hard unless you talk me out of it."

"You called the wrong guy to talk you out of it," Kitchens replied. "My feeling is we hit him with everything we got right now. We stop his momentum."

To boost attention, Wray gave advance notice of the ad to Greg Hilburn, Gannett Newspapers' respected Capitol reporter, whose articles appeared in daily newspapers in Lafayette, Alexandria, Shreveport, Monroe, and Opelousas. His story, posted on Friday, November 6, provoked an immediate reaction on social media. "Gloves off," @usatoday2016 said in one Tweet.

"BAM!" wrote @BossMedia Comm.

Arsement's ad, titled, "The Choice," aired the next evening during the highly anticipated LSU–Alabama football game. That was also the day early voting began across the state. "The choice for governor couldn't be more clear," a female narrator began, with the words placed against a black backdrop. Viewers then saw photos of the Democratic candidate in uniform as the narrator said solemnly, "John Bel Edwards, who answered our country's call and served as a Ranger in the 82nd Airborne Division…or"—as dark music played and an image of Vitter appeared, on his cell phone in a dark trench coat—"David Vitter, who answered a prostitute's call minutes after he skipped a vote honoring 28 soldiers who gave their lives in defense of our freedom." The ad showed a frowning Vitter. "David Vitter chose prostitutes over patriots. Now, the choice is yours."

State Representative Cameron Henry, a conservative Republican supporting Vitter, was watching the LSU game at a friend's house in Metairie when the ad appeared on the screen. All the adults in the room grew quiet. When it was over, they agreed that the ad would backfire by tarnishing Edwards' clean-cut West Point persona. They also quietly hoped that none of the children would ask questions about the prostitution part. And it wasn't just those children. The attacks against her husband had become so intense that Wendy Vitter had taken to asking staffers which cable channels were included in certain ad buys so she could shield her teenage son and daughters from hearing the rough language.

Orleans Civil District Court Clerk Dale Atkins was watching the game at home when the ad aired. Atkins, a stalwart Democrat who helped elect Kathleen Blanco as governor in 2003, had been assisting the Edwards campaign. "Damn!" she said to herself. Her phone began blowing up with text messages from friends who had seen the ad and thought it was a brutal blow against Vitter.

Liz Mangham, a Baton Rouge lobbyist who had gotten to know Kitchens while working for Democrats years earlier, sent the pollster a two-word text: "kill shot."

"I think this might be the most vicious negative ad ever," NBC's Meet the Press host Chuck Todd said the next morning, just before showing the 30-second spot to his national audience.

The Vitter campaign did its best to counter the ad's blunt-object impact. It publicized a letter sent to Edwards by Kim Florich, whose son, Thomas, had been among four Louisiana National Guardsmen killed during a stateside training mission in March. Florich asked Edwards to pull the ad, writing that it offended her because the image of Vitter talking on a cell phone came with Arlington National Cemetery as a backdrop. She noted that Vitter had helped secure her son a burial plot at Arlington after Army officials initially said he didn't qualify.

"When my husband and I see your commercial, we are both uncomfortable and disappointed to see the Arlington National Cemetery used for politics," she wrote in the letter. That put Edwards in an uncomfortable position, since he had repeatedly highlighted his bio as a West Point grad and former Army Ranger captain. He resisted Florich's request for a day, saying the ad was an appropriate and accurate response to Vitter's attacks against him. Then, the following day, he had a change of heart. He told Arsement to edit out the cemetery image—but to continue running the ad as planned.

The controversy proved minor. Moreover, subsequent poll numbers proved Arsement and Kitchens were right in pushing to run the ad. Before the spot ran, Vitter had improved his favorable-to-unfavorable ratio to 40 percent favorable to 49 percent unfavorable. Five days later, Kitchens found that it had dropped to 37–56 percent.

On Sunday, November 8, the day after the ad first aired, Edwards visited five African-American churches in New Orleans. He was feeling increasingly confident that he would defeat Vitter. At each stop, the pastor invited the candidate to the lectern to offer remarks. "We've got the ball on the five-yard line," Edwards told the packed house at New Home Ministries in the Central City neighborhood. "We are going to score on November 21st!" The congregants stood and cheered.

That afternoon at the home of Jim Thorns, a real estate appraiser, Edwards took part in a fundraiser that drew a large crowd of movers and shakers in the African-American community. Later, at 6 p.m., another fundraiser followed at James Carville's spacious home in Uptown New Orleans. Bradley Beychok, a Democratic campaign operative, knew the event was successful when he had to park blocks away—farther than ever before for a fundraiser at Carville's. The strategist who had managed Charlie Melancon's unsuccessful 2010 Senate campaign against Vitter, Beychok had provided one of the best lines of the gubernatorial primary when he told *Politico* about the difficulty in taking down Vitter.

"This is Godzilla," Beychok said. "To slay Godzilla, you got to go directly at him. You can't slay a dragon by chopping at his feet."

Carville's home was jammed. The close circle of people who had been with Edwards from the beginning couldn't help but notice all the folks who had been doubters for so long. But this was no night for recriminations. Everybody was feeling good. Mitch Landrieu, who had called his top donors to invite them to the event, stood on the landing of the stairs leading upstairs, next to Carville and Edwards. "I had doubts about how the race would turn out," Landrieu later told the crowd. "Not because of this man but because of the nature of the state. I was wrong. This guy will be elected governor." A rare *mea culpa* from Landrieu, it prompted cheers from the crowd. His sister Mary, who had tried to get Edwards out of the race in July, to his utter dismay, would deliver her own apology. The event raised nearly $500,000 for Edwards' campaign.

One person who didn't partake in the good time was Josh Standifer. Dressed in a Tennessee Titans jersey, he stood outside Carville's front yard, filming guests with a hand-held camera as they walked to the host's waist-high black gate, passed through it, and climbed the front steps. Standifer was well known to Edwards and his team, and they weren't about to let him onto Carville's property, much less inside his house.

Campaign aides, reporters, and candidates all knew him as "Josh the Tracker." He was working for America Rising, a conservative political advocacy group based in Alexandria, Virginia. The pro-Vitter super PAC, the Fund for Louisiana's Future, had, according to its campaign finance report, paid America Rising $80,000 since February for "consulting and research services." Lanky, with brown hair and a taciturn manner, careful not to divulge much, the twenty-something Josh had studied at an Evangelical university in Tennessee. During the governor's race, he turned up at every campaign event of Vitter's three main rivals.

"He was everywhere we were," Dardenne said at one point. "I thought he must have been cloned." To be sure, American Bridge—a national group that supports Democrats—had a tracker periodically videotaping Vitter as well.

Footage from Josh had already appeared in negative commercials against all three candidates, including the Vitter ad that began airing two days into the runoff, accusing Edwards of wanting to release 5,500 "dangerous thugs" from prison.

Advocate columnist Stephanie Grace had first encountered Josh at a mid-June Alario Center campaign forum in Westwego, when she noticed him filming her as she spoke with Jay Dardenne. Grace couldn't believe the intrusiveness.

Edwards thought Josh often failed to respect personal boundaries.

He said the young man typically filmed him during the legislative session when he left the House Chamber to talk to constituents in the hall. "Some of the conversations were very, very private," Edwards said. "He was very aggressive. I do believe he crosses the line." Edwards once told a reporter that he wanted to conduct an interview in the House Chamber, rather than in the hall, to avoid having Josh record it. Cathy Dardenne, the lieutenant governor's wife, said she found Josh "very unnerving." So did some of the guests arriving for the Carville fundraiser. A few stopped to greet or taunt him. Josh took it all in stride.

With just days remaining in the runoff, Vitter began making himself more available to reporters, after dodging them for years. He didn't exactly invite *The Question*, but his campaign regularly told reporters where he would be. At those events, he answered off-the-cuff questions. At the same time, instead of skipping candidate forums, he sought every opportunity to go one-on-one with Edwards. That's why the two candidates appeared together for a mini-debate at the Press Club of Baton Rouge luncheon on November 9—before a packed house inside a conference room at the Belle of Baton Rouge casino hotel. The encounter turned out to be a revealing one.

Each candidate sat alone at a table on either side of the podium, taking turns to stand and speak into a bank of microphones. In his opening remarks, Edwards called himself a uniter who would govern Louisiana in a bipartisan fashion. Jay Dardenne's endorsement four days earlier was an example of that, he said. "After eight years of failed policies from Bobby Jindal, and benign neglect from someone who would rather be in New Hampshire than Baton Rouge," Edwards said, "I will be a leader who puts Louisiana first."

Then it was Vitter's turn. "The two candidates for governor," the senator said, "could not offer a more starkly different voting record and political philosophy. His campaign is built on a myth that he's some sort of a conservative and that we don't differ much on the issues. We do."

Vitter desperately needed the election to turn on each man's voting record, because he was the more conservative candidate in a conservative state. He sought to drive home the point by noting that Edwards had a lifetime score of 23 percent from the National Federation of Independent Business, versus his own 98 percent. The Louisiana Association of Business and Industry scored Edwards at 25 percent, versus Vitter's 95 percent. Edwards' score from LABI, Vitter noted, "is lower than clear proven liberals like Mary Landrieu, Mitch Landrieu, and Bill Jefferson." Vitter jabbed one more time. Edwards, he said, "actively carries forth the trial lawyer agenda and the union agenda."

Vitter had ducked *The Question* in 2007, in 2010, and as much as possible during the recent primary. One reporter who knew this first-hand was WAFB-TV anchorman Greg Meriwether. In 2010, when Vitter was running for re-election to the Senate, Meriwether had asked him during a televised debate to explain his "serious sin." When Vitter dodged the question, Meriwether then asked whether he had violated the law. Vitter stonewalled him. Now, five years later, Meriwether tried again, at the Baton Rouge Press Club forum, with a similar question: "Was that the end of the behavior then? Your 'serious sin.' Are you telling voters that nothing else happened since then and it's time to move on?"

"Yes, Greg," Vitter said, "I made that very clear then, and I'll make it very clear now. The answer is absolutely yes. I've learned that life isn't just about our faults. What's more important in life is how we respond, how we get up, how we earn redemption, how we take responsibility and ask for forgiveness. That was the most serious mistake of my life, clearly. But the aftermath of that, how I healed with my family, how I learned from that and grew was the single most positive experience of my life, bar none. That response and that growth, that receiving of forgiveness and that acknowledgement and taking of responsibility was the single most important and positive step in my life. I've learned a lot in that sense in terms of what life is about. It's all about how you learn, grow and earn—and I underscore earn—redemption."

As Arsement had predicted, his "prostitutes over patriots" ad had dramatically refocused attention on Vitter's character.

Associated Press reporter Melinda Deslatte asked about the two candidates' differences on reforming criminal sentencing laws, noting that Vitter had aired a television ad on that subject. Vitter responded that Edwards had "pandered" to an audience at Southern University— in remarks captured by Josh the Tracker—that he wanted to reduce Louisiana's incarceration number by 5,500 inmates.

Edwards countered, "It is an act of desperation for him to come here and act like I went to Southern to pander to some group," Edwards then said. Josh the Tracker, he said, had "filmed me about 50 times making the same talk."

The hour-long forum was nearing its end, when Jim Engster asked another question that focused on Vitter's character and judgment in the context of the October 23 Spygate incident at the Royal Blend coffee shop in Metairie.

"Part of what you're referring to is this silly coffee shop incident," Vitter responded.

"A silly coffee shop incident?" asked a disgusted Edwards "What kind of a Nixonian system would we have in Louisiana?"

After closing remarks, the two men shook hands. The campaign's temperature was clearly rising with just 12 days to go, and Edwards' repeated smack-downs of Vitter on the character issue continued to script the runoff narrative.

Vitter's prospects didn't get any better the next day, November 10. Newell Normand called a mid-afternoon press conference at his office across the Mississippi River from New Orleans. The Jefferson Parish sheriff had supported fellow Republican Jay Dardenne in the primary, but Normand loathed Vitter—even before he caught Frenzel recording his conversation with John Cummings at the Royal Blend on the day before the primary election.

At his press conference, Normand revealed more sensational developments. Frenzel's cell phone was actually a video camera that contained footage of Wes Bearden, his boss at the Dallas-based private detective agency, talking with a woman named Kelly at the Hammond IHOP on October 20. Three days earlier, Jason Brad Berry had posted videos on his *American Zombie* blog of the interview in which Ellis claimed she had borne Vitter's love child and then put the child up for adoption. Bearden's conversation with Kelly had occurred while news outlets were still weighing whether to report Ellis' salacious allegations. The Vitter campaign was desperate to keep the Ellis matter under wraps. Privately, though, Normand hinted that Frenzel's device contained recordings of other potentially embarrassing conversations, but he never made any of them public.

One recording, according to Normand, showed Bearden at the IHOP giving Kelly an affidavit aimed at destroying Berry's credibility. Though Bearden and Kelly hadn't met before, the affidavit had already been typed. All Kelly had to do was sign it.

"You are the hero here," Bearden told her. "You are the linchpin. Things are spiraling out of control. We have been controlling this. But I don't know how much longer I can control this. I need to keep the stuff out of the paper for the next seven to eight days." Keeping Ellis' allegations out of the mainstream media for that long would move the Vitter campaign past the October 24 primary.

Bearden, according to Normand, wanted Kelly to lie about Berry. "I'd like you to say that Jason Berry has made a payment to several witnesses," Bearden said. "That would be kind of true, too. If I could show them that Jason Berry is paying people off, that would kill this story."

Bearden wanted her to go further. "Let's try to see if we can trap him and hopefully he offers you some money," the P.I. said.

Normand was outraged as he disclosed to reporters what Bearden had said. "My own investigators have said in all the years of their experience, they've never seen an interview that was so suggestive in coaching the person being interviewed as to what to say," Normand said. "The manner in which they procured the affidavit was incredibly flawed and very, very suggestive." The sheriff's news conference lasted almost an hour. He dismissed suggestions that he might be shilling for Edwards, but that's how the Vitter campaign and others saw it.

"John Bel Edwards' political allies are clearly using their badges to play politics, which is horrible," the Vitter campaign said in a statement.

During the Baton Rouge Press Club forum the day before, Vitter had attempted to put a new spin on the Spygate story. He said he had given affidavits and documentation gathered by Frenzel and Bearden to the FBI and the United States Attorney's office in New Orleans. "[Frenzel] was researching a serious matter of what I believe is an illegal scheme between a business associate and major donor of John Bel Edwards and a private investigator, to pay for false testimony from witnesses against me," Vitter said.

Immediately after the Press Club forum, the Vitter campaign disclosed that its target was New Orleans attorney John Cummings, who had attended the Royal Blend coffee klatch on the day before the primary. Cummings, who had donated $25,000 to Edwards' campaign under his name, his wife's name, and via his law firm, owned a sand and gravel company in Amite called Tangi Holdings. Edwards acknowledged after the forum that his law firm had handled the paperwork for Tangi Holdings but said Cummings had taken ownership of the company afterward. The Vitter campaign apparently believed that Cummings was behind Wendy Ellis' sudden appearance in the gubernatorial campaign. Danny DeNoux, the P.I. who had located Ellis, consistently denied that Cummings was the "businessman" who had hired him.

Normand, at his November 10 press conference, said he, too, was turning over his evidence from Robert Frenzel's arrest to the FBI. No one on the outside knew which federal crimes either camp believed might have been committed, but their political motives were clear. Vitter, weary of fending off accusations that he had hired prostitutes, hoped to turn the tables by suggesting his political enemies were paying for slanderous stories. Normand—who now was saying that Vitter would be the "worst governor in the history of the state of Louisiana"—was charging the Vitter campaign's chief investigator, Bearden, with pressuring a "witness" to sign a false affidavit.

Normand's press conference on November 10 was dramatic,

but it was just a warm-up for the main event that night, the runoff's first televised debate between Vitter and Edwards. Louisiana Public Broadcasting and the Council for A Better Louisiana, a Baton Rouge-based nonprofit that advocated for charter schools and a more business-friendly state, sponsored the event.[8] Inside LPB's studio, Edwards and Vitter sat facing each other at opposite ends of a rectangular table.

After the often-stilted primary debates, this showdown had a format guaranteed to produce fireworks: The two candidates would ask each other questions and rebut the responses. Vitter started off by saying that Edwards had opposed legislation that would require sacrifices of public officials and had voted in favor of a pay raise for state legislators. Vitter then asked how the public could trust Edwards not just to look out for himself as governor.

"Senator Vitter, you've been lying sideways in the public trough since 1992," shot back Edwards.

"I've always fought against the political establishment," Vitter said during the 30 seconds he had to respond. "I led the fight to establish term limits in Louisiana."

Over the next 40 minutes, the two men took turns answering serious questions on Medicaid expansion, the Common Core education standards, taxes, and the budget—while bad-mouthing each other at every opportunity. Then Vitter left an opening while complaining about the "prostitutes over patriots" ad.

"You act holier than thou," he said to Edwards. "Well, in fact, you have the most vicious negative ad up right now that veterans have been offended by…. You're not living by the Honor Code, John Bel. You're living by the lawyer's code, trying to parse words and trying to create technicalities that don't exist."

"With respect to the negative ad," replied Edwards, "if it's a low blow, that's only because that's where you live, senator. It's 100 percent truthful. You didn't say it was untrue. You want me to take it down because you don't like that. I understand that you don't like it. *It hits you where you live.*"

"I'm not talking about me saying anything, John Bel," responded Vitter. "I'm talking about what veterans say."

"Hundreds of veterans have contacted me," Edwards shot back, "and they wanted to know that you were missing out on your public performance of your duties in Congress in order to engage in those extra-curricular activities that you don't want to admit to. You will say anything at any time. You are unconstrained by the truth."

---

[8] Co-author Jeremy Alford served as one of two journalists who posed questions to the candidates during the debate.

They began talking over each other until moderator Beth Courtney of Louisiana Public Broadcasting stepped in. "Gentlemen, let's stop here," she said.

It was Vitter's turn again. "You're being completely disingenuous," he said to Edwards. "You're not living by some Honor Code. You're living by some lawyers' code of technicalities."

Edwards wagged his finger at Vitter. "And with respect to the Honor Code, Senator, the last part of it is: *I will not tolerate those who do.* You are a liar. And you are a cheater, and I don't tolerate that."

Edwards' punches had landed. In every campaign debate of Vitter's 24-year career in politics, he had always had the upper hand and always exuded supreme confidence. Oftentimes he flat-out intimidated his opponents. Not this time. Vitter delivered a shaky closing statement. "His campaign," the senator said of Edwards, "is built on some sort of myth that he's a conservative, that we don't differ much on the issues, when we do."

Edwards' close was crisp. "When I decided to serve our country," he said, "nobody asked me whether I was a Republican or a Democrat. This election, too, isn't going to turn on party. It's going to turn on leadership and character, which candidate is best able to lead this state right now after eight years of miserable, failed policies under Bobby Jindal, leadership to unite our people, bring our people together, forge consensus, tackle our biggest problems and challenges, and provide real opportunity for our children in Louisiana. That is my record in the Legislature. It is a leader. It is a uniter. I will fight against anyone of any party when they mean to do harm to Louisiana. And I will stand up and fight alongside of anyone of any party when they want to do our state good. I will always be honest with you. I will never embarrass you. I will always fight to put Louisiana first."

Vitter's team scrambled to find a formula to reel in Edwards. In one commercial, the senator sat at what appeared to be his kitchen table expressing his sorrow for having failed his family, while adding that he was grateful for the lessons that failure had taught him. He pushed the same theme in another ad in a totally different setting, with Willie Robertson of "Duck Dynasty" fame. The two men wore camouflage jackets, trying to look as if they had just come from a hunt.

"David and I have been out in the woods today," Willie said. "I know he's made some mistakes, but who hasn't? The whole story of the Bible is about redemption."

Leaders of the state's business groups, meanwhile, were nervous about an Edwards administration and felt far more comfortable with Vitter. They liked the senator's vow to limit lawsuits by trial lawyers, his pledge of an even hand in changes to the tax system, and above all his proven record of working with business interests. The political arm of the Louisiana Oil and Gas Association immediately came through with an endorsement and pledges of money for the runoff. The National Federation of Independent Business followed suit, but an even bigger nod was on the way. Faced with the possibility of Edwards' winning in November, LABI, the statewide business group that held considerable sway at the Capitol, decided it was time to get involved. LABI had played in only three elections for governor in recent history and had always picked a winner; in most elections, however, the group had focused on legislative races.

Because LABI's rules require super-majorities to endorse, rounding up the votes took almost three weeks—but ultimately Vitter got the nod on November 11, with just 10 days left in the runoff. The members of LABI's four political action committees saw that their natural enemies, unions and trial lawyers, had lined up behind Edwards. Many PAC members were quick to note that they liked Edwards personally and that he had some conservative credentials on social issues, but they would qualify those remarks in private by saying Edwards' election would mark a sad day for the business community.

Also on November 11, Sheriff Normand returned to bedevil Vitter. This time, he bad-mouthed the senator in a pro-Edwards Gumbo PAC television ad paid for by the Democratic Governors Association. It aired exclusively in the New Orleans media market, where Normand was arguably the most popular and influential public official around. He had just won re-election with 88 percent of the vote.

In the ad, decked out in his sheriff's full-dress white uniform, with four gold stars on each collar and shoulder and a large, shiny badge, Normand said of Vitter, "I've watched him for many years. David Vitter is all about David Vitter. He's not about anybody else. It's important that this is not about the party. This is about the individual. And in this particular race, David Vitter is not that individual that is going to be able to lead Louisiana."

The ad ended with a still shot of Vitter with the tagline: "How can Louisiana trust David Vitter as governor?"

Normand said he had withheld permission from Gumbo PAC to air the ad until after he had turned over the evidence related to Frenzel to the FBI. "The Gumbo PAC folks were actually pissed at me because of that," Normand said later. "Then Vitter announced he was turning everything over to the FBI. When he did that, I said, 'Fine. I'll turn everything I have over to the FBI too.' At that point, there was no longer a conflict, so I then released the ad to run. But if Vitter had not turned over the whole thing to the FBI, that ad would never have run, because my office would have been conducting an investigation."

Still, the ad prompted criticism from Vitter supporters that Normand was suggesting to reporters the possibility that the senator had engaged in criminal activity while the sheriff was actively campaigning against him. In the opinion of Team Vitter, Normand was misusing the power of his office.

Then, on Thursday, November 12, the day after Gumbo PAC began airing the Normand ad, the race took another strange turn. The events were set in motion in August, when a white New Orleans-area attorney named Dan Robin Jr. heard from African-American friends that Edwards didn't have much of a presence in the African-American community in Orleans, Plaquemines, and St. Bernard Parishes. Robin, a 44-year-old criminal defense attorney who handled mostly drug cases in St. Bernard, agreed with them that Edwards needed to appear at an event that would attract a large crowd of African-American voters. The organizers agreed that the Lyve Nite Club on Tulane Avenue would be a great venue because it could hold a big crowd.

In late October, Robin called the Edwards campaign scheduler, John Walsh, to ask if he could add an event to the candidate's schedule. Robin had some pull because his father, Dan Sr., had been an early supporter of Edwards and was one of his biggest fundraisers. Walsh said Edwards could attend an event at Lyve from 4 p.m. to 5 p.m. on November 12, between two other events.

In the days leading up to the candidate's appearance, Robin and others posted fliers touting his visit. Kenya Taylor, a member of the planning group, secured a bus from a colorful local operator named Andrew Honeycutt, who went by the moniker "DJ Whatever," to give folks who didn't have transportation a ride to the Lyve event. Honeycutt's old school bus had been repainted purple and repurposed as a party bus—for people of all ages, including children and seniors. The plan was that after Edwards' appearance, the hosts would drive the African-American voters from Lyve to New Orleans City Hall so they could cast ballots during early voting, which was underway for two more days.

Honeycutt called his bus "Club Whatever." He had stripped out the seats and replaced them with benches along the sides, while the middle featured two poles that could either help steady people during the ride or serve as props while they danced to the music.

Dan Robin Jr. arrived at Lyve at about 2:30 p.m., a half-hour before the event was scheduled to begin. Everything appeared in order. His dad had purchased a spread of food, and Dan Jr. had paid for a batch of Edwards For Governor t-shirts to give away. Edwards was expected to arrive at 4 p.m., but he was running late at an event in Metairie. In the meantime, Donna Edwards showed up at about

4:10 p.m. As Robin greeted her, he spotted the purple party bus, now plastered with blue-and-white Edwards campaign signs and pumping music. Robin also noticed the poles. Something about the bus made him uneasy.

Noticing Josh the Tracker, Robin immediately instructed the security guards not to allow Josh onto the bus, just to be sure. Robin was more concerned about the small crowd inside Lyve. Only about 50 people had gathered when Donna arrived. Robin had expected at least 300 people. When the candidate arrived about 20 minutes after his wife, Robin rushed him inside. The Most Wanted Brass Band began playing an up-tempo song, and DJ Whatever, shaking a decorated umbrella, began leading a second-line, New Orleans style. Robin had seen recognition of the low turnout register in Edwards' eyes. His heart sank, but the candidate showed no concern. He began dancing with DJ Whatever and then grabbed his wife to move in time to the music. Edwards couldn't stay long, though. The brass band stopped, and he delivered a few remarks about the need to make sure that government benefitted everyone, not just the wealthy. Afterward, people waited in line to greet him.

Edwards thanked everyone and headed out the door at 5 p.m. He needed to get ready for a major fundraiser that Dan Robin Sr. was hosting that evening at Arnaud's Restaurant in the French Quarter. About a dozen people at Lyve boarded the purple party bus, and it took off for City Hall. Dan Jr. headed to his home in New Orleans on Park Island, a home he had bought from former Mayor Ray Nagin, who was now housed in a federal prison.

Unbeknownst to Dan Jr., while Edwards was at Lyve Nite Club, *The Hayride* had posted a scathing article that would cause a major ruckus. The article, by John Binder, included a copy of the invitation to Edwards' event from the club's Instagram page. The article also posted Instagram photos that showed other events at the club—and those events posed a problem. As Binder described it, "The rest of the Lyve New Orleans' Instagram account includes a multitude of photos of scantily clad women showcasing their derrieres." Binder's article provided four of the photos, and, indeed, there were derrieres galore.

The post exploded on conservative social media sites. Mary-Patricia Wray, the Edwards campaign's communications director, quickly got word. She turned to Walsh, the scheduler. "John, what the fuck is going on?" she asked. He said he had no idea.

"Donna was there," noted Bruce Parker, another campaign aide, "and so was a preacher."

Wray called Dan Robin Jr., who was just pulling up to his house. She introduced herself and said, "We have a problem."

"What's the problem?" replied Robin, immediately put off by her brusque tone.

"Well, you got the governor showing up at a strip club on Tulane Avenue," she said.

"Excuse me?" responded Robin.

"Have you seen the Instagram page?"

"I don't even have Instagram."

"And there's this purple party bus with stripper poles, and you really put us in a hell of a situation." Her voice was rising.

"First of all, in an hour and a half, I'm going to hand your boss a check for $400,000," Robin said. His voice was rising, too. "So that effectively makes me your boss. So don't talk to your boss that way. Secondly, the people who helped organize that event don't have the money to rent out the lobby of the Ritz-Carlton or the Windsor Court Hotel. I'm sorry we didn't have a more formal limousine bus to take people to the early polling stations. You told me you're the communications director? And you have to deal with problems like this? Kiss my ass! Do your job and deal with it!" Robin hung up. Wray thought she might get fired.

After Robin got to Arnaud's, he had a friend pull up the Lyve Nite Club Instagram page. "Holy shit," he said aloud. Then he called Lester Wheeler, a friend who had helped organize the event. "Has this ever been a strip club"? he asked.

"No," replied Wheeler.

Robin explained the situation and asked Wheeler to have people who took pictures and video at the event to send them to him. He would forward all of it to Wray to show that Edwards was dancing with his wife in front of a brass band. There were no strippers.

"Don't worry about what happened earlier," Donna Edwards told Robin when she saw him at Arnaud's.

"I can assure you it's not a strip club," Robin said.

"Don't worry about it," she repeated.

Her husband told him the same thing. Robin felt better. All 80 seats at Arnaud's were taken, and then some. His father's fundraiser was a grand success, adding $500,000 to the Edwards campaign treasury.

The Hayride sought to keep the controversy alive the next afternoon with another Binder post. The article claimed that Edwards had skipped a Louisiana Family Forum event that Vitter had attended on the night of the Lyve Club event. It didn't mention that Edwards had attended the Arnaud's fundraiser during the Family Forum event. Embedded in Binder's article were three short videos shot by Josh the Tracker. Despite Dan Robin Jr.'s order that he not be allowed on the purple party bus, Josh had slipped on board and offered viewers a tour. "That's awesome," Josh could be heard telling DJ Whatever as he got off.

A second video captured Edwards' arrival at the club.

A third showed DJ Whatever moving the purple party bus after being told that he had illegally parked it outside of City Hall. At one point, Josh zoomed in and caught the strobe lights twinkling inside the bus. The blog post and the videos ricocheted through conservative social media. *Breitbart.com* sought to fan the flames by reporting that Edwards had attended a meet and greet "at a New Orleans strip club joint."

The uproar rattled Wray and other staffers, but Edwards was unfazed. He had gone to Lyve with Donna in the mid-afternoon. No strippers took part. He had given an interview to a Christian radio station. He didn't think Vitter had the moral standing to make an issue of it. Besides, so much money was flowing into his campaign that he had at least $2 million more than the $4 million originally budgeted for the final four weeks. Jared Arsement couldn't even find enough available TV time to spend it all. Everything was going Edwards' way. Now he was the juggernaut and Vitter the underdog.

The hour was indeed getting late for Vitter. His campaign desperately needed something—anything—that could propel the senator back ahead of Edwards before the November 21 runoff. A day later, just eight days before Election Day, Team Vitter finally caught a break—a bombshell from the unlikeliest source imaginable.

23

"It's a Hail Mary Pass"

The Stade de France, the French national sports stadium in a northern suburb of Paris, was packed to capacity on Friday night, November 13. Two of the world's great soccer teams—France and Germany—were playing a friendly match. French President Francois Hollande was among the 81,000 spectators.

At 9:20 p.m., about 20 minutes into the game, a security guard patted down a man with a ticket as he attempted to enter the stadium. The man was wearing a bulky vest. Suspicious, the guard denied him entry. The man took several steps back and detonated the vest, which contained a bomb. The suicide bomber and a bystander died. Ten minutes later, a second bomber blew himself up outside the stadium, followed by a third nearby 23 minutes after that. Meanwhile, at 9:25 p.m., attackers with assault rifles sprayed fire on people having drinks outside Le Carillon, a café and bar, before crossing the rue Bichat and gunning down diners inside the restaurant Le Petit Cambodge. Those attacks killed another 15 while leaving 100 injured. Within minutes, terrorists launched three more attacks in the City of Lights. When the horrific night was over, the death toll would reach 130, and nearly 400 more would be injured. The attacks were the deadliest on French soil since World War II, and the deadliest in the European Union since the Madrid train bombings in 2004.

The next day, the Islamic State group claimed responsibility for the attacks, calling them retaliation for the French airstrikes on ISIS targets in Syria and Iraq. President Hollande called the attacks an act of war. News reports noted that more than one of the terrorists had come to France from Syria, posing as refugees fleeing that country's civil war. That revelation had immediate repercussions in the United States. Governors across the country—particularly Republican governors—unilaterally issued statements saying they would bar Syrian refugees from their states, even though constitutional scholars said the governors had no right to take such action. The politicians' statements reflected widespread public fear, if not panic, that foreign-born terrorists might strike inside the United States.

In Louisiana, Governor Bobby Jindal released a statement the day after the Paris attacks. He wrote President Obama to express "my grave concern about the unreported diffusion of Syrian refugees in the United States." Under pressure from the United Nations to aid in the refugee crisis—the worst since World War II, with four million Syrians displaced by the civil war—Obama had instructed his administration in September to accept at least 10,000 Syrians over the next fiscal year, starting in October. During the previous year, the United States had received fewer than 2,000 Syrians, according to *The New York Times*.

"Last week," Jindal wrote, "the city of New Orleans began receiving its first wave of Syrian refugees. As with former immigration crises and federal relocation policy, Louisiana has been kept in the dark about those seeking refuge in the state. It is irresponsible and severely disconcerting to place individuals, who may have ties to ISIS, in a state without the state's knowledge or involvement. As governor of Louisiana, I demand information about the Syrian refugees being placed in Louisiana in hopes that the night of horror in Paris is not duplicated here." Jindal then asked four questions related to admitting Syrian refugees into the United States and said he wanted answers.

David Vitter weighed in with a Facebook post that same afternoon. "After yesterday's devastating terror attacks," he wrote, "we cannot forget the importance of protecting ourselves here at home. Obama wants to let 10,000 Syrian refugees into the U.S., and a lot of them are already coming into Louisiana. I want to make sure that the people entering our country are exactly who they say they are—not ISIS terrorists…I am committed to keeping us safe at home." In his initial post, Vitter did not take a position on whether to continue resettling Syrian refugees in Louisiana.

John Bel Edwards' campaign also posted a statement on Facebook that day. "As governor," it said, "I will continue to be an active participant in the ongoing conversation with federal authorities so that we can be partners in the effort to both accommodate refugees who are fleeing from religious persecution and ensure that all of our people are safe." Conservatives on Facebook and Twitter immediately began ripping Edwards' softer response. Unnerved, his campaign replaced "accommodate" in its post with the slightly less friendly "assist."

Mary-Patricia Wray, the Edwards campaign's communications director, had approved both Facebook posts—the initial one written by two lower-level staffers—without getting Edwards' okay. She typically didn't seek his approval for Facebook posts. She knew how her candidate thought and had a good sense of what worked on social media.

That evening, facing withering criticism from conservatives, the Edwards campaign revised its position once again, now taking a tougher stance: "In light of the recent tragedy in Paris, it's imperative for us to pause the influx of refugees flowing into our state without more information on the security measures in place. Gov. Jindal has requested additional information from the President on how the federal government is handling the refugees being sent to Louisiana, and I think the President has an obligation to provide answers before we move any further." The changing positions put Wray and other top campaign staffers on edge.

As it happened, *The Hayride's* John Binder had posted a story on November 2—11 days before the attacks—reporting the Obama administration's plan to resettle 10,000 Syrian refugees in the United States and noting that three Louisiana cities—New Orleans, Baton Rouge, and Lafayette—were among the 180 cities nationwide slated to receive them. Twenty-four hours later, Binder posted another story reporting that Syrian refugees had already been resettled in Louisiana.

"Catholic Charities, which receive federal grants from U.S. Department of State/Bureau of Population, Refugees, and Migration, have apparently taken in two Syrian refugee families already and are expecting many more," he wrote. Binder's post attracted some attention, but interest had tailed off before the terrorists attacked in Paris. Then page views spiked, especially after two national conservative pundits mentioned his post. "And then it went viral on social media," *The Hayride's* Scott McKay wrote in another blog post. "So much so that the rumor was started to the effect that 10,000 Syrians had already been brought to New Orleans."

On Sunday, November 15—six days before the gubernatorial primary—*Times-Picayune* reporter Michelle Hunter tried to set the record straight. "Despite blog posts and social media rumors indicating that thousands of Syrian refugees had already arrived in the New Orleans area, the U.S. State Department reported only 14 Syrian nationals have resettled in Louisiana since Jan. 1," Hunter reported. In a sign of the heightened tensions and passions, readers shared Hunter's story an astounding 10,700 times. It also prompted 833 reader posts, many of them part of the tit-for-tat insult battle that controversial topics typically provoke online.

That same day, Vitter toughened his position, calling the plan to accept 10,000 Syrian refugees in the United States "outrageous and irresponsible." He also sought to fan the flames by sending an open letter to New Orleans Mayor Mitch Landrieu and the city's police chief.

"As you know," he wrote, "New Orleans is expecting an influx of Syrian refugees, some of whom have already arrived. Based on all the information available to me, I have no confidence that these refugees are being fully and properly vetted to ensure they contain absolutely no terrorists elements. Please join me and others in demanding that President Obama stop accepting these Syrian refugees immediately, and stop settling any into New Orleans, given this unacceptable lax security and lack of full vetting on their backgrounds."

Vitter noted that New York City was deploying counter-terrorism measures to guard against a possible terrorist act. "We, too, are a port city and a major tourist destination, and as such, I request that the City of New Orleans and the New Orleans Police Department to deploy any and all counter-terrorism and public safety resources to crowded areas around the city, particularly the French Quarter."

Vitter also started a petition drive on Facebook entitled, "Tell Obama: No Syrian refugees in Louisiana!" It drew dozens of supportive comments.

Late that Sunday evening, Vitter finally found a way to use the Syrian refugees issue to batter Edwards. Luke Bolar, the Vitter campaign's press secretary, sent out an email reprinting Edwards' Facebook post from the preceding day—the one in which Edwards said he wanted to "accommodate" the refugees. Bolar provided what he called a translation of what Edwards was really saying: "I will continue to work with Barack Obama to bring Syrians to Louisiana." Saturday's weak initial postings had given Vitter an opening. The senator and his campaign staff were too battle-hardened to let that opportunity pass.

Times-Picayune op-ed columnist Bob Mann couldn't help but point out the one weakness, if not irony, in Vitter's hard-liner response to the Syrian refugee issue—Wendy Vitter was the general counsel for the Catholic Archdiocese of New Orleans, the very organization that had resettled most of the 14 Syrian refugees who had come to Louisiana since January 2015. "Why Vitter didn't ask his wife about those refugees was puzzling, unless one understands that Vitter's letter was about nothing more than reviving his gubernatorial campaign by injecting terror into the state's political bloodstream," Mann wrote in a column in *Salon*. Mann's piece was headlined "David Vitter's desperate last stand: He throws his wife under the bus—again."

Mann and Team Edwards could throw anything they wanted at Vitter on this issue, thought the senator's campaign manager, Kyle Ruckert. It wouldn't do much good. After beating each other up on a daily basis since the primary election, with very little sticking to Edwards, Ruckert was finally seeing overnight polling numbers that revealed a vulnerability. "His image with voters was upside down on this," Ruckert said later, referring to Edwards. This was especially true among white voters, whose support was critical to both campaigns.

On Monday morning, Vitter sent out a statement under his name that kept up the pressure. "This is a dangerous policy and exactly why we need to defeat Edwards," he said. "These Syrians have already started arriving in Louisiana. That needs to stop immediately, and I will continue to lead that fight and protect the people of Louisiana." Trailing his Democratic opponent, with less than a week before Saturday's runoff election, Vitter launched a Hail Mary pass. For once, the Edwards and Vitter campaigns actually agreed on something— with just days remaining in the race, the "Syrian issue" could resurrect Vitter's chances of winning.

Louisiana was full of fear and loathing in those fitful days. The mainstream media's assurances to the contrary notwithstanding, conservative blogs continued to report that 10,000 Syrian refugees were already arriving in Louisiana. According to WWL-TV, those reports were based on "an image, purportedly of Syrian men in New Orleans, which actually is a photograph of migrants protesting outside of a train station in Budapest, Hungary, on Sept. 3."

When David Aguillard, the executive director of Catholic Charities in Baton Rouge, arrived to work on Monday, he found the phone ringing off the hook from frightened callers wanting to know more about his agency's plans to resettle Syrian refugees. Aguillard tried to calm them by explaining that all refugees had to undergo multiple security checks before they could be resettled in the United States. That reassurance mattered little. Panic continued, and, consequently, few politicians dared to inject reason into the public discourse. Later that same day, Governor Jindal issued an executive order forbidding the resettlement of Syrian refugees in Louisiana. Never mind that resettlement was entirely a federal matter.

Mike Edmonson, the superintendent of Louisiana State Police, sought to tamp down the fear that same day, a Monday. At a press conference in Baton Rouge, he said that a briefing from the FBI in New Orleans had led him to believe that Louisiana faced no threat from the 14 refugees there already.

Despite Edmonson's assurances, and no doubt still reeling from Team Vitter's criticism on this issue, Edwards ramped up his position on the refugees just after noon on Monday by (for once) echoing Jindal: "Louisiana should hault [sic] completely the entry of refugees from Syria." It was Edwards' fourth statement on the Syrian issue in 48 hours. Each successive statement was clearly calibrated to strengthen the candidate's "soft" initial position in the face of public hysteria and an inevitable attack by his Republican opponent. To political insiders, the momentum shift was palpable.

Then the inevitable happened: Team Vitter launched a TV ad campaign at mid-afternoon on Monday highlighting the threat posed by Syrian refugees. It began dramatically, with the boom of an explosion, a quick clip of a French soccer player ending in a "freeze frame," followed by another quick clip of worried fans who had been evacuated onto the soccer pitch. Next came clips of a speeding police car, lights flashing, and a burning building, apparently following one of the terrorist attacks.

"Now Obama is sending Syrian refugees to Louisiana," said a male narrator. "David Vitter warned Obama (of) the dangers of Syrian refugees weeks ago," the narrator continued, as viewers saw images of a letter that Vitter purportedly wrote in September to the administration, "and promised as governor no Syrian refugees will enter Louisiana."

Images of Vitter speaking to supporters flashed on the screen. "John Bel Edwards has pledged to work with Obama, to bring Syrian refugees to Louisiana," the narrator said, as an image of Edwards alone segued into one of Edwards and Obama on a split screen. Text on the screen cited his Facebook post on Saturday. Viewers then saw a clip of Edwards from the October 1 WDSU-TV gubernatorial debate saying, "I supported the president," as the announcer concluded, "He always does."

Wray was keeping vigil for Vitter's next move on Syria while gathering materials for the campaign's last big event—the second and final televised debate that night between her boss and Vitter. She was sitting in Edwards' shotgun house on North Eighth Street in Baton Rouge with Richard Carbo, an Alexandria native who had just come aboard from the Democratic Governors Association to assist her with the media. Carbo saw a mention of Vitter's TV ad on social media at about 2:30 p.m., and he and Wray watched it together on his cell phone. After she saw that the ad referenced Edwards' initial weak statement Saturday on Facebook—a post she had okayed without his approval— Wray immediately felt ill. The campaign had been remarkably gaffe-free until then. Now it seemed to be unraveling, and that meant the tide could suddenly—and dramatically—turn in Vitter's favor. If that were to happen, if Vitter were to get back into the race, she knew that she would be to blame. Wray excused herself and went outside to cry.

Wray had gone across the street to the campaign office when Edwards and Donna arrived a few minutes later, in the back seat of a State Police SUV. The candidate was exhausted. He and Donna had visited five African-American churches the day before in Monroe, spent the night at a friend's house there, and attended a plant opening at CenturyLink in the morning. They then flew on a private plane to Lafayette.

"You're not well," Donna told him during the flight. In Lafayette, Edwards spoke at a luncheon the district attorneys' association had hosted at its fall meeting. On the drive to Baton Rouge, the SUV got stuck in traffic and arrived later than planned. "He won't make it through the debate," Donna thought to herself. Her husband, who hadn't been sleeping or eating well, had lost 30 pounds during the previous two or three months.

Even more urgent than all those concerns, Edwards had to figure out how respond to Vitter on Syria—while Wray, his top message strategist, was an emotional wreck. Inside his shotgun house, Edwards removed his button-down shirt and, wearing a white undershirt, sat at one of the two folding tables that formed a "T" in the front room. He watched Vitter's ad and felt the gut punch. He gathered his team and asked for an explanation of how the campaign had responded to the Syria bombing. He wanted to see each statement, one by one. Wray printed them out for him. Edwards scanned the first Facebook post, put the paper aside, and looked at the second one. Frowning, he saw how the campaign had defensively tried to address the mistake of the first post by changing "accommodate" to "assist." Holding the sheet of paper in his left hand, he flicked it with his right forefinger. "This is what it's all about," he said with disgust. "Unforced error."

Wray fled outside and, sitting on the front steps, bawled until she had dry heaves. She hadn't eaten in 24 hours. State Representative Karen St. Germain, a Cajun from Pierre Part who was part of Edwards' inner circle, followed her out. Seeing Wray's distress, St. Germain fetched a cup of water and a wet towel that she put around the sobbing aide's neck. "I have to resign," Wray said between sobs. "It's all my fault."

"You're going to be fine, and the campaign is going to be fine," St. Germain said soothingly.

"No, I need to quit," Wray said.

State Representative Sam Jones came outside at one point to check on her. "Sam, I need two minutes with John Bel alone," Wray said.

"Why?" he asked.

"I want to resign and be the fall guy so we can wipe the slate clean."

Jones refused that request. Resigning wouldn't help anything, he said.

Still sobbing, Wray made her way into the campaign finance

office and haltingly told campaign manager Linda Day and campaign treasurer Andrew Edwards what had happened. Edwards, Wray said, should fire her to deflect attention from the error so the campaign could move forward. Day felt bad for Wray and wrapped her in a hug. She knew that Wray had been a stalwart worker throughout the campaign, staying up late each night to handle the press and daily messaging. "We'll correct the mistake," Day told her. "You can't resign."

"John Bel does not throw his people under the bus," interjected Andrew Edwards. Wray looked up.

"MP, did you hear me?" he repeated. "John Bel does not throw his people under the bus."

Across the street, the candidate and his top advisers were debating how to respond to the Vitter ad. Donna stayed out of the discussion but waited close by, knowing that her presence was a calming influence on her husband. She gathered the little items that he liked to have in the breast pocket of his jacket for a debate—Kleenex, lozenges for a dry mouth, and mints. With nothing else to do, she began ironing his shirt for that evening.

In the makeshift war room, while nobody said it aloud, all of Edwards' advisers feared that Vitter had tapped an explosive vein of voter hysteria, one that just might propel him past the Democrat by Election Day—notwithstanding Vitter's "very serious sin" and glaring character flaws. When voters are scared, they embrace candidates who exude strength. What should Team Edwards do?

Someone suggested responding with another Facebook post to avoid elevating the issue further. No, someone else said, they should completely ignore the Syrian refugees and keep the focus on their candidate's honor and integrity.

"It's a Hail Mary pass," Edwards said matter-of-factly. "Only a small percentage of them are successful. It's our job to make sure that it doesn't happen here."

Edwards didn't see how voters could believe that a West Point grad and former Army Ranger captain who was the son, brother, grandson, and great-grandson of sheriffs, would try to smuggle dangerous refugees from Syria into Louisiana.

Ad man Jared Arsement arrived for debate prep. Instead, he watched the ad on Sam Jones' cell phone. "We need to respond to that," Arsement told Edwards.

"Yes, we do," the candidate agreed.

"I need to go write a spot," Arsement said.

"Well, what are you waiting for?"

As Arsement drove back to Lafayette, he remembered how David Treen's grandson had gone missing late in the campaign when Treen faced Vitter in the 1999 special congressional election to replace Bob Livingston. Treen lost momentum and ultimately lost by two percentage points. Could eleventh-hour lightning possibly strike twice for Vitter?

Arsement's thoughts turned to that evening's gubernatorial debate. He feared that the flap over Syria was leaving Edwards woefully unprepared for whatever Vitter might throw at him. Edwards had been so focused and well-prepared for the other debates. On this afternoon, Arsement thought, his candidate seemed tired, distracted.

The other advisers at the candidate's house on North Eighth Street also feared that Edwards seemed unprepared, and they agreed to move on from Syria. They began a belated debate prep. Wray had formulated a list of questions that Edwards should expect. She and several others went over the material with him, including questions about Syria. At about 5 p.m., Edwards was ready to head out but confessed to Sam Jones that he didn't feel completely ready and wished he could skip the debate. With a solid lead in Jim Kitchens' tracking poll, Edwards had seemingly nothing to gain and everything to lose.

Edwards and Jones had fought dozens of political battles over the past four years, and they sat down one last time. Jones asked him how he planned to answer a question on the Syrian refugees. It would come up, without a doubt. Edwards gave his answer. Jones jumped out of his chair. "That was perfect," he said. "This debate prep is over. Just go be yourself. You'll be fine."

Edwards rode with Donna in the State Police SUV to the Dunham School, a Baton Rouge K–12 Christian academy hosting the debate. It would air statewide. Donna was nervous, feeling as though she were accompanying her husband as he went off to battle. Edwards was nervous, too. He had always gotten jittery before his high school football games, and these debates were no different. He also knew that just as the nervousness disappeared after the first hit in a football game, the butterflies, too, would go away after the debate began. When Vitter hit him on Syria, Edwards was determined to hit him back.

Edwards and Donna were led to the green room. Mark Beard, their pastor from their home church, St. Helena Catholic in Amite, prayed with them. At a few minutes before 6 p.m., Edwards got word to take his place on the stage. He kissed Donna. She went to her seat in the auditorium, confident in her husband but with a sense of foreboding.

24

What Goes Around

The second and final televised debate—five days before the runoff election—had the electric air of a heavyweight championship fight. Each man took a corner at the end of a four-foot-long black table. Sitting at angles, they faced the moderators—WVLA-TV anchor Fred Hickman of Baton Rouge and Jacque Jovic, an anchor for KTAL-TV in Shreveport—who sat on the other side of the table. Hickman and Jovic had their backs to the crowd of 400 that filled the auditorium. The two moderators and two candidates sat on a raised stage. Hickman began by asking the crowd to hold its applause—a futile request of an audience primed for a title bout.[9]

There would be no opening statements. It was as if a bell rang and the fight began.

"What do you think is the best way to approach the Syrian refugees?" asked Hickman.

Vitter answered first, jabbing immediately. He criticized Obama's decision to resettle 10,000 Syrian refugees in the United States and said he wouldn't allow any more to come to Louisiana. "My opponent has staked out a very different position," Vitter said. "In fact, he's staked out *four*. Last night, he said he would fully cooperate with President Obama, including in relocating Syrian refugees." Vitter's comments misrepresented Edwards' Facebook posts in terms of both timing and substance. But that did not matter to the senator.

Vitter added, "Today, he's trying to change his tune. He's now had four different positions in 48 hours. I don't know where he is. But I know we can't trust where he might end up, because he has always consistently supported President Obama, including in terms of immigration enforcement or I should say non-enforcement."

When it was Edwards' turn to respond, he too came out punching.

"As I told all of the people in Louisiana to start the runoff," he

---

[9] Co-author Jeremy Alford, through a contract with Nexstar Broadcasting, served in a paid advisory role for the debate, writing questions and conducting research.

said, referring to his opening TV ad, "David Vitter is desperate. He will lie. He will distort. It's what he does. It's who he is because he lacks a moral compass.

"On Saturday, I called for a halt to all Syrian refugees coming into Louisiana."

Edwards, too, understood that this fight was not following the Marquess of Queensbury rules. He ignored his weak Facebook posts from Saturday and misstated his actual call that night for a "pause" in admitting refugees.

"This is about public safety, the number one issue that we face as a government," Edwards continued. "As governor, I will take it seriously. It's who I am. I know a little thing or two about protecting American lives. I'm a graduate of the United States Military Academy. I commanded paratroopers. I have the support of the sheriffs' association [and] the Louisiana State Troopers Association because they know that as governor, I will partner with them and work every day to keep them safe."

As he concluded, Edwards sought to put Vitter on the defensive. "Senator, you missed key votes in Congress when you could have stopped this," he said, referring to information released by Team Edwards that day. In researching Vitter's voting record, Edwards' staff had found that the senator had missed a hearing on Syrian refugees that the Senate Judiciary Subcommittee on Immigration and the National Interest held on October 1, as well as a Senate vote that day to fund military construction, the Department of Veterans Affairs, and related agencies.

Vitter was actually in New Orleans for the WDSU-TV debate on the day of the missed hearing and vote, which is why he missed official Senate business. He had, however, skipped three other televised debates during the primary, citing the press of his work in the Senate.

Hickman told Vitter that he could have 15 seconds to respond.

"Look at John Bel Edwards' Facebook post yesterday," Vitter said, referring to Saturday's post two days earlier. "It says very clearly he would fully cooperate with President Obama, including in resettling refugees here. That's what it says. I realize he tried to change that tune today. Again, four different positions in 48 hours."

Hickman gave Edwards 10 seconds. "That's not what the Facebook says," the Democrat responded. "It says we will have a conversation to get the information about those refugees who are here. It uses the word *conversation*. He skips what I said Saturday. He skips what I said today."

Vitter jumped back in. "Fred, I don't want to have a conversation," he said. "I want to put a halt to this. I have said that consistently."

Vitter partisans disregarded Hickman's earlier request and applauded and cheered.

"We're going to put a halt to this," Vitter repeated. His partisans cheered again.

The first round was over. Hickman thanked them both. But Vitter kept throwing punches. "I think it's also significant," he said, "that I said that *way* before the Paris bombing, when the Syrian refugees first came up in September."

"We're moving on now," Jovic said.

"Senator," Edwards said, talking over Jovic, "you missed three committee hearings where you could have done something about this in the Senate, including the placement of refugees in Louisiana." The hosts tried to get the two men to stop, while the crowd yelled for its favorite. Edwards kept going—and began shouting to be heard. He then threw a verbal punch from the "prostitutes over patriots" ad: "I answered the call. You don't show up for work. That's the difference between us." Hickman and Jovic tried again to stop them as Vitter explained that he had missed the committee hearing because he had attended the gubernatorial forum.

The two men finally backed down, not unlike fighters when a referee breaks up a clinch.

Jovic next asked about their positions on abortion. Vitter noted that he had a consistent anti-abortion voting record but portrayed Edwards as soft on the issue because he hadn't called for defunding Planned Parenthood, hadn't opposed the opening of a new clinic in New Orleans that would perform abortions—Vitter called it "an abortion mill"—and had the support of Planned Parenthood's Gulf South president Melissa Flournoy, a former state representative.

"There you go again, Senator," began Edwards, noting that he had a 100 percent anti-abortion voting record with Louisiana Right to Life.

"I don't sit there and say you're less committed to life because you supported Rudy Giuliani," he said, referring to the former New York City mayor who ran for president with Vitter's support in 2008, "who was both pro-choice and anti-gun...because I don't believe that to be your position. But I will say this to you, Senator, you're a hypocrite."

Now it was the Edwards' partisans who erupted into cheers, as Vitter shook his head.

"John Bel," replied Vitter, "you can throw every ugly insult my way. I'm perfectly comfortable with who I am, with my family's love for me, and my work for the people of Louisiana, including on the issue of life." Now he had to speak over the raucous cheers of his supporters. "I've been a leader on the issue of life."

Hickman now had a question for Edwards.

The anchorman noted that LABI had given the Democrat a failing grade during the 2015 legislative session and asked whether Edwards would raise taxes on business.

Edwards began by saying that LABI had assigned a grade of *failure* to about 90 legislators because they hadn't taken a "cuts-only approach" to the latest state budget.

He noted that the Legislature had trimmed business tax breaks to prevent deeper cuts to public colleges and universities.

"They didn't like that," Edwards said of LABI. "I understand that they don't like that. It's time to put Louisiana first." His supporters cheered.

"John Bel has a lifetime rating from that organization of 27 percent," Vitter responded. "When I went to school, that wasn't only an *F.* I thought you got more points for putting your name right on the test."

As Vitter's supporters hooted and hollered, Hickman told Edwards that he had 15 seconds to respond.

"I'll just tell you, Fred," Edwards said, and trotted out one of his favorite lines, with a twist. "I give 100 percent to my wife. That's who I give 100 percent to." Edwards pointed at Vitter. "Senator, you ought to try it."

Vitter looked stunned. He could not believe how quickly Edwards had pivoted from holding up West Point's Honor Code to savaging the senator's marriage. Vitter had undoubtedly known that he would have to answer questions about his past—maybe even *The Question*—but he was taken aback by what he saw as Edwards dragging Wendy Vitter into the fight.

Cheers and catcalls rained down from the crowd.

Hickman tried to move on, but Vitter began talking over the anchorman.

"As I said before," he said, "you can hurl nasty insults," and he waved his right hand toward Edwards in disgust.

"We're moving on to the next one," Jovic said, speaking over Vitter without success.

"But the fact is that was 15 years ago," Vitter continued.

"We must move on," Hickman tried again without success.

"I give 100 percent to my family today," Vitter added, now visibly angry as he wagged his index finger at Edwards. "Don't you ever suggest otherwise. Don't do it."

Edwards leaned toward Vitter and said over the crowd, "You can never be 100 percent in that category. You can never be 100 percent again there, Senator."

Another clinch, and again the two men backed apart.

Round two was over, but Vitter's inner circle was deeply insulted by what they considered Edwards' attack on Wendy Vitter and the Vitter children. They rightly predicted that the state's political press would give Edwards a pass. Not everyone agreed, however, that Edwards had attacked Wendy Vitter. Edwards' supporters maintained he had focused laser-like on the senator's behavior.

Jovic then asked Vitter what he could do to energize his Republican base, when 500,000 registered Republicans didn't vote in the primary—and Jay Dardenne had since endorsed Edwards.

"I thought you were talking about *real* Republicans," Vitter responded with a rare smile but hallmark sarcasm, "but then you brought up Jay Dardenne, so I'm a little confused."

He went on to say he was consolidating Republican support, with the race pitting what he called "a Louisiana conservative versus a pro-Obama liberal. That's the choice."

More Democrats than Republicans turned out during the early voting period, Jovic pointed out, and a survey by pollster John Couvillon showed Edwards with a 15-point lead. "With five days left, what can you do to get Republicans energized?" she asked.

An experienced boxer knows that when throwing a punch, he cannot leave himself exposed. In his response, Vitter left himself open.

"The early vote was certainly influenced by a lot of things," Vitter said, "including huge Democratic money on the street. For instance, they paid for that purple party bus last Thursday in New Orleans." Vitter smiled again, relishing the imagery conjured by *The Hayride* blog's treatment of the sparsely attended party at the Lyve Nite Club in New Orleans.

"John Bel Edwards hosted voters, gave them free drinks, at a *very* adult New Orleans nightclub, to pack them into a party bus to go early vote. So that's affecting early voting." Vitter was still smiling, as if he thought he had turned the tables on his opponent. "But, you know what," he continued, "I'd much rather depend on the hard work, the perspiration, the dedication of our volunteers, and on our advocates than that purple party bus."

"Senator," replied an incredulous Edwards, "I was at that place with my wife, with my wife. I gave an interview on a Christian radio station."

"Quite an interesting date night," interrupted a smiling Vitter.

"Not as interesting as your date night, Senator, let me tell you," Edwards jabbed back. The blow wiped the smile from Vitter's face.

The senator's supporters booed the Democrat, but virtually every

TV and print reporter used that line in their stories on the debate.

"Let's move on," Hickman said. "We're going to move on, gentlemen."

The candidates spent the next 10 minutes jabbing at each other over taxes and the budget. Jovic then returned to Vitter's weak spot. She could not avoid asking *The Question*. "The allegations of prostitution have come to the forefront in recent weeks," Jovic said. "You've said you've been forgiven by your family, and you're looking to the future. We want to ask you a couple of questions about an ad your opponent released."

"Move on," a woman from the crowd could be heard yelling.

"Get over it," another woman yelled.

Jovic pressed on. "Why did you miss that vote? Did you take that vote? And what was the purpose of the call?"

"I've spoken about this directly with the people of Louisiana for some time," Vitter responded. His supporters applauded. "I humbly apologized to them directly and, just as importantly, I committed to rebuild their trust by working hard every day. I've tried like heck to do that. I've tried to re-earn that trust, and I'm hopeful I'm on that path based on the vote of confidence they placed in me with my Senate re-election. I know that answer is not good enough for my political opponents. I know that it's not good enough for the gotcha media, who wants to make headlines, who wants to make a splash and build a name for themselves." His supporters applauded again.

"But everybody understands the circumstances of that part of my life 15 years ago. So if that's not good enough for you, I'm sorry. It is good enough for Wendy. It is good enough for our family. And as I travel the state, I have town halls in every parish of the state. Voters come up to me with all sorts of concerns and tough questions. You know, Jacque, it's never that. It's about their future." His partisans cheered. "It's about their family. So I understand that the gotcha media is never going to be satisfied with that answer."

Jovic, however, wasn't finished. A graphic appeared on the screen showing that 55 percent of voters said the prostitution allegations would make them less likely to support Vitter, versus 6 percent more likely and 39 percent undecided.

"What would you say to those 55 percent who would not vote for you because of those allegations?" she asked. "This is your opportunity."

"I'm speaking on television directly to those people right now," Vitter replied. "I've explained to them how I've worked hard to earn the redemption from that low point in my life and that life, in my experience, isn't just about your falls. The good news is, it's more

important about how you get up, how you learn from those falls"—
by now his supporters were applauding again—"how you earn
redemption." More applause.

"Redemption and forgiveness, the good news is, is something
that people all around Louisiana can relate to, maybe not on the level I
had to experience it. But they appreciate it. They relate to it. They tell
me that every day in terms of my service."

"We're all obligated as Christians to forgive," countered
Edwards. "But that doesn't have to mean we forget. There is certainly
no obligation to vote for someone who commits a crime and refuses to
talk about it and refuses to answer any questions."

Vitter supporters tried to shout him down.

"He has never answered the question about whether he committed
a crime. The sad fact for Senator Vitter is we have congressional
records showing when votes are cast or not cast, and we have cell
phone records showing when phone calls are accepted or made. That's
the truth of the matter."

Vitter partisans called on the moderators to move on, and they
did.

Vitter landed a shot at Edwards, saying he was beholden to "a
three-legged stool"—trial lawyers, public employee unions, and
teacher unions.

Hickman said Edwards had 15 seconds to reply.

"I understand that David Vitter isn't proud to be a lawyer," he
said. "In fact, he's not a lawyer. He surrendered his law license rather
than answer questions, not about a sin, but about a crime."

On the split screen, Vitter could be seen grimacing and then
shaking his head as the crowd hooted and hollered again.

Jovic immediately went on to a question about the TOPS
scholarship program, not giving Vitter a chance to respond. He
had explained before that he had asked the Louisiana State Bar
Association to allow his license to lapse in 1999 because he was no
longer practicing law.

The two candidates jabbed at each other several more times during
the next 10 minutes, and then the brawl reached its final round. Jovic
asked each candidate to explain his wife's role during the campaign.

"What's more important to me is what my wife means to me and
my family," Vitter said, beginning an unusually personal response,
with a brightness that was rarely seen in his face during the election's
televised debates. "The campaign, win, lose or draw, that's secondary
to our kids, our family, and everything Wendy's meant." His supporters
applauded once again. "And Wendy, quite frankly, has been the rock of
our family. She's got us through good times, and she's got us through

bad times. Fifteen years ago, she offered her love and her forgiveness to me, and in the process, our kids learned an unbelievable life lesson. Of course, I wish they didn't need to learn it that way. But Wendy used the opportunity, and she sure as heck taught them and me that life lesson."

Edwards also spoke warmly of Donna, crediting her with keeping him grounded on education because of her role as a teacher. "Donna has been the partner in my life for 26 years," he said.

Edwards returned to a familiar theme in his close. "I will be a uniter," he promised.

Vitter chose to address once again how he had learned from the prostitution scandal. "Fifteen years ago," he said, "I faced my darkest day in life when I had to look my kids in the eye and tell them how badly I had failed my family. What they gave me in return was the best day of my life, when they and Wendy offered complete love and forgiveness. And that was absolutely the single best day of my life and the most powerful motivator I have for the rest of my life."

As Hickman and Jovic signed off, cheers from supporters of both candidates nearly drowned them out.

Immediately after the debate, union officials inundated state AFL-CIO President Louis Reine with phone calls. Reine had been one of Edwards' early supporters, at a time when few were aboard. If any doubts remained, Edwards' performance during the debate assuaged their concerns. "You didn't tell me this guy had a crawfish sack of nuts," said one union official.

Vitter was not giving up. The day before, he had begun airing an unusual spot that addressed Edwards' attacks on his character. The ad featured the senator's youngest child, Jack, who was spending as much time on the campaign trail as his school schedule allowed, including working phone banks. In the spot, Jack spoke directly into the camera, wearing a blue polo shirt. "Whether or not you vote for him, we love our dad," Jack said, as viewers saw Vitter affectionately rubbing his son's back and smiling. Jack sat on one side of Vitter and one of the senator's daughters sat on the other side. "Because he's a great dad. He'll be an awesome governor. And if anyone tries to tell you otherwise, just tell them to call me."

"It's a cute ad, and it's aimed at doing two things," wrote *The Hayride*. "First, softening Vitter's image—the *Daily Kos* called it his 'I'm not a complete a**hole!' campaign, which comes off a little like projection. And second, it's an effort at showing persuadable voters who the people are catching collateral damage from all the deeply personal shots demonizing him."

More than anything else, Vitter was trying to find another way to undermine his opponent. On the morning after the WVLA debate, his Senate office sent out a press release announcing that Vitter was introducing a bill that day to toughen the rules for permitting Syrian refugees to enter the country.

"We need to make sure that every person stepping onto American soil is exactly who he says he is," Vitter said in a statement, "and right now we don't have the necessary verification safeguards in place to make that determination, not by a long shot. My legislation will help protect Americans here at home."

He flew to Washington that day to dramatize his position on the Senate floor. Meanwhile, the Fund for Louisiana's Future, the super PAC supporting Vitter, aired an ad that added to the drumbeat against the Democrat. Edwards, the ad said, "would be partners with Obama and accommodate Syrian refugees." Several hours before Vitter's scheduled speech, he threw more gasoline on the flames with a tweet at 1:51 p.m. "Spoke w/LA State Police. They don't know where Syrian BR refugee is except that he was headed to DC & no gov agency is in contact with him."

As word spread of his tweet, calls began pouring into State Police offices from citizens in a panic. Some said they were arming themselves. Catholic Charities of Baton Rouge received more phone calls. Some callers pledged to cut off their funding. Then someone called in with a death threat.

Mike Edmonson, the superintendent of Louisiana State Police, went to Catholic Charities' offices that afternoon to obtain more information. He learned that the Syrian refugee who had left Baton Rouge was not on the loose. He had received government permission to resettle in the Washington, D.C., area. That information put Edmonson in a ticklish position. Vitter still had a chance of becoming the next governor, and Edmonson wanted to keep his job after Bobby Jindal left office.

Edmonson called a press conference that evening. "I've personally received numerous phone calls from people that said, 'I'm worried there's a Syrian loose and you don't know where it is,'" Edmonson said. "That is a mischaracterization. That is just simply not true."

David Aguillard, Catholic Charities' executive director, added, "The Syrians that we have resettled in Louisiana are not out wandering willy-nilly around the country."

Meanwhile, John Bel Edwards began Tuesday by speaking to supporters at the Grand Opera House of the South in Crowley, in the heart of Cajun country. He then went to the home of Jared Arsement's parents in Lafayette to tape a response to Vitter on the Syrian refugees. Arsement had written the script the night before, while his candidate squared off against Vitter in the final debate.

Standing in what appeared to be a study, with an American flag in the background, Edwards said he wanted no more Syrian refugees to come to Louisiana and accused his opponent of distorting his position on the issue. Vitter, he said, was "trying to use this tragedy to save his desperate campaign." Edwards promised that as governor he would protect the people of Louisiana. The ad began airing that afternoon.

From Lafayette, the Democrat went to Abbeville, another Cajun town, where he ordered an oyster po' boy at a restaurant filled with the courthouse crowd.

Then, just as suddenly and unforeseeably as the Syrian refugee panic had breathed life back into Vitter's faltering campaign, another unforeseen event all but took that issue off the table. It literally knocked the refugees out of the news cycle: Bobby Jindal announced he was "suspending" his presidential campaign.

"I've come to the realization that this is not my time," Jindal said on Fox News. "We spent a lot of time developing detailed policy papers. Given this crazy, unpredictable election season, clearly there wasn't an interest in those policy papers."

Jindal's long-shot presidential bid had never gotten off the ground among the 17 Republicans vying for the party's nomination. He had announced his candidacy in June and then spent most of his time campaigning in Iowa to win the endorsement of the state's social conservatives. That strategy clearly wasn't working. Jindal had bet that a strong finish in the Iowa Caucuses in February would generate the media attention and money that his campaign needed to make him a serious contender, but he could never break into the top tier, the main stage at the Republican debates. Instead, Jindal found himself relegated to the so-called "kiddie table" with the other also-rans.

Jindal's decision—to end his presidential campaign—immediately emerged as the top news story in Louisiana. It didn't just knock the Syrian refugee "crisis" out of the top spot on the evening news; it completely removed it from the first "block" of news as TV stations first reported Jindal's decision and then followed with several stories analyzing why and what it meant to have him back in Louisiana. This was a major break for Edwards, and some assumed its timing was deliberate.

"It smothers the news cycle," said James Carville. The timing, he said, "will help John Bel. When you're behind, you need to win the news cycle. If you're Vitter, the last thing you want is to see Bobby Jindal in the news."

"Time is not on Vitter's side," said Joshua Stockley, a political science professor at the University of Louisiana at Monroe. "For John

Bel Edwards, Election Day can't get here soon enough."

"I wish he would have chosen another time to do that," Kyle Ruckert, Vitter's campaign manager, later said of Jindal's decision to drop out of his race. Though pure speculation, it was widely assumed that Jindal's timing was the governor's final "up yours" to Vitter in their tit-for-tat game of one-upmanship, a sparring that began when Vitter timed his first post-scandal press conference at the exact moment of Jindal's New Orleans announcement for governor in 2007.

If that was Jindal's purpose, he timed his move brilliantly and in the process illustrated one of the oldest rules in politics: What goes around comes around.

On the same afternoon that Jindal announced his withdrawal from the presidential race, Wendy Vitter and a handful of campaign volunteers arrived at a campaign rally for Billy Nungesser, candidate for lieutenant governor and a fellow Republican. They were unannounced but hardly unnoticed in the large "Vitter For Governor" motorhome that they parked directly across the street from the rally, which was held at Gattuso's, a neighborhood bar and grill on a busy corner in downtown Gretna, in Jefferson Parish. Not unnoticed, because David Vitter's arch-enemy, Jefferson Sheriff Newell Normand, along with several other parish officials, was lead sponsor of the Nungesser rally.

Standing outside Gattuso's, Normand's chief deputy Craig Taffaro watched in muted astonishment. "Can you believe they showed up and parked right there?" Taffaro said, turning to West Bank businessman Craig Clark. "If Billy pulls up and sees this, he's gonna have a fit."

"Go tell 'em to move," Clark said, half asking and half suggesting.

"We can't do that," Taffaro replied, sensitive to the strained relations between his boss and Vitter.

"I'll handle this," Clark said.

Clark then crossed the street and tapped on the driver's side window. "Hey, man, you gotta move," he said. "This is Billy's reserved parking spot." His message was clear: *You're not welcome here.*

Undeterred, the Vitter crew moved the large RV in search of another parking spot. By the time they found one and returned on foot to work the crowd, Normand had arrived with Nungesser. They were all standing on the patio as the senator's wife approached.

"Hi, I'm Wendy Vitter," she said to Clark. "How are you?"

"I'm Craig Clark," he replied in a pleasant but knowing tone. "I don't think it's gonna be a real good night for you because nobody here is gonna vote for your husband."

"Oh?" Wendy replied, just as nicely.

Behind the smiles, it was all frost. Wendy turned and, with her troops in tow, walked into Gattuso's to mix with the crowd. All the while, Nungesser kept his distance. Although Vitter had supported Nungesser for lieutenant governor against Dardenne in 2011, the two men were now estranged politically.

Meanwhile, Normand and Taffaro were laughing at the exchange between Clark and Wendy. "Guys, this is *war*," Clark said, to more chuckles.

As if to prove his point, Clark entered Gattuso's and began trailing Wendy, occasionally re-introducing himself by saying, with the same grin, "Hey, I'm Craig. I'm still not voting for your husband."

Nungesser later recalled how, during his speech at the rally, he had acknowledged by name all of the public officials in the room— except one, whom he forgot. His omission was pointed out to him as soon as he came off the stage.

"Why didn't you recognize us?" Wendy asked Nungesser, clearly hurt by the snub. Her husband was none too pleased when he got word. In a late-night text, he called Nungesser "truly gutless" and then concluded with a barb for his old foe, Normand: "Give Newell my best."

On Wednesday, the next day, Vitter continued to hammer Edwards on the Syrian refugees, with "media availabilities" in Bossier City, West Monroe, and Lafayette, but journalists, echoing Carville's comment, were more interested in speculating why Jindal had timed his announcement when he did. That gave the governor's withdrawal from the presidential race another full day at the top of the news cycle—completely overshadowing the Syrian refugee issue with just three days left in the campaign.

Still, just to make sure, Gumbo PAC launched its own Syrian refugee ad to give Edwards added cover. "David Vitter's lying again," an announcer told viewers, "this time about Syria." The announcer then said Edwards opposed relocating more Syrian refugees in Louisiana.

"Never in our wildest dreams did we think we'd be running a commercial about Syria in the final days of the campaign," Gumbo PAC's Trey Ourso said later.

At that stage, the Edwards campaign began rolling out robocalls featuring Donna Edwards, West Point pal Murray Starkel, and the candidate himself. Louisiana Families First, the pro-Edwards super PAC funded mostly by national unions, aired an ad tying Vitter to Bobby Jindal. "Remember," said an announcer, "a vote for David Vitter is a vote for Bobby Jindal's third term."

The governor's decision to end his presidential campaign was actually hurting Vitter, his Republican rival, as his "homecoming" gave the Edwards super PAC grounds for hanging the wildly unpopular Jindal around the senator's neck. Again, the first rule of knife fights applied: There are no rules.

Edwards, meanwhile, spoke before a noontime throng of supporters in Houma that day. "The polls look good," he told a packed room at the Holiday Inn. "But the only poll that matters is the one on Saturday."

In an interview afterward, Edwards didn't hide his disgust with Vitter's having said repeatedly that the Democrat wanted to admit more Syrian refugees. "He's a habitual liar," Edwards said. Then he recalled an old country saw his dad had taught him years earlier. "David Vitter," Edwards said, "is the kind of person who would climb naked to the top of a thorny tree just to tell a lie when he could stand flat-footed and clothed on the ground and tell the truth."

It wasn't just Vitter who was prompting derision. Sheriff Newell Normand was dismayed that the Louisiana Republican Party, his party, had sent out an email that day repeating a now-disproven claim that "there is an unmonitored Syrian refugee who is walking around freely, and no one knows where he is."

"Somebody's going to get killed" because of this kind of thing, Normand said, noting that a Catholic Charities office had received at least one death threat.

Jim Duffy, a national Democratic media consultant who had gotten his start in Louisiana, was one of many Louisiana expatriates watching the race closely. Duffy had worked for Mayor Moon Landrieu in the 1970s before settling in Washington. He called Kitchens, a long-time friend, to ask about the race. "I am going to be 70 next year," Duffy told Kitchens. "I told my wife that I didn't think I'd live to see another Democrat elected governor of Louisiana. Am I wrong?"

"Unless you die before Saturday," Kitchens said, "you're going to live to see another Democrat elected governor of Louisiana."

Kitchens' tracking poll that day, the Wednesday before the election, showed that after redistributing the undecided African-American vote in favor of Edwards, his candidate led Vitter 52 percent to 35 percent. The Syrian refugees issue had probably helped Vitter, but not nearly enough.

That evening, Edwards went to the Baton Rouge office of veteran lobbyist Randy Haynie, who operated from a house behind Capitol Lake that formerly belonged to Earl Long's widow, Blanche. Haynie had invited some clients to give last-minute checks to Edwards. Also gathered there in a conference room were nearly all of the 20 or so businessmen and women who funded Verne Kennedy's monthly poll, including *Advocate* owner John Georges.

Kennedy sat in front of his laptop and ran through a series of slides in a PowerPoint presentation that he projected onto a screen.

The last slide contained the numbers everyone wanted—his tracking poll from Wednesday through Friday the previous week. Straight up, Edwards was leading Vitter by 45 percent to 41 percent.

But when Kennedy adjusted the votes to give 90 percent of the African-American vote to Edwards, the Democrat led 50 percent to 40 percent, with African Americans accounting for only 20 percent of the overall turnout. If they accounted for 26 percent of the turnout—which was more in line with historic turnout patterns, Edwards led 53 percent to Vitter's 38 percent.

Kennedy noted that the tracking poll preceded Vitter's attempt to bludgeon Edwards with the Syrian refugees. But Kennedy didn't foresee that issue changing much. Edwards had a very high probability of winning, Kennedy said, unless something unusual happened before Saturday's election.

Then Team Edwards got a scare. Greg Rigamer, a demographer and pollster in New Orleans, emailed Wednesday's tracking numbers to his clients in Baton Rouge. On that night, among the 200 voters surveyed, Edwards led Vitter only 46 percent to 41 percent. Rigamer's clients were a group of Baton Rouge-based lobbyists. Like Kennedy, Rigamer had been polling 200 people per night to get an 800-person "rolling sample." Though the 200 voters he interviewed each night provided an indication of the direction in which the race was moving, the sample was too small by itself to be definitive. That's why Rigamer and other pollsters always folded each night's results into the three previous nights' results to obtain a more accurate 800-person poll.

On Monday night, November 16, Rigamer had found that Edwards led among the 200 people sampled that night, 50 percent to 37 percent, but that he had had a slightly bigger advantage over the previous four nights, 52 percent to 35 percent. At 9:11 p.m. on Wednesday night, after Kennedy had presented his numbers at Haynie's house, Rigamer emailed tracking numbers that showed the race tightening significantly, 46 to 41 percent among those sampled that night. Though Rigamer emphasized that the four-night sample of 800 showed Edwards with a healthy 51 percent to 36 percent advantage, that did little to reassure Sam Jones and others in Edwards' inner circle, who received Rigamer's numbers within minutes.

The Wednesday night tracking number, suggesting that Vitter was closing the gap, sent shivers through Edwards' team. The sample was only 200 people, with a large margin of error. Still, could the Syrian refugees gambit actually be paying off for Vitter?

"This is a serious dip here," Jones told Edwards.

The candidate went to bed around midnight but woke up a couple of hours later, worrying about Rigamer's poll and running scenarios through his mind about how to stop a Vitter surge. He never did fully fall back to sleep that night.

Edwards' advisers agreed that Arsement ought to take the $400,000 remaining in the campaign's bank account and spend more money on Edwards' rebuttal to Vitter on the refugees as well as a revival of the "prostitutes over patriots" ad.

In stark contrast to the cold, impersonal numbers that pollsters, candidates, and clients were tossing about, Wednesday also saw one of the campaign's few moments of warmth—a tender, emotional appeal on Facebook from one of Vitter's 18-year-old twin daughters, Lise, who posted a description of her father that no campaign consultant had ever captured:

> *Some of you know David Vitter—or at least think ya'll do— from the articles, commercials, or phone calls throughout the years—either for or against him. But the David Vitter I know is not the man many of you think you know. The David Vitter you think you know is the one that the media wants you to see—both in a positive and negative light. Ya'll have seen him fight for our state, but also got to see him make a huge, public mistake—a mistake that may have caused some of you to lose faith in him, and I don't blame you. But I do hope you see past it because trust me, there is so much more to my dad than a mistake. What the media or his opponents won't show you is each painstaking moment throughout the years that he has spent making it right again. The thing is, despite his mistakes, he is an amazing leader and an even better dad. So if you'll listen, I'd like to tell you who David Vitter is, not as a politician, but as just another guy.*

> *He's the guy who stood in our kitchen next to my mom rapping for my friends the first (and last) time I had friends over. He's the guy who dedicates three full days every year hosting "prank wars" with my brother against the rest of our family. He's the nerdy guy who's worn faded, somewhat acid-washed jeans with white sneakers for as long as I can remember (he still sometimes does). He's the guy who encouraged me to go to the college I thought fit me best—and then nearly cried when he found out I'd be with him in DC. He's the guy who took me alligator hunting the week before I left for college because of my incessant complaints that my little brother got to do all the cool stuff. And yes, he's the guy who made a mistake—a mistake I'm sure he will never forget and will spend the rest*

of his life making right. And there is no doubt in my mind that he will make it right because he has dedicated every day since to gaining your trust back, to gaining my whole family's trust back. My dad has spent his entire life teaching my siblings and me to defend what we believe in, against all adversity. And I think it's time I defend my dad because there is no one I believe in more. There comes a point where we all have to decide—to either fall back on the comfort of what we've known, or to step up and embrace something new, something scary. The choice is ours—to hold on to past mistakes or have faith that the future, however risky, is worth investing in. This isn't a political statement; I don't know the first thing about politics. This is a daughter letting you know how weird, embarrassing, thoughtful, and inspiring her dad is to her and how much he has brought to her life, to Louisiana's life. So vote for my dad. Don't vote for my dad. Agree with my dad. Disagree with my dad. But please, whatever you decide—I hope that you know who David Vitter is—a man who has and will continue to dedicate his life to making it right and a man worth far more than his past mistakes.

On Thursday, Edwards, still feeling anxious, asked his brother Daniel to campaign with him as he made stops in Alexandria and Marksville. Vitter's counterattack on the Syrian refugees and the drop in Rigamer's tracking poll the night before weighed on Edwards. "I wish the election would be today," he told Daniel at one point.

"Me, too," Daniel replied. "But it will be here Saturday, and it will be fine."

With Treasurer John Kennedy at this side, Vitter held a press conference that day on the steps of the state Capitol to draw attention to his promise to fix the state's budget problems. The Joint Legislative Budget Committee would meet the following day, and Vitter, through the media, urged its members to reject Jindal's plan for plugging the state's $500 million deficit.

But that suggestion ended up playing second fiddle to Vitter's political proclamations. He told reporters that the Jindal administration was withholding budget information from his campaign and recommended that the governor appoint Bill Fenstermaker, who owned a Lafayette-based engineering firm, as interim commissioner of administration. Jindal's sitting Commissioner of Administration Stafford Palmieri, who had been on the job for only a month, didn't take kindly to that suggestion. She turned to Twitter and invited Vitter to a private meeting.

Then, to Edwards she tweeted, "You are of course invited as well but I know you'd probably call me instead of holding a presser." The result was an all-out Twitter war that pulled in former staffers of both Jindal and Vitter.

This being Louisiana, many voters kept their sense of humor—and their sense of history—about the campaign. State Senator Norby Chabert, a Democrat-turned-Republican from Chauvin, a coastal town in Terrebonne Parish, was paying an insurance bill on Thursday when an elderly woman stopped him to talk about the election. As they said goodbye and Chabert headed for his truck, the woman harkened back to a saying immortalized in the infamous David Duke–Edwin Edwards runoff in 1991. "Vote for the Boy Scout," she called out. "It's Important!"

Rigamer emailed his final tracking numbers to his clients that evening, two days before the election, at 9:28 p.m. The Thursday night sample of 200 showed Edwards leading again by a healthy margin, 52 percent to 37 percent. Edwards' cumulative advantage over the last four nights was 52 percent to 36 percent. "Last night's track was a bit lower than what we have seen," Rigamer said in his email, "but that is not unusual with a nightly track—the variance was in the margin of error of the survey. Tonight's rebound confirms his position in the race." Rigamer predicted that Edwards would be the next governor. "It is not unusual for me to go out on a limb but I feel pretty safe on this one."

Vitter's Hail Mary pass had fallen incomplete.

On Friday, Vitter made campaign appearances in Abbeville, Jennings, and Gonzales. Edwards held a press conference after the Joint Legislative Budget Committee hearing in the state Capitol. Former General Russel Honoré endorsed Edwards in a spot that aired on African-American-oriented radio stations.

The campaign had been long and arduous for John Bel Edwards. He had begun the governor's race in mid-2012 as the longest of long shots, an afterthought even in the Democratic Party. David Vitter was the prohibitive favorite. Few people wanted to stand in the senator's way, given his reputation for vindictiveness and his track record of always getting what he wanted. To have a chance, Edwards needed to do everything right *and* catch a few lucky breaks.

He needed to have no big-name Democrat enter the race against him. *Check.* He needed to have at least several major Republicans enter and draw Republican votes from Vitter. *Check.* He needed to have none of the Republicans beat *him* up in the primary. *Check.* He needed to face Vitter, and not Scott Angelle or Jay Dardenne, in the runoff. *Check.*

Even so, it wasn't until Edwards led the primary field with a stunning 40 percent of the vote—and Vitter trailed far behind with just 23 percent—that a win for the small-town Democrat in the GOP stronghold of Louisiana seemed possible. Even then, many in the political arena still wondered if he could beat Vitter.

By the end of the second debate, Vitter's strategy of angling for the little-known Democrat opponent in the runoff had backfired—and his assumption that his "very serious sin" was behind him was fatally off the mark. Ironically, had Vitter offered a more forthcoming admission of wrongdoing—and a genuine *mea culpa*—to voters and the media back in 2007 when he first faced reporters about the sex scandal, and if in 2015 he had not so ham-fistedly dodged reporters and forums on *The Question* throughout the campaign, he likely would have withstood Democrats' efforts to club him with the scandal. In retrospect, he might even have taken the issue off the table entirely by *inviting* questions about it from Day One, just to inure the voters. That strategy, however, might have failed, due to his never answering the question of whether he had violated the law.

Instead, Vitter blindly adhered to the template that had worked for him in 2010 and for Bill Cassidy in 2014. In doing so, he ignored two time-honored political maxims: (1) Every election is a unique event; and (2) it's damn near impossible to keep secrets in politics. Vitter mistakenly believed that President Obama's unpopularity would trump any concerns about his own past and that he could turn a local election for governor into a national campaign played out in Louisiana. He also mistakenly believed that skipping forums and dodging reporters would somehow keep a lid on his past transgressions. Vitter had planned to serve as the most powerful—and most transformative—Louisiana governor since Huey Long, and he threw everything he had at Edwards during their four-week runoff.

Little of his strategy went as planned, however, and now the country lawyer from Amite was just one day away from up-ending the man who had looked and acted like a political juggernaut just a few months earlier. Edwards would get credit for pulling off a stunning upset, but in truth he couldn't have done it had Vitter not made some fundamental miscalculations.

Edwards ate dinner Friday night at his home in Rosedale. His brother Daniel brought over steaks, tomatoes, okra, a big salad, and bread pudding. Murray Starkel and two other West Point buddies—Doug Gillem and Michael Holland—joined them. The guys wore jeans and polo shirts—except for the candidate, who was still wearing his suit pants and dress shirt from the final day of campaigning. They ate Daniel's food on the deck by the swimming pool and laughed over old stories about their days together at West Point and their careers in the Army. Edwards occasionally tossed more wood on the fire. At one point, he threw a football with his 14-year-old son, John Miller.

The candidate betrayed his nervousness about the next day's forecast of rain, the bane of Democrats who need a big turnout, but otherwise he tried to remain calm. He would need a good night's rest. Tomorrow would be a long day for the long shot.

25

"Na Na Hey Hey Goodbye"

At about 9:30 a.m. on Saturday, November 21, in a light rain, Dan Foley walked out of his house in the Lakeview neighborhood of New Orleans and got behind the wheel of his wife's SUV. Edwards for Governor yard signs filled the back of the vehicle. A former clerk of Orleans Parish Civil District Court, an elected position, and now a successful trial attorney, Foley had been a strong supporter and financial backer of John Bel Edwards since 2013. He knew that the latest tracking polls showed that his candidate was poised to win that day, but the 67-year-old Foley was old school about elections: You always run scared until the last votes are counted. So he put up yard signs for several hours, knowing they might yield a few more votes for Edwards. Besides, Foley was nervous, and the work would occupy his time.

Joining him were two buddies, Henry Flanagan, a friend and engineering inspector from the Irish Channel, and Edwin Murray, an attorney who was leaving the state Senate because of term limits. The three men drove around Lakeview, stopping every few minutes to poke the metal frames of the Edwards signs into front yards and neutral grounds. Between stops, they toweled off the rain.

At about 11:15 a.m., Foley's cell phone rang. "What are you doing?" asked Edwards. The candidate was on Interstate 10 on his way to New Orleans with his son, John Miller. "Want to grab lunch?" Edwards asked, adding that he could get there quickly. Foley suggested they meet at Mandina's, a favorite of the attorney's, a place where power brokers ate New Orleans food in a casual setting. Foley called the restaurant. "I know it's busy," he told the manager who answered. "You need to hold a table for eight people."

That would be difficult, the man said.

"Well, I've got John Bel Edwards, the next governor of Louisiana, with me," Foley said.

"We'll hold a table for you," the man said.

Heads turned when Edwards and John Miller entered, followed by two State Police troopers and a photographer. Foley, Murray, and Flanagan were already seated. The candidate said he was feeling good, but looking out the big windows facing Canal Street, he said he wished it would stop raining. As they ate, diners stopped to greet Edwards and wish him good luck. At one point, Foley motioned over a waitress who wanted to meet the candidate. At another point, Edwards told John Miller that he needed to get his hair cut that afternoon because they would be on live statewide television that night. John Miller resisted the idea. Foley leaned over and said with a laugh, "Just because you're going to be governor doesn't mean you can make your son get a haircut."

David Vitter, meanwhile, had been on the move since early that morning. With a group of supporters, he waved signs at the intersection of Clearview Parkway and Veterans Boulevard in Metairie, in his home parish of Jefferson, and then did the same thing at nearby Causeway Boulevard and Veterans. Vitter arrived to vote at the Metairie fire station around 9:30 a.m., accompanied by his wife and their four children. Holding hands with Wendy, he wore jeans, a checkered shirt, a light jacket, and tennis shoes. After he voted, press secretary Luke Bolar took a photo of the family together. Vitter posed with a thumbs up. "It's a big day," he told a small group of reporters. "We're all very excited by the response we've been getting over the last eight days."

A reporter asked Wendy if she had anything to say. "I know that David's the right person," she said, adding, "We'll be fine either way tomorrow."

Elsewhere around the state, the Democratic Governors Association and its team were overseeing more than 5,000 door-knockers and phone-bankers in a major GOTV effort. The air war was over; now it was time for the ground assault, especially after the lackluster effort for Mary Landrieu the year before. While Edwards' supporters had focused on Baton Rouge, Shreveport, and New Orleans, they now mounted a bigger than usual push for Democrats in rural areas. They had especially high hopes for the parishes south of Interstate 10, particularly in the Acadiana regions of southwest and south central Louisiana, and in the River Parishes between New Orleans and Baton Rouge.

The Louisiana Federation of Teachers and the Louisiana Association of Educators had pooled their resources for the first time ever for a joint GOTV effort. The pro-Edwards Louisiana Families First super PAC had spent $322,000 the week prior on voter outreach, including a telephone program, direct mail, and $30,000 to the Service Employees International Union Local 21 in New Orleans, which provided canvassing services. The PAC also went on television for the first time in the preceding days in select markets, spending $208,000 on the ad that tied Vitter to Jindal.

Still, Edwards worried about the rain. Turnout was below expectations by mid-afternoon, especially among African Americans, the Democrats' most reliable voting bloc. Edwards met with Congressman Cedric Richmond at the Spears & Spears law firm in New Orleans to make phone calls and send encouraging texts to supporters. The Edwards campaign played its final trump card: a robocall secretly recorded by President Obama urging African-American households to vote for the Democrat. The Edwards campaign had to trigger the robocall early enough to be effective but late enough to prevent his more conservative supporters from learning of the help from Obama, who once again, during the Syrian refugee dustup, had surfaced as the GOP bogeyman. The Vitter campaign would surely love another Hail Mary if it could find one. The President's robocall went out at 5:30 p.m.

Edwards was attending a Catholic Mass at St. Louis Cathedral in the French Quarter, with 20 family members and friends, when the president's robocalls began. When Mass ended, he and Donna walked to the front of the church, lit a candle, and said a prayer. Afterward, Edwards stood near the confessional in the back of the church and remembered the long cast of doubters who had told him he couldn't win. "I was told that over and over and over," he recalled. "I said, 'You just wait and see. It's going to come together. We're going to work really hard. We're going to be smart.'"

Edwards recalled the meeting in July when two "very, very influential powerful people in Louisiana and Democratic politics" tried to get him out of the governor's race. "That was the worst for me," he said, declining to identify them. (Others subsequently said they were Mary Landrieu and Karen Carter Peterson.)

Edwards' West Point sense of duty, he said, kept him going. "I have never backed out of any commitment I've ever made in my life," he added. "I have never failed at anything that I set to accomplish either."

Donna interrupted him to say that the Cathedral was closing and he needed to go outside. As he passed through the doorway, a young man recognized him and, nearly hyperventilating, asked if he could get a selfie with the candidate.

"You can, you can," Edwards gently replied.

They posed together.

"It's such a pleasure," said the man, shaking the next governor's hand.

Edwards walked toward an awaiting State Police SUV parked at the corner of St. Ann and Chartres streets. He stopped in front of the 19th Century Presbytere to elaborate on why he hadn't dropped out. He had made a commitment to people throughout Louisiana, Edwards said, to "people who had been hurting, school teachers, middle class people, poor people. There are a lot of people out there who have been left behind over the last eight years. I had gone around the state and talked to thousands of those people. There's no way I was backing out. That was never going to happen. I had accepted that I might lose. But I would be able to go home and look at my children and tell them that I had done my best. When you quit, you have not done your best."

It was 6 p.m., and Edwards admitted to being nervous—but he said he was not as nervous as Vitter was at that moment. He would watch the returns at the Hotel Monteleone on Royal Street, the favored election night headquarters of the other Governor Edwards, who typically holed up in a 15th-floor suite as donors and office-seekers lined up in the hall outside for a few minutes of his time. The hotel held such a special meaning for Edwin Edwards that he got married there in 2011 after his release from federal prison.

That John Bel Edwards ended up at the Monteleone on election night happened by chance, as it had the biggest available ballroom in New Orleans that Mary-Patricia Wray could book. Edwards liked the choice. His grandfather Frank Edwards had stayed at the hotel when he was elected sheriff of Tangipahoa Parish for the first time in 1927. "He brought my grandmother to the Hotel Monteleone on the afternoon of Election Day," Edwards told *Times-Picayune* reporter Julia O'Donoghue. "They got up the next morning and bought *The Times-Picayune* to see whether he had won."

From St. Louis Cathedral, John Bel Edwards rode with his brother Daniel through the French Quarter to Galatoire's 33 Bar & Steak on Bourbon Street. Video poker lobbyist Alton Ashy had texted Edwards that he and other supporters would be watching the LSU–Ole Miss football game there on the first floor. Everyone applauded when Edwards walked in. "Do you want a drink?" asked Ashy.

"I better wait until later," he said.

"How's it going? What do you think?" Ashy asked.

"The rain has stopped," Edwards replied. "The lines are around the block. I think I'm going to kick his ass."

Edwards returned to the Monteleone and installed himself in Suite 1450. Wray brought him his victory speech. Five days earlier, Wray had been so afraid that the errant Facebook post on the Syrian refugees had given Vitter a late opening that she had dissolved in tears and told others that Edwards should fire her to deflect attention from the error. That now seemed like a lifetime ago.

"Well, Mary-Patricia," Edwards said, "we're gonna win this thing."

"You're sure?" she asked.

"I'm sure. I've had all the reports that I need to know. It's in the bag."

"Well, I'll wait till it's official."

"I want you to know that I appreciate your sacrifice. I know it wasn't always easy. I couldn't have done it without you."

They hugged, and they both teared up.

At 7:30 p.m., Edwards called Jay Dardenne, who had issued a key endorsement 16 days earlier. Dardenne was watching the returns at his father-in-law's camp in St. Francisville, a two-hour drive northwest of New Orleans. Edwards thanked Dardenne for his support and said he wanted to talk with the outgoing lieutenant governor after the election about a role in his administration.

Scott Angelle and his wife Dianne were on a mini-vacation, spending the night at a hotel in Destin, Florida. Vitter, meanwhile, was holding his election night party at the Airport Hilton in Kenner, just as he had in the primary.

At 8 p.m., the polls closed. "Now the waiting begins," tweeted *The Advocate's* Elizabeth Crisp, who was in the Monteleone's packed La Nouvelle Orleans Ballroom on the second floor.

No one had to wait long. She tweeted again at 8:05 p.m.: "Crowd just went wild as TV showed early vote way up for @JohnBelforLA Cheers, bell ringing."

At 8:21 p.m., WWL-TV called the lieutenant governor's race. Billy Nungesser, the Republican, had trounced Kip Holden, the Democrat.

At 8:40 p.m., Edwin Edwards strolled into the Monteleone on the arm of his 36-year-old wife Trina. They had left baby Eli had home. Well-wishers crowded around them, asking for selfies with the former governor.

At 8:52 p.m., *Advocate* reporter Will Sentell captured a campaign running on empty at the Airport Hilton. "Vitter watch party subdued," Sentell tweeted. "Guests munching at buffet and drinking $3.25 bottled water. Cash bar."

In his suite at the Monteleone, Edwards watched the returns while sitting on a three-legged stool covered by an Edwards campaign t-shirt. The stool had been a favorite perch of his grandfather's and then his father's at an Amite restaurant called Ardillo's. The candidate was surrounded by his family, friends, and senior aides.

WWL-TV called it at 9:02 p.m. John Bel Edwards would be

the next governor of Louisiana. The crowd in Suite 1450 erupted in cheers. Edwards hugged and kissed Donna. She became teary-eyed.

When the news appeared on the giant TVs scattered throughout the La Nouvelle Orleans Ballroom, the crowd practically lifted the roof with its roar. The Most Wanted Brass Band burst into the room and paraded through the crowd while playing the New Orleans favorite, "When the Saints Go Marching In." Amidst the whooping and hollering, the seven-member band added an extra bit of local flavor with a chant that riffed on New Orleans Saints fans' favorite cheer: "Who Dat say dey gonna beat John Bel! Who Dat! Who Dat!" Supporters waved their hands in the air, some holding yellow handkerchiefs branded with Edwards' name and others brandishing thin sticks with a cut-out photo of the governor-elect attached.

Celebrating two blocks away were roughly 75 Edwards supporters packed into a second-floor dining room at Galatoire's. The crowd included Newell Normand, Danny DeNoux, state Senator Danny Martiny, and John Cummings—all of whom, five weeks earlier, were having breakfast at the Royal Blend coffee house in Metairie when the Vitter campaign's hapless private investigator got too close with his spy camera. John Georges, one of Galatoire's owners, who had sat with Edwin and Trina Edwards during their dinner, had drifted upstairs to the celebration. Alton Ashy, who had reserved the dining room, stood on a chair, got everybody to quiet down, and said, "You know, for once in our lives, the good guy wins." The group cheered again. Then Normand stood on a chair, held a glass of red wine in the air, and asked everyone to join him in toasting the victory.

Waiters bearing trays entered and handed out glasses of champagne. Ashy got up a second time. "I especially wanted to thank John Georges for paying for the champagne," he said. The group hooted its approval. Georges gave a sheepish wave and grin. Though he hadn't planned on it, he picked up the bill.

Jason Brad Berry, who had released the Wendy Ellis videos on his *American Zombie* blog, gathered with friends at his home in Algiers. He was drinking Stone Pale Ale and Maker's Mark whisky, celebrating his not having to face the wrath of Governor Vitter.

Dan Moldea, the investigative reporter who in 2007 broke the sex scandal when he found the D.C. Madam's calls to Vitter, spent the night at his Washington, D.C., apartment eating carry-out Chinese food. He got the election result from CNN.

At about 9:20 p.m., Vitter called Edwards and graciously offered congratulations and best wishes.

At 9:27 p.m., the senator appeared from behind a curtain at the Airport Hilton and made his way through the crowded stage, high-fiving a couple of supporters as if he had won. "David! David!" chanted the crowd, which greeted him with sustained applause. "We came up short tonight," he began. "Let me rephrase that. I came up short. You all were fabulous." Two minutes later, Vitter dropped a bombshell—he would not seek re-election to the Senate in 2016. He said that when he decided to run for governor, he and Wendy had agreed that he would end his Senate career, no matter what.

"I had reached my personal term limit," he told the crowd and smiled. "I'm genuinely excited with Wendy about starting a new chapter of my professional life, and all the fun and reward and challenge that will bring." He thanked Wendy, kissed her on the cheek, and they shared a long embrace.

In the La Nouvelle Orleans Ballroom, though no one could hear the sound on the TV screens, the on-screen ticker flashed the news that Vitter would not seek re-election next year. The gasp was audible. The Edwards supporters, however, were not in a forgiving mood. The crowd spontaneously broke into song: "Na Na Na Na! Na Na Na Na! Hey Hey Hey! Goodbye!"

Louisiana voters might have been willing to send Vitter to Washington to do battle with Obama, but they clearly did not want him to occupy the Governor's Mansion and directly influence their day-to-day lives. Now Vitter was about to exit the political stage he had held for more than 20 years.

He was beaten.

At 9:38 p.m., just after Vitter finished his remarks at the Airport Hilton, Edwards and his family climbed onto the La Nouvelle stage from a back entrance. "I did not create this breeze of hope that's blowing across our beautiful and blessed state," he told the jubilant crowd. "But I did catch it."

Several minutes later he pledged, "I'm going to be the governor of all the people. And I'm speaking to everybody in Louisiana right now, whether you voted for me or whether you didn't, or whether you didn't vote. I'm going to be your governor. And I'm going to work hard for you just as I'm going to work hard for those people who have been supporting me from the very first day."

When he finished speaking, he grabbed a yellow second-line umbrella made especially for the occasion and second-lined through the crowd with the brass band again playing "When the Saints Go Marching In." Celebrating the victory in the back of the ballroom was Trey Ourso, who had created Gumbo PAC, which had teamed with the Democratic Governors Association during the runoff to hammer Vitter.

The final results:

	Votes	%
John Bel Edwards	646,929	56.11
David Vitter	504,940	43.89

Turnout was 40.2 percent of registered voters, up slightly from 39.2 percent in the primary.

Edwards' victory was so complete that he even carried Vitter's home parish of Jefferson. The Democrat got his 141,989-vote margin by demolishing Vitter with 73 percent of the vote in the 10 parishes that President Obama had won in 2012. In those 10 parishes, Edwards led by 146,225 votes. In the 54 parishes Mitt Romney had carried in 2012, Vitter won by less than 1 percent, or 5,241 votes.

Edwards had broad geographic support, winning a majority of the vote in six of the state's seven media markets, falling short only in the Monroe market, while running strongest in the Baton Rouge and New Orleans markets.

The winning Democratic formula called for Edwards to win at least 33 percent of the white vote, for African Americans to account for 30 percent of the overall turnout, and for Edwards to win at least 90 percent of the African-American vote. He met or exceeded all three goals.

According to demographer John Couvillon, he won 37 percent of the white vote, African Americans accounted for 30 percent of the turnout, and he won 97 percent of the African-American vote.

One more measure: Vitter needed at least 75 percent of the voters who supported Scott Angelle and Jay Dardenne in the primary. Couvillon estimated that he got only 60 percent.

Edwards had become the first Democrat to win statewide office since 2008.

Some labeled his victory a work of political art and strategy. Others called it a fluke, a product of political optics and Louisiana's jungle primary system. Either way, the race was the most expensive contest for governor in Bayou State history. Candidates, super PACs, political parties, and others spent nearly $50 million trying to influence the outcome, shattering the previous $32 million record set in 2007, when Bobby Jindal won his first term.

While Edwards and his supporters celebrated, Vitter gathered with about 75 people—close friends, family, and campaign aides—in a suite upstairs at the Airport Hilton. "In a way, I'm really relieved for your family," state Representative Mike Johnson told Vitter. "You can go back and have a normal life again."

"You know what, you're right," Vitter replied.

Johnson was struck by how Vitter and Wendy, too, seemed almost relieved. Vitter certainly seemed more relaxed than Johnson had seen him in a long time.

At about midnight, the true believers who had been with Edwards throughout—Sam Jones, Jared Arsement, Mary-Patricia Wray, Jim Kitchens, and Kathleen and Coach Blanco—posed for photos in the now-deserted ballroom.

Afterward, the Blancos sat on a bed in their 14th floor room in the Monteleone and reflected on their early decision to back Edwards. "We had been watching John Bel," recalled Kathleen. "He was one voice in the wilderness saying: 'Stop the madness.' He understood that the Jindal policies were destructive." The former governor and her husband reflected on the turning points of the race. One, they agreed, was the "prostitutes over patriots" ad during the runoff. They remembered that the decision to run it had provoked a strong debate among Edwards' inner circle. "John Bel made the call," Kathleen said. "You got to show that you've got—" She paused. "I don't want to say the word."

"Balls," offered Coach.

"He had to show he was tough," affirmed Kathleen.

Coach was asked why Vitter was smiling as he entered the stage to concede. "He can now throw off the demons and the unhappy life he's been living!" Coach shouted. "He's free!"

Down the hall, in suite 1450, as state troopers stood watch outside, friends and family streamed past to join the party inside. A waiter pushed a cart into the suite with a resupply of liquid refreshments. Inside, Edwards, his jacket off, collected hugs and handshakes. The result was still sinking in for everyone.

At about 3 a.m., Edwards was ready for bed. But his three West Point classmates reminded him that he had promised to smoke a victory cigar with them. "Come on, Ranger," Doug Gillem said. "A promise is a promise. We got a cigar to smoke and some scotch to drink. Let's go to the roof."

As they stood near the Monteleone's rooftop pool, the four men were about as giddy as West Point graduates could be. They lit up their cigars to honor the one-time long shot's improbable victory, then FaceTimed another West Point buddy, Pat Gary, waking him up in North Carolina so he could enjoy the revelry in New Orleans.

The chilly wind didn't bother the men. At one point, Edwards walked to the roof's edge. He looked down. Some people were going home; others were going to work. "This is a tremendous responsibility," he thought to himself, "a sacred responsibility."

He and his buddies called it a night at 4 a.m.

Edwards awoke at 7:30 a.m. *Did I really win?* That was his first thought as he gained his bearings. He got out of bed and opened the door to the living room of his suite. Strewn about the room were empty bottles of beer and champagne, half-filled drink glasses, unlit cigars that supporters had dropped off as gifts—all the signs of a victory party. He smiled, reassured.

Someone had placed a copy of that morning's *Times-Picayune* newspaper on a coffee table. "GOVERNOR," read the large headline in block leaders. "Edwards takes reins of deeply red state after beating Vitter in runoff," read a sub-headline. Dominating the front page was a giant photograph of Donna pressing her cheek against his in a celebratory hug.

Yes, he really *did* win.

Epilogue

Plus ça change

There would be no honeymoon period for John Bel Edwards. That became evident shortly after his historic win. Despite Edwards' lopsided margin of victory, partisan anger lingered among die-hard Republican lawmakers, particularly in the GOP-dominated state House of Representatives. Many if not most Republican House veterans won office with David Vitter's help in prior election cycles. In the summer and early fall of 2015, they looked forward to Vitter's election as governor and to helping him, in their new roles as his legislative allies, transform Louisiana into a conservative model of budgetary restraint and political reform. Their candidate for governor may have lost his election, but that didn't mean they had to roll over for Democrat Edwards—even though Louisiana governors had traditionally hand picked the House and Senate leadership. Like everything else in politics, that time-honored tradition was subject to change, which it did as Edwards prepared to take his oath of office. The new governor would soon learn that politicians who don't recognize—and quickly adapt to—such seismic changes in the political landscape pay a heavy price.

In the Louisiana governor's race of 2015, David Vitter failed to grasp that voters no longer tolerated his past sins. He also mistakenly assumed the template that had worked so well for him in past "national" elections for the Senate would work again in the decidedly "local" election for governor. That mistake cost Vitter dearly. For his part, Governor-elect John Bel Edwards would fail to recognize that the Louisiana House of Representatives—the body he had been a part of for eight years—had declared its independence from the governor. Edwards mistakenly assumed that he could anoint Democrat Walt Leger III of New Orleans as the next speaker, despite the lower chamber's GOP majority. That mistake would cost Edwards dearly.

"We'll of course have that honeymoon," Edwards told reporters at the outset of 2016. No, he would not. The warning signs came early, but the handwriting was plainly on the wall in, of all places, St. Joseph's Cathedral in Baton Rouge on the morning of Edwards' inauguration on January 11, 2016.

Edwards, his family, and friends arrived at St. Joseph's early for the traditional Inauguration Mass, which began at 8 a.m. Bishop Robert Muench welcomed everyone, rattling off names and titles of distinguished guests. "For those of you not mentioned, I promise you an abundance of goodness," Muench said to laughter. Mass proceeded with bipartisan lectors, until 8:50 a.m., when the strains of "You Satisfy A Hungry Heart" echoed above the bowed heads of those in line for communion. Then another queue took form.

A second-term House member left the church early with his wife, followed by a freshman, then a term-limited representative. One by one they left—House Republicans all. They made their way to another important gathering, this one scheduled to begin at 9:15 a.m. in the Capitol's Ellender Room. There they convened to derail Edwards' choice for speaker with an eleventh-hour stratagem, one that reflected both the GOP delegation's political agility and a fatal flaw in the governor-elect's handle on the vote count.

Edwards had spent the preceding weeks meeting with Republican lawmakers, telling them that Leger, the speaker pro-tempore in the previous term, would be their next speaker. In earlier times, a word from the incoming governor would have been enough, though occasionally some arm-twisting was necessary. This time the incoming governor encountered more resistance as his team lobbied lawmakers. Sometimes he met with House members one-on-one; other times Leger was present alongside Chief of Staff Ben Nevers, a Democrat who had just left the state Senate. Joining them on other occasions was former state Senator Robert Adley, a north Louisiana Republican whom Edwards had tapped to serve as a political troubleshooter. If needed, Adley followed up with GOP lawmakers. They were all old hands at counting votes, and they knew it would be important to have more than just a simple 53–vote majority in the 105-member House.

Counting votes, it's said, is like growing figs: You have to make sure you grow enough for yourself *and* enough for the birds—because the birds are going to get theirs. A comfortable margin for Leger and Edwards would be somewhere around 60 votes, leaving some for the birds. They were aware that Leger's main rival, Republican state Representative Cameron Henry of Metairie, who was widely reported to have been David Vitter's choice for speaker, was too strident to beat the more moderate Leger. The fact that upwards of 20 Republican House members had promised to back Leger over Henry gave Team Edwards a misplaced sense of confidence. What the governor-elect didn't know was that Henry and other GOP House leaders had hatched an alternate plan the night before Inauguration Day. The final pieces were coming together in the Ellender Room while the governor-elect sat in the front pew of St. Joseph's awaiting Bishop Muench's final blessing. Sitting in the front row, Edwards hadn't noticed the Republican exodus from the pews behind him during communion.

At the Capitol, Henry and Republican Delegation chair Lance Harris of Alexandria headed downstairs to the Ellender Room. There, Henry explained to the group that there would be two other candidates for speaker besides himself and Leger—Representatives Taylor Barras of New Iberia and Neil Abramson of New Orleans. Barras was a one-time Democrat who had switched to Republican before the 2011 elections. Abramson was a Democrat. It was no coincidence that the delegation meeting was called for 9:15 a.m. Henry didn't want any lag time between the end of that gathering and the House convening at 10 a.m. That way no one could alert the governor-elect, who might yet be able to twist some arms for Leger—or worse, draft his own Republican candidate for the job.

"If my vote and Taylor's vote equal or combine to 53, we will have a Republican speaker," Henry said to start that final meeting. "But it won't be me."

For once, a meeting room filled with Republican House members went silent. In that moment, Henry actually envisioned a pin dropping with a thunderous plunk. The plan was for Henry to drop out of the race if he ran second and Barras ran third, forcing a Leger–Barras runoff. Barras would then carry all of Henry's votes. Henry had accepted that he could not cobble together a majority, so his decision to step aside was a sacrifice for the GOP team.

The vote went down exactly as planned. On a second ballot, Barras won 56 votes to 49 for Leger.

This meant that Edwards took office as the first Louisiana governor in modern history who did not handpick the House speaker. Just as elections at the ballot box have consequences, so, too, do elections for legislative leadership. Leger's defeat meant Edwards would have no say in who got chairmanships or committee assignments—and therefore relatively little direct influence in the House. The vote was an early sign of turbulent times to come, and a harsh reminder of the two kinds of politics in American democracy: the politics of elections and the politics of governance. The two intersect occasionally and overlap frequently, but they require very distinct skill sets. Edwards had proven he knew how to win a tough election. His first attempt at governing did not go so well.

Even before the crushing loss in the speaker's race, Edwards received disturbing news about the state's finances. Just about every legislator who had served under Governor Bobby Jindal knew that Jindal was fudging the numbers to create the illusion of a balanced budget. What no one knew until shortly before Edwards took office was the size of the budget hole. The "real numbers" came as a gut punch: Revenues in the then-current fiscal year, which would end June 30, 2016, were *at least* $750 million short—and up to $2 billion short for the fiscal year beginning July 1. Louisiana was in a fiscal free fall, and the new governor was coming aboard mid-descent. Worse yet, he would have to cover those deficits by asking a Republican-majority Legislature—one that now had a House speaker installed by David Vitter's allies—to raise taxes.

No honeymoon, indeed.

When Edwards announced that the state would need new taxes to cover the deficit, his Republican foes pounced, saying he had already violated his much-ballyhooed Honor Code by "lying" when he said during the campaign that he would not raise taxes. He responded directly in a statewide televised address, saying, "I am fully aware that I did not campaign on a platform of raising taxes, but the state's deficit is now more than twice as big as anyone ever anticipated, so clearly when the facts surrounding the problem change so dramatically, so must the solutions."

His reasoning was sound, but that didn't matter to his adversaries. He got dinged on talk radio and on conservative blogs, and LABI, which had supported Vitter in the election, chimed in by opposing any efforts by the governor to end business tax breaks.

The attacks grew louder when news broke over the salary that Edwards would pay his commissioner of administration, his top appointee. Republican Jay Dardenne, who had finished fourth in the primary and then endorsed Edwards, would receive $33,000 more than the previous commissioner, for a total salary of $237,500. In her news story, Associated Press reporter Melinda Deslatte noted that Edwards, during the November runoff, had "bristled" at the salaries Bobby Jindal paid his top aides. "They're exorbitant. They're too high. We're going to reduce those costs right off the top," Edwards said at the time. Deslatte, reflecting on that promise, wrote, "But since becoming governor, Edwards, who receives a $130,000 salary outlined in state law, appears to have changed his mind."

Edwards enjoyed a brief respite a few weeks later at the 2016 Washington Mardi Gras. Bobby Jindal had skipped the festivities during the past three years. He had been too busy running for president.

Unlike the previous year, when Edwards was all but ignored, he was now a dignitary. He conducted meetings at several federal agencies to discuss transportation and health care policy—and none of those meetings was canceled. A year earlier, he and campaign aides had worked into the night hanging Mardi Gras beads bearing his campaign logo on doors at the Washington Hilton. Now that he was *The Governor*, doors opened for him.

David Vitter was serving his final year as captain of the Mystick Krewe, which organizes the three-day party. Vitter's involvement was more restrained than ever—a sign, perhaps, that he was looking forward to his departure from Washington. He did not join the rest of the congressional delegation in hosting an open hospitality suite. No one could remember when a senior Louisiana senator had not rolled out the welcome mat. Months later, *Politico* would quote a tipster as saying that Vitter was having preliminary talks about a potential lobbying job on K Street. Vitter's staffers and close friends called the report ridiculous. On that point, the senator's supporters and critics totally agreed: No one could imagine Vitter, who always railed against the establishment, trying to lobby his former colleagues.

Meanwhile, by early February, Edwards had released his recommendations for fixing the budget deficits. In addition to $160 million in cuts, he proposed adding a penny to the state's 4-cent sales tax, hiking the cigarette tax by 22 cents, and limiting corporate and personal income tax breaks. In the eyes of conservatives, that cemented their view of him as a liberal tax-and-spend Democrat. State Treasurer John Kennedy delivered the GOP response to Edwards' televised statewide address, calling the governor's proposals "the largest tax increase in Louisiana history." He was not wrong; he merely ignored the part about Bobby Jindal's leaving the biggest deficit in Louisiana history.

Edwards summoned lawmakers into a special session that began on Valentine's Day, February 14. No one sent flowers in either direction. His message on Opening Day was simple, and it echoed one of his campaign themes: "I am asking everyone to shed partisan labels and blinders and work with me to repair the state we all love. I will do the same." Not everyone got the message.

As he delivered his speech, the Louisiana Republican Party debuted an online attack ad that replayed clips of candidate Edwards promising not to raise taxes. Nothing about this session was going be easy, members of Team Edwards thought, but they had no idea just how bad things would get. The governor would ultimately keep lawmakers in session for 19 consecutive weeks, eventually calling a second special session after the annual regular session—a record three sessions in less than six months.

Greek tragedies had better endings than the conclusion of

Edwards' first special session. His legislative hands fumbled key policy initiatives, and many of the taxes lawmakers agreed to pass were only temporary. The Legislature gave him $60 million less than what he said he needed for the current fiscal year and $800 million less than what he sought for the next. Worse, communications and trust broke down completely between the conservative House and the Edwards-friendly Senate. Edwards did moderately better in the regular annual session, but the real showdown came in the second special session, when he tried to convince lawmakers to pass another $600 million in taxes and received less than half that much.

After all three sessions, though Edwards got about $1.5 billion in taxes out of $2 billion that he had requested since taking office, most of those taxes were temporary, making for a steep fiscal cliff that would surface by 2018. He was learning harsh lessons about the politics of governance.

Louisiana's fiscal troubles were not the only challenges that Edwards would face in his early months as governor. In March, more than 20 inches of rain brought widespread flooding to north Louisiana. In Bossier City, residents were stranded as floodwaters reached four feet. When the waters finally receded, more than 5,000 homes, farms, and businesses had been damaged or destroyed. At least four people died.

Soon after the governor entered the new fiscal year, he had to confront another crisis, this one unfolding in Baton Rouge but before a worldwide audience. On July 5, two white Baton Rouge police officers shot an African-American man named Alton Sterling at close range. Witnesses had earlier reported seeing Sterling with a gun, but cell phone videos taken at the scene created a firestorm of criticism that spread quickly on social media. The videos showed officers holding Sterling down on the ground and screaming "Gun!" before firing, and then taking something out of Sterling's pocket. The United States Justice Department immediately launched a civil rights investigation. Edwards, knowing that protests with choruses of "Black Lives Matter" had already started, urged calm.

"I know that there are protests going on," Edwards said, "but it's urgent that they remain peaceful." The governor added, "I have full confidence that this matter will be investigated thoroughly, impartially, and professionally. I have very serious concerns. The video is disturbing, to say the least."

The situation in Baton Rouge took a dark turn less than two weeks later, on July 17, when 29-year-old Gavin Eugene Long, a former Marine sergeant from Missouri, shot six police officers, three of whom died: East Baton Rouge Parish sheriff's deputy Brad

Garafola and Baton Rouge City Police officers Matthew Gerald and Montrell Jackson. A law enforcement sniper then took down Long, who apparently had come to Baton Rouge with a twisted plan to avenge Alton Sterling's death at the hands of cops. The shootings once again thrust Baton Rouge—and Edwards—into a national debate over police violence, race relations, and gun control. Edwards sought to turn the heartrending events into a teachable moment.

"We cannot allow this tragedy to define us," he said during a memorial attended by Vice President Joe Biden, "but we can allow it to direct us."

On August 11, the same Baton Rouge region that had been torn apart by the July shootings was inundated by what meteorologists called a 1,000-year flood event. An intense rain system dumped almost two feet of rain on a wide swath of Louisiana in 48 hours. The footprint of the catastrophe spanned from parishes near the Texas line eastward to Tangipahoa Parish. More than a half-dozen river gauges hit record highs. Even Edwards and his family had to be relocated after the basement of the Governor's Mansion flooded, damaging its electrical system. Within a week, the flood swamped at least 134,000 households, caused at least $8.8 billion in damages, and killed at least 13 people.

During the first eight months of 2016, President Barack Obama issued disaster declarations covering north, central, and south Louisiana. In handling those disasters and the shootings in Baton Rouge, Edwards had stood tall as a calm voice of reason in the midst of crisis. His military training had prepared him to lead, and polls showed a majority of Louisiana voters giving him high marks. The triumphs of the campaign were giving way to the hard-earned lessons of governing. John Bel Edwards was growing into the job.

Politicians, like all human beings, are imperfect creatures. Nonetheless, revelations of a politician's moral failures or political inconsistencies leave many voters profoundly disappointed. For those who live and work in the belly of the beast known as the political arena, such revelations are just another day at the office. Or, as the French tell us, *Plus ça change, plus c'est la même chose* ("The more things change, the more they stay the same").

So it was that as the August 2016 floodwaters receded, Edwards faced another political storm, this one of his own making. He had promised to govern in a manner different from his predecessors, but news reports surfaced about business-as-usual decisions in the dispensing of patronage. Edwards cleaned house at the Louisiana Stadium and Exposition District, the official name of the board that oversees management of the state-owned Mercedes-Benz Superdome and the Smoothie King Arena in New Orleans. That board, in turn, fired its long-standing attorneys and hired the law firm that employed Jefferson Parish Sheriff Newell Normand's wife, Shawn Bridgewater. The sheriff's wife was a respected corporate attorney with an A-List of local business clients, but the press gave the story Page One treatment.

In an even bigger story, Edwards appointed a handful of politically connected trial lawyers—most of them among his top campaign donors—as counsel for the state in a controversial lawsuit against oil and gas companies. One "hook" of the story was that Edwards had appointed former state Representative Taylor Townsend, who had been one of the new governor's key campaign fundraisers, as lead counsel in the case. Unlike the other trial attorneys named in the story, Townsend was not known as an environmental lawyer—but he did serve as a co-chair of Edwards' transition team and, in early 2016, he stepped in as chair of the governor's super PAC, Louisiana Families First. Townsend, in his capacity as lead counsel, hired the other attorneys as highly qualified "subcontractors."

Another hook of the story: The contract for legal services included provisions for attorneys fees that oil and gas advocates thought were too generous, triggering a public spat between Edwards and new Attorney General Jeff Landry, who came into office with solid backing from energy interests. The story raised a host of red flags.

"There is a perception that the governor is turning his office into a private law firm," Melissa Landry of Louisiana Lawsuit Abuse Watch told WWL-TV, which broke the story with *The Advocate*. The governor, she added, "is quietly handing no-bid legal contracts to his campaign supporters."

One name among the trial attorneys Townsend hired practically jumped off the page to those who followed the election closely: James Garner, the David Vitter campaign attorney who had worked so hard to keep the Wendy Ellis allegations out of the mainstream press. Politically, that was the biggest red flag of all. How did *David Vitter's lawyer* get such a patronage plum from the man who had just beaten Vitter? The answer was as old as politics itself. After the election, Garner reached out to Team Edwards via New Orleans attorneys Gladstone Jones and Dan Robin Jr., who had worked on separate legal matters with Garner's firm in the past.

More important, Jones and Robin were early and fervent supporters of Edwards. Robin also knew Neal Kling, a member of Garner's firm. The two lawyers were happy to help Garner extend an olive branch. What resulted was a match made in political heaven: Garner's firm announced on January 22, 2016 its "affiliation" with Robin & Associates—"a governmental relations firm in Louisiana and

Washington, D.C., headed by Dan A. Robin Sr., along with Ted Jones and Dan A. Robin Jr."

Robin *pere et fil* had shown their fundraising prowess during the campaign. Now it was Garner's turn to show what he could do, and he delivered. Garner raised at least $25,000 for Edwards' transition team, and in early September 2016 he generated a significant portion of the more than $1 million in ticket sales for an Edwards fundraiser hosted by Dan Robin Sr. at Arnaud's Restaurant in the French Quarter. Garner's work was perfectly legal and, to political insiders, perfectly understandable. His firm had a bevy of big-name corporate clients eager to have a friend in the Governor's Mansion, and the new governor saw the wisdom of turning a savvy former adversary like Garner into a newfound ally—especially one who could help fill campaign coffers. Money, after all, is the mother's milk of politics.

Speaking of money, Garner's was not the only olive branch extended to the new governor. Within a month of Edwards taking office, various oil, gas, and chemical associations—whose members had opposed him during the campaign—were likewise eager to help him replenish his campaign war chest. Political action committees for the Louisiana Mid-Continent Oil and Gas Association and the Louisiana Chemical Association sponsored a joint fundraiser on January 26 in Baton Rouge. Two days later, the PAC for the Louisiana Oil and Gas Association held its own fundraiser at the group's annual meeting at the Golden Nugget Casino in Lake Charles.

"They opposed me last year, and I'm governor this year," Edwards told *The Advocate* when asked about the fundraisers. To no one's surprise, the groups later opposed much of the governor's tax proposals in subsequent legislative sessions, notwithstanding their recent willingness to shower him with campaign checks.

In politics, battle lines and olive branches—much like time-honored traditions—inevitably dissolve with the passage of time. Only the game itself endures, because human nature is immutable.

Plus ça change, indeed.

Acknowledgements

Turning **Long Shot** into reality required the assistance of several hundred people. We owe them a huge debt of gratitude. But no one deserves our thanks more than Clancy DuBos, who served as our editor. Both of us have known Clancy as a friend who is always ready to discuss the latest political developments. He is likewise a colleague, as we have written pieces for *Gambit* that he has edited.

Co-authoring a book, however, is something like getting married: You don't know how it will turn out until you've lived through a few chapters. Simply put, Clancy was a perfect match. He provided a narrative arc to several chapters that recited too many facts without shape. He line-edited the manuscript to eliminate unnecessary words and sections. He added material, sometimes from his knowledge, sometimes from additional reporting. He corrected our factual errors and insisted on fair, balanced reporting.

To accomplish this wedding of our work, Clancy relied on his deep knowledge of the 2015 governor's race and recent Louisiana political history. Both of us hate to think how the book would have turned out, minus his steady, experienced hand.

We would like to thank Jim Brown of Lisburn Press. For Jim, publishing is more a labor of love than a financial enterprise. We're happy that he published **Long Shot**, which meant handling lots of unglamorous production and printing tasks. David Kroll of *Gambit* and Sarah Powell with Compose Digital oversaw the book's design elements, and the numerous revisions we kicked their way. Patricia Stallman copyedited the book, insisting that we minimize the passive voice, weak verbs, and unnecessary words. She was consistently on mark. Those who helped us worked hard under a difficult and compressed timeframe, and we are forever grateful.

We also thank James Carville and Mary Matalin for contributing such wonderful Forewords to this book. We likewise are grateful to Jonathan Martin, Charlie Cook, Ron Faucheux and Buddy Roemer for offering generous praise in their advance reviews.

Tyler would like to thank editor Peter Kovacs and managing editor Fred Kalmbach at *The Advocate* for assigning him to cover the governor's race. He would also like to thank Mark Ballard, Elizabeth Crisp, Will Sentell, and Marsha Shuler—*The Advocate's* Capitol News bureau in 2015—for their assistance and good reporting from the campaign trail. Tyler would also like to thank Kovacs for making *Advocate* photos available for the book and John Balance, Director of Photography, and Jill Arnold, Data Systems Manager, for digging them out of the paper's digital archive. Thanks to Amy Mikler for letting us use her evocative 2011 photo of John Bel and *John Miller* Edwards, and Mo. Tyler would like to offer special thanks to his wife, Cecilia Tait. Given the intense focus this long process requires, working on a book means forgoing family outings, nights out, and, at times, the presence of loved ones. *Mil disculpas!* Daughter Luciana, who also had to bear with an absent father, did so with love and kindness.

Jeremy would like to thank Jackie Drinkwater Maginnis, who was among the early believers in this project and invested in it, and the team members who helped produce *LaPolitics.com*, *LaPolitics Weekly*, and *Tuesday Tracker* during the 2014 and 2015 election cycles, including Kelly Spires, Jeremy Harper, Fred Mulhearn, and Jennifer LeJeune. But it was the *LaPolitics* family of subscribers, sponsors, and readers who made the initial reporting and travel for this book possible. Above all others, though, Jeremy would like to thank his wife Karron Clark Alford, who went to incredible lengths while her husband lived out of a suitcase covering the race for governor in 2015—and during the extra 10 months we needed in 2016 to finish the project. As for son Keaton Alford, Jeremy would like to thank him for making off with and hiding two notebooks of interviews and observations. They remain missing. And to daughter Zoe Alford, whose knowledge of and love for Louisiana blossomed during the production of this book. And finally, to mother Dora Alford, whose strength and love lifted all hearts throughout this process.

The authors also particularly found useful the reporting by several Capitol bureau reporters: Greg Hilburn with the *USA Today Network* of Louisiana newspapers; Melinda Deslatte with the Associated Press; Jim Beam with the *Lake Charles American Press*; and Julia O'Donoghue and Kevin Litten with *The Times-Picayune*. We are also grateful that our colleagues at the Capitol from time to time delved into their memories of the 2015 campaign to answer our questions and fill in a few gaps.

We interviewed more than 100 people for the book, including Governor John Bel Edwards, who submitted to seven different interviews, both in his fourth floor office in the Capitol and over the phone; and Donna Edwards, his wife, who sat for a 2 ½-hour interview one evening in the family quarters of the Governor's Mansion. Others of Team Edwards who were particularly generous with their time were Mary-Patricia Wray, Sam Jones, Jim Kitchens, Jared Arsement, Andrew Edwards, and Linda Day. From Team David Vitter: Kyle Ruckert, John Diez, and Luke Bolar. From Team Scott Angelle: Roy Fletcher and Ryan Cross. From Team Jay Dardenne: Marsanne Golsby, Cody Allen Wells, and George Kennedy. From the super PACs: Trey Ourso, Joel DiGrado, Charlie Spies, Bill Skelly, Ben Nevers, John Loe, Brandon Moody, Travis Smith, and Jeff Roe.

Others we interviewed for the book, both during and after the election, are: Stephen Handwerk, Beau Tidwell, Rene Lapeyrolerie, Kyle Gautreau, Chris Binder, Doug Menefee, Eric Foglesong, Gene Reynolds, Jack Montoucet, Arthur Morrell, James Hallinan, Buddy Leach, Jennifer Smith, Bob Mann, Chris Frink, Brendan McCarthy, Kate Moran, Karen St. Germain, Robert Travis Scott, Rob Green, Rob Stutzman, Marty Wilson, Adam Rosenblatt, Chris Whittington, Katie Moore, Kevin Franck, Fred Herman, Greg Meriwether, Chris Tidmore, Bradley Beychok, Pat Smith, Vincent Bruno, Derek Myers, Newell Normand, Danny Martiny, Danny DeNoux, Eric LaFleur, Rock Palermo, Mark Vining, Brad Stevens, Mark Armstrong, Louis Reine, Cameron Henry, Kathleen Blanco, Raymond Blanco, Richard Carbo, Andre Stolier, Verne Kennedy, Randy Haynie, Jim Duffy, Jason Doré, Lane Grigsby, Jason Redmond, Paul Hollis, Billy Nungesser, Dan A. Robin Sr., James Garner, Charles E. "Peppi" Bruneau Jr., Ryan Berni, Bernie Pinsonat, John Couvillon, Craig Clark, Scott Sternberg, Jeff Wiley, Johnny Berthelot, Wendy Vitter, James T. Hannan, Chris John, Rob Maness, Eva Kemp, Fred Mills, Austin Stukins, Tyron Picard, Brent Littlefield, Bud Courson, Stephen Ortego, Kim Carver, Kenny Havard, Joe Harrison, Taylor Barras, John Carmouche, Don Carmouche, Ravi Sangisetty, Robert Johnson, Laura Veazey, Karmen Blanco, J. Bennett Johnston, James Carville, Stephanie Grace, Dan Foley, Walt Leger III, Glenn Armentor, Daniel Edwards, Alton Ashy, Jack Capella, Tony Clayton, Jason Williams, Rick Gallot, Dan Robin Jr., Tiger Hammond, Russ Herman, Sandra Herman, Phil Cossich, John Georges, Jay Luneau, Steve Monaghan, Stephanie Riegel, Mark Ballard, Dora Jean Edwards, Murray Starkel, Gary Bennett, Michael Ranatza, Anagene Mobley, Dick Covington, Donald Cravins Sr., Ryan Gatti, JP Morrell, Mike Johnson, Ted Jones, John Binder, Jason Engels, David Aguillard, Frank Edwards III, Ronnie Anderson, Timmy Teepell, Russel Honoré, Dale Atkins, Norby Chabert, Melissa Flournoy, Jim Engster, John Anzalone, Zac McCrary, Kenya Taylor, Corey Platt, Christian Garbett, Carey Martin, Jason Brad Berry, Edwin Murray, Ersel Bogan III, Bruce Parker, Lance Harris, Pat Gary, James Garner, and Robby Carter.

We would also like to thank the many librarians, editors, and archivists who helped us, including: Frances Thomas, director of the David R. Poynter Legislative Research Library; Bud Johnson, former LSU Sports Information Director; Bonnie Dier, librarian at the Washington Parish Public Library; Judy Jumonville, library manager of *The Advocate*; Melinda Giardina, editor of the *Amite-Tangi Digest;* Bill Dorman, librarian in the genealogy department, Tangipahoa Parish Public Library; and Francis J DeMaro Jr., Public Affairs Specialist at the United States Military Academy Public Affairs Office.

To those who didn't make the list due to confidentiality, you know who you are.

Editor's Note

For years I had the pleasure of editing Jeremy Alford's weekly columns and Tyler Bridges' occasional stories in my alt-weekly newspaper, *Gambit*. Both authors are first-rate journalists and terrific storytellers. When they asked me to edit *Long Shot*, I was honored.

From the outset, they knew that collaborating on this epic story would present challenges as unique as Louisiana's storied brand of politics. Jeremy and Tyler have very distinct writing styles, for starters, and each has his own "take" on Bayou State politics. In the end, their commitment to this project overcame every obstacle. Above all, they did a magnificent job of giving this book one "voice." In doing so, they made my job easy—and a genuine pleasure.

I also challenged the authors to tell the story in a way that would appeal to readers outside Louisiana. I believed from the get-go that while this tale should capture Louisiana's colorful characters and unrivaled mystique, the fundamental lessons inherent in John Bel Edwards' improbable victory hold true in all 50 states. They met that challenge and more.

Perhaps our biggest challenge was the uncomfortable task of objectively telling a story occasionally shaped by one or more of us—particularly the chapter chronicling blogger Jason Brad Berry's posts featuring Wendy Ellis and her explosive allegations against Senator David Vitter. Tyler and I were privy (as were several other traditional journalists) to Jason's videos before he posted them, and we each influenced how our respective publications reacted to those posts. To help us tell that story as honestly as we could, we turned to Jerry Ceppos, dean of LSU's Manship School of Mass Communication and a respected former newspaper editor. Jerry's sage advice helped guide us to what we hope is an impartial account of what happened, and why. We cannot thank him enough.

I leaned on several people in the course of fulfilling my duties as editor, mostly my long-suffering wife Margo, who patiently tolerated my late-night conference calls and months-long lack of focus around the house. She is a saint. I also thank my dear friends, James Carville and Mary Matalin, for generously providing the wonderful Forewords after I gave them all of two weeks' notice. They are great Louisianans.

I'm fond of saying there's never a recession in Louisiana politics. The events recounted in *Long Shot* prove that beyond all doubt.

— Clancy DuBos

Notes

A note on the notes: We spend so much time working digitally now that, in most instances, we used the headlines and dates from the online versions of the articles cited. We should note that dates for *Advocate* articles might be wrong in some cases. A digital remap by the newspaper in 2016 changed the publication dates on articles from 2015 and perhaps earlier years. We did our best to get all of the correct dates and hope *The Advocate* will correct its online articles one day soon for future researchers.

Chapter 1

The layers of chatter rose: **Long Shot** co-author Jeremy Alford covered the induction ceremony and reception

Whereas other states are majority: United States Census, 2010; Louisiana Secretary of State, statewide voter registration file, October 1, 2015; James Minahan, **Encyclopedia of the Stateless Nations: A-C**, Greenwood Publishing, 2002; Wayne Parent, **Inside the Carnival: Unmasking Louisiana Politics**, LSU Press, 2006; A.J. Liebling, **The Earl of Louisiana**, LSU Press, 1959 (Since the 1960s, Louisiana has consisted of three main voting blocs: African Americans, rural WASPs, and Cajuns, with the Catholic urban vote in and around New Orleans loosely associated with the Cajuns. Since that time, Louisiana has been "suburbanized," giving rise to a fourth—and very important—demographic. The white voters clustered in and around Louisiana's major cities now comprise a significant "metropolitan vote" equal in size yet quite distinct from conservative rural white voters and the "swing voters" in mostly Catholic Acadiana. Voter registration figures from the Louisiana Secretary of State's office bear out these numbers along the lines of race and party affiliation. Rural whites outside of Acadiana, white voters in the "Cajun Triangle" of south Louisiana, and white voters in metropolitan areas, including suburban precincts, each comprise 20 percent to 22 percent of the electorate. —**Long Shot** editor Clancy DuBos)

He was facing, for the 2015–16: Steve Sanoski, "Jindal administration begins work to close $1.4B budget gap," *Baton Rouge Business Report*, December 11, 2014

The go-to factoid of the afternoon: Eric Benson, "Last Of The Red Hot Poppas," *Oxford American*, August 11, 2014

Between 2004 and 2015: Robert Mann, "Louisiana Democrats' best hope to beat David Vitter? Vote Republican," *The Times-Picayune*, May 15, 2015

In 1978, 90 percent: Marsha Shuler, "Democrats lose voter majority: GOP, others more than 50% of La. voters," *The Advocate*, August 14, 2011; Louisiana Secretary of State statewide voter registration file, October 1, 2015

Louisiana also had a massive: Nick Corasaniti, "Louisiana: Democrats in Registration Only," *FiveThirtyEight: Nate Silver's Political Calculus*, July 30, 2012

Meanwhile, African American registration: Louisiana Secretary of State statewide voter registration file, October 1, 2015; Louisiana Secretary of State statewide voter registration file, October 2, 2007; Jeremy Harper, "The (Slowly) Changing Racial Makeup of Louisiana Voters," *LaPolitics.com*, July 27, 2015

Women, who accounted for: Louisiana Secretary of State statewide voter registration file, October 1, 2015

Every early poll: Jeremy Alford, "Vitter, Nungesser-Young Lead Early 2015 Poll," *LaPolitics Weekly*, November 13, 2014; Elizabeth Crisp, "Poll: David Vitter is early frontrunner for governor in 2015," *The Advocate*, December 19, 2014

Though the cumulative number: Promotional pamphlet, Louisiana Political Museum and Hall of Fame, 499 East Main Street, Winnfield, Louisiana, 71483

In the end, the two men: Louisiana Ethics Administration, 2014 and 2015 campaign finance reports, John Bel Edwards and David Vitter

Besides Edwards' storybook upset: Louisiana Ethics Administration and Federal Election Commission, 2014 and 2015 campaign finance reports, Louisiana Families First, Gumbo PAC, Louisiana Water Coalition PAC, Louisiana Rising PAC, Now or Never PAC, Democratic Governors Association, Republican Governors Association and Fund for Louisiana's Future

Chapter 2

The Democratic volunteers working: Interviews with Eric Foglesong, John Bel Edwards, Karen St. Germain, Pat Smith and Sam Jones

Jindal was hailed: Robert Travis Scott, "Gov. Bobby Jindal takes center stage in 60 Minutes profile," *The Times-Picayune*, March 1, 2009

When the recovery money: Gordon Russell, *"Louisiana Gov.* Bobby Jindal pivots on tax credits, marking a big change in philosophy," *The Advocate; March 1, 2015*

Republicans picked up: Bill Barrow, "Louisiana Republicans take first House majority since Reconstruction with latest party switch," *The Times-Picayune*, December 17, 2010

Jindal helped push: Walter Pierce, *The IND Monthly*, "Gautreaux resigns, Perry to seek seat," December 22, 2010

At their request: Interviews with Raymond Blanco and Jack Montoucet

Kitchens was a: Interview with Jim Kitchens

Mad Dog's lead: Interview with Jennifer Smith

The best message: Interview with Foglesong

Another picture: Interviews with Foglesong and Amy Mikler

Montoucet, 63: Interview with Montoucet

The attack mailers: Interviews with Edwards, Foglesong, Smith and Chris Binder

On October 22: Interviews with Foglesong, Smith and Binder

As Eric Foglesong: Interviews with Foglesong and Edwards

Chapter 3

The water tower behind: Interviews with John Diez

The evening before, in the: "Prep football capsules for October 28, 2011," *The Advocate*, October 28, 2011

As Diez pulled: Interviews with John Diez

The Republicans took the House: Bill Barrow, "Louisiana Republicans take first House majority since Reconstruction with latest party switch," *The Times-Picayune*, December 17, 2010

the GOP had captured the: Jan Moller, "Senate election completes Republican takeover of Louisiana government," *The Times-Picayune*, February 21, 2011

As he parked his truck: Interviews with John Diez

Nungesser, who had developed: Marsha Shuler, "Vitter chooses in GOP conflict," *The Advocate*, September 26, 2011

Though Vitter was not on the ballot: Interviews with John Diez

When Dardenne vacated the seat: Jeremy Alford, "Secretary of state wants to stay in office," *Houma Courier*, October 14, 2011

The bad blood between them: Alexis Levinson, "Why Bobby Jindal and David Vitter Hate Each Other: Louisiana's two most powerful Republicans are also bitter enemies, and it's hurting both of their careers," *National Journal*, February 25, 2015; Marin Cogan, "Whatever Happened to Bobby Jindal?: The feud that helped knock the shine off a Republican golden boy," *New Republic*, July 7, 2013

By late afternoon, Diez: Interviews with Ascension Parish Sheriff Jeff Wiley and John Diez

At that very moment, Vitter: Interviews with Kyle Ruckert

Former Gonzales Mayor Johnny Berthelot, who: Interview with Johnny Berthelot

"You know you: Interviews with Ascension Parish Sheriff Jeff Wiley, John Diez and Kyle Ruckert

Joel DiGrado, Vitter's communications director, joined: Interviews with Joel DiGrado, Kyle Ruckert and John Diez

Diez began cleaning up: Interviews with John Diez

The Vitter–Ruckert–Diez game plan: Interviews with Joel DiGrado, Kyle Ruckert and John Diez

Judging by their unspoken: Secretary of State, election results, October 22, 2011

At 10:45 p.m., Vitter: Interviews with Kyle Ruckert

a total gain of 10 seats: Mark Ballard, "New face of party discipline, big-business style," *The Advocate*, July 10, 2016

Term limits had not: Interviews with Kyle Ruckert

Chapter 4

On the morning: Interviews with John Bel Edwards
R-Day: http://www.johndlock.com/#!78-beast-barracks/c1vbb;
http://westpointcadet.blogspot.pe/2013/02/r-day.html

exactly 1,460: July 5, 2016, email from Francis J. DeMaro Jr.,
Public Affairs Specialist at the United States Military Academy
Public Affairs Office

Many had been Tories: Samuel C. Hyde Jr., **Pistols and Politics:
The Dilemma of Democracy in Louisiana's Florida Parishes,
1810-1899**, LSU Press 1998

Millard Edwards: obituary of Millard Edwards, *The Era-Leader of
Franklinton*, January 12, 1928

One of Millard's sons: "Former Senator Frank Edwards dies in
Orleans," *Morning Advocate*, February 4, 1961

"He was gorgeous: Interview with Dora Jean Edwards

Children in the: Interviews with John Bel Edwards, Daniel
Edwards, Dora Jean Edwards and Frank Edwards III

When Sheriff Edwards: Articles from *Hammond Daily Star*,
October, November, December 1979; Stephanie Warren, "Longtime
Tangipahoa Parish Sheriff Frank Edwards dies," *Amite-Tangi Digest*,
April 17, 2014; 2014 obituary of Frank Edwards Jr. published by
McKneelys Funeral Home,
http://www.mckneelys.com/home/index.
cfm?action=public%3Aobituaries.view&o_id=2485668&fh_
id=10545

After his loss: Interviews with John Bel Edwards and Frank
Edwards III

He went on: Articles from *Hammond Daily Star*, October and
November 1983

When Frank Edwards: Interviews with Dora Jean Edwards, John
Bel Edwards and Frank Edwards III

By the early 1980s: Interviews with John Bel Edwards, Dora Jean
Edwards, Daniel Edwards, Mark Vining and Donna Edwards; Kevin
Litten, "John Bel Edwards brings home-grown compassion to role as
Louisiana governor," *The Times-Picayune*, January 8, 2016
he gave his sixth grade: Interview with Anagene Mobley

John Bel made it through: Interviews with John Bel Edwards,

Murray Starkel and Dora Jean Edwards

During the fall semester: Interviews with John Bel Edwards; https://www.army.mil/ranger/

He was away training: Interviews with Donna Edwards
on the first day of classes: Interviews with John Bel Edwards, Donna Edwards, Ryan Gatti and Christian Garbett

After graduation: Interviews with John Bel Edwards and Robby Carter

Chapter 5

Late one afternoon: Interviews with John Bel Edwards and Sam Jones

The aspiring candidate: Interviews with John Bel Edwards and Donna Edwards

One hot Friday: Interviews with John Bel Edwards, Brad Stevens and Daniel Edwards

On July 20: Interviews with Kathleen Blanco and Raymond Blanco

In the coming months: Interview with Andrew Edwards

In January 2013: Interviews with Chris Binder and Mary-Patricia Wray

There Edwards met: Interviews with Jared Arsement and John Bel Edwards

Edwards took a seat: Audio of February 20, 2013, interview on Jim Engster radio show, http://wrkf.org/post/wednesday-state-rep-john-bel-edwards-metro-councilwoman-c-denise-marcelle?nopop=1#stream/0

She silently cheered: Interview with Mary-Patricia Wray

He drove to: Interviews with Sam Jones, Kathleen Blanco, Raymond Blanco, Jared Arsement, Eric Foglesong and Mary-Patricia Wray

On March 21: Interviews with Tiger Hammond and Louis Reine

The Edwardses attended: Interviews with Kathleen Blanco, Raymond Blanco, Karmen Blanco, John Bel Edwards and Donna Edwards

Two weeks later: Interview with Brad Stevens

of 27 percent: "Gov. Bobby Jindal's 27% approval rating in Louisiana is sign of bipartisan dissatisfaction," *Gambit*, March 16, 2015

According to annual: Lanny Keller, "Last year's drop showed future in Jindal polls," *The Advocate,* April 10, 2013

Before the governor: John Maginnis, "Gov. Jindal park his tax plan, gives legislators the wheel," *The Times-Picayune*, April 8, 2013

Later in the: Tyler Bridges, "Fiscal Hawks flew high in legislative session now ended, defying Jindal," *The Lens*, June 6, 2013

He accepted speaking invitations: Interviews with John Bel Edwards, Sam Jones, Jared Arsement, Buddy Leach and Chris Binder

Middendorf's: Interviews with Brad Stevens and John Bel Edwards

St. Dominic's School: Interview with Dan Foley

in the town of Kinder: Interview with Donna Edwards

Chapter 6

David Vitter didn't know it yet: 2016 C. Alvin Bertel Award Ceremony & Luncheon honoring U.S. Senator David Vitter, https://www.youtube.com/watch?v=j_wz43UikuA; Interviews with Luke Bolar; Vitter declined all interview requests made after the November 21, 2015, runoff election (Subsequent endnotes noting interviews with Vitter were conducted during or prior to the 2015 election cycle)

The massive blue-and-beige: Big River Coalition email to members, from Sean M. Duffy Sr., January 17, 2012

River pilots and others: The Editorial Board, "Ship that ran aground in the Mississippi River is a sign of danger," *The Times-Picayune*, June 20, 2011

"Mike, good morning: 2016 C. Alvin Bertel Award Ceremony & Luncheon honoring U.S. Senator David Vitter, https://www.youtube.com/watch?v=j_wz43UikuA; Interviews with Luke Bolar

Roughly 12 hours later, large: Bruce Alpert, "Corps of Engineers sends dredging vessel to Mississippi River's Southwest Pass," *The Times-Picayune*, January 18, 2012

If asked to explain David: Elizabeth Crisp, "Gubernatorial frontrunner David Vitter: 'I have great friends who support us'," *The Advocate*, October 5, 2015

Those who knew Vitter as a young adjunct: Interview with David Marcello

That's one reason his political: Garry Boulard, "'Tuition-Gate' Scandal Hits Louisiana Politicians," *Christian Science Monitor*, July 15, 1993

He once said that his favorite: Interviews with David Vitter; Jeremy Alford, "The Men Behind the Ads," *Gambit*, November 2, 2010

Reporters found him: Interviews with Jim Engster and Marsanne Golsby

The youngest of six children: Interviews with David Vitter; Vitter family genealogy, www.Vitter.org

Every year Audrey and Al: Vitter family Christmas cards, www. Vitter.org

When he was a schoolboy: Greg Hilburn, "Vitter: Politically fractious, yet pragmatic?," *Monroe News-Star*, September 19, 2015

He attended De La Salle: Interviews with David Vitter; Jeremy Alford, "The Men Behind the Ads," *Gambit*, November 2, 2010

In his later high school years: Interviews with Kyle Ruckert

Young David had an independent streak: Vitter family genealogy, www.Vitter.org; Interviews with Kyle Ruckert

In England, Vitter's politics: Stephanie Grace, "Straight Arrow Aims For Congress; Vitter Has Built Vocal Reputation," *The Times-Picayune*, April 17, 1999

The late 1980s and early 1990s: Tina Dupuy, "Buddy Roemer's Long Road to Reform: How the ex-Louisiana Governor channeled his political and personal demons into a rabble-rousing presidential campaign," *Mother Jones*, May 31, 2012

During this same period, Vitter: Interview with Wendy Vitter

"We both went to Tulane: Jeremy Alford, "Candidates' Wives Key In Governor's Race," *The Daily Advertiser*, November 4, 2015

Wendy was only six: Bruce Eggler, "Wendy Vitter has never been shy about standing her ground," *The Times-Picayune*, July 23, 2007

She began her law career: Interview with Wendy Vitter

His target was another guy: John Maginnis, **Cross To Bear: America's Most Dangerous Politics**, Darkhorse Press, 1992

While Duke's win: Interviews with Kyle Ruckert

The year before, in 1990: Louisiana Secretary of State, election results, October 6, 1990

In contrast to most states: Bill Barrow, "Department of Justice gives approval to Louisiana's open primaries," *The Times-Picayune*, February 8, 2011

Vitter captured 68 percent: Louisiana Secretary of State, election results, October 19, 1991

"the runoff from hell": John Maginnis, **Cross To Bear: America's Most Dangerous Politics**, Darkhorse Press, 1992

In Vitter's first year: Ron Gomez, **My name is Ron, and I'm a recovering legislator: Memoirs of a Louisiana State Representative**, iUniverse, 2000

When Edwards and his: Tyler Bridges, **Bad Bet on the Bayou: The Rise of Gambling in Louisiana and the Fall of Governor Edwin Edwards**, Farrar, Straus and Giroux, 2001

As staunchly as he opposed: Interview with Charles E. "Peppi" Bruneau Jr.

"He did not make a lot: Craig Malisow, "Syndicated columnist addresses Rotarians," *The Hammond Daily Star*, February 28, 2002

He shamed legislators into: Scott Dyer, "Scholarship Controversy Grows," *The Advocate*, June 17, 1993; "'Tuition-Gate' Scandal Hits Louisiana Politicians," *Christian Science Monitor*, July 15, 1993

Jefferson Parish Sheriff Harry Lee: Deno Seder, **Wild About Harry: A Biography of Harry Lee**, Edition Dedeaux, 2001; S.L. Alexander, **Courtroom Carnival: Famous New Orleans Trials**, Pelican Publishing Company, 2011

Although Vitter's scholarships: Stephanie Grace, "Old rivals renew fight with U.S. Sen. David Vitter," *The Advocate*, March 21 ,2016

On that note: David Vitter, Op-Ed, *The Times-Picayune*, October 29, 1998

In the early spring of 1999: Stuart Rothenberg, "Hot race for Livingston's Louisiana House seat," *CNN.com*, April 13, 1999

For his part, Vitter: Interviews with Kyle Ruckert

Vitter's gamble paid: Louisiana Secretary of State, election results, May 1, 1999

A tight runoff followed between: B. Drummond Ayres Jr., "Political Briefing; Putting Family First In a Louisiana Race," *The New York Times*, May 27, 1999

Vitter had called Treen: The Associated Press, "David Duke fails in bid at House seat in Louisiana," *The Southeast Missourian*, May 3, 1999

Vitter won—barely: Louisiana Secretary of State, election results, May 29, 1999

Wendy Vitter, whose interest: Interview with Wendy Vitter

In Washington, the new: Interviews with Kyle Ruckert
Wendy showed her own: Carrie Budoff Brown, "GOP senator admits link to escort service," *Politico*, July 9, 2007

Though now a congressman, Vitter: Wayne Wynn Williams III, "A Historical Perspective of Governor Mike Foster's 'Live Mike' Radio Program," Thesis submitted to the Graduate Faculty of the Louisiana State University and Agricultural and Mechanical College, August 2004

In June 2002, the: Christopher Tidmore, "Congressman is accused of having an alleged affair with prostitute," *Louisiana Weekly*, June 3, 2002

Vitter suffered a devastating: Interviews with Kyle Ruckert

Vitter, who quickly: Charles S. Bullock and Mark J. Rozell, **The New Politics of the Old South: An Introduction to Southern Politics**, Rowman & Littlefield Publishers, 2007

He craftily flipped the seat red: Louisiana Secretary of State, election results, November 2, 2004

John admitted later: Interviews with Chris John and Jason Redmond

The Democratic Senatorial Campaign Committee did: Mary Jacoby, "There is a house in New Orleans: Rumors involving a prostitute and a secret alliance with neo-Nazi David Duke trail the Republican Senate candidate in Louisiana," *Salon.com*, Oct. 29, 2004

The Senate race was: Interviews with Kyle Ruckert

Chapter 7

Other than one article: Christopher Tidmore, "Congressman is accused of having an alleged affair with prostitute," *Louisiana Weekly*, June 3, 2002

mentions on talk radio: Jefferson Parish Republican Party activist Vincent Bruno discussed the allegation on Jim Engster's "Louisiana Live!" talk show on April 26, 2002; caller David Bellinger asked Vitter about the allegation on Jeff Crouere's "Ringside with a Punch!" talk show on July 25, 2002; on that show, Vitter called Bruno "a thug and a liar"; Bruno then responded to Vitter's comments on Engster's "Louisiana Live!" show later that day

Dan Moldea was a veteran: Interviews with Dan Moldea; Dan E. Moldea, **Confessions of a Guerrilla Writer**, self-published, 2013

she had seemed less charitable: Joel Roberts, "Senator caught in 'D.C. Madam' scandal," *CBS News*, July 9, 2007

interview with Jeanette Maier: "Canal Street Madam says Vitter was a client," *WDSU-TV,* July 10, 2007

made five separate calls: Bill Walsh, "Vitter had five calls with D.C. Madam," T*he Times-Picayune*, July 11, 2007

Journalists and pundits: Adam Nossiter, "A senator's moral high ground gets a little shaky," *The New York Times*, July 11, 2007

Cortez, the prostitute: Kate Moran, "Prostitute describes Vitter affair," *The Times-Picayune,* July 12, 2007

Had burned the photos: Gary Scheets, "Prostitute describes Vitter affair," *The Times-Picayune*, July 12, 2007

Congressman Richard Baker: "Louisiana Republicans offer guarded support for Vitter," *The Times-Picayune*, July 13, 2007

Jindal struck a cautious note: "A hard fall," *The Ind*, July 18, 2007

The Times-Picayune dispatched: Interviews with Brendan McCarthy and Katie Moore

Vitter and his wife: https://www.youtube.com/watch?v=QufjIbBH9lU

alongside Hustler owner: Kate Moran, "Former prostitute details Vitter affair," *The Times-Picayune*, September 11, 2007

"He nailed it: Interviews with Kyle Ruckert

His colleagues lifted: Marianne Means, "Republicans celebrate hypocrisy," *Times-Herald Record*, July 23, 2007

Some senators kept: Dana Milbank, "In Whole or in Part, a Missing Vitter," *The Washington Post*, July 11, 2007; Max Blumenthal, **Republican Gomorrah: Inside the Movement that Shattered the Party**, National Books New York, 2009

five-page nude: Mark Johnson, "Senator David Vitter's Secret Lover Revealed," *Hustler*, January 2008

one-time treatment: Bruce Alpert, "Magazine puts Vitter back in spotlight," *The Times-Picayune*, November 7, 2007

Another break came: Colley Charpentier, "Ethics committee drops complaint against Vitter," *The Times-Picayune*, May 8, 2008

he filed 34 bills: Jonathan Tilove, "David Vitter stuffs slew of bills in Senate hopper," *The Times-Picayune*, January 8, 2009

Hillary Clinton: "Senate confirms Clinton as secretary of state," *The Associated Press*, January 21, 2009

"Forgotten Crimes: https://www.youtube.com/watch?v=JpsCbXdqbY8

Melancon campaigned: Interview with Bradley Beychok

In one ad: Jan Moller, "Sen. David Vitter rips Rep. Charlie Melancon in two new TV commercials," *The Times-Picayune*, September 24, 2010

Melancon hit Vitter: Scott Conroy, "Melancon Hammers Vitter Over Scandal," *Real Clear Politics*, October 28, 2010

That same evening: Interview with Greg Meriwether; Jan Moller, "David Vitter sex scandal gets spotlight again in debate with Charlie Melancon," *The Times-Picayune*, October 28, 2010

After the debate ended: Interview with Kyle Ruckert

Five days later: Jan Moller, "Sen. David Vitter wins re-election in remarkable comeback," *The Times-Picayune*, November 2, 2010

One of them: Interview with Greg Meriwether

"It's my personality translated: Jeremy Alford, "Kingmaker David – Marginalized after a 2007 prostitution scandal, U.S. Sen. David Vitter is consolidating his power and picking his battles with an eye to the future, which could include an eventual run for governor," *Baton Rouge Business Report*, October 18, 2011

Wendy had taken time: Interview with Wendy Vitter

Pundits back home: Interviews with Bernie Pinsonat

Chapter 8

State Representative Paul Hollis closed the windows: Interviews with Paul Hollis

In 2012 he penned: Jeremy Alford, "U.S. Senate Field Not Cleared," *LaPolitics.com*, November 11, 2013

Hollis' phone rang: Interviews with Paul Hollis

Hollis broke the news: Jeremy Alford, "Hollis Withdraws From U.S. Senate Race," *LaPolitics.com*, July 14, 2014

Vitter was on Twitter: https://twitter.com/DavidVitter/status/488700316247146496?ref_src=twsrc%5Etfw

"He's the Michael Jordan: Jeremy Alford, "Vitter Rising: Senate victory would be his too," *LaPolitics Weekly*, October 16, 2014

The senator and the governor couldn't stand: Alexis Levinson, "Why Bobby Jindal and David Vitter Hate Each Other: Louisiana's two most powerful Republicans are also bitter enemies, and it's hurting both of their careers," *National Journal*, February 25, 2015; Marin Cogan, "Whatever Happened to Bobby Jindal?: The feud that helped knock the shine off a Republican golden boy," *New Republic*, July 7, 2013

The senator crafted Cassidy's strategy: Jeremy Alford, "Vitter Rising: Senate victory would be his too," *LaPolitics Weekly*, October 16, 2014; interviews with Kyle Ruckert, Joel DiGrado and Luke Bolar

In stark contrast to the colorful: Jeremy Alford, "Congressman engaged in health care: Though he's seeking a third term in Congress, this fall is the first time Rep. Bill Cassidy will be seeking votes in Terrebonne and Lafourche parishes," *The Houma Courier*, October 1, 2012

Cassidy secured victory: Louisiana Secretary of State, election results, December 9, 2006

narrowly defeated incumbent Don: "La. Democrats blame independent for Congress loss," *The Associated Press*, November 6, 2008

"Family Fun Day": Cassidy for Congress, press release, July 17,

2009

Though he came off as: Julia O'Donoghue, "Bill Cassidy wants to be the doctor he believes the U.S. Senate needs," *The Times-Picayune*, October 16, 2014

Louisiana at the time had three physicians: Jeremy Alford, "Dr. Smith goes to Washington, via Louisiana," *The Times-Picayune*, September 16, 2014

campaign made background calls: Bruce Alpert, "Senate candidate Bill Cassidy discloses that his teenage daughter is pregnant," *The Times-Picayune*, July 3, 2014

Founder Charlie Cook: Gregory Roberts, "Why Bill Cassidy's low-key strategy to defeat Mary Landrieu seems to be working," *The Advocate*, December 4, 2014

"Cassidy is as bland: Campbell Robertson and Jonathan Martin, "Louisiana's Rogues Yield to National Issues," *The New York Times*, October 29, 2014

"He's weird: Burgess Everett, "Is this guy too boring for Louisiana?," *Politico*, October 15, 2014

True believers like: Interviews with Jason Doré

Democratic operatives were eyeing: Jeremy Alford, "Senate Race Already Reaching Down to the Parish Level," *LaPolitics Weekly*, June 19, 2014

Doré and the Cassidy: Interviews with Jason Doré

"Mary Landrieu supports: Bruce Alpert, "What's behind the 97% support for President Obama cited by GOP against Mary Landrieu and other Democrats?," *The Times-Picayune*, October 21, 2014

Now seeking a fourth: Jeremy Harper, "After 18 Years, Mary Landrieu Reaches The End of the Line," *LaPolitics.com*, December 6, 2014

The oldest of nine: Jason Berry, "Mary and the Landrieus: A dynasty bruised but standing, *Politico*, December 7, 2014

The following year, Landrieu: Jeremy Harper, "After 18 Years, Mary Landrieu Reaches The End of the Line," *LaPolitics.com*, December 6, 2014

With her husband, Frank Snellings: Jeremy Alford, "Adopting and adapting," *Gambit*, February 12, 2013; Interview with Mary Landrieu

By August 20, the first: Jeremy Alford, "Money Trends, Debates Divide Senate Candidates," *LaPolitics.com*, August 21, 2014

On that first day of qualifying: Melinda Deslatte, "Landrieu, Cassidy qualify on opening day," *The Associated Press*, August 20, 2014; Mike Hasten, "Field crowded in major congressional races," *Opelousas Daily World*, August 23, 2014

She eventually paid back: Deborah Barfield Berry and Mike Hasten, "Landrieu pays back nearly $34K for charter flights," *USA Today*, September 12, 2014

"The Wobble": Julia O'Donoghue, "Mary Landrieu does the 'Wobble' at Southern University tailgate," Julia O'Donoghue, *The Times-Picayune*, October 9, 2014

young man do a keg stand: Peter Sullivan, "Landrieu's GOP challenger comes out as anti-keg stand," *The Hill*, September 24, 2014

"They need to get a sense of a humor": "Quote of the week," *Gambit*, September 29, 2014

Then, for the first time: Ashley Killough, "CNN Poll: Tight Louisiana Senate race sets stage for runoff," *CNN.com*, September 28, 2014

The Democratic Senatorial Campaign Committee countered: Jeremy Alford, "Landrieu Goes on the Attack," *LaPolitics Weekly*, September 25, 2014

When voter registration closed: Jeremy Alford, "What Happened?," *LaPolitics Weekly*, November 6, 2014

For her final primary push, Landrieu: Interviews with Ryan Berni

While the Landrieu team: Interviews with Bernie Pinsonat

The only poll that mattered: Louisiana Secretary of State, election results, November 4, 2014

Equally important, Cassidy: Jeremy Alford, "What Happened?," *LaPolitics Weekly*, November 6, 2014

finally endorsed Cassidy: Julia O'Donoghue, "Bobby Jindal endorses Bill Cassidy in Louisiana Senate race," *The Times-Picayune*, November 5, 2014

With Republicans now controlling: Dan Roberts, "Republicans win majority in US Senate, giving party full control of Congress," *The Guardian*, November 5, 2014

Though the reason wasn't known: James Hohmann, "DSCC left with $20.4M in post-election debt," *Politico*, December 9, 2014

staged a "Unity Rally": Jeremy Alford, Issue 1004, *LaPolitics Weekly*, November 13, 2014

Despite her best efforts: Louisiana Secretary of State, election results, December 6, 2014

poured onto a small stage: **Long Shot** co-author Jeremy Alford covered Bill Cassidy's election night party

Chapter 9

On a sweltering July midday: Interviews with Scott Angelle; https://www.youtube.com/watch?v=DFulzrN4nlk

The headlines the next day: The Associated Press, "Deepwater drilling moratorium targeted by rally in Lafayette," July 21, 2010

While Jindal got the: Ben Rooney, "Louisiana governor: Let's start drilling," July 21, 2010

He had learned the trade: Jeremy Alford, "Touched by an Angelle," *The Independent*, December 15, 2010; Interviews with Scott Angelle

always aware of his ancestry: Ken Stickney, "Angelle: Guy with a long-term vision," *The Monroe News-Star*, August 30, 2015; Interviews with Scott Angelle

Burton Angelle taught his: Jennifer Picard Angelle, **Traditions & Feasts: Derived from J. Burton & Shirley Dauterive Angelle**, self-published, 2010

For "Scotty," the: Ken Stickney, "Angelle: Guy with a long-term vision," *The Monroe News-Star*, August 30, 2015

"Where ya from? Who's ya daddy? Are ya Catholic?": Kelly Connelly, *"LaPolitics Newsmaker: Scott Angelle," LaPolitics.com*, December 18, 2013

played basketball in junior: Ken Stickney, "Angelle: Guy with a long-term vision," *The Monroe News-Star*, August 30, 2015

"I told her: Julia O'Donoghue, "3 Louisiana governor candidates talk state finances, with David Vitter absent," *The Times-Picayune*, October 07, 2015

In 1987, at age: Jeremy Alford, "Touched by an Angelle," *The*

Independent, December 15, 2010; interviews with Scott Angelle

  switched from Democrat to Republican: Scott McKay, "BREAKING: Angelle Switches Parties To GOP," *TheHayride.com*, October 26, 2010

    back of a cocktail napkin: Interview with Reggie Dupre

    "Scott's 'I'm Home Early, Mom's: Jennifer Picard Angelle, **Traditions & Feasts: Derived from J. Burton & Shirley Dauterive Angelle**, self-published, 2010

  strike out on his own: Heather Miller, "Angelle running for PSC," *The Independent*, August 9, 2012

  Roy Fletcher had served: Interviews with Roy Fletcher
  influenced younger consultants: Interview with Timmy Teepell

  "I want to hire you: Interviews with Roy Fletcher

  Angelle had reported: Jeremy Alford, "Angelle Still Feeling Out Statewide Races," *LaPolitics Weekly*, March 24, 2014

  Reporters around the state: Interviews with Fred Mills

  The campaign team that: Interviews with Roy Fletcher and Ryan Cross

  The campaign truly kicked off: **Long Shot** co-author cover the Angelle kickoff event at the Evangeline Downs Event Center

  what Hunter S. Thompson: Hunter S. Thompson, "The Kentucky Derby Is Decadent and Depraved," *Scanlan*, June 1970

  Joe Harrison from the: Interview with Joe Harrison

  Occupying half of the: **Long Shot** co-author Jeremy Alford covered the Angelle kickoff event at the Evangeline Downs Event Center

  a young consultant: Interviews with Ryan Cross

  a campaign rain dance: Interviews with Roy Fletcher

  arrived at a farm owned: Interviews with Roy Fletcher and Ryan Cross

  Edwards was the first to go negative: Jeremy Alford, "Edwards' Radio Ad Hits Angelle, Jindal," *LaPolitics.com*, February 26, 2015; https://lapolitics.com/wp-content/uploads/2015/02/JBE_Radio_1.mp3

  While Angelle's $200,000: Jeremy Alford, "Angelle Unleashes Six-Figure TV Buy," *LaPolitics.com*, February 20, 2015

Chapter 10

Two carloads of LSU: Interviews with Jay Dardenne

"You Are My Sunshine: Richard Severo, "Jimmie Davis, Louisiana's Singing Governor, Is Dead," *The New York Times*, November 6, 2000

On that autumn afternoon: Interviews with Jay Dardenne

win the 1971 Democratic runoff: Peter Applebome, "Blacks and Affluent Whites Give Edwards Victory," *The New York Times*, November 18, 1991

As they waited for the governor: Interviews with Jay Dardenne

When he finally won his: Marsha Shuler, "Lt. Gov. Jay Dardenne has shown an independent streak in his political career," *The Advocate*, October 5, 2015

"I learned there is a green: Jeremy Alford, "They Said It," *LaPolitics Weekly*, February 5, 2015

Dardenne was Jewish: Tyler Bridges, "Can Jay Dardenne Become the First Jewish Governor of Louisiana?," *Forward* magazine, July 18, 2015

At the end of each legislative session: Interviews with Jay Dardenne

As was the case with: Ed Anderson, "Two stand between Dardenne, full term," *The Times-Picayune*, September 27, 2007

"A lot of people: Jeremy Alford, "Behind the Kingfish's Desk," *Gambit*, April 17, 2007

But Dardenne's attention turned: Interviews with Jay Dardenne

On Dardenne's 56th birthday: Michelle Krupa and Frank Donze, "Mitch Landrieu wins New Orleans mayor's race," *The Times-Picayune*, February 6, 2010

Dardenne officially announced: *The Associated Press*, "Jay Dardenne announces candidacy for lieutenant governor," February 12, 2010; Jeremy Alford, "Jay Dardenne already woven into political fabric," *The Houma Courier*, October 25, 2010

Dardenne beat Fayard: Ed Anderson, "Jay Dardenne elected to lieutenant governor's post," *The Times-Picayune*, November 2, 2010

be his most agonizing: Mark Moseley, "Dardenne, Nungesser race for lt. governor gets down and dirty," *The Lens*, October 19, 2011 *some disturbing news*: Interviews with Jay Dardenne

freshly re-elected David: Capitol News Bureau, "Vitter endorses Nungesser," *The Advocate*, September 1, 2011

surgeons at Tulane: Interviews with Jay Dardenne

entertaining PowerPoint presentation: **Long Shot** co-author Jeremy Alford covered a "Why Louisiana Ain't Mississippi" presentation during the 2015 election cycle

Dardenne was a good fit: Interviews with Jay Dardenne

Edwards appeared on The: Audio of February 20, 2013, interview on Jim Engster radio show, http://wrkf.org/post/wednesday-state-rep-john-bel-edwards-metro-councilwoman-c-denise-marcelle?nopop=1#stream/0

In November 2013, Southern: Jeremy Alford, "Vitter Leads Governor's Race in Poll," *LaPolitics Weekly*, November 21, 2013

released an internal poll: Jeremy Alford, "Vitter Leads Landrieu, Dardenne in New Governor's Poll," *LaPolitics.com*, December 17, 2013

de facto water-walker: Interviews with George Kennedy

In all of 2014, Dardenne: Louisiana Ethics Administration, 2014 campaign finance reports, Scott Angelle, Jay Dardenne, and David Vitter

On March 20, 2015: Jeremy Alford, "ADVANCE: Dardenne Announcement Speech (4/6/15)," *LaPolitics.com*, Jeremy Alford

a key campaign hire: Interviews with Marsanne Golsby

Chapter 11

From his perch on a curved bench: **Long Shot** co-author Jeremy Alford covered 2015's Washington Mardi Gras

Nearly 3,000 people: Jeremy Alford, "Money Gras Mambo: Fundraising, state budget the talk of D.C. Carnival," *LaPolitics Weekly*, January 22, 2015

The Saturday evening ball: Interviews with Tyron Picard

Stukins, a native: Interview with Austin Stukins

instead on the campus of LSU: Rosalind S. Helderman, "At controversial prayer rally, Jindal calls for spiritual revival," *The Washington Post*, January 24, 2015.

Looking dapper: Interview with Austin Stukins

A good spot: Interviews with Tyron Picard

team was riding high: Interviews with Luke Bolar

couldn't use his federal money: Jeremy Alford, "Vitter Unwraps Governor's Race," *LaPolitics Weekly*, December 18, 2014

shoved under their doors: Jeremy Alford, "Pro-Dardenne Super PAC Emerges," *LaPolitics Weekly*, January 22, 2015

candidates, save Dardenne: Interviews with Jay Dardenne

farther away he was: Interviews with Joel DiGrado

such as YouTube: Interviews with Ryan Cross

could get stressful before: Interviews with Tyron Picard

Caldwell serenading: Jeremy Alford, "Web Ad Pairs Up Caldwell, Landrieu," *LaPolitics Weekly*, November 19, 2014

Edwards made his presence: Interviews with Jared Arsement

"I was acting governor: Interviews with Jay Dardenne

Historians note that: Mystick Krewe of Louisianians, historical overview, http://mkofl.com/heritage

covered the ball in 1975: "THE CAPITAL: Mardi Gras on the Potomac," *Time* magazine, March 4, 1975

Long had taken over: Jeremy Alford, "Throw Me Something, Senator!," *The Independent*, February 14, 2007

As Picard and Vitter: Interviews with Tyron Picard

their heads away from the pomp: Interviews with Stephen Ortego and Robert Johnson

went to a dark corner: Interviews with Tyron Picard

Chapter 12

When the two men: Interview with John Bel Edwards

Edwards congratulated Landrieu: "State Rep. Edwards jabs Mitch Landrieu about governor's race," *Associated Press*, February 3, 2014; interview with Raymond Blanco

Edwards' small team of advisers: Interviews with Sam Jones, Remy Starns, Mary-Patricia Wray and Daniel Edwards

From his home: Interviews with Jim Kitchens

By the time the Police Jury Association: **Long Shot** co-author Jeremy Alford covered the Police Jury Association annual convention

Upon arriving: Interview with Walt Leger III

Another potential spoiler: Interview with Russel Honore

Honore appeared: https://www.youtube.com/watch?v=ScHAL9e87Oc

Donald Cravins Sr.: Interview with Donald Cravins Sr.

State Senator Rick Gallot: Jeremy Alford, "Recruiting Gets Serious For Black Governor's Candidate," *LaPolitics Weekly*, February 26, 2015

Montana Governor: "DGA Leaders Talk Up Manchin and Heitkamp for Governor in 2016," *National Journal*, February 21, 2015

To get the DGA: Interviews with John Bel Edwards, Mary-Patricia Wray and Sam Jones

But Steve Monaghan: Interview with Steve Monaghan

Monaghan turned for help: February 3, 2015, letter from Steve Monaghan to Louis Reine; interviews with Louis Reine and Steve Monaghan

After Edwards departed: Interview with Louis Reine

Six days afterward: Interview with Kathleen Blanco

The second maneuver: Interviews with John Bel Edwards, Sam Jones, Mary-Patricia Wray and Stephen Handwerk

The executive committee members: Interviews with John Bel Edwards, Arthur Morrell, Kyle Gautreau;"AFL-CIO endorses John Bel Edwards," *Action News 17*, March 10, 2015

he told reporters afterward: Julia O'Donoghue, "Louisiana Democrats pick John Bel Edwards in hopes of clearing field in governor's race," *The Times-Picayune*, March 28, 2015

she told Mark Ballard: Interview with Mary-Patricia Wray

explained in an article: Julia O'Donoghue, "Louisiana Democrats pick John Bel Edwards in hopes of clearing field in governor's race," *The Times-Picayune*, March 28, 2015

crowded out Mitch Landrieu: Mark Ballard, "Mitch Landrieu says commitment to New Orleans will keep him out of governor's race,"

The Advocate, April 27, 2015; Clancy DuBos, "Can anyone beat David Vitter?" *The Ind*, June 2, 2015

Edwards was sharing: Interviews with John Bel Edwards, Sam Jones and Jim Kitchens

Armentor threw: Interview with Glenn Armentor

During the forum: Interview with Robert Travis Scott

Southern Media: Greg Meriwether, "Poll: Gov. Jindal's low approval rating similar to Blanco, Edwards," *WAFB-TV*, May 15, 2015

Bob Mann made note: Bob Mann, "If history is any guide, Sen. David Vitter should be nervous, *The Times-Picayune,* May 9, 2015

the Yellow House: Interviews with Mary-Patricia Wray and Linda Day

But the Southern Media: Interview with Bob Mann; Bob Mann, "Louisiana Democrats' best hope to beat David Vitter? Vote Republican," *The Times-Picayune*, May 15, 2015

Mann's column sent shivers: Interviews with John Bel Edwards, Donna Edwards, Mary-Patricia Wray and Jared Arsement

The pundit was expecting: Interview with Bob Mann

Three days after: Stephanie Grace, "Question of whether a Democrat, any Democrat, can win a Louisiana race these days hangs over John Bel Edwards' campaign," *The Advocate*, May 21, 2015

from another flank: Jeremy Alford: "Clayton considering run for governor," *Baton Rouge Business Report*, May 22, 2015

whom Clayton would undercut: John Binder, "How Tony Clayton's Run for Governor Could be a Gift for Jay Dardenne," *TheHayride.com*, May 22, 2015

inadvertent dig at Edwards: Jeff Singer, "The Louisiana gubernatorial race may get interesting after all," *The Daily Kos*, May 26, 2015

Edwards holed up: Interviews with Sam Jones and Mary-Patricia Wray

Vitter had to request a meeting with Clayton: Interviews with Kyle Ruckert

Clayton went on: Jim Engster Show, June 9, 2015, http://www.jimengster.com/jim-engster-podcasts/2015/6/9/tuesday-prosecutor-tony-clayton-and-political-consultant-c-b-forgotston

That left one: Jeremy Alford, "Citizen Georges," *Gambit*, October 2, 2007; Stephanie Riegel, "Baton Rouge's new power broker—Who is this businessman from New Orleans? How did he make his millions? And what are his plans for The Advocate?" *Baton Rouge Business Report*, May 13, 2013

Given his desire: Interviews with John Bel Edwards and John Georges

Chapter 13

at the Alario Center: **Long Shot** co-author Tyler Bridges and editor Clancy DuBos covered this event for their respective publications

Louisiana Farm Bureau: Interviews with Ronnie Anderson, Carey Martin and Jim Engster; audiotape of Vitter's answer: https://www.dropbox.com/s/ulcon0wvm30gxh1/LFBF%20Gubernatorial%20Forum%20Vitter%20Answer.mp4?dl=0

Less than three weeks later: Interviews with John Bel Edwards, Ted Jones, Louis Reine, Andre Stolier, Steve Monaghan, Corey Platt and J. Bennett Johnston

Edwards' mood quickly soured: Interviews with John Bel Edwards, Karen Carter Peterson (she confirmed the meeting but wouldn't discuss details) and Mary Landrieu (she later confirmed the meeting in a text, said she had expressed her concerns to Edwards and said she was happy to have been wrong)

could hear the pain: Interviews with Linda Day, John Bel Edwards and Ted Jones

Edwards called his pollster: Interview with Jim Kitchens

Edwards needed to raise more money: Interviews with John Bel Edwards, Andrew Edwards, Sam Jones and Mary-Patricia Wray (LA Harris declined to be interviewed)

The sheriffs' endorsement: Interviews with Glenn Armentor, Newell Normand and Daniel Edwards

Vitter texted: July 16, 2015, text from David Vitter to sheriffs

The sheriffs issued: Jeremy Alford, "Sheriffs Deny Vitter on Early Endorsement," *LaPolitics*, August 18, 2015

Kennedy faced questions: Interview with Verne Kennedy

May/June/July polling numbers: April 26, 2016, email from Verne Kennedy

Kennedy traveled to Metairie: Interview with Verne Kennedy

Ruckert sent an email blast: August 6, 2015, email from Kyle Ruckert

Kennedy also issued a point by point: Rebuttal contained in April 26, 2016, email from Verne Kennedy

On August 19: https://www.youtube.com/watch?v=kzKDj9TJVOg

His second spot: https://www.youtube.com/watch?v=v77eX0qjjvM

His third spot: https://www.youtube.com/watch?v=QuTiPU_sexo

Angelle's late August spot: http://thehayride.com/2015/08/video-scott-angelle-has-a-new-ad-out-and-its-pretty-good/

by WRKF Radio: Sue Lincoln, "Dardenne Solos at Forum, Fires on Vitter," *WRKF*, August 31, 2015

Jason Williams: Jeff Adelson, Governor's race could look radically different if New Orleans City Council President Jason Williams jumps in, *The Advocate*, August 8, 2015

Williams officially ended: Richard Rainey, "New Orleans City Councilman Jason Williams quashes rumors over 2015 governor's race, *The Times-Picayune*, August 20, 2015

the campaign's first poll: January 18, 2016, email from Jim Kitchens

In a strategy memo: Memo contained in April 16, 2016, email from Jim Kitchens

flew to Washington: Interviews with John Bel Washington, Corey Platt and Andre Stolier; Cedric Richmond and Karen Carter Peterson declined to be interview for this book

Chapter 14

An early riser: **Long Shot** co-authors Tyler Bridges and Jeremy Alford covered the first day of qualifying for their respective publications; Mark Ballard, "Some candidates met by protesters as they qualify for Oct. 24 elections, including governor, Legislature, BESE, other statewide offices," *The Advocate*, September 8, 2015

For those who hadn't: Julia O'Donoghue, "We have six candidates in the Louisiana governor's race: Here's what you need to know," *The Times-Picayune*, September 8, 2015

across the aisle: Burgess Everett, "Vitter in the Senate: Gadfly, deal-maker wrapped in one," *Politico*, November 18, 2015

One other incident: Tyler Bridges, "Baton Rouge television reporter claims his firing connected to confrontation with U.S. Sen. David Vitter," *The Advocate*, September 9, 2015; Christina Wilkie, "David Vitter tweet to young woman was 'inadvertent staff' mistake, spokesman says," *Huffington Post,* August 24, 2015; https://www.youtube.com/watch?v=xAWpS4PMxio&feature=youtu.be

one big-name potential candidate: The account of John Georges' possible candidacy comes from interviews with Georges, Mark Ballard, Jack Capella, Mark Armstrong, Stephanie Riegel and Verne Kennedy; Stephanie Riegel, "Georges reconsidering run for governor; has paperwork ready to file, pollster says," *Baton Rouge Business Report*, September 10, 2015; Amber Stegall, "John Georges will not qualify to run for Louisiana governor," *WAFB-TV*, September 10, 2015; https://twitter.com/cenlamar/status/642046860241203200

Burl Cain: Interview with Burl Cain

Chapter 15

One day in May 2015: Interviews with John Carmouche and Don Carmouche

On March 13: https://www.youtube.com/watch?v=sKTBp1WJNSA&feature=youtu.be

The Carmouches: Interviews with John Carmouche and Don Carmouche

They created a super PAC: http://www.cleanwaterandland.com/about/

spent $486,124: Jim Mustian, "In battle over 'forced recusals,' Louisiana Supreme Court justice takes his case to federal court," *The Advocate*, January 5, 2016

the brainchild of Trey: Interviews with Trey Ourso

Vitter spokesman Luke Bolar: Elizabeth Crisp, "PAC takes aim at David Vitter in Louisiana gubernatorial race," *The Advocate*, May 13, 2015

Ourso later called it: Trey Ourso, "Engineering a surprise Dem victory in the Deep South," *Campaigns & Elections*, December 24, 2015

One day at the Capitol: Interview with Trey Ourso

By then, the Carmouches: Interviews with John Carmouche, Don Carmouche, Robert Green, Rob Stutzman, Adam Rosenblatt and Marty Wilson

"The People vs. David Vitter: https://www.youtube.com/watch?v=dCZ69Bl6w_U&feature=youtu.be

Kyle Ruckert: Interview with Ruckert

Rocky Daboval: Tyler Bridges, "Anti-Vitter ads taken off the air at least temporarily," *The Advocate*, September 10, 2015

Four days after: Tyler Bridges, "David Vitter murky past with prostitution focus of campaign behind campaign," *The Advocate*, September 13, 2015

A day later: Tyler Bridges, "David Vitter on forum question asking if he's broken law: 'I really don't appreciate the games,'" *The Advocate,* September 14, 2015

Chapter 16

In May 2014: Bruce Alpert, "New Orleans judge frees Vitter super PAC to solicit donations over $100,000," *The Times-Picayune*, May 2, 2014

Vitter and DiGrado: Interview with Joel DiGrado

"reformer with results: https://www.youtube.com/watch?v=VbI93PqMGiU&feature=youtu.be

another super PAC: https://www.youtube.com/watch?v=AOxJf4MRIzc

Grigsby asked: Interviews with Lane Grigsby and Kyle Ruckert

It featured a woman: Tyler Bridges, "TV ad war underway between Louisiana gubernatorial candidates," *The Advocate*, September 15, 2015; https://www.youtube.com/watch?v=dAo8ZPfIy84

Dardenne became the last candidate: https://www.youtube.com/watch?v=i7k7BZaQTXM

The pro-Vitter super PAC: https://www.youtube.com/

watch?v=9HM1XBSEDkY; https://www.youtube.com/
watch?v=iENzuEisCNI

DiGrado went after both men: Interview with Joel DiGrado

Louisiana Families First: Interview with Laura Veazey

Vitter's first attack ad: https://www.youtube.com/
watch?v=YDpTl1Enh7Y

the best Dardenne could do: Tyler Bridges, "David Vitter attack ads portray Republican opponents in governor's race as liberal, Obama-like," *The Advocate*, September 19, 2015

On September 19: https://www.youtube.com/watch?v=sU8OF_vSAYA

"Scott's Sinkhole: Tyler Bridges, "David Vitter attack ads portray Republican opponents in governor's race as liberal, Obama-like," *The Advocate*, September 19, 2015; https://www.youtube.com/
watch?v=lI-eFSaWa4I

slammed him again on September 22: https://www.youtube.com/
watch?v=MtTI37IBJbk&feature=youtu.be

It was Angelle's turn: http://hueystate.com/2015/09/angelle-releases-new-ad-tell-the-truth/

"Jay's Birthday Bash: http://www.cajunconservatism.com/
blog/2015/10/1/jay-dardennes-birthday-bash

The ad infuriated Dardenne: October 1, 2015 press statement from the Dardenne campaign

In addition to letting Vitter: Federal Election Commission, 2014 and 2015 campaign finance reports, David Vitter

on his own petard: Interview with Kathleen Blanco

McCollister had founded: Rolfe McCollister, "Two faces of John Bel Edwards," *Baton Rouge Business Report*, September 30, 2015

A poll taken by Rob Green: December 14, 2015 email from Adam Rosenblatt

His 33-year-old: Interviews with Jared Arsement

Viewers around the state: https://www.youtube.com/
watch?v=Fwat5MaBFhg

aired on September 21: https://www.youtube.com/
watch?v=SakubgecrJ4

During their drive: Interviews with Jared Arsement

Donna had told her daughter: Interview with Donna Edwards

Jones previewed: Interview with Sam Jones

Edwards and Donna: Interviews with Jared Arsement, John Bel Edwards, Jim Kitchens and Rock Palermo

Donna Edwards sat alongside: https://www.youtube.com/watch?v=bE-340ZRJhE

The ad particularly resonated: January 18, 2016 email from Jim Kitchens

At one meeting with Mitch: Interview with John Bel Edwards; Mitch Landrieu declined an interview request for this book

Ruffino's: Interviews with Russ Herman, Sandra Herman, Melissa Flournoy and several sources on background

believed Vitter would triumph: "Political experts weigh in on governor's race," *KATC-TV*, September 29, 2015

Chapter 17

Faucheux found that: Elizabeth Crisp, "Poll: Among David Vitter, John Bel Edwards, Scott Angelle, Jay Dardenne, two lead in Louisiana governor's race with fierce runoff looming," *The Advocate*, September 27, 2015

"On top of all that: Clancy DuBos, "WWL-TV/Advocate poll very bad news for Vitter," *Gambit*, September 28, 2015

Larry J. Sabato's: Kyle Kondik and Geoffrey Skelley, "Louisiana Governor: Ganging up on Vitter," *Larry J. Sabato's Crystal Ball*, October 1, 2015

He faced the six candidates: **Long Shot** co-authors Tyler Bridges and Jeremy Alford covered the debate; Tyler Bridges, Debate: GOP foes balk as David Vitter says he's the true conservative; John Bel Edwards says he differs with national Democrats," *The Advocate*, October 1, 2015; http://www.wdsu.com/article/2015-wdsu-louisiana-gubernatorial-debate-part-1/3216902; https://www.youtube.com/watch?v=VogLfco8PMM; https://www.youtube.com/watch?v=gmcKB-5dhQ8; https://www.youtube.com/watch?v=v0iDjQs9MPM

Commentators on both: Tyler Bridges, "WDSU defends handling of Louisiana governor's debate following criticism on social media but second-guesses one issue," *The Advocate*, October 2, 2015

They thought their first: Interviews with John Carmouche and Don Carmouche

For the third ad: Interview with Rob Stutzman

PJ Clarke: Clarke provided background in June 18, 2016 email

The ad aired on October 6: https://www.youtube.com/watch?v=4WkAV5fuiUA

offered John Couvillon: Interviews with John Couvillon

Kevin Wise: https://www.youtube.com/watch?v=K-cVhSvaqTs

Wendy Vitter, its best asset: https://www.youtube.com/watch?v=h4NgzbR46U8

Kyle Ruckert believed: Interview with Kyle Ruckert

Bill Cassidy: Interview with Bill Cassidy

Timmy Teepell: Interview with Timmy Teepell

The first of three RGA ads: https://www.youtube.com/watch?v=PwCpYYANq2E

One ad took a clip: https://www.youtube.com/watch?v=roBmEm-nAHo&feature=youtu.be

testimonials from West Point buddies: https://www.youtube.com/watch?v=yGLngm4EwWM

Coach Blanco loved the spot: He showed it to **Long Shot** co-author Tyler Bridges, among others

The spot featured Dardenne: https://www.youtube.com/watch?v=KUoVuzu_rXc

Cattle Festival: **Long Shot** co-author Tyler Bridges covered the event

The other three candidates: Tyler Bridges, "David Vitter's absence from gubernatorial debates has become campaign issue, drawing criticism from other candidates," *The Advocate*, October 13, 2015

Louisiana Tech University: **Long Shot** co-author Jeremy Alford covered the event; interviews with Elizabeth Crisp, Greg Hilburn, and Mary-Patricia Wray; Elizabeth Crisp, "What if they held a debate and no one was there to see it? Why some Louisiana governor's candidates are upset," *The Advocate*, October 15, 2015; Julia O'Donoghue, "Other Louisiana governor candidates blame

David Vitter for closing off debate," *The Times-Picayune*, October 15, 2015; Melinda Deslatte, "Vitter squares off with opponents in his second TV debate, *The Associated Press*, October 15, 2015

Later, after the campaign ended: Interview with Luke Bolar

The other big takeaway: Post-debate press conference covered by book co-author Jeremy Alford

at the Governor's Mansion: **Long Shot** co-author Jeremy Alford covered the event; *Elizabeth Crisp*, "Three Louisiana governor candidates criticize David Vitter's absence from Monday's debate: 'We have a candidate who has no courage to come here,'" *The Advocate*, October 19, 2015

Chapter 18

Originally from Kentucky: Interviews with Jason Brad Berry

Berry was credited by Gambit: Clancy DuBos, "Interview with the Zombie," *Gambit*, February 14, 2014

from the LSU Health Sciences Center: Jason Brad Berry, "Bill Cassidy's questionable billing—Lamar fills in more blanks," *TheAmericanZombie.com*, November 25, 2014

Berry began chasing rumors: Interviews with Jason Brad Berry

Danny DeNoux: Interviews with Danny DeNoux
morning, *DeNoux and Berry:* Interviews with Danny DeNoux and Jason Brad Berry

Phone call from James Garner: Interviews with James Garner and Jason Brad berry

Berry spoke with Scott Sternberg: Interviews with Jason Berry and Scott Sternberg

In the posted segments: http://www.theamericanzombie. com/2015/10/david-vitter-interview-with-wendy-ellis.html

Lamar White Jr., a liberal: Lamar White Jr., "Bombshell in Louisiana governor's race: Former mistress alleges David Vitter asked her to get an abortion," *CenLamar.com,* October 17, 2015

A day later: White: Lamar White Jr., "Wendy Ellis' sordid story about David Vitter unravels," *CenLamar.com*, October 18, 2015

Another media outlet: Jonathan Shelley, "Vitter accuser claims pregnancy; some claims contradicted by legal documents," *WDSU-*

TV, October 17, 2015

The next morning: **Long Shot** editor Clancy DuBos provided the account on the dealings between *Gambit* and the Vitter campaign; Clancy DuBos, "Vitter update: inconsistencies come to light," *bestofneworleans.com*, October 18, 2015

at an LSU forum: Peter Kovacs made his comments on November 30, 2015; https://vimeo.com/album/3696451

at LSU's Manship School: **Long Shot** co-author Jeremy Alford covered the event; Elizabeth Crisp, "Scott Angelle launches most pointed attack yet on David Vitter's prostitution scandal in final debate before Saturday election," *The Advocate*, October 21, 2015; http://www.lsureveille.com/tigertv/newsbeat/tiger-tv-presents-the-gubernatorial-debate-full/youtube_680be702-78ed-11e5-8060-d75995992b5d.html

Chapter 19

Royal Blend coffee shop: Interviews with Newell Normand, Danny Martiny, Danny DeNoux, Jason Brad Berry, Luke Bolar, and Kyle Ruckert; John Cummings declined an interview request; Jefferson Parish Sheriff's Office arrest report, October 23, 2015; Jim Mustian and Tyler Bridges, "Man arrested after trying to record Jefferson Sheriff Newell Normand and his breakfast club; sheriff suspects David Vitter behind it," *The Advocate*, October 23, 2015; Jim Mustian, "Prominent lawyer targeted by David Vitter private eye says 'something very, very strange' about 'naughty' senator," *The Advocate*, October 28, 2015; Tyler Bridges, "Newell Normand: David Vitter's private eye video shows campaign operatives urge woman to discredit prostitute claims," *The Advocate*, November 10, 2015

Normand got a phone call from John Fortunato: Russell Jones, "Vitter driver involved in Metairie crash," *WBRZ-TV*, October 23, 2015

the Angelle campaign released: October 23, 2015 email from Angelle campaign

Dardenne followed: October 23, 2015 email from Dardenne campaign

Chapter 20

Not shy about discussing: Interview with Ryan Cross

Looked straight into the camera: https://www.youtube.com/watch?v=sFJ0h1JwsAg&feature=youtu.be

The pro-Angelle super PAC: https://www.youtube.com/watch?v=BTnUnu54I3U

Dardenne said in the video: Email from Dardenne campaign, October 24, 2015

Louisiana Carpenters' Union: Interviews with Louis Reine, Jason Engels and Tiger Hammond

Plumbers and Steamfitters: **Long Shot** co-author Tyler Bridges covered the event; interviews with Louis Reine and Donna Edwards

The University of New Orleans: Tyler Bridges, "Gubernatorial candidates make last-minute appeals for undecideds," *The Advocate*, October 22, 2015

Jim Kitchens' poll: Interview with Jim Kitchens

As Vitter and his family: **Long Shot** co-author Tyler Bridges covered Vitter at the fire station and talked to voters afterward

At 8:15 p.m.: The Twitter feeds from *The Advocate* and *The Times-Picayune* provide a news feed of events that night; http://theadvocate.com/news/acadiana/13776741-93/live-updates-analysis-from-governors; http://www.nola.com/politics/index.ssf/2015/10/louisiana_election_results.html

additional election night coverage: **Long Shot** co-authors covered the Vitter election night gathering; Julia O'Donoghue, "John Bel Edwards, David Vitter advance to runoff in governor's race," *The Times-Picayune*, October 25, 2015; Mark Ballard, "Off and running: It's John Bel Edwards vs. David Vitter in the race to be Louisiana's next governor," *The Advocate*, October 24, 2015; David Weigel, "Democrats see strange new hope in two red state races," *The Washington Post*, October 26, 2015; Secretary of State, election results, October 24, 2015; https://www.youtube.com/watch?v=qar5-3g3vbs

Chapter 21

On the afternoon: **Long Shot** co-author Jeremy Alford covered

John Bel Edwards' press conference

Bob Mann: Interview with Bob Mann; Bob Mann, "I was wrong: John Bel Edwards can win the Louisiana governor's race," *BobMannBlog.com*, October 25, 2015

Lod Cook Hotel: Interviews with Daniel Edwards and Andrew Edwards

Edwards authorized cousin: Interviews with John Bel Edwards and Andrew Edwards

In his first runoff ad: https://www.youtube.com/watch?v=VqdY9-z8UTQ

As if on cue: http://www.politico.com/video/2015/10/david-vitter-ad-accuses-edwards-of-wanting-thugs-out-of-prison-030693

The Edwards campaign immediately: October 27, 2015, email from Edwards campaign

The ad also offended: Jarvis DeBerry, "David Vitter's thugs ad offends—and ignores a shameful Louisiana problem," *The Times-Picayune*, October 30, 2015

Vitter used a softer approach: October 25, 2015, text from David Vitter to sheriffs

The sheriffs met the next morning: October 26, 2015, press release from the Louisiana Sheriffs Association; interview with John Bel Edwards

The Republican Governors Association: https://www.youtube.com/watch?v=IGiCWwumBkk&feature=youtu.be

Democratic Governors Association: Interviews with Trey Ourso, Corey Platt, John Anzalone, Zac McCrary

Gumbo PAC's 30-second ad: https://www.youtube.com/watch?v=4Osxl8YfV2Q&feature=youtu.be

Ourso would write later: Trey Ourso, "Engineering a surprise Dem victory in the Deep South," *Campaigns & Elections*, December 24, 2015

Angelle refused to take his calls: A source close to Scott Angelle

Dardenne took the call: Interview with Jay Dardenne

Landrieu joined six other mayors: October 30, 2015, email from Edwards' campaign

Landrieu flew with John Bel: Interview with John Bel Edwards

The party was hosted by James Carville: Interviews with James Carville, John Bel Edwards, J. Bennett Johnston and Bradley Beychok

Mike Johnson: Interview with Mike Johnson; https://www. facebook.com/MikeJohnsonLouisiana/posts/502465596582095

Edwards was not happy: Interviews with Mike Johnson and John Bel Edwards

Edwards was close to the video poker industry: Interview with Alton Ashy

Released on November 2: Interview with John Couvillon

It featured four sheriffs: https://www.youtube.com/ watch?v=NJitV_bemQw&feature=youtu.be

Jay Dardenne had officially endorsed: Interview with Jay Dardenne; https://www.youtube.com/watch?v=a50WAc88B1Q

Dardenne's decision outraged: Jeremy Alford, "Picking Sides For Governor," *LaPolitics Weekly*, November 5, 2015

Jay Luneau: Interview with Jay Luneau

Rothenberg & Gonzales: Eli Yokley, "Louisiana Governor's Election Continues Tradition of Unusual Party Splits," *Roll Call*, November 5, 2015

Chapter 22

In mid-January 2015: Interviews with Jared Arsement and Mary-Patricia Wray; Joel Roberts, "'D.C. Madam' called Vitter during votes," *CBS News*, July 13, 2007

House Concurrent Resolution: https://www.congress.gov/ congressional-record/2001/02/27/house-section/article/H426-1

Nearly all of them: Interviews with John Bel Edwards, Donna Edwards, Andrew Edwards and Daniel Edwards

Raymond Blanco: Interview with Raymond Blanco

Arsement, however: Interviews with Jared Arsement, Jim Kitchens and John Bel Edwards

Wray gave advance notice: Greg Hilburn, "Edwards ad: Vitter chose prostitutes over patriots," *Gannett Newspapers*, November 6, 2015

provoked an immediate reaction: Tyler Bridges, "New John Bel

Edwards campaign ad states rival David Vitter 'chose patriots over prostitutes," *The Advocate*, November 6, 2015

> *Arsement's ad:* https://www.youtube.com/watch?v=RpzMQ-z-QsY

> *Cameron Henry:* Interview with Cameron Henry

> *Dale Atkins:* Interview with Dale Atkins

> *Liz Mangham:* November 7, 2015, text to Jim Kitchens

> *Chuck Todd:* http://www.nbcnews.com/meet-the-press/meet-press-transcript-november-8-2015-n459476

> *Kim Florich:* Kevin Litten, "John Bel Edwards to remove Arlington Cemetery images in ad against David Vitter," *The Times-Picayune*, November 9, 2015

> *Five days later, Kitchens found:* Interview with Jim Kitchens

> *On Sunday, November 8:* **Long Shot** co-author Tyler Bridges covered John Bel Edwards as he visited the churches

> *Bradley Beychok:* Interview with Bradley Beychok; Kevin Robillard, "Vitter's past at center of governor's race," *Politico*, October 24, 2015

> *Carville's home was jammed:* Interviews with Mary-Patricia Wray, Bradley Beychok and James Carville

> *Josh Standifer:* Tyler Bridges, "Meet Louisiana's most prominent 'tracker'—video camera-toting person who films political candidates to capture their every word, misstep," *The Advocate*, October 30, 2015

> *Stephanie Grace:* Interview with Stephanie Grace

> *Edwards thought Josh:* Interview with John Bel Edwards

> *Press Club of Baton Rouge:* **Long Shot** co-authors Tyler Bridges and Jeremy Alford covered the event; Tyler Bridges, "Prostitution scandal comes up at David Vitter, John Bel Edwards debate," *The Advocate*, November 9, 2015; https://www.youtube.com/watch?v=vD8oPr7_T6s

> *At his press conference:* Tyler Bridges, "Newell Normand: David Vitter's private eye video shows campaign operatives urge woman to discredit prostitute claims," *The Advocate*, November 10, 2015

> *the runoff's first televised debate:* http://www.lpb.org/index.php?/site/programs/the_governor_debate_2015

> *In one commercial:* http://www.nola.com/politics/index.

ssf/2015/11/david_vitter_acknowledges_pros.html

Willie Robertson: http://www.politico.com/story/2015/11/david-vitter-duck-dynasty-willie-robertson-campaig-ad-215805

Sheriff Normand returned: https://www.youtube.com/watch?v=0xPztS2_FG4

Normand said he had withheld: Interview with Newell Normand

the race took another strange turn: Interviews with Dan Robin Jr., Andrew Honeycutt, Kenya Taylor, John Bel Edwards and Donna Edwards

Unbeknownst to Dan Jr.: John Binder, "Apparently John Bel Edwards hosted a 'meet and greet' at a New Orleans club," *TheHayride.com*, November 12, 2015

She turned to Walsh: Interviews with Mary-Patricia Wray and Dan Robin Jr.

Embedded in Binder's article: http://thehayride.com/2015/11/exclusive-heres-all-the-videos-of-john-bel-edwards-nola-night-club-campaign-rally-and-his-early-vote-party-bus/

but Edwards was unfazed: Interview with John Bel Edwards

Chapter 23

Bobby Jindal released a statement: Jed Lipinski, "Jindal demands Obama provide more information on Syrian refugees in U.S.," *The Times-Picayune*, November 14, 2015

David Vitter weighed in: Scott McKay, "If the Syrian migrant issue matters to Louisiana voters, John Bel Edwards has some problems," *TheHayride.com,* November 16, 2015

Mary-Patricia Wray: Interview with Mary-Patricia Wray

As it happened: John Binder, "Flood of migrants from the Muslim world may be coming to Baton Rouge, Lafayette and Metairie," *TheHayride.com*, November 2, 2015

Binder posted another story: John Binder, "Syrian refugees from the Muslim world are arriving in New Orleans," *TheHayride.com*, November 3, 2015

"And then it went viral: Scott McKay, "If the Syrian migrant issue matters to Louisiana voters, John Bel Edwards has some problems," *TheHayride.com,* November 16, 2015

Michelle Hunter tried to set: Michelle Hunter, "How many Syrian refugees are in the New Orleans area? 13, officials say, *The Times-Picayune*, November 15, 2015

He also sought to fan the flames: November 15, 2015, email from the Vitter campaign; Rich Rainey, "Mitch Landrieu, David Vitter tussle over Syrian refugees in New Orleans after Paris attacks," *The Times-Picayune*, November 16, 2015

Vitter also started a petition drive: https://www.facebook.com/DavidVitter/posts/10153731884352964

Late that Sunday evening: November 15, 2015, campaign email from Luke Bolar

Bob Mann couldn't help: Bob Mann, "David Vitter's desperate last stand: He throws his wife under the bus—again, *Salon*, November 18, 2015

Ruckert was finally seeing: Interview with Kyle Ruckert

Vitter sent out a statement: November 16, 2015, Vitter campaign email

According to WWL-TV: Danny Monteverde, "Officials: 14 Syrian refugees get access to Louisiana this year," *WWL-TV*, November 16, 2015

When David Aguillard: Interview with David Aguillard

Mike Edmonson: Elizabeth Crisp, "Bobby Jindal issues executive order to block Syrian refugees," *The Advocate*, November 16, 2015

Edwards ramped up his position: November 16, 2015, Edwards campaign email; David Weigel, "David Vitter, trailing in gubernatorial race, wants to make it about Syrian refugees," *The Washington Post*, November 17, 2015

Team Vitter launched a TV ad: https://www.facebook.com/DavidVitter/videos/vb.53906687963/10153733183282964/?type=2&theater

Wray was keeping vigil: Interviews with Mary-Patricia Wray, Richard Carbo, John Bel Edwards, Donna Edwards, Karen St. Germain, Sam Jones, Andrew Edwards, Linda Day and Jared Arsement

Chapter 24

The second and final televised debate: **Long Shot** co-author

Jeremy Alford helped write questions for the debate and covered it; Kevin Litten, "Louisiana governor candidates John Bel Edwards and David Vitter clash in heated final debate," *The Times-Picayune*, November 16, 2015,: https://www.youtube.com/watch?v=Ajwzlc26n68

AFL-CIO President Louis Reine: Interview with Louis Reine

Jack spoke directly into the camera: http://thehayride.com/2015/11/video-jack-vitter-weighs-in/

His Senate office sent out: November 17, 2015, Vitter Senate office email

that added to the drumbeat: Kevin Litten, "Gubernatorial candidates continue to spar over Syrian refugees," *The Times-Picayune*, November 18, 2015

he threw more gasoline: Kevin Frey, "Catholic Charities of Baton Rouge receives threat over Syrian refugee," *WAFB-TV*, November 18, 2015; Melinda Deslatte and Kevin McGill, "Refugee flap overtakes state issues in La. governor's race," *The Associated Press*, November 19, 2015

Arsement had written the script: Interview with Jared Arsement

Edwards said he wanted no more Syrian refugees: https://www.youtube.com/watch?v=vPqlo71Hr0o&feature=youtu.be

Ordered an oyster po' boy: Campbell Robertson, "David Vitter wages uphill bid for governor in solidly red Louisiana," *The New York Times*, November 19, 2015

Bobby Jindal announced: Elizabeth Crisp, "Bobby Jindal suspends presidential campaign: 'This is not my time,'" *The Advocate*, November 17, 2015; Philip Rucker, Robert Costa, David Fahrenthold, "Jindal suspends presidential campaign: 'This is not my time,'" *The Washington Post*, November 17, 2015

This was a major break: Tyler Bridges, "Did Bobby Jindal time his announcement to upstage David Vitter days before runoff? Maybe, one analyst says," *The Advocate*, November 18, 2015

Kyle Ruckert: Interview with Kyle Ruckert

Gattuso's: Interviews with Billy Nungesser, Newell Normand and Craig Clark

Gumbo PAC launched: https://www.youtube.com/watch?v=4jCakfTZ_Ug

"Never in our wildest dreams: May 5, 2016, email from Trey Ourso

Louisiana Families First: https://www.youtube.com/ watch?v=gNy-8LtZ9yE

Holiday Inn: **Long Shot** co-author Tyler Bridges covered the event

"Somebody's going to get killed: Clancy DuBos, "Vitter, GOP resort to hysterical lies about Syrian refugees in Louisiana," *Gambit,* November 18, 2015

Duffy told Kitchens: Interviews with Jim Duffy and Jim Kitchens

Haynie had invited: Interviews with Randy Haynie, John Georges, John Bel Edwards, Sam Jones and Verne Kennedy

Greg Rigamer: Nightly tracking poll numbers from Greg Rigamer from November 11, 2015 thru November 19, 2015

Jones told Edwards: Interviews with Sam Jones and John Bel Edwards

Lise: Facebook post from Lise Vitter, November 18, 2010, https://www.facebook.com/jvitter8/posts/802389569872057

asked his brother Daniel: interviews with John Bel Edwards and Daniel Edwards

Vitter held a press conference: Jeremy Alford, "Budget Fight Becomes Gubernatorial Sideshow," *LaPolitics Weekly,* November 19, 2015; Elizabeth Crisp and Mark Ballard, "David Vitter, John Bel Edwards both seek to reject Gov. Bobby Jindal's plan to plug $500 million deficit," *The Advocate,* November 19, 2015

"Vote for the Boy Scout: Interview with Norby Chabert

Daniel brought over: Interviews with Daniel Edwards, John Bel Edwards, Donna Edwards and Murray Starkel

Chapter 25

At about 9:30 a.m.: Interviews with Dan Foley, Edwin Murray and John Bel Edwards

Vitter arrived to vote: **Long Shot** co-author Tyler Bridges covered him at the fire station

Louisiana Families First: Interview with Laura Veazey

recorded by President Obama: Interview with Dale Atkins

Edwards was attending a Catholic Mass: **Long Shot** co-author Tyler Bridges accompanied John Bel Edwards and his family to the Mass and interviewed him afterward

That John Bel Edwards ended up: Julia O'Donoghue, "Why John Bel Edwards chose Hotel Monteleone for his election night party," *The Times-Picayune*, November 21, 2015

Everyone applauded when: Interviews with Alton Ashy, John Bel Edwards and Daniel Edwards

Edwards returned to the Monteleone: Interview with Mary-Patricia Wray; http://www.jimengster.com/jim-engster-podcasts/2015/11/23/1123-monday-john-bel-edwards-wins-the-gubernatorial-election-local-cancer-survivor-jeff-sirlin-and-john-bel-edwards-campaign-manager

Edwards called Jay Dardenne: Interview with Jay Dardenne

Scott Angelle and his wife Dianne: Interview with Scott Angelle

At 8 p.m.: http://www.theadvocate.com/baton_rouge/news/politics/elections/article_69f2c7f2-f0a5-5131-968a-ff61d4c190be.html

WWL-TV called it: **Long Shot** co-authors Tyler Bridges and Jeremy Alford covered the Edwards campaign victory night party at the Monteleone

The crowd in Suite 1450: Interviews with John Bel Edwards, Donna Edwards, Murray Starkel, Sam Jones and Mary-Patricia Wray

Celebrating two blocks away: Interviews with Alton Ashy, Newell Normand, Danny DeNoux, Danny Martiny and John Georges

Jason Brad Berry: Interview with Jason Brad Berry

Dan Moldea: Interview with Dan Moldea

the senator appeared: https://www.youtube.com/watch?v=etKo-qhgr5o

"I did not create this breeze of hope: https://www.youtube.com/watch?v=IHcaSXZwIVU

Trey Ourso: Interview with Trey Ourso

The final results: Secretary of State, election results, November 21, 2015

in the 10 parishes: Dante Chinni, "How John Bel Edwards won Louisiana," *The Wall Street Journal*, November 23, 2015; demographer John Couvillon supplied additional analysis

Mike Johnson told Vitter: Interview with Mike Johnson

Afterward, the Blancos: Interviews with Raymond Blanco and Kathleen Blanco

At about 3 a.m.: Interviews with Murray Starkel, John Bel Edwards and Jared Arsement

Edwards awoke at 7:30 a.m.: Interview with John Bel Edwards

Epilogue

no honeymoon period: Jeremy Alford, "Honeymoon over for Edwards," *USA Today,* November 24, 2015

That became evident: Richard Fausset and Jeremy Alford, "New Louisiana Governor, John Bel Edwards, Is Off to a Volatile Start," *The New York Times*, January 14, 2016;

at the outset of 2016: Pre-inauguration walkthrough and press conference on the State Capitol steps, January 2016

for the traditional Inauguration Mass: **Long Shot** co-author Jeremy Alford covered the mass

in the Capitol's Ellender Room: Jeremy Alford, "UNLIKELY SPEAKER: Barras Over Bel," *LaPolitics Weekly*, January 14, 2016

At the Capitol, Henry and Republican: Between January 11, 2016, and January 14, 2016, **Long Shot** co-author Jeremy Alford interviewed more than 20 sources for their accounts of the speaker's race and to obtain multiple confirmations on the meetings and events described

were at least $750 million: Press release from the Office of Governor John Bel Edwards, "Gov. Edwards Testifies Before House Appropriations Committee," April 12, 2016; Elizabeth Crisp, "Thousands of students could lose TOPS scholarships under latest 'very nasty' proposed budget cuts," *The Advocate*, April 16, 2016

Republican foes pounced: Kevin Boyd, "VIDEO: LAGOP Cuts An Ad Blasting John Bel Edwards For Lying About Not Raising Taxes," *TheHayride.com*, February 15, 2016

"I am fully aware that I: Tanya Sinkovits, "Governor John Bel Edwards: 'Say farewell to college football next fall' if no new revenue is raised," *WGNO-TV*, February 11, 2016

chimed in by opposing: Julia O'Donoghue, "Louisiana big business doesn't like John Bel Edwards' June special session," *The*

Times-Picayune, May 4, 2016

broke over the salary: Melinda Deslatte, "Edwards keeps Jindal-era salaries he criticized," *The Associated Press*, January 26, 2016

respite a few weeks later: **Long Shot** co-author Jeremy Alford covered the 2016 Washington Mardi Gras festivities

Vitter's involvement was: Jeremy Alford, "Politics On Parade: D.C. Mardi Gras kicks off," *LaPolitics Weekly*, January 21, 2016

would quote a tipster: Isaac Arnsdorf, "Vitter tests the water," *Politico*, March 10, 2016

released his recommendations: Julia O'Donoghue, "John Bel Edwards' budget-fixing proposal: Sin tax hikes," *The Times-Picayune*, February 19, 2016

"the largest tax: Jeremy Alford, "Takeaways From Thursday Night's Speeches," *LaPolitics.com*, February 11, 2016

As he delivered his speech: "VIDEO: LAGOP Cuts An Ad Blasting John Bel Edwards For Lying About Not Raising Taxes," *TheHayride.com*, February 15, 2016

19 consecutive weeks: Jack Richards, Manship School News Service, "LINGERING LAWMAKERS: Days In Session An All-Time Record," *LaPolitics.com*, June 5, 2016

Greek tragedies had better: Jeremy Alford, "Holding Their Noses, Louisiana Officials Act to Narrow State Budget Gaps," *The New York Times*, March 9, 2016

legislative hands fumbled: Tyler Bridges, "How Louisiana special session ended disgusts some, pleases others; here's what's next," *The Advocate*, March 11, 2016

20 inches of rain: The Associated Press, "3 dead, 1 in northern Louisiana, from torrential rains," *The Times-Picayune*, March 9, 2016

man named Alton Sterling: Richard Fausset, Richard Perez-Pena and Campbell Robertson, "Alton Sterling Shooting in Baton Rouge Prompts Justice Dept. Investigation," *The New York Times*, July 6, 2016

took a dark turn: Nicole Hensley, "Baton Rouge shooter Gavin Eugene Long—retired Marine—was outraged at police for Alton Sterling death, *New York Daily News*, July 18, 2016

"We cannot allow this tragedy: Jeremy Alford, "Joe Biden and

Loretta Lynch mourn officers at Service in Baton Rouge," *The New York Times,* July 29, 2016

inundated by what meteorologists: Madeline Farber, "Here's how Baton Rouge floods rank among worst U.S. natural disasters," *Fortune*, August 25, 2016

Edwards cleaned house: Gordon Russell, "Wife of sheriff, who helped Gov. John Bel Edwards win election, lands Superdome contract months later, *The Advocate*, September 1, 2016

politically connected trial lawyers: Gordon Russell and David Hammer, "Gov. Edwards quietly picks top donors to handle coastal suit that could result in big payday, *The Advocate*, August 31, 2016

governor's key campaign fundraisers: Maya Lau, "Top donor to governor also hired to investigate possible improper donations to Edwards, other politicians," *The Advocate*, September 3, 2016

"There is a perception: David Hammer and Gordon Russell, "Critics say Gov. Edwards is running his own 'buddy system,'" *WWL-TV*, September 6, 2016

Vitter campaign attorney: David Hammer, "Lawyer drops claims against state, can now join governor's team," *WWL-TV*, September 2, 2016

More important, Jones: Interviews with Dan A. Robin Sr. and James Garner

replenish his campaign war: Tyler Bridges, "Louisiana Gov. John Bel Edwards' energy opponents now friends, especially when it comes to fundraising," *The Advocate*, March 21, 2016

INDEX